HUMBERSIDE LIBRARIES

BAXTER, R E. & Volume
PHILLIPS, C.   Ports,
                Civil

GW01557944

29 APR 1980

Kingston upon Hull City Libraries
WITHDRAWN
FROM STOCK

FOR SALE

ALS No.   H1237186

This item should be returned on or before the last date stamped above. If not in demand it may be renewed for a further period by personal application, by telephone, or in writing. The author, title, above number and date due back should be quoted.

LS/3

REVIEWS OF UNITED KINGDOM STATISTICAL SOURCES

VOLUME X

PORTS AND INLAND WATERWAYS
AND
CIVIL AVIATION

REVIEWS OF UNITED KINGDOM STATISTICAL SOURCES

Editor: W. F. Maunder

Vol. I   1. Personal Social Services, B. P. Davies

         2. Voluntary Organizations in the Personal Social Service Field, G. J. Murray

Vol. II   3. Central Government Routine Health Statistics, Michael Alderson

         4. Social Security Statistics, Frank Whitehead

Vol. III   5. Housing in Great Britain, Stuart Farthing

         6. Housing in Northern Ireland, Michael Fleming

Vol. IV   7. Leisure, F. M. M. Lewes and S. R. Parker

         8. Tourism, L. J. Lickorish

Vol. V   9. General Sources of Statistics, G. F. Lock

Vol. VI   10. Wealth, A. B. Atkinson and A. J. Harrison

         11. Personal Incomes, T. Stark

Vol. VII   12. Road Passenger Transport, D. L. Munby

         13. Road Goods Transport, A. H. Watson

Vol. VIII   14. Land Use, J. T. Coppock

         15. Town and Country Planning, L. F. Gebbett

Vol. IX   16. Health Surveys and Related Studies, M. Alderson and R. Dowie

Vol. X   17. Ports and Inland Waterways, R. E. Baxter

         18. Civil Aviation, Celia M. Phillips

REVIEWS OF UNITED KINGDOM STATISTICAL SOURCES

Edited by W. F. MAUNDER

*Professor of Economic and Social Statistics
University of Exeter*

VOLUME X

PORTS AND INLAND WATERWAYS

by

R. E. BAXTER

*Director of Economics and Statistics
National Ports Council*

and

CIVIL AVIATION

by

CELIA M. PHILLIPS

Lecturer in Statistics, London School of Economics

Published for
The Royal Statistical Society and
the Social Science Research Council

PERGAMON PRESS

OXFORD · NEW YORK · TORONTO · SYDNEY · PARIS · FRANKFURT

U.K.	Pergamon Press Ltd., Headington Hill Hall, Oxford OX3 0BW, England
U.S.A.	Pergamon Press Inc., Maxwell House, Fairview Park, Elmsford, New York 10523, U.S.A.
CANADA	Pergamon of Canada, Suite 104, 150 Consumers Road, Willowdale, Ontario M2J 1P9, Canada
AUSTRALIA	Pergamon Press (Aust.) Pty. Ltd., P.O. Box 544, Potts Point, N.S.W. 2011, Australia
FRANCE	Pergamon Press SARL, 24 rue des Ecoles, 75240 Paris, Cedex 05, France
FEDERAL REPUBLIC OF GERMANY	Pergamon Press GmbH, 6242 Kronberg/Taunus, Pferdstrasse 1, Federal Republic of Germany

Copyright © 1979 Royal Statistical Society and Social Science Research Council

All Rights Reserved. No part of this publication may be reproduced, stored in a retrieval system or transmitted in any form or by any means: electronic, electrostatic, magnetic tape, mechanical, photocopying, recording or otherwise, without permission in writing from the copyright holders

First Edition 1979

British Library Cataloguing in Publication Data

Reviews of United Kingdom statistical sources.
Vol. 10: Ports and inland waterways; and, Civil Aviation.
1. Great Britain—Statistical Services.
I Maunder, Wynne Frederick II Baxter, Ron Eric III Phillips, Celia M IV Royal Statistical Society V Social Science Research Council (Great Britain)
314.1   HA37.G7   78-40506

ISBN 0-08-022460-1

For Bibliographic purposes this volume should be cited as: Baxter R E and Phillips Celia M *Ports, Inland Waterways and Civil Aviation* Pergamon Press Limited on behalf of the Royal Statistical Society and the Social Science Research Council, 1978

Reproduced, printed and bound in Great Britain by Fakenham Press Limited, Fakenham, Norfolk

VOLUME CONTENTS

Foreword   vii

Introduction   xi

Review No. 17: Ports and Inland Waterways   1

Subject Index to Ports and Inland Waterways   105

Review No. 18: Civil Aviation   111

Subject Index to Civil Aviation   299

FOREWORD

The Sources and Nature of the Statistics of the United Kingdom, produced under the auspices of the Royal Statistical Society and edited by Maurice Kendall, filled a notable gap on the library shelves when it made its appearance in the early post-war years. Through a series of critical reviews by many of the foremost national experts, it constituted a valuable contemporary guide to statisticians working in many fields as well as a benchmark to which historians of the development of Statistics in this country are likely to return again and again. The Social Science Research Council and the Society were both delighted when Professor Maunder came forward with the proposal that a revised version should be produced, indicating as well his willingness to take on the onerous task of editor. The two bodies were more than happy to act as co-sponsors of the project and to help in its planning through a joint steering committee. The result, we are confident, will be adjudged a worthy successor to the previous volumes by the very much larger 'statistics public' that has come into being in the intervening years.

Dr C. S. SMITH

Secretary
Social Science Research Council

April 1978

R. F. A. HOPES

Honorary Secretary
Royal Statistical Society

April 1978

MEMBERSHIP OF THE JOINT STEERING COMMITTEE
(April 1978)

Chairman: Miss S. V. Cunliffe

Representing the Royal Statistical Society:
Mr M. C. Fessey
Dr S. Rosenbaum

Representing the Social Science Research Council:
Mr A. S. Noble
Mrs J. Peretz
Dr W. Taylor

Secretary: Mr D. E. Allen

INTRODUCTION

In the Introduction to Volume VII, which contained two reviews on the statistics of Road Transport, it was foreshadowed that further work was following and that eventually the intention was to cover the whole of the subject matter of Order XXII of the Standard Industrial Classification. The present volume is a further step in the realization of this plan although the order of topics has been slightly rearranged.

The primary aim of this series is to act as a work of reference to the sources of statistical material of all kinds, both official and unofficial. It seeks to enable the user to discover what data are available on the subject in which he is interested, from where they may be obtained, and what the limitations are to their use. Data are regarded as available not only if published in the normal printed format but also if they are likely to be released to a *bona fide* enquirer in any other form, such as duplicated documents, computer print-out or even magnetic tape. On the other hand, no reference is made to material which, even if it is known to exist, is not accessible to the general run of potential users. The distinction, of course, is not clear-cut and mention of a source is not to be regarded as a guarantee that data will be released; in particular cases it may very well be a matter for negotiation. The latter caution applies with particular force to the question of obtaining computer print-out of custom-specified tabulations. Where original records are held on magnetic tape it might appear that there should be no insuperable problem, apart from confidentiality, in obtaining any feasible analysis at a cost; in practice, it may well turn out that there are capacity restraints which override any simple cost calculation. Thus, what is requested might make demands on computer and programming resources to the extent that the routine work of the agency concerned would be intolerably affected.

The intention is that the sources for each topic should be reviewed in detail, and the brief supplied to authors has called for comprehensive coverage at the level of 'national interest'. This term does not denote any necessary restriction to statistics collected on a national basis (still less, of course, to national aggregates) but it means that sources of a purely local character, without wider interest in either content or methodology, are excluded. Indeed, the mere task of identifying all material of this latter kind is an impossibility. The interpretation of the brief has obviously involved discretion and it is up to the users of these reviews to say what unreasonable gaps become apparent to them. They are cordially invited to do so by communicating with me.

To facilitate the use of the series as a work of reference, certain features have been incorporated which are worth a word or two of explanation.

First, the text of each review is designed, in so far as varying subject matter permits, to follow a standard form of arrangement so that users may expect a similar pattern to be followed throughout the series. The starting point is a brief summary of the activity concerned and its organization, in order to give a clear background understanding of how data are collected, what is being measured, the stage at which measurements are made, what the reporting units are, the channels through which returns are routed and where they are processed. As a further part of this introductory material, there is a discussion of the specific problems of definition and measurement to which the topic gives rise. The core sections on available sources which follow are arranged at the author's discretion—by origin, by subject subdivision, or by type of data; there is too much heterogeneity between topics to permit any imposition of complete uniformity on all authors. The final section is devoted to a discussion of general shortcomings and possibly desirable improvements. In case a contrary expectation should be aroused, it should be said that authors have not been asked to produce a comprehensive plan for the reform of statistical reporting in the whole of their field. However, a review of existing sources is a natural opportunity to make some suggestions for future policy on the collection and publication of statistics within the scope concerned.

Secondly, detailed factual information about statistical series and other data is given in a Quick Reference List (QRL). The exact nature of the entries is best seen by glancing at the list and accordingly they are not described here. Again, the ordering is not prescribed except that entries are not classified by publication source since it is presumed that it is this which is unknown to the reader. In general, the routine type of information which is given in the QRL is not repeated verbally in the text; the former, however, serves as a search route to the latter in that a reference (by section number) is shown against a QRL entry when there is a related discussion in the text.

Third, a subject index to each review acts as a more or less conventional line of enquiry on textual references; however, it is a computerized system and, for an individual review, the only peculiarity which it introduces is the possibility of easily permuting entries. Thus an entry in the index to the first review in this volume is:

National Ports Council surveys of facilities

which is also shown as:

Surveys of facilities, National Ports Council

as well as:

Facilities, National Ports Council surveys of

The object at this level is merely to facilitate search by giving as many variants as possible. In addition, individual review subject indexes are merged into a cumulative index which is held on magnetic tape and may possibly be used to produce a printed version from time to time if that seems desirable. Computer print-outs of the cumulative index to date are available on application to me at the Department of Economics, University of Exeter. In addition, selective searches of this index may be made by the input of key-words; the result is a print-out of all entries in which the key-word appears in the initial position in the subject index of any review. Like the cumulative index itself, this is a facility which may be of increasing help as the number of reviews in print grows.

Fourth, each review contains two listings of publications. The QRL Key gives full details of the publications shown as sources and text references to them are made in the form [QRL serial number]; this list is confined essentially to data publications. The other listing is a general bibliography of works discussing wider aspects; text references in this case are made in the form [B serial number].

INTRODUCTION

Finally, an attempt is made to reproduce the more important returns or forms used in data collection so that it may be seen what tabulations it is possible to make as well as helping to clarify the basis of those actually available. Unfortunately, there are severe practical limitations on the number of such forms that it is possible to append to a review and authors perforce have to be highly selective.

If all or any of these features succeed in their intention of increasing the value of the series in its basic function as a work of reference it will be gratifying; the extent to which the purpose is achieved, however, will be difficult to assess without 'feedback' from the readership. Users, therefore, will be rendering an essential service if they will send me a note of specific instances where, in consulting a review, they have failed to find the information sought.

As editor, I must express my very grateful thanks to all the members of the Joint Steering Committee of the Royal Statistical Society and the Social Science Research Council. It would be unfair to saddle them with any responsibility for shortcomings in execution but they have directed the overall strategy with as admirable a mixture of guidance and forbearance as any editor of such a series could desire. Especial thanks are due to the Secretary of the Committee who is an unfailing source of help even when sorely pressed by the more urgent demands of his other offices.

The authors join me in thanking all those who gave up their time to attend the seminar held to discuss the first drafts of their reviews and which contributed materially to improving the final versions. We are most grateful to Mr Thomas Dalby of Pergamon Press Ltd. for all his help, particularly during the vital production stages. The subject index entries for both reviews in this volume were compiled by Mrs Juliet Horwood who has also been responsible for many other aspects of the work. Our thanks go also to Mrs Gill Skinner, of the Social Studies Data Processing Unit at the University of Exeter, who has written the computer programs for the production of the subject indexes. Finally, we also wish to record our appreciation of the permission granted to us to reproduce certain copyright material by the Controller of Her Majesty's Stationery Office, by the Civil Aviation Authority, by the National Docks Labour Board and by the National Ports Council.

University of Exeter   W. F. MAUNDER
January 1978

17: PORTS AND INLAND WATERWAYS

R. E. BAXTER
Director of Economics and Statistics
National Ports Council

REFERENCE DATE OF SOURCES REVIEWED

This review is believed to represent the position, broadly speaking, as it obtained in 1976. Later revisions have been inserted up to the proof-reading stage (October 1978), taking account, as far as possible, of any major changes in the situation.

LIST OF ABBREVIATIONS

AMLBO	Association of Master Lightermen and Barge Owners
BACAT	Barge Aboard Catamaran
BHP	Brake Horse Power
EEC	European Economic Community
ISO	International Standardization Organization
LASH	Lighter Aboard Ship
LO/LO	Lift-on/lift-off
MLH	Minimum List Heading
MLWS	Mean Low Water Springs
NDLB	National Dock Labour Board
NPC	National Ports Council
NRT	Net Registered Tonne
NSTR	Nomenclature Uniforme de Marchandises pour les Statistiques de Transport, Revise
PIAC	Petroleum Industry Advisory Committee
PLA	Port of London Authority
RDW	Registered Dock Worker
RO/RO	Roll-on/roll-off
SIC	Standard Industrial Classification
SITC(R)	Standard International Trade Classification (Revised)
WPSWL	Winter Partially Smooth Water Limit

ACKNOWLEDGEMENTS

I would like to record my thanks to the many friends in the ports and inland waterways industry and government departments who gave so much help and encouragement to me during the preparation of this review. If there are any errors, they all did their best to prevent my making them.

I am particularly grateful to Bill Eadie for his close support at the National Ports Council and to Ralph Schiller for his patient guidance through the sections concerned with HM Customs statistics.

Finally, I would like to acknowledge my appreciation of the contribution made by my secretary, Angharad Thomas, who not only survived, but also prepared, the Quick Reference List and Bibliography.

London

1978

R. E. BAXTER

National Ports Council

CONTENTS OF REVIEW 17

1.	**Introduction**	7
2.	**Statistics of Port Enterprises**	10
2.1.	*Introduction*	10
2.2.	*Sources and data*	13
2.3.	*Foreign traffic by commodity*	15
2.4.	*Coastwise traffic by commodity*	17
2.5.	*Special traffic*	19
2.6.	*Scheme and non-scheme port traffic*	19
2.7.	*Container and roll-on traffic*	20
2.8.	*Contents of containers*	23
2.9.	*Driver accompanied and unaccompanied road goods vehicles*	24
2.10.	*Restow movements*	24
3.	**Transhipment and Transit Movements**	25
4.	**Fishery Traffic**	27
5.	**Passenger Traffic**	28
5.1.	*Accompanied vehicles*	29
6.	**Statistics of Customs Ports**	30
6.1.	*Foreign trade*	30
6.2.	*Container and roll-on statistics*	32
7.	**Manpower**	34
7.1.	*National Ports Council*	34
7.2.	*Non-scheme ports*	37
7.3.	*The National Dock Labour Board*	37
7.4.	*Department of Employment*	38
7.5.	*Accident statistics*	39
8.	**Inland Water Transport**	42
9.	**Shipping Movements**	47
9.1.	*Pilotage*	50

10.	**Port Facilities**	51
11.	**Finance**	54
12.	**Current and Proposed Developments**	55

Quick Reference List   59
Key to Publications   68

Bibliography   72

Appendices   73

Subject Index   105

CHAPTER 1

INTRODUCTION

1.0.0. There are about 800 ports and shipping places in the United Kingdom which accept vessels from time to time and of this total about 180 have a significant level of commercial (non-fishery) traffic. Every conceivable type of legal ownership is represented in the ports from those owned by the Government directly to private non-statutory companies. Out of a total of 184 significant commercial ports, 29 are nationalized, 31 are owned by their local authority, 50 are Public Trusts, 13 are Statutory Companies, 59 are Non-statutory Companies and 2 are owned and operated directly by the Government. Within the Statutory Company group there are two special cases, the Mersey Docks and Harbours Company and the Manchester Ship Canal Company. In the former, the Secretary of State for Transport is represented on the Board and in the latter, Manchester Corporation have the right by Statute to appoint a majority of the Board. Most of the Non-statutory Companies are small or single user own account undertakings. Felixstowe is the only port of any size which is a Statutory Company. Not all dock workers are employed by the port authorities. About 35 per cent of the registered dock labour force are employed by private companies who are engaged in cargo handling.

1.0.1. The Harbours Act of 1964 [B 10] established the National Ports Council as an advisory body, on port matters in Great Britain, to the Secretary of State for Transport. Under Section 9 of that Act no capital project may be undertaken in the commercial ports if it exceeds £1 million without the Secretary of State's approval. The Secretary of State is required to seek the Council's advice before making a decision. This control applies to all schemes however they are financed, whether private or public, in those ports within the responsibility of the Department of Transport. The control applies equally to an oil jetty, specific to a refinery (constructed, owned and operated by an oil company) as it does to a general cargo berth of a statutory port authority. The Council is not required to advise on matters relating to industrial relations and the employment of registered dock workers. These are the responsibility of the National Joint Council of the Port Transport Industry and the National Dock Labour Board, respectively. The National Ports Council has the statutory duty under the 1964 Act to collect information necessary for it to carry out its function as defined in the Act.

1.0.2. Apart from the restrictions imposed by the Act in relation to the areas in which the Council may be called upon to give advice mentioned above, the Council's authority does not extend to Northern Ireland, nor to fishery harbours in England and Wales which are the responsibility of the Ministry of Agriculture, Fisheries and Food, nor to marine works in Scotland, for which the Secretary of State for Scotland is responsible. Finally, the inland waterways, although they have close economic ties with the ports, also fall outside the institutional structure outlined above. Many of the commercial waterways are owned and operated by the British Waterways Board.

1.0.3. Since 1964 the National Ports Council has developed port statistics on a national basis. The Council has co-operated closely with HM Customs and Excise in respect to statistics of international traffic and has brought together into one publication a range of data obtained by the other institutions concerned with port matters. This development of statistical information since 1964 has been against the background of major changes in the economy of the ports.

1.0.4. The industry's activity is the physical transfer of goods, passengers and the vehicles on which they are carried, between land and sea transport. Port traffic generally is predominantly international trade although other movements are important, i.e. coastwise, transhipment and Continental Shelf traffic. In the transportation of bulk commodities such as oil, ores, cereals, and fertilizers, the major influence has been the increase in vessel size. Large bulk carriers have been introduced on those routes where the length of voyage and the level of traffic are sufficient for their potential economies of scale to be realized. This development has had two effects on the British ports. Firstly, relatively greater capital investment is required both to enable the ship to berth and to stockpile its cargo on delivery. Secondly, it has caused transhipment (e.g. via the Continental ports such as Rotterdam and Antwerp to Britain) to become cheaper than the direct route to a British port. Nevertheless already the trend has begun to change. Worldwide the increase in bulk ship sizes has reached a plateau and at home the development of offshore oil will change the port distribution and level of foreign crude-oil imports.

1.0.5. There have been significant changes in the distribution of traffic between the different ports mainly because of the shift in the pattern of UK trade in favour of the Continental members of the European Economic Community and the rapid advance of container and roll-on/roll-off methods of cargo handling and transport. The latter has also had a major impact on employment in the industry, with the numbers employed falling by about 50 per cent in the last decade.

1.0.6. The Rochdale Committee Report of 1962 [QRL 30] upon which was based the Harbours Act of 1964 [B 10] laid particular emphasis on the lack of co-ordinated statistics on a national basis of port traffic and port facilities. The National Ports Council has been able to remedy that deficiency by defining and collecting statistics using its statutory powers where applicable in relation to port undertakings in Great Britain. Later, with the development of unit-load methods of cargo handling, greater reliance has been placed on obtaining information on a voluntary basis from shipping lines operating unit-load services. From the beginning, the Council in conjunction with the Department of Trade and HM Customs and Excise was able to derive tonnage port foreign traffic by trade route from Customs data.

1.0.7. In inland waterway statistics a major difficulty has been the lack of national coverage. This has been partly as a result of the fact that the British Waterways Board does not cover the whole range of inland waterways, and partly the difficulty of definition of inland waterway movements. There is a considerable gap in the coverage of statistics in regard to movements, for instance, on the major rivers and estuaries. In addition the introduction into service of the technological innovation of ship–barge systems, such as LASH (Lighter Aboard Ship) and BACAT (Barge Aboard Catamaran), has raised problems of definition as well as highlighting in themselves the commercial importance of inland waterway movements.

CHAPTER 2

STATISTICS OF PORT ENTERPRISES

2.1. Introduction

2.1.0. As mentioned in the first chapter, standardization, collection, and collation of port statistics on a national basis were not being carried out when the Committee of Inquiry into the Major Ports of Great Britain (under Lord Rochdale) made their investigations in 1962 [QRL 30]. (It was in the light of the Committee's recommendations that the Government of the day established the National Ports Council under the Harbours Act of 1964 [B 10].) At least in so far as the commercial ports (excluding Fishing Harbours) in Great Britain are concerned, the Council has been able to act as the central co-ordinating body for the development of statistics for the ports industry. The Council's first *Digest of Port Statistics* [QRL 14] published in 1966 contained statistics of port goods traffic in 1965 of a kind which had not previously been available. Port Traffic Statistics in Northern Ireland are the responsibility of the Statistics Branch of the Department of Commerce, Belfast.

2.1.1. For information about the British ports in the period prior to 1965 reference should be made to the Rochdale Report [QRL 30] as the Committee made the first attempt to collect together on a consistent and a national basis statistics of port goods traffic. Appendix C of that report describes the sources and methods used by the Committee in compiling their statistics.

2.1.2. There are two prime sources of foreign goods traffic statistics, that of HM Customs and Excise and that of Port Authorities and port enterprises. It is important to note the fundamental differences between the two sources. The basic unit of measurement of port traffic is of weight in tonnes (metric or long tons). This is because in addition to the physical characteristics of commodities, it is their weight which directly or indirectly influences the nature and extent of harbour facilities. Statistics in weight terms are available both from Customs and from Port Authorities and enterprises but the former are in terms net of immediate packaging and the latter are gross, inclusive of such packaging. The packaging referred to is *immediate*, that is in neither case does the weight include the weight of the unit-load device (e.g. an ISO container) in or on which the commodity is transported.

2.1.3. HM Customs and Excise ports do not necessarily coincide geographically with Port Authority areas of statutory jurisdiction. For instance, the Customs Port called Cardiff includes, in addition to the port of Cardiff, the port of Barry. Again, until 1974 the Customs Port of London included Sheerness which is within the ownership and control of the Medway Port Authority (MPA) and not the Port of London Authority (PLA).

2.1.4. Some goods are excluded by Customs as not entering international trade because no commercial transaction is involved, e.g. waste material, British military supplies (details of these exclusions are given in paragraph 15 of the Notes to the monthly *Overseas Trade Statistics* [QRL 23]), transhipment or transit traffic (see paragraph 2.1.16), personal and professional effects and trade samples. These are all included in port statistics.

2.1.5. The basic measure of 'activity' or output of the ports is the tonnage of goods (or the number of passengers) moved across the quays or jetties. The quay or jetty with its associated support facilities (e.g. cranage, transit sheds, stacking areas) is the main 'production' unit of the industry, although, of course, the vessels loading or discharging goods or passengers play a complementary role in the activity. The methods employed in moving the goods or passengers across the quays determine the nature of the port facilities and the nature of the vessels used.

2.1.6. Many factors will influence the choice of the mode of transport of commodities through the ports. However, modal choice is significantly determined by the tonnage, the physical characteristics and the overseas origin and destination of commodities. The Council's first aim in 1964, therefore, was to establish a system for the collection on a standardized basis of statistics for the industry which would illuminate these factors.

2.1.7. It is necessary to distinguish certain categories of traffic. The UK has only one land boundary, that with the Republic of Ireland. Therefore, apart from a relatively small though valuable quantity of goods traffic which moves by air freight and that moving across the land boundary, almost the whole of UK visible foreign trade by weight passes through the ports. (Any offshore natural gas or crude oil landed by pipeline from wells outside the British sector are not, of course, part of port traffic although included in Customs statistics.) In practice the ports do not have any competition from other transport enterprises in foreign trade. Changes in the UK's international trade therefore have an important effect on activity in the ports and it is necessary to distinguish foreign imports and foreign exports as a category of traffic. Foreign traffic is defined as traffic which passes to or from countries outside the UK (that is, outside Great Britain, Northern Ireland, the Isle of Man and the Channel Islands). Foreign trade, however, although a major part of port traffic is not by any means the whole of it. About one-third of port traffic is currently *coastwise* and *special* traffic.

2.1.8. *Special* traffic is traffic in sea-going vessels other than foreign and coastwise. This traffic includes the following:
(a) dredged sand and gravel and other material landed at a port for commercial purposes (e.g. it excludes material derived from maintenance or capital dredging of shipping channels);
(b) motor vehicles, including tourist motor cars, roll-on/roll-off vehicles and trailers not themselves subject to commercial transactions;
(c) used packaging and containers not themselves subject to a commercial transaction;
(d) petroleum and coal bunkers for a ship's own use on voyage;
(e) fish landings from fishing grounds;
(f) traffic to and from offshore installations;
(g) material shipped for dumping at sea.

2.1.9. *Coastwise* traffic is traffic in sea-going vessels passing between ports in the United Kingdom (that is between ports in Great Britain, Northern Ireland, the Isle of Man and the Channel Islands; and between ports in Great Britain). Traffic between the mainland and islands within Great Britain (e.g. Shetland) is coastwise. It should be noted, however, that sea-going vessels are vessels which actually go to sea. Traffic which moves from one port to another port within the same estuary is not included in *coastwise* even if the vessel used is designed for sea voyages.

2.1.10. One of the objectives of the Statistical Office of the European Communities is to reach agreement among the member countries on the standardization as far as practicable of nomenclature used in national statistics. Consideration is being given to the definitions used for 'non-foreign' traffic. In particular it is felt that the traffic covered by the definition of coastwise (see paragraph 2.1.9) used in UK port statistics should more appropriately be termed 'national' or 'domestic' with perhaps an extension to include the special traffic (see paragraph 2.1.8) so that in effect it becomes all traffic other than foreign.

2.1.11. The terminology 'coastwise' or 'coastal' traffic could be retained and defined as 'domestic' traffic excluding 'special' traffic and traffic between Great Britain and Northern Ireland (carried between ports in Great Britain or between ports in Northern Ireland). All these definitions relate to traffic in 'sea-going vessels'—that is to traffic which is actually carried out to sea. Such a definition has the added advantage of bringing the ports (and shipping) into correspondence with the general transport economy. The coastal trade of Great Britain, for instance, could be viewed as traffic passing between points which could be connected by land or inland waterway transport and therefore operating within clearly defined boundaries within which different modes of transport are or could be in competition.

2.1.12. It should be noted that because all the traffic categories above (see paragraph 2.1.7 et seq.) refer only to sea-going vessels, the three categories together do not give a complete coverage of traffic movement at ports. Traffic moving by barges unsuitable for sea-going voyages between wharves and ports connected by inland waterways are excluded (see paragraph 8.0.0 et seq. for a description of available inland waterway statistics) as are, also, any traffics carried, say, between ports within the same estuary in vessels which *could* go to sea.

2.1.13. The interpretation of the meaning of 'sea-going' vessel became ambiguous with the introduction of LASH (lighter aboard ship) and BACAT (barge aboard catamaran) vessels. The barges of these vessels travel along inland waterways, are picked up by the mother ship and are taken out to sea. In a sense, therefore, these barges are 'sea-going' in that they do actually go to sea. This issue was raised in 1975 when Barge Aboard Catamaran (UK) Limited, Patrederiet Rudkøbing VI and the British Waterways Board objected under Section 31 of the Harbours Act, 1964 [B 10] to the dues charged by the British Transport Docks Board at Hull, Grimsby, Immingham, Goole and on the Rivers Humber and Ouse. In Appendix VII of the Inspector's report of the Inquiry dated 7 April 1975 [B 13], the solicitor to the National Ports Council, the appellate body, advised that the expression vessels '*passing* from the River Humber to the sea' used in the relevent Acts should be taken to mean a vessel passing when it it itself on the water and does not include a vessel passing by being transported in a larger vessel. He concluded that BACAT and LASH barges did not 'go to sea' as far as the local Acts of Parliament relevant to the Humber were concerned.

2.1.14. It was pointed out in paragraph 2.1.5 that the basic unit of measurement is the tonnage of cargo moved across the quays. The categories of cargo defined in paragraphs 2.1.7 et seq. cover all (sea-going) traffic which passes through the ports from a sea mode of transport from/to a land mode. In order to complete the total of measurement of port activity it is necessary to add restow and transhipment movements.

2.1.15. Restow movements arise when a vessel has more than one port of call but the cargo has not been stowed in sequence with these ports of call. Cargo, therefore, has to be removed to reach cargo stowed lower in the hold and then restowed for discharge at the next port of call. Movements of this kind are particularly common with container vessels. The cargo does not leave the berth at which it is temporarily unloaded, nevertheless the movements do give rise to a claim on resources at the port in terms of cranage and stacking area as well as labour. It is not a trivial movement. At some ports in Britain, restows account for 10 to 15 per cent of the total tonnage shifted at some container berths.

2.1.16. Transhipment traffic is defined as traffic which is discharged at a port but rather than passing from a sea mode to a land mode of transportation passes to a sea mode for the next leg of its journey. This traffic may be discharged overside from one vessel to another without being landed to quay, or it may be traffic transported by sea mode to be discharged to the Dock Estate and loaded to sea-mode transport subsequently. Transit traffic is traffic which although transferring to a land mode is transported to another port of loading for onward movement by sea without breaking Customs seal. Commodities transported in this way are not enhanced by any added value within the UK and are not included by HM Customs and Excise as part of the UK's visible trade (see paragraph 2.1.4). These movements are generally included in the statistics of traffic obtained from the ports (see paragraph 2.1.2). In some ports, e.g. London, some goods transhipped at the port do not attract any port dues or charges and consequently the port authority does not record the movement at all even aggregated in other traffic figures. They are not, however, in any case separately distinguishable in UK port statistics (see paragraph 3.0.0 et seq.). Transhipment traffic is of interest to ports as a sub-category because individual ports see it as an area in which they are particularly sensitive to competition. There is some evidence of substantial tonnages of bulk commodities which are transhipped to the UK via ports in Continental Europe. Deep sea shipping services avoid calling at the large ports of the UK such as London and feed the UK market with small ships from Europe calling at the smaller UK ports. There has been some controversy about the extent of this kind of movement in the general cargo (as opposed to the bulk) trades and whether any significant upward trend has emerged in recent years (see paragraph 3.0.0 et seq.).

2.2. Sources and Data

2.2.0. We deal under this heading with traffic statistics derived from sources other than HM Customs and Excise (see paragraph 6.1.0 et seq.). In pursuance of the Harbours Act, 1964

[B 10], the National Ports Council has become the central authority for the collection, development and publication of the statistics of the commercial ports and harbours in Great Britain. The Council has no jurisdiction in Northern Ireland (see paragraph 2.2.3), the Isle of Man or the Channel Islands. Further, the Council has regard to the 'commercial' ports only. Fishery Harbours in England and Wales as defined in Section 21 of the Sea Fish Industry Act, 1951 [B 20] are the responsibility of the Ministry of Agriculture, Fisheries and Food. A list of Fishery Harbours is given in the Fourth Schedule of the 1951 Act [B 20]. Similarly, in Scotland, the National Ports Council's authority does not embrace 'marine works'. These are defined as harbours, ferry or boatslips in Scotland which are principally used for the fishing industry or which are required for the maintenance of communications in the Islands. (See Section 57 of the Harbours Act, 1964 [B 10] for a full definition.)

2.2.1. The National Ports Council has the power under Section 41 of the Harbours Act, 1964 [B 10] to obtain information by notice in writing served on a person engaged in a harbour activity in Great Britain. A person failing to comply with the notice is guilty of an offence. The Council does not have any authority to serve such a notice in respect to a fishery harbour or a marine work. A fishery harbour or marine work may, of course, have some commercial traffic and likewise a commercial port is not precluded from having some fishery business. Although the Council cannot by statute insist on the completion of its statistical returns by people engaged in fishery harbour or marine work activity, in practice it has been able to cover these on a voluntary basis. This has been sufficiently successful for the Council to be confident that only the most trivial tonnage of commercial traffic is not being recorded.

2.2.2. The coverage of the Council's statistics has not always been so complete. In 1972 the Council carried out a special analysis of 'scheme' and 'non-scheme' ports (see paragraph 2.6.0 et seq.) which brought to light a significant gap in the Council's statistical coverage. In particular many wharves along the Rivers Trent and Ouse had previously been overlooked. This survey discovered about 3 million tonnes of traffic which had previously been unrecorded. For details of this traffic, reference should be made to the Council's annual *Digest of Port Statistics* 1972, Tables 57A and 57B [QRL 14]. There is therefore a discontinuity in the historic time series in 1972.

2.2.3. Traffic statistics for the ports in Northern Ireland have been collected continuously since 1930. The responsibility for collecting these statistics rests with the Statistics Branch of the Department of Commerce which receives periodic traffic returns from all the 25 ports in Northern Ireland. These ports are required to supply information by statute under the Harbours Act (Northern Ireland), 1970 [B 11].

2.2.4. The National Ports Council first requested port authorities and other bodies to submit annual statistical returns under the authority of Section 41 of the Harbours Act [B 10] in 1966. The results of this request were published in the Council's first issue of its annual *Digest of Port Statistics* [QRL 14] which was published in 1966 and contained data for the year 1965. However, in any historical study it is preferable to assume that the series began with the year 1966, as the data for 1965 were in many ways suspect. This was because a number of port authorities had not by that year introduced information systems which were adequate to meet the demands laid upon them by the Council's returns. By the following year, 1966, the ports had had time to learn and adjust and, it is generally believed, were able by then to meet the Council's statistical requirements at least up to the point that they would ever meet them. The Council's *Annual Digest of Port Statistics Volume I* [QRL 4] contains an alphabetical list of the ports, shipping places and port authorities in the UK. This list also records those enterprises which submit returns to the Council.

2.2.5. In 1975 the National Ports Council obtained the agreement of the British Ports Association that the major and medium-size ports in Great Britain should submit traffic returns quarterly on a voluntary basis. The detail and coverage were decided initially by statistics which each port already collected for its own management purposes. The Council began publishing the data in a quarterly bulletin in 1976.

2.2.6. For the ports in Northern Ireland, the Department of Commerce collects yearly traffic data. Annual data for these ports were published in *The Trade of Northern Ireland* [QRL 39] available in a series dating from 1930 to 1974—the last year for which detailed commodity information was collected (see paragraph 2.4.7). There was, however, a change in commodity classification in 1968 with the introduction of an SITC based commodity code.

2.3. Foreign Traffic by Commodity

2.3.0. Statistics of foreign traffic (see paragraph 2.1.7) are submitted to the National Ports Council annually by port undertakings in Britain, on Council forms P.S.3a (for imports) and P.S.3b (for exports). (See Appendix 1 for a sample of these returns.) They are obtained under statutory notice from those ports and harbours over which the Council has jurisdiction and on a voluntary basis from others (see paragraph 2.2.1). For the difference between these statistics and those collected by HM Customs and Excise see paragraphs 2.1.2 et seq.

2.3.1. These returns are compiled by port undertakings from records maintained of the dues levied on their goods traffic, supplemented by figures supplied by shipowners, shippers, stevedores, wharfingers and HM Customs and Excise. These returns give exports and imports in gross tonnages (i.e. including immediate packaging) by commodities classified by an NPC code based on SITC(R). (See Appendix 2 for the commodity classification used by the National Ports Council.) This classification was designed so that the major commodity categories of traffic could be determined, e.g. dry bulks, general cargo and fuels, and at the same time retaining sufficient detail to preserve the major economic characteristics of the classification of SITC(R). The prime source publication for these data is the National Ports Council's *Digest of Port Statistics* [QRL 14] for the period up to 1972 and the *Annual Digest of Port Statistics Volume I* [QRL 4] for statistics for the years 1973 and after. This publication includes the complete data (see Appendix 1 for the sample returns) for each major and medium-size port in Great Britain and summary data for the small ports. The only exceptions to publication are those cases in which there would be a breach of confidence because to do so would reveal the traffic of a specific undertaking from whom the Council has not obtained permission to publish. (In practice, this does not lead to a serious loss of published information in this area. It is a more important constraint in the publication of unit-load statistics (see paragraph 2.7.0 et seq.).)

2.3.2. It should be noted that the Port of London Authority is an exception in that the PLA does not submit to the National Ports Council the statistical returns P.S.3a and P.S.3b. This is because the PLA has never had a charging system for foreign trade in any way related to the commodity classification required by the Council and was unable to establish systems which would meet the requirement. This is due to the complexity of activity within the PLA jurisdiction involving 'overside' as well as 'over quay' operations and including many operators along the river independent of PLA management although within their statutory boundary. The NPC publish in their *Digest* [QRL 4] data for London based on HM Customs and Excise returns. As a result, up to 1975, the London figures were in *net* tonnes and not gross tonnes as for the other ports.

2.3.3. A more serious difficulty has emerged over the years. The commodity classification was established by the Council before the unit-load services had become the important mode of sea transport they are today. The P.S.3 series of returns are designed to cover the whole of port traffic and the commodity analysis in particular to apply equally to that whole. The prime sources, however, of the information are charges and cargo-handling records. Generally, the ports do not keep information for these purposes related to the commodity carried in unit loads (e.g. a roll-on/roll-off vehicle or an ISO container) and so, with the growth of this type of traffic, other methods of collecting this information have had to be devised.

2.3.4. For a commodity analysis of the content of unit-loads, the ports make use of the shipping manifest which records in detail the commodities and tonnages loaded in each container or RO/RO vehicle carried by the ship. Ships' manifests, however, do not follow any standard commodity classification system and some ports do not collect such information on a continuous census basis but rely on sampling methods to obtain their commodity classification of the contents of unit-loads. As an example, the latter method was carried out by the Mersey Docks and Harbours Company for the years 1973 and after, in order to complete the P.S.3 returns. (See mimeograph paper by National Ports Council staff on the use of *Ships Manifests as a Source of Statistical Information*, E. Hunter [B 3], and *The Sampling of Mersey Docks and Harbours Company Ship Manifests*, 1973, by W. T. Eadie [B 2].)

2.3.5. The commodity content of unit-loads is needed by the ports industry for both marketing and planning purposes. However, as from 1975, HM Customs and Excise are able to supply such information because of the requirement to specify unit-load devices on the basic Customs documentation (see paragraph 6.2.0). Given a satisfactory outcome of the development of this new source, the National Ports Council is considering a revised commodity classification for the P.S.3 returns which will not apply to cargo carried by unit-loads such as container and roll-on/roll-off movements.

2.3.6. In Northern Ireland, as foreign traffic accounts for only about 35 per cent by weight of total port traffic, the Department of Commerce does not collect detailed commodity information about foreign traffic movements from port enterprises. The only source of detailed commodity information about foreign traffic of these ports is that obtained by HM Customs and Excise (see paragraph 6.1.0 et seq.).

2.4. Coastwise Traffic by Commodity

2.4.0. Statistics of coastwise traffic (see paragraph 2.1.9 et seq.) are submitted annually to the National Ports Council by port undertakings in Great Britain on Council forms P.S.3c (for inwards movements) and P.S.3d (for outward movements). (See Appendix 3 for a sample of these returns.) Quarterly returns are also submitted by the major ports. They are obtained under statutory powers from those ports and harbours over which the Council has jurisdiction and on a voluntary basis from others (see paragraph 2.2.1). The sources of information used by the port undertakings and the commodity classification adopted are identical to those of foreign traffic and are explained in paragraph 2.3.1. In addition, the difficulties that are being met with by ports in completing the returns in respect of unit-load movements which are explained for foreign traffic in paragraphs 2.3.3 and 2.3.4 also apply to coastwise movements. Coastwise unit-load movements are significant because the definition includes traffic between Great Britain and Northern Ireland (see paragraph 2.1.9). In this case, of course, the new information which it is hoped will be derived from the new Customs documentation (see paragraph 2.3.5) will not apply.

2.4.1. Coastwise traffic is traffic in sea-going vessels passing *between ports* in the United Kingdom (see paragraph 2.1.9). In theory, therefore, coastwise inwards movements should balance coastwise outwards. Coastwise statistics by commodity and by port published in the National Ports Council's *Annual Digest of Port Statistics Volume I* [QRL 4] are for Great Britain. They cover coastwise movements—that is movements within the United Kingdom recorded only at ports in Great Britain. This means that the outwards traffic includes traffic *to* the Channel Islands, the Isle of Man and Northern Ireland *from* ports in Britain. However, the inwards traffic excludes the traffic arriving *at* those destinations. In order to obtain balance, therefore, the coastwise traffic recorded at the ports in Northern Ireland (see paragraph 2.4.5), the Channel Islands and the Isle of Man should be included.

2.4.2. Nevertheless it is true that, even when such adjustments as outlined in paragraph 2.4.1 are made, there still remains a gap between the two figures and between the figures for specific commodities. A number of explanations are possible:

(a) The P.S.3c and P.S.3d returns do not give a complete coverage (but see paragraph 2.2.1).
(b) Timing for certain flows may be such that an outward movement is recorded in one year and the inward movement in the following year.
(c) Some transhipment movements may not be recorded (see paragraph 2.1.16).
(d) There may be some misclassification of commodities (this may be quite substantial, e.g. between crude petroleum and petroleum products).

2.4.3. It is not possible to match individual outward with individual inward movements because port undertakings do not keep records of movements on this basis. There is a strong case, however, for the collection of such information if coastwise shipping movements are redefined along the lines debated within the EEC as described in paragraphs 2.1.10 and 2.1.11. In that context, coastal trade is seen as part of a competitive transport system including road, rail and inland waterways. Statistics of port origin and destination of coastal movements would be necessary before any intermodal studies could fruitfully be launched. There is a basic source of such information in the Customs document called the 'transire'.

This is a document which must be completed and held by the master of a vessel in the coastal trade carrying any cargo except coal. The document shows the ports of loading and discharge and is issued either for a specific journey between two ports or for a series of ports of call (a 'general transire') (specimen copies are at Appendix 4).

2.4.4. Statistics of total coastal traffic in tonne kilometres are published in the *Annual Abstract of Statistics* [QRL 3]. Statistics of petroleum and petroleum products traffic carried coastwise in tonne kilometres are published in the *Digest of UK Energy Statistics* [QRL 16]. The Departments of Industry, Trade, and Prices and Consumer Protection (and predecessors), Statistics (Shipping) Division collected data from 1945 until the first quarter of 1976 of dry cargo coastwise traffic carried by UK vessels. The returns were made monthly by shipping lines on a voluntary basis. These returns showed for each vessel and each voyage:

(1) date cargo loaded,
(2) date cargo discharged,
(3) loading port,
(4) discharging port,
(5) nature of cargo.

These statistics were used to calculate the aggregate tonne-kilometre figures published in the *Annual Abstract of Statistics* [QRL 3]. No further details were published. The detailed information was confidential. Because the returns were made voluntarily and excluded foreign shipping lines, only a proportion of the trade was covered. The statistics of coastwise movements of petroleum and petroleum products traffic published in the *Digest of UK Energy Statistics* [QRL 16] are made available to the Departments of Energy and Transport by the Petroleum Industry Advisory Committee (PIAC).

2.4.5. The Statistics Branch of the Department of Commerce, Belfast, does not collect statistics of traffic between ports in Northern Ireland but this traffic is believed to be insignificant. The Department does, however, collect statistics of the traffic between the ports of Northern Ireland and the ports of Great Britain. These figures include foreign imports and exports of Northern Ireland shipped from/to overseas countries through Britain without breaking Customs seal (see paragraph 2.1.16 on transhipment and transit traffic). These statistics have been collected since 1930.

2.4.6. Returns of traffic between Britain and Northern Ireland were in the past submitted to the Department of Commerce monthly by the five major ports of Belfast, Larne, Londonderry, Warrenpoint and Coleraine; quarterly by a further 15 ports and annually by the remaining five. The returns, one for inwards and one for outwards traffic, recorded the gross tonnes, kilogrammes, or numbers of units of traffic for commodities specified in a coded 'Goods Schedule Index'. Traffic was broken down into 235 commodity headings based on the SITC(R) on the returns and the 'Goods Schedule Index' contained about 2000 separate references to assist the ports in the correct classification of commodities. Statistics of the total cross-Channel traffic inwards and outwards in gross tonnes between Northern Ireland and British ports analysed into the National Ports Council's commodity groups (see Appendix 2) were published in the Council's *Annual Digest of Port Statistics Volume I* [QRL 4] in 1973 and 1974 and, prior to 1973, in the *Digest of Port Statistics*

[QRL 14]. The Department of Trade's publications *The Trade of Northern Ireland* [QRL 39] included only total imports and total exports (i.e. foreign plus cross-Channel) in gross tonnes for each of the five major ports (mentioned above) plus Newry and for all the ports in Northern Ireland in total. The publication of *The Trade of Northern Ireland* was discontinued after 1974 and the collection of commodity data from ports ceased.

2.4.7. The collection of commodity data from the ports of Northern Ireland ceased because it was becoming increasingly difficult to obtain accurate information on cross-Channel trade, which accounts for about 80 per cent of Northern Ireland's total. Since Customs documentation is not required for cross-Channel trade, the necessary information had to be obtained from ships' manifests. Owing to the growth of containerization with its mixed consignments for which descriptions are usually too general to provide the necessary detailed analysis, the Department decided that the overall accuracy of the information available was no longer good enough for statistical purposes.

2.5. Special Traffic

2.5.0. Statistics of special traffic (see paragraph 2.1.8 et seq.) are submitted annually to the National Ports Council by port undertakings on Council form P.S.3e. (See Appendix 5 for a sample of this return.) Tonnage of used packaging and containers, not themselves subject to a commercial transaction, are collected for foreign traffic on forms P.S.3a and P.S.3b (see paragraph 2.3.0 et seq.), for coastwise traffic on forms P.S.3c and P.S.3d (see paragraph 2.4.0 et seq.), for the cross-Channel traffic with Northern Ireland on the forms issued by the Department of Commerce (see paragraph 2.4.5). Information about special traffic is obtained under statutory notice from those ports and harbours over which the National Ports Council has jurisdiction in Britain and the Department of Commerce in Northern Ireland, and on a voluntary basis from others (see paragraph 2.1.1). The sources of information used by the port undertakings to complete these returns are the records of charges and dues levied on goods and vessels and cargo-handling records.

2.5.1. Special traffic statistics (for Great Britain only) are published annually by commodity and for each port in the National Ports Council's *Annual Digest of Port Statistics Volume I* [QRL 4]. They have been collected and published annually by the Council since 1966 except the commodity breakdown which was introduced in 1975 (see paragraph 2.2.4) and except for the two items 'material shipped for dumping at sea' and 'traffic with offshore installations' which were introduced for 1973.

2.6. Scheme and Non-scheme Port Traffic

2.6.0. 'Scheme' ports are defined as all ports and undertakings where cargo-handling work is subject to the provisions of the Dock Labour Scheme (see paragraph 7.3.0). In 1972 the Minister for Transport Industries invited the National Ports Council to carry out a study of the relative position of scheme and non-scheme ports. The terms of reference of the study were to examine:

(i) the traffic handled by non-scheme ports (in which term are included wharves and jetties not operated under statutory powers). A clear distinction should be drawn between common user and single user facilities;

(ii) their significance for the capacity of the ports industry and their effect upon adjacent ports;

(iii) the finances and labour costs of such undertakings,

with a view to tendering advice including advice as to whether in the national interest such undertakings, or any of them, should be brought within the control of the larger ports which provide a full range of services.' The National Ports Council completed its study in 1973 and published its report in two volumes (*Survey of Non-Scheme Ports and Wharves*, Preliminary and Final Reports) [QRL 37].

2.6.1. The Council sent out a questionnaire (see Appendix 6) to a total of 226 non-scheme port and wharf undertakings. The list of addresses was drawn up from official sources (see paragraph 7.1.3) and the Council was satisfied that all non-scheme ports of any significance were included. Of the 226 undertakings to whom the questionnaire was sent, 63 replied that they no longer handled traffic. Of the remainder, 23 replies were not received but all these were regarded as of no importance. Information was, therefore, obtained for 140 non-scheme undertakings. This survey revealed that the Council had not been adequately covering the commercial ports with its P.S.3 series of returns (see paragraph 2.2.2).

2.6.2. The Council was hesitant about sending a questionnaire which would be regarded as too irksome, dealing as it was with a subject which was politically sensitive. To quote the Preliminary Report [QRL 37]: 'The questionnaires were deliberately kept as simple as possible, in order to facilitate speedy response and analysis.' In the event, from a statistical point of view, they probably gave overmuch weight to the requirement of a 'speedy response' and too little to the needs of 'analysis'. In addition, the emphasis of the study was to isolate 'own account' from 'third party' activities. (See the *Preliminary Report* of the *Survey of Non-Scheme Ports and Wharves* for a definition of these terms [QRL 37].) As a result, a breakdown only of fuel and the main bulk cargoes was called for, without any split inwards/outwards, coastwise, foreign or special and even that breakdown was only for 1971. For earlier years only total tonnages were recorded. The result was that the survey could not be used to fill the gap in the statistical coverage it itself had revealed. This could only be done from 1972 onwards, when the P.S.3 returns could be sent out to the newly uncovered addresses.

2.6.3. Traffic at non-scheme ports in 1971 analysed by Fuel, Main Dry Bulks and General Cargo and divided between single-user (own account traffic) and third-party traffic was published in the *Preliminary Report* of the *Survey of Non-Scheme Ports and Wharves* [QRL 37]. A time series, 1966 to 1971, of non-scheme third party and own account traffic was published in the *Final Report* [QRL 37].

2.7. Container and Roll-on Traffic

2.7.0. Statistics of container and roll-on traffic are submitted annually by port undertakings to the National Ports Council on Council forms P.S.48 (Revised) and P.S.48 Annexes A, B and C. (See Appendix 7 for samples of these returns.) They are obtained on a voluntary basis from all ports having unit-load services in Great Britain. The basic data sources used by the ports are varied, depending on the nature of the information required. Information is available to them either from their own financial records—their charges are levied on, for instance, numbers of containers moved—or their own operational records which monitor movements at and across the berths, or they may request the shipping lines to complete the relevant returns. It should be noted in the latter context, that a separate return is requested for each shipping company or consortium and each service route. Statistics are also collected on a quarterly basis by the Department of Transport of (driver) accompanied and unaccompanied road goods vehicles, trailers and semi-trailers on specialized roll-on services (see Appendix 8 for specimen form). This return is obtained by the Department of Transport from shipping lines. The prime publication for all these statistics, on an annual basis, is the National Ports Council's *Annual Digest of Port Statistics, Volume I* and *Volume II* from 1973 onwards [QRL 4]. Prior to that year, the figures were published in the Council's *Container and Roll-on Port Statistics, Great Britain* [QRL 12], the first issue of which was in 1970, carrying data for 1965 to 1969. The port authorities which submit P.S.48 returns to the National Ports Council are listed in the *Annual Digest of Port Statistics* [QRL 4]. (The earlier publications were *Port Traffic on Unit Transport Services, Great Britain, 1965 and 1966* [QRL 27], *Port Unit Transport Statistics, Great Britain, 1968* [QRL 28] and *Port Unit Transport Statistics, Great Britain, 1969* [QRL 28].)

2.7.1. There is no international standardization of definitions covering unit-load statistics (see paragraph 6.2.0 for Customs definition). The definitions used by the National Ports Council which are applied by the port undertakings and shipping lines completing the P.S.48 (Revised) returns (see also paragraph 2.7.6) are as follows. Container and Roll-on traffic statistics are classified into three groups:

(1) 'Roll-on Services'—those services on which all the vessels have ramp loading.
(2) 'Special Lift-on Services'—those services on which all the vessels are specially constructed or adapted for the carriage of containers (q.v.) and normally do not carry any 'break bulk' cargo.
(3) All other (conventional) services—those conventional dry cargo vessels which carry some containers in addition to predominantly break bulk cargo.

2.7.2. In addition the 'type of unit' is divided into five classes:

(1) Railway Wagons—all railway wagons carried on train ferries.
(2) Road Goods Vehicles and Trailers—including those carrying class (3) except dockside or ships' trailers.
(3) Lancashire Flats—including those carried on dockside or ships' trailers but not by class (1) or class (2).
(4) Bulk Liquid Containers—with a capacity of at least 500 gallons but excluding those carried by class (1) or class (2).
(5) A freight container—except those carried on class (1) or class (2) defined by B.S. 3951, that is 'an article of equipment having an overall volume greater than 8 cubic metres, either rigid or collapsible, suitable for repeated use in the carriage of materials in bulk or package form and capable of transfer between one or more forms of transport'.

2.7.3. The traffic is recorded by overseas country and it should be particularly noted that this is the country where goods are discharged from/loaded aboard that vessel which took them from/brought them to a British port. The term refers to the overseas country of *shipment*. The traffic is not, therefore, recorded by country of origin/destination or country of consignment. The latter is the definition used by HM Customs and Excise for their foreign trade statistics (see paragraph 6.1.0).

2.7.4. The National Ports Council publishes all statistical data collected on the P.S.48 returns and Annexes subject to the overriding constraint of confidentiality of commercial information. The 'rule of three' is applied both in relation to the data of shipping lines and also to port undertakings. In practice this constraint limits the detail published in two ways. Firstly, data are published generally by individual port and these are grouped by regions in Britain. However, a number of ports have to be grouped within each region in order to lose identity. For instance, the traffic of Harwich, Parkeston Quay and Ipswich is grouped together under 'East Midlands and East Anglia—Others'. Felixstowe which is in this region can be shown separately. Secondly, it also happens that to publish statistics for a specific trading route or mode could reveal commercially confidential information of particular shipping lines. As far as possible, analyses are published for each overseas country of shipment but in some cases data for only a broad grouping of countries can be revealed. For this purpose, but also for the purposes of analysis, routes are grouped into the following categories:

(1) Coastwise—see paragraph 2.1.9 for a discussion of the definition of this term. Statistics for Northern Ireland are shown separately.
(2) Foreign—non-coastwise traffic by country of shipment (see paragraph 2.7.3) of which:

Near Sea   Republic of Ireland, France, Netherlands, Western Germany and Belgium.
Short Sea   Europe (other than near sea), Scandinavia and the Mediterranean countries.
Deep Sea   All countries outside Europe and the Mediterranean.

2.7.5. The statistics for the years 1965 and 1966, which were published in the National Ports Council's *Port Traffic on Unit Transport Services, Great Britain, 1965 and 1966* [QRL 27] were based upon estimates made by port authorities and the Council. A description of the methods used may be found in that publication (see paragraph 2.7.0). Statistics for 1967 and later years have been based on the P.S.48 series of returns. The P.S.48 return was revised, to the basis shown in the sample at Appendix 7, to take effect from 1969.

2.7.6. Prior to 1969, unit-load traffic was divided into two classes:

(1) Roll-on/roll-off units, on wheels integral to the transport unit, i.e. railway wagons, road goods vehicles and trailers (including those vehicles carrying Lancashire flats, bulk liquid containers and other loaded freight containers).
(2) Other transport units (Lancashire flats, bulk liquid containers and other freight containers).

This classification was found inadequate to distinguish the two major modes of unit transport operation, i.e. lift-on/lift-off and roll-on/roll-off. It is this distinction which is clearly most relevant to unit-load operations both in terms of the type of vessel employed and the type of port facility required. Unit-loads are carried aboard roll-on/roll-off vessels on special ships' trailers or dockside-only trailers. These movements were recorded as 'other transport units' although they required a shore-linked ramp for the vessel and were in fact a roll-on/roll-off operation. Data derived from the pre-1969, P.S.48 return overestimated the volume of traffic over lift-on/lift-off port facilities.

2.7.7. The pre-1969 P.S.48 returns were not made for each individual service. Route analysis is available for this period only for foreign and coastwise services. In addition, the revised P.S.48 return extended coverage for the first time to include 'accompanied cars and buses', the numbers of ISO containers by size and numbers of empty containers.

2.7.8. Each of the ports of Northern Ireland returns the following details to the Statistics Branch of the Department of Commerce, Belfast:

	Number Loaded/Empty	Tonnes Tare weight	Tonnes Weight of goods carried
Unit load traffic (inwards and outwards)			
Roll-on/Roll-off:			
Road goods vehicles/trailers			
Other (flats, containers, etc.)			
Lift-on/Lift-off:			
Flats, containers, etc.			

2.8. Contents of Containers

2.8.0. A commodity analysis of unit transport traffic for 1970 was published in the National Ports Council's *Container and Roll-on Port Statistics, 1971* Part 2 [QRL 12]. This analysis was derived from the information on ships' manifests at 14 ports in Britain. The commodity classification was that of the National Ports Council (see Appendix 2) and gave a breakdown between foreign and coastwise traffic. A further analysis of the commodity content of containers based on ships' manifests was made of exports to and imports from North America for the years 1969, 1970 and 1971. The results were published in *Container and Roll-on Port Statistics, 1973* Part 2 [QRL 12].

2.8.1. The average weight of container contents, sizes of containers and movements by trade route have been published by the National Ports Council since 1968. These data are supplied by port authorities from their own records which form the basis of their charges to shipping lines. They may be regarded as reasonably accurate for route and average tonnage of contents but may be less accurate as regards the numbers of non-standard sizes of containers. For instance, it is believed that the figures are reasonably accurate for the standard container sizes, e.g. $40 \times 8 \cdot 5 \times 8$ ft and $20 \times 8 \times 8$ ft, but may be less accurate for less frequently observed non-standard sizes because the basic records at some port authorities do not distinguish every container with unusual dimensions.

2.8.2. Statistics of the average weight of contents of containers analysed by size of container and by trade route have been collected by the National Ports Council and published in *Container and Roll-on Port Statistics, 1971* Part 2 and *1973* Part 2 [QRL 12]. These figures were based on samples of containers, viz. 98,968 containers in 1968; 160,225 containers in 1969; 320,531 containers in 1970 and finally 141,591 containers in 1972. No survey was conducted in 1971 or after 1972. The samples were derived from information held by shipping lines which carried a particular size of container rather than a mix of container sizes. By 1972 an increasing number of shipping lines was carrying a mixture of sizes so that this source of information ceased to be satisfactory.

2.9. Driver Accompanied and Unaccompanied Road Goods Vehicles

2.9.0. In 1972 the National Ports Council carried out a survey of shipping companies carrying commercial road goods vehicles/trailers in order to determine the proportion of driver accompanied vehicles. An overall response rate of 95 per cent of the number of movements during 1972 was achieved. The results were published in *Container and Roll-on Port Statistics, 1973* Part 2 [QRL 12]. This publication includes tables of the proportion of unaccompanied Road Goods Vehicles by trade route for each year 1970, 1971 and 1972. Subsequently, the Department of Transport took over responsibility for the collection of this information from shipping lines. The prime source of the latter information is the National Ports Council, *Annual Digest of Port Statistics, Volume I* [QRL 4] (see paragraph 6.2.1).

2.10. Restow Movements

2.10.0. Annex C of P.S.48 (Revised) (see Appendix 7) was first introduced in 1974 by the National Ports Council. It is completed by port authorities from their own operating records. It had become evident in the ports that restows could amount to a significant movement of containers (see paragraph 2.1.15). Consideration is being given to publishing these data.

CHAPTER 3

TRANSHIPMENT AND TRANSIT MOVEMENTS

3.0.0. Containers are particularly well suited for the employment of transit movements of freight without breaking Customs seal. Containers may pass in transit from one foreign country to another through Britain. Containers may therefore arrive at one British port and be moved overland to another British port for onward delivery or be transhipped outwards at the port of entry without passing through the port gates (see paragraph 2.1.16).

3.0.1. In 1971 the National Ports Council and HM Customs and Excise at London carried out a special survey to determine the extent of these transit movements through that port. All transits of loaded containers are recorded on Customs forms XS48-1, transhipment bills, which are required to be completed by the shipper so that Customs can keep the movement under surveillance until the container is reshipped abroad. The survey covered all loaded containers received for transit or transhipment within the Customs Port of London during March 1971. A total of 358 containers of 20 ft and 40 ft size were recorded in that month, an amount which was regarded by HM Customs and Excise officials as normal. The results were analysed by port of entry and port of exit from Britain by number of containers and by country to and from shipped. The results were published in *Container and Roll-on Port Statistics, 1971* Part 2 [QRL 12].

3.0.2. There is a box 'Port or place of foreign loading' on import document C10 and a box 'Port/airport of discharge' on export form C273 (see Appendix 9). In theory, therefore, there is some basis on the documentation for deriving transhipment traffic as the ports of loading and discharge could be linked up with the information on the document of country of consignment. The difficulty is that this information must be entered in the form of a code for computer analysis. There are a great number of ports/airports in the world which could be candidates for a code number. These numbers could take up such space on the documents as to require them to be redesigned. The documents are, however, a part of an aligned series so that this cannot necessarily easily be done. This problem is now being considered by HM Customs and Excise, Government Departments, the National Ports Council and other interested bodies.

3.0.3. The lack of statistical information for the UK on transhipment movements is partly met by a study specially commissioned by the National Ports Council, and partly by foreign port traffic statistics. A report prepared in 1969 for the National Ports Council by Management Sciences Limited, entitled *An Initial Study of the Likely Effect of Transhipment on Bulk Cargo Deep Sea Berth Requirements of the UK* [QRL 19] estimated the quantities of bulk commodities imported into the UK via transhipment at the Dutch ports of Rotterdam and Amsterdam. A description of the statistical sources and data showing tonnages of bulk commodities transhipped via Dutch ports to the UK is given in the Management Sciences Limited report [QRL 19]. The data are given for each year 1950 to 1967 for each of the following products: grain, bauxite, soya beans, crude oil, sulphur, potassium, phosphates, iron ore and manganese ore. The monthly Statistical Bulletin of International Port Traffic (*Statistiek van het International Zeehavenvervoer* [QRL 35]) and the annual Statistical Bulletin of International Trade of Rotterdam and Amsterdam (*Statistiek van het International Goendenvervoer in de Havens Rotterdam en Amsterdam* [QRL 34]) published by the Netherlands Central Bureau of Statistics (Central Bureau voor de Statistiek) give information for each Dutch port and each product group, the tonnage carried by sea, canal, rail or road. Country of consignment is given as is also movements into and out of bond and in transit. UK transhipments via these Dutch ports can be derived from these publications. Similarly, statistics published by the National Institute of Statistics, Belgium (Institute National de Statistique), in *Statistique annuelle du Trafic International des Ports* [QRL 36] give data for UK imports and exports transhipped via Antwerp to/from the UK. These give a broad commodity breakdown by SITC(R) chapter heading.

3.0.4. Statistical information about UK transhipment traffic may also be obtained from the United States Department of Commerce. The annual publications, *US Waterborne Exports; Outbound in-transit Shipments, and Supplement—Department of Defense and Special Category Cargo* [QRL 40] and *US Waterborne General Imports and Inbound in-transit Shipments* [QRL 41] give the following information:

For Exports
(1) Type of service; US Customs district, port of loading, foreign port or country/area of unloading, country of destination and country of origin, by commodity.

For Imports
(2) Type of service, US Customs district, port of unloading, foreign port of loading and country of origin by commodity.

Detailed explanation of coverage and methods adopted for the collection of these statistics are set out in the US Department of Commerce publication *Guide to Foreign Trade Statistics* [B 9]. These statistics are available annually.

3.0.5. It is possible to extract from the US publications referred to in paragraph 3.0.4 [QRL 40, 41] the following information for the UK:

(i) USA imports transhipped through UK ports by country of origin and by commodity in tons;
(ii) USA exports transhipped through UK ports by country of destination and by commodity in tons;
(iii) USA imports from the UK transhipped via the North European ports by commodity in tons;
(iv) USA exports to the UK transhipped via the North European ports by commodity in tons.

CHAPTER 4

FISHERY TRAFFIC

4.0.0. Annual returns of the tonnage of fish landed are made by port authorities to the National Ports Council on form P.S.3e (see Appendix 5 and paragraph 2.5.0). The tonnage is recorded for 'fish, whales and natural produce of the sea landed direct from fishing vessels and fish carrier vessels'. However, as explained in paragraph 2.2.0, the NPC has no locus in respect of the Fishery Harbours in England and Wales and 'Marine Works' in Scotland. Accordingly the data received by the NPC on their P.S.3e forms give an incomplete picture of the fishery traffic at ports in Britain.

4.0.1. Statistics derived from returns submitted to the Ministry of Agriculture, Fisheries and Food showing landings of fish in Great Britain by vessels of all nationalities are published annually in tonnes for each place of landing and Economic Planning Region in the National Ports Council's *Annual Digest of Port Statistics, Volume I* [QRL 4]. The Council's *Digest* is the prime source publication for these figures. In addition, landings of fish in Great Britain by British vessels only are given annually in weight and value for each major port and by kind of fish in the Ministry of Agriculture, Fisheries and Food's *Sea Fisheries, Statistical Tables* [QRL 31]. More detailed information may be obtained from the Secretary, Ministry of Agriculture, Fisheries and Food, Fishery Statistics Section.

CHAPTER 5

PASSENGER TRAFFIC

5.0.0. Statistics of passenger traffic by sea have been collected by the Board of Trade (Departments of Industry, Trades, and Prices and Consumer Protection) for 70 years. The Secretary of State has statutory authority under Section 76 of the Merchant Shipping Act, 1906 [B 14] to direct ships' masters to make returns of passengers carried. Currently there is a single form which must be completed for each voyage. This form asks for the following information:

(a) name and nationality of ship (including hovercraft);
(b) port and date of arrival/departure of vessel;
(c) for each port of embarkation in the UK, numbers of passengers travelling to each port of disembarkation outside the UK;
(d) for each port of disembarkation in the UK numbers of passengers travelling from each port of embarkation outside the UK.

5.0.1. This form was introduced in April 1973, replacing six separate documents, but generally this has not led to any discontinuity in the series. A possible exception is the treatment of cruises. Prior to 1973 there was a separate form for cruises, so that it was for the ship's master to decide what voyages should be classified as such. Since 1973 the decision rests with the Departments of Industry, Trade, and Prices and Consumer Protection. Cruise figures have not been published in the past but the 1976 *Annual Abstract of Statistics* [QRL 3] contains cruise figures with a run back to 1964.

5.0.2. The prime source publication for passenger statistics prior to 1964 was the *Board of Trade Journal* [QRL 9] in which they appeared quarterly. This was stopped in 1964 from which year they were published in the *Annual Abstract of Statistics* [QRL 3] and the *Monthly Digest of Statistics* [QRL 20]. The *Annual Abstract of Statistics* included an analysis by ports of arrival and departure by three broad routes, viz. UK and European Continent; UK and non-European Continent; UK and the Republic of Ireland, until 1967. Thereafter, the prime source publication for this port analysis has been the National Ports Council, *Annual Digest of Port Statistics* [QRL 4].

5.0.3. The National Ports Council's *Annual Digest of Port Statistics, Volume I* [QRL 4] contains tables showing passenger movements by sea at ports of the United Kingdom (of which 12 are separately specified) and for the main areas of landing and embarkation, viz. Republic of Ireland; Europe and the Mediterranean and the Rest of the World. These statistics are also available quarterly on request from the National Ports Council. Publication of these statistics is subject to the approval of the Departments of Industry, Trade and Prices and Consumer Protection in order to ensure the preservation of confidentiality.

5.1. Accompanied Vehicles

5.1.0. The National Ports Council has collected statistics of accompanied vehicle traffic since 1969, through their P.S.48 series of returns to port authorities (see paragraph 2.7.0 for a description of these returns and Appendix 7 for a sample form). Initially no figures were collected of accompanied cars and coaches separately. The available 1969 statistics were published in *Container and Roll-on Port Statistics, Great Britain, 1970* [QRL 12]. This publication gave numbers of accompanied cars and buses in aggregate carried on roll-on/roll-off services, inwards and outwards by trading area, e.g. Foreign, Coastwise, Near Sea, Short Sea, Northern Ireland, and the Netherlands. As from 1970, the returns were revised to give a split between Accompanied cars and Accompanied buses/coaches, and between roll-on/roll-off services and hovercraft services. Data by trading area and by port or port group have since been published annually in the *Container and Roll-on Port Statistics, Great Britain* [QRL 12] until 1973, after which they appear in the National Ports Council's *Annual Digest of Port Statistics, Volume I* [QRL 4]. The more recent publications have been able to extend the number of trading areas for which numbers are published separately to show France, Belgium, the Netherlands and West Germany, Republic of Ireland, Northern Ireland, and Scandinavia.

CHAPTER 6

STATISTICS OF CUSTOMS PORTS

6.1. Foreign Trade

6.1.0. HM Customs and Excise collect and publish statistics of the foreign trade of the United Kingdom. Statistics of imports and exports by commodity, defined by the SITC(R) until the end of 1977 and SITC(R2) from 1978, showing values, units of weight and occasionally other units of quantity by country of consignment (see paragraph 6.1.3), are published in the *Overseas Trade Statistics of the United Kingdom* [QRL 23] every month. The data are shown for the current month and the cumulative figure for the year to that date. The year 1974 was the first in which all commodities were given in weight units. In earlier years only a mix of units—weights, physical units and values—was available. It was necessary prior to 1974 to apply special conversion factors in order to get the statistics on to a common weight (tonnage) basis. Statistics of imports and exports at each Customs port by SITC division and section heading in value terms and statistics by Customs port (see paragraph 2.1.3) showing imports and exports by five-digit SITC(R) heading showing a mix of units and also values have been published in the HM Customs and Excise *Annual Statement of the Overseas Trade of the United Kingdom, Volume V* [QRL 7] up to 1974 (see paragraph 6.1.3). These volumes appeared about 2 years after the year to which the statistics referred. HM Customs and Excise discontinued production of the *Annual Statement* after that for 1975. Commencing with data for the first quarter of 1976, HM Customs now publish a quarterly and annual series called *Statistics of Trade through United Kingdom Ports* [QRL 33]. These volumes contain tables showing total imports and exports for each Customs port and economic planning region; the analysis of trade by overseas area for each port; and for each division of SITC(R) imports and exports for each port. Further information about individual ports, commodities and countries may be obtained from HM Customs and Excise, Bill of Entry Service on payment of a fee.

6.1.1. As explained in the Introduction, the Rochdale Committee [QRL 30] had drawn attention to the fact that there were no suitable statistics of the ports on a national basis. One of the first tasks of the National Ports Council when it was established in 1964 was to co-operate with HM Customs and Excise in order to establish a system based on Customs data which would yield information of more relevance to the ports. The major problem was the fact that Customs documents did not require every entry in weight units at that time. Consequently the data were in a mix of units (e.g. values, numbers, volume as well as weights). An agreement was reached between HM Customs and Excise, Board of Trade (now the Department of Industry, Trade, and Prices and Consumer Protection) and the National Ports Council. The Boards of Trade were included in the agreement because they required a similar analysis for their Flag Statistics (i.e. statistics of vessels by nationality of registration) and also because they could assist with the conversion factors which were required. These factors were decided for each item in the export and import lists. They were the estimated weight in tons for each unit declared. They were updated each year and checked with industry sources. These factors were applied by HM Customs and Excise through a special computer program. This program produced a matrix in tons, by port by commodity by country. The prime source of this information is the National Ports Council's *Digest of Port Statistics* [QRL 14] and the *Annual Digest of Port Statistics, Volume II* [QRL 4]. These annual digests published tabulations of commodities by port by overseas trading country, tabulations of port by commodity by overseas trading country, and tabulations of country by port by commodity. The published commodity classification was the same as that used for port enterprise statistics (see Appendix 2). The groupings of overseas countries, are defined in Appendix E of the *Annual Digest of Port Statistics, Volume II* [QRL 4]. Specific details for each of the countries in the list and for each of the commodities of the National Ports Council classification for each Customs port (see paragraph 2.1.3) may be obtained from the Council for a fee.

6.1.2. Data obtained from HM Customs and Excise of the kind explained in paragraph 6.1.0 are also published by the British Ports Association (formerly the Docks and Harbour Authorities' Association) in their publications entitled *Port Statistics for the Foreign Trade of the United Kingdom* [QRL 26]. These show imports and exports at the twenty principal ports of the UK for each SITC(R) division; selected specific commodities imported and exported at the 20 principal ports of the UK together with the 10 principal countries concerned and imports and exports at individual ports for each SITC division of external trade. It should be noted that the physical units are not necessarily in weight terms in these publications. The publication is mainly useful for the selected commodity detail (down to five digits of the SITC(R)).

6.1.3. Following the entry of the United Kingdom into the European Economic Community (EEC) certain revisions were introduced by HM Customs and Excise into their procedures. For exports (form C273, see Appendix 9) country of destination has been asked for since January 1974 rather than country of consignment. For imports (form C10, see Appendix 9) both country of origin and country of consignment are recorded. As from 1 January 1974, it also became a requirement for the shipper to enter on the basic documents not only the value of the exported or imported commodity but also its net weight. This means that there should be a greater accuracy in the tonnage trade statistics compared with the period up to 1973 in which recourse had to be made to estimating conversion factors. This could lead to a significant discontinuity in the time series particularly for those commodities (such as chemicals) for which conversions had previously to be made from value figures only. Statistics for the year 1974 on this revised basis were published in the National Ports Council's *Annual Digest of Port Statistics, Volume II, 1974* [QRL 4] and will continue to be published in this volume in future years.

6.1.4. The revised Customs documentation also means that for the first time a monthly tonnage series of UK port traffic could be derived from the monthly Overseas Trade Accounts. In the event the weight statistics in the first year, 1974, of the new system must be regarded as nothing but very provisional as far as the monthly data are concerned because of various 'start-up' problems. Although subject to later correction, monthly data may increasingly be used with more confidence as a guide to short-term foreign traffic trends.

6.2. Container and Roll-on Statistics

6.2.0. It will be noted that the Customs documents shown at Appendix 9 include boxes to indicate whether the commodity is imported or exported in a 'container' and whether by 'roll-on/roll-off' methods. The definition used by Customs for 'container' is wider than that used by the National Ports Council for its port enterprise statistics (see paragraph 2.7.2). The Customs definition, as set out in HM Customs and Excise Tariff, includes:

   (i) large containers designed to be transported by road or rail,
   (ii) road vans and enclosed trailers,
   (iii) road and rail tank wagons and large portable tanks,
   (iv) rail wagons.

Unlike the British Standards definition of a container, used by the National Ports Council, the Customs definition is not confined to sizes in excess of 8 cubic metres; and portable tanks are not restricted by the Customs definition to sizes above 500 gallons. Customs have revised their definition of a container for statistical purposes, bringing it closer to the British Standard definition, with effect from 1978.

6.2.1. Similarly, the definition used by Customs for the roll-on/roll-off entries, also given in HM Customs and Excise Tariff, is very broad. Firstly a split is requested between '*road vehicle*' and 'other means' (which includes rail roll-on/roll-off). However, Customs plan to distinguish rail separately from the beginning of 1978. If the import was by road vehicle a further breakdown was asked for in 1974 and 1975, viz.:

   (i) UK registered powered vehicle on 'own account'.
   (ii) UK registered powered vehicle on 'hire or reward'.
   (iii) UK registered powered-vehicle type of operation 'not known'.
   (iv) Foreign registered powered vehicle.
   (v) Unaccompanied trailer.

For exports the breakdown was as follows:

   (i) UK registered powered vehicle.
   (ii) Foreign registered powered vehicle.
   (iii) Unaccompanied trailer.

In 1976 HM Customs and Excise simplified this further breakdown of roll-on/roll-off by road vehicle and now ask, both for imports and exports, for a distinction between (i) powered vehicle and (ii) unaccompanied trailer.

6.2.2. Experience has shown that it is often difficult for a shipper to be able to complete the roll-on/roll-off entry. In fact as far as exporters are concerned HM Customs and Excise apparently foresaw this difficulty as the following extract from the Customs Tariff indicates: 'The co-operation of exporters and agents in providing the information under this heading is requested, but if the information is not known at the time goods must be entered, entries will not be refused because of the omission. Provision of this information is not to be made a reason for delaying the submission of a form in the C273 series beyond the statutory period of 14 days after clearance outwards.' In the event the data derived from this source should be treated with extreme caution, since their accuracy remains in doubt.

6.2.3. HM Customs and Excise expect to have a satisfactory analysis of container data showing commodity and country of consignment and port available from 1975 onwards. This information will be available annually from the Bill of Entry service although quarterly figures may become available in the future. Container analyses may eventually appear in the quarterly publication which Customs launched in 1976 (see paragraph 6.1.0). It may also be published in the National Ports Council *Annual Digest of Port Statistics, Volume II* [QRL 4]. Analyses are available quarterly from 1975 from the National Ports Council on payment of a fee.

6.2.4. The container statistics based on the data collected through the C10 and C273 Customs documents (see paragraph 6.1.3) will fill an important gap in the coverage of port statistics. As explained in paragraph 2.3.4 et seq., it has become difficult for port authorities to obtain information about the commodity content of boxes from their own records. (This lack of information is not true of all port authorities because some regularly extract this information from ships' manifests since they regard the data as necessary for their marketing departments.) The information is required for the general forward planning of the industry because it is only from such data that estimates can be made of the penetration of container traffic into the conventional general cargo markets. It is clearly vital to be able to make realistic forward estimates of the split between container and other transport modes because of the considerable impact these different demands have on capital investment and labour requirements in the industry.

6.2.5. The commodity classification used by Customs for the container and roll-on/roll-off statistics is as far as possible the EEC transport classification NSTR. By 1978 Customs will have incorporated the EEC Nimexe into the UK Overseas Trade Classification, from which the NSTR classification can be derived exactly. From 1975 the container statistics are also available in the NPC classification (see Appendix 2).

CHAPTER 7

MANPOWER

7.0.0. There are three sources of information for manpower statistics, reflecting the institutional structure of the industry; the National Ports Council, in relation to its statutory duty to promote training and education (except in relation to registered dock workers), the National Dock Labour Board (NDLB), in relation to the administration of the Dock Labour Scheme, and the Department of Employment for information covering the whole of MLH 706.

7.1. National Ports Council

7.1.0. The Harbours Act, 1964, Section 3(1) [B 10] defined the duties of the Council in relation to training and education as the promotion of 'the training and education (except to do, or in the doing of, work that usually falls to be done by dock workers) of persons employed or to be employed in doing work falling to be done in the course of the management of harbours or the carrying out of harbour operations'. The general restrictions relating to the jurisdiction of the National Ports Council are set out in paragraph 2.2.0. The term 'dock worker' is defined by Section 6 of the Dock Workers (Regulation of Employment) Act, 1946 [B 5] (see paragraph 7.3.1).

7.1.1. One of the National Ports Council's first tasks was to try to fill the information gap that existed at its inception. There were no detailed figures of the numbers of employees in the ports industry by grade and skills when the Council was established in 1964. The National Ports Council carried out the first manpower census of the ports industry for 12 January 1966. Questionnaires were completed and returned by 118 port authorities and 480 other port employers. The returns covered all persons actually employed on the census date whether permanent, temporary or casual. The following classes of occupations were defined for the census:

(a) Managerial—including superintendents, heads of departments and all staff of managerial status, excluding foremen.
(b) Professional and Technical—including engineering, scientific, medical, veterinary and qualified members of chartered and incorporated bodies, draughtsmen and technicians.
(c) Clerical and Commercial—including all office staff, shorthand typists; progress clerks, representatives, personnel, welfare, etc.
(d) Dock Workers (distinguishing between RDWs and others)—including
  (1) Foremen—including boss gangers and chief clerks.

(2) Dockers and Stevedores—including tally clerks and registered dock worker operatives.
(3) Riggers, Trimmers—including deal porters or carriers and other specialist grades of dock worker.
(4) Lightermen and Watermen—including tugmen and all other employees working in floating craft such as dredgers.
(5) Operatives, if non-registered dock workers—including drivers of cranes, fork-lift trucks, etc.
(6) Dockgatemen—including all persons primarily engaged in the movement of a vessel within a dock, such as berthing assistants and boatmen.

(e) Non-dock Workers, including
(1) Foremen (not in charge of dockers or stevedores).
(2) Maintenance workers.
(3) Labourers, Storemen, Cleaners, etc.
(4) Police, Security and Firemen.
(5) Canteen workers.
(6) Others.

7.1.2. The prime source publication for the information derived from the 1966 census is the National Ports Council's *Digest of Port Statistics, 1966* [QRL 14]. This *Digest* includes two tables showing (a) the number of employees by occupational group by port and economic planning region and (b) the number of dock workers by specific occupation, registered and unregistered for each port and economic planning region.

7.1.3. The National Ports Council conducted a further census on 10 January 1968 in order to monitor the changes taking place in the industry but also to get more detailed information about managerial and supervisory grades of staff than had been obtained from the 1966 census. Returns were requested from port employers for all persons engaged wholly or mainly on a permanent, temporary or casual basis, 'wholly or mainly engaged' being defined as more than half of a person's working time. One deficiency of the 1966 census had been the inadequacy of the available register of port employers. This had been improved by 1968 and had been supplemented by a list of applicants for licences to employ registered dock workers under the Dock and Harbours Act, 1966; a list of frontagers to the River Thames supplied by the Port of London Authority (PLA) and the list of undertakings within the area of the 72 harbour authorities named in the Minister of Transport's policy statement on nationalization (*Ports Reorganisation*, July 1967 [B 18]). Nevertheless there still remained some undertakings which were overlooked (see paragraph 2.6.1).

7.1.4. A total of 1861 undertakings were sent questionnaires and 1483 replies were received. The high non-response rate was partly because of the difficulty of compiling an up-to-date register but was probably also due to the current nationalization plans. The following categories of employee were defined for the survey:

(1) Managers, classified as to
(a) Operational, commercial and 'general'. The latter were defined as 'managers concerned with controlling a range of activities embracing more than one specialist function and which includes the integration of these functions into overall requirements of the organisation'.

(b) Financial.
(c) Engineering.
(d) Other.

(2) Supervisory grades defined as 'all those who controlled a working group on a direct and frequent face to face basis', within which were distinguished:
   (a) Gangers, hatch bosses or similar.
   (b) Other supervisors of stevedores and dock workers, e.g. shed foremen, quay foremen, ship's foremen.
   (c) Maintenance supervisors.
   (d) Clerical and office supervisors.
   (e) Supervisors of nautical and docking operations.
   (f) Other supervisors not covered above.

(3) All other staff employed on port transport work. Within this, the following categories were distinguished:
   (a) Registered dock workers (other than those included in supervisory grades).
   (b) Other permanent workers.
   (c) Temporary and casual workers.

The management grades were also classified by three salary groups and both the management and supervisory grades by 10 age groups.

7.1.5. The results of the 1968 survey were published in the National Ports Council's *Digest of Port Statistics, 1968* [QRL 14] in six tables; for each port and economic planning region the following information was given:

(a) employees by grade and by salary of managers,
(b) management grades by age,
(c) management grades by salary, function and age,
(d) supervisory grades by age,
(e) supervisory grades by category and age,

and, for economic planning region, the number of undertakings by number of employees.

7.1.6. The third census by the National Ports Council was carried out for 14 January 1970. This census sought information, additional to that covered by the 1968 census, on the qualifications of managers, on the numbers of tradesmen by category and by age and on the numbers of clerical workers by age. Information from this census was not published but tabulations of data are available on request from the National Ports Council. The information covered by the census comprised:

(a) Management grades by salary range and membership of professional bodies.
(b) Supervisory grades, as defined in paragraph 7.1.4, distinguishing between registered and non-registered dock workers.
(c) Dock workers, registered and non-registered, of which:
   (1) skilled tradesmen and apprentices by trade and by age,
   (2) clerical workers by age,
   (3) others.

7.1.7. The fourth census was carried out by the National Ports Council for 16 June 1975. The results of this census were published in the National Ports Council's *Annual Digest of Port Statistics, Volume I, 1975* [QRL 4]. (A copy of the census form is at Appendix 10.)

7.2. Non-Scheme Ports

7.2.0. As explained in paragraph 7.0.0, the National Dock Labour Board collects statistics relating to labour employed at Scheme ports and these statistics are described in paragraph 7.3.0 et seq. In 1972 the Minister for Transport Industries called upon the National Ports Council to carry out a survey of those ports in Britain which were outside the Scheme. It will be seen from the sample questionnaire at Appendix 6 which the National Ports Council sent out to the non-Scheme ports that a number of questions were asked concerning labour in these ports and the conditions of employment. (See paragraph 2.6.0 et seq. for further details about this survey.)

7.2.1. Statistics derived from this questionnaire were published in the National Ports Council's *Survey of Non-Scheme Ports and Wharves*, 1973 [QRL 37]. Tables in that publication cover (a) numbers of regular and casual workers employed at 'own account' and 'third party' facilities, and (b) basic hours worked, basic wages and average earnings by type of facility.

7.3. The National Dock Labour Board

7.3.0. The National Dock Labour Scheme was set up in 1947 under the provisions of the Dock Workers (Regulation of Employment) Act [B 5]. (The Scheme was revised under Dock Workers (Regulation of Employment) (Amendment) Order, 1967 [B 6]. Under this order every registered dock worker was allocated to permanent employment.) The Scheme applies to about 80 ports in Great Britain. (A list of ports covered by the Scheme is given in the *Annual Reports of the National Dock Labour Board* (NDLB) [QRL 6] and also in the National Ports Council's *Annual Digest of Port Statistics, Volume I* [QRL 4].) The National Dock Labour Board, through its local boards, is responsible for administering the Scheme. The objects of the Dock Labour Scheme are 'To ensure greater regularity of employment for dock workers and to secure that an adequate number of dock workers is available for the efficient performance of dock work'. The Scheme is based on the following:

(a) limitation of entry to dock work by the registration of both employers and dock workers and the restriction of employment on dock work to registered dock workers (RDWs);
(b) centralized hiring of labour;
(c) payment for attendance for work if no work is available;
(d) a guaranteed minimum weekly wage for all who report regularly for work.

7.3.1. In order to carry out its function of administering the dock labour scheme, the NDLB collects statistics relating to the availability and demand for RDWs, their average earnings, and of stoppages of work in which they are directly involved. A dock worker is defined in the Dock Workers (Regulation of Employment) Act, 1946 [B 5] as 'a person employed or to be employed in or in the vicinity of any port on work in connection with the loading, unloading, movement or storage of cargo or work in connection with the preparation of ships or other vessels for the receipt or discharge of cargoes or for leaving port'.

7.3.2. Since the revision of the Scheme in 1967, statistics have been collected from port employers by the local Dock Labour Boards on a weekly basis relating to the Dock Labour force. These statistics are returned by employers on NDLB Form B50 (a copy of which is shown at Appendix 11). It will be seen that data are returned, for each day, of the number of permanent, supplementary and temporarily unattached workers, reasons for absence and changes in the Register, labour shortages and numbers in dispute. A copy of this return is sent to the local Dock Labour Board. Each local Dock Labour Board summarizes the employer B50 returns on Form B51 which is sent to the NDLB weekly. (See Appendix 12 for a copy of form B51.)

7.3.3. The data from these returns are published annually in the *Annual Reports of the NDLB* [QRL 6] which is the prime source publication, and in the National Ports Council's *Annual Digest of Port Statistics, Volume I* [QRL 4]. The NDLB Annual Reports include four tables of information from these returns:

(a) Changes in the Register during the year by local Board; permanent, temporarily unattached, and supplementary workers.
(b) Analysis of intake and outflow by Register.
(c) Comparison of Register and labour requirements by Board.
(d) The disposition of the Workers Registers.

7.3.4. In addition, weekly returns are submitted by individual employers of earnings and hours of work for permanent and supplementary workers. These returns now cover about 97 per cent of the total number of employers. Figures of average gross earnings and hours worked per man (with overtime hours shown separately) are published in the *Annual Reports of the NDLB* [QRL 6] for each quarter of the year. These figures also appear in the National Ports Council *Annual Digest of Port Statistics, Volume I* [QRL 4].

7.3.5. Finally, the NDLB carry out an Annual Survey of Dock Workers to determine the age distribution of workers of the Register. The results of the survey are published in the *NDLB Annual Report* [QRL 6] and also in the National Ports Council *Annual Digest of Port Statistics, Volume I* [QRL 4].

7.4. Department of Employment

7.4.0. The Department of Employment (for Great Britain) and the Department of Manpower Services (for Northern Ireland) carry out annual censuses of employment. The results of these annual censuses are first published in the *Department of Employment Gazette* (formerly *Ministry of Labour Gazette*) [QRL 13] and subsequently in the *British Labour Statistics Yearbook* [QRL 11]. Historical data are available in *British Labour Statistics: Historical Abstract 1886–1968* [QRL 10]. (From 1948 to 1971 the main annual series of employment statistics were based on counts of National Insurance cards. The new series derived from Censuses of Employment began in 1971. A description of the Census and of discontinuities between the census results and earlier sources was published in the *Department of Employment Gazette* in January 1973 [QRL 13]. The first census results appeared in August 1973.) The *Gazette* gives data for the total number of employees in port and inland water transport (MLH 706) analysed by region in Great Britain and also numbers of male, female, full- and part-time employees in the industry in the United Kingdom. Information from the June 1974 census was published in the June and July 1975 issues of the *Department of Employment Gazette* [QRL 13].

7.4.1. Figures of unemployed are published monthly in the *Department of Employment Gazette* [QRL 13]. Numbers of unemployed for MLH 706 are shown for Great Britain and the United Kingdom, males and females. The percentage of insured workers unemployed for each year from 1923 to 1939 in 'docks, harbours, canals, etc.' are quoted in *British Labour Statistics: Historical Abstract 1886–1968* [QRL 10]. These statistics are derived from *Abstract of British Historical Statistics*, by B. R. Mitchell with the collaboration of Phyllis Deane (Cambridge University Press, 1962) [QRL 1]. (For a review of the methods and principles of the statistical measurement of the unemployed generally see *Unemployment Statistics*—Report of an Inter-Departmental Working Party, November 1972, Cmnd. 5157 [B 24].)

7.4.2. Stoppages of work in MLH 706 are published monthly in the *Department of Employment Gazette* [QRL 13]. Statistics are given of the number of stoppages beginning in the period covered, the number of workers involved in stoppages in progress. Information relating to the definitions and qualifications applying to these statistics are set out in the *Department of Employment Gazette* report on the annual returns; for instance, in the report for the year 1974 contained in the June 1975 issue of the *Gazette*.

7.5. Accident Statistics

7.5.0. The *Report of the Committee of Inquiry into the Major Ports of Great Britain* (the Rochdale Report) of 1962 [QRL 30] referred to the inadequacy of the available statistics of accidents in the port transport industry. The prime and main source of such statistics was, and still is, the *Annual Report of HM Chief Inspector of Factories* [QRL 5]. Under the Factories Act of 1961 [B 8] every fatal accident and every accident which disables a worker for more than 3 days from earning full wages at the work at which he was employed must be reported to HM Inspector of Factories for the district on a specified form (F.43). Statistics of the numbers of fatal accidents and of all accidents are published in the *Annual Report of HM Chief Inspector of Factories* [QRL 5] (Health and Safety Commission since the Health and Safety at Work Act, 1974 [B 12]) and quarterly in the *Department of Employment Gazette* [QRL 13]. These statistics are classified by industry and by process. The *Annual Report of HM Chief Inspector of Factories* [QRL 5] gives figures by industry classified by minimum list heading, including MLH 706. These statistics cover work at 'docks, wharves and quays (other than shipbuilding) defined under Section 125 of the Factories Act 1961' [B 8]. The provisions apply to the process of loading, unloading or coaling of any ship in any dock, harbour or canal, and to all machinery or plant used in those processes. This definition is not coincident with that used for Manpower statistics generally. The Rochdale Report [QRL 30] pointed out that it was not possible to compare statistics of accidents to dock workers with those in other industries. The Factory Inspector's accident statistics cover not only dock workers but all workers employed within the defined premises. The figures include, for instance, railway employees and lorry drivers and any persons employed by firms with premises in the docks. These accident figures therefore cannot be compared with employment statistics for MLH 706, without reservations.

7.5.1. The Factory Inspectorate (Health and Safety Executive) also analyses data by process classification. The Inspector's classification refers to specific processes used in each factory or other premises subject to the Factories Act, 1961. This classification includes 'docks and inland warehouses' falling under Section 125 of the Act. The *Department of Employment Gazette* [QRL 13] gives the number of fatal accidents and the number of all accidents by process. The *Gazette* gives separate figures for 'work at docks, wharves and quays (other than shipbuilding)' and 'work at inland warehouses'. More detailed statistics may be obtained from the Health and Safety Executive, Accident Statistics Unit, London. Tabulations are available of accidents by type for MLH 706 and for the 'docks, wharves and quays (other than shipbuilding)' process for adults and young persons, males and females separately; dangerous occurrences by process groups; all reported accidents by primary cause and by district by industry.

7.5.2. Accident statistics for registered dock workers only have been compiled since 1964 on a quarterly basis by the National Association of Port Employers from returns submitted by their Accident Prevention Committees. These statistics give the number of industrial accidents to registered dock workers which caused absence from work for more than 3 days. These data are not published.

7.5.3. Statistics of accidents have also been available since 1951 from the analysis of 'Certificates of Incapacity' carried out by the Department of Health and Social Security. These statistics were published annually from 1951 to 1972, in *Digest of Statistics Analysing Certificates of Incapacity* [QRL 15]. They are based on a sample of the certificates of incapacity for work submitted by persons claiming benefit under the National Insurance Acts. A full description of the methods employed and definitions used in deriving the statistics is given in the *Digest* [QRL 15].

7.5.4. The Department of Health and Social Security *Digest* [QRL 15] gives estimates for MLH 706, although there is a warning that the allocation of the statistics into industry groups is liable to a wide margin of error. The *Digest* gives the following information for MLH 706:

(1) Number of spells resulting from fresh accidents by age group and by type of accident and disease resulting from accidents; males and females.
(2) Number of days of certified incapacity by type of accident and disease resulting from accidents; males and females.
(3) Number of spells of certified incapacity terminating in the review period by duration of spell; males and females.
(4) Number of spells of certified incapacity occasioned by accidents, by external cause of injury; males and females.

(A 'spell' means a continuous period of incapacity for work.)

7.5.5. A statistic is allocated to port and inland waterways as defined by the SIC and is the industry in which the claimant for injury benefit worked at the time of the accident. However, to quote the *Digest* [QRL 15] itself, 'There is reason for thinking that the quality of the information by which the attributable industry is classified is to some extent defective, so that the statistics should be regarded as approximate only.' Although, therefore, in theory accident figures from this source can be compared to a population at risk defined to make comparisons possible across industries, the information in the source documents is so doubtful as to make such comparisons suspect. Since 1972 the *Digest of Statistics Analysing Certificates of Incapacity* [QRL 15] has been replaced by the annual *Social Security Statistics* of the Department of Health and Social Security [QRL 32]. This annual does not give information at the MLH level.

7.5.6. It should be noted that the statistics recorded in the *Digest of Statistics Analysing Certificates of Incapacity* [QRL 15] are based on claims for benefit under the National Insurance Acts. These do not coincide with the number of injuries reported under the Factories Act, 1961. One reason for this is that not all accidents which should be recorded under the Factory Act were in fact so recorded. For a full discussion on the reliability of official statistics and recommendations for improvement see *Safety and Health at Work, Report of the Committee 1970–1972*, Cmnd. 5034 [B 19]. Finally, an *Explanatory Note on Statistics of Accidents Notified under the Factories Act* is available from the Health and Safety Executive, London [B 7].

CHAPTER 8

INLAND WATER TRANSPORT

8.0.0. The Transport Act, 1947 [B 21] vested in the British Transport Commission 2172 miles of inland waterway. The Act nationalized 17 independent undertakings covering 1138 miles of waterway; the railway owned or controlled canals (965 miles) and the Caledonian and Crinan Canals in Scotland (69 miles) which were government owned. The British Waterways Board inherited these canals when the British Transport Commission was wound up by the Transport Act of 1962 [B 22]. A list of the inland waterways vested in the Board is published in the Board's Annual Reports [B 25]. It is important to note that not all inland waterways have been nationalized. Apart from the many navigable rivers such as the Thames, a number of canals are also excluded from the British Waterways Board's control (e.g. the Manchester Ship Canal). In total, these independent waterways form an important part of the industry.

8.0.1. The Transport Act of 1968 [B 23] classified the British Waterways Board waterways into three groups: 'commercial', 'cruising' and 'remainder'. The 'commercial' and 'cruising' waterways were specifically listed in the Act [B 23]. A commercial waterway is principally available for the commercial carriage of freight, and the cruising waterways principally available for cruising, fishing and other recreational purposes. The remainder are those not defined as commercial or cruising. The Secretary of State for Transport is empowered to transfer a waterway from one group to another. It is the duty of the British Waterways Board to maintain commercial waterways in a suitable condition for use by commercial freight-carrying vessels and to maintain the cruising waterways suitably for vessels constructed or adapted for the carriage of passengers and driven by mechanical power. Commercial traffic is not, *ipso facto*, precluded from cruising waterways, nor are pleasure craft prohibited on commercial waterways. The Board controls about 360 miles of commercial and 1500 miles of cruising waterway.

8.0.2. In 1974 a report, *Barges or Juggernauts* [QRL 8], was published by the Inland Shipping Group of the Inland Waterways Association in which it was estimated that the 'commercial' waterways of the British Waterways Board carried only about 11 per cent of the total inland waterway freight traffic of Great Britain. The Inland Shipping Group based this estimate on returns of traffic received from a special survey which they carried out of navigation authorities and inland waterway carriers. No statistics are collected nationally on a regular basis covering the whole of the inland waterways industry. The official published inland waterway statistics relate only to the inland waterways of the British Waterways Board.

8.0.3. The British Waterways Board submits a monthly (four weekly) return to the Department of Transport, statistics from which are published in the *Monthly Digest of Statistics*

[QRL 20] and the *Annual Abstract of Statistics* [QRL 3]. The monthly returns show the tonne/kilometres and tonnage of freight passing along the British Waterways Board's commercial and other waterways. Freight is divided into three categories, viz. coal, coke and patent fuel; liquids in bulk; general merchandise, and is recorded for each of 11 waterways. These figures include traffic carried in craft operated by organizations other than the British Waterways Board.

8.0.4. A monthly return is also submitted by the British Waterways Board covering freight traffic conveyed by the Board's craft only, whether owned or hired by the Board. These figures include freight carried on waterways other than those controlled by the Board because in most cases craft moving from the Docks to Inland Terminals have to traverse other water routes before they reach the Board's waterways. A breakdown of the freight is given for coal, coke and patent fuel; and general merchandise. In addition these figures are also split between 'compartment boats' and 'general merchandise craft'.

8.0.5. Finally the British Waterways Board submits monthly to the Department of Transport a return of staff employed at the end of the period. This return gives numbers recruited, wastage and transfers during the period. These numbers are also divided between operating, maintenance, and administrative, technical, clerical and miscellaneous grades. The operating personnel are subdivided into:

(a) Supervisory;
(b) Waterways lock, weir, bridgekeepers, reservoir attendants, etc.;
(c) Boat and tug crews;
(d) Warehouse and depot;
(e) Dock, pierhead, etc.

The maintenance personnel are divided into:

(a) Supervisory;
(b) Engineering;
(c) Boat builders and repairers;
(d) Dredgermen.

8.0.6. The returns completed by the British Waterways Board are the source of the statistics published in the *Monthly Digest of Statistics* [QRL 20] and *Annual Abstract of Statistics* [QRL 3]. The *Monthly Digest* publishes under the heading 'British Waterways' the British Waterways Board freight statistics described in paragraph 8.0.3 above, showing the tonnage of general merchandise, liquids and coal, coke, etc., separately, together with an aggregate in tonne/kilometres for each 4-week period. The *Annual Abstract* publishes only the annual tonnage and tonne/kilometres of freight carried. It should be noted that these published figures of the traffic of 'British Waterways' cover in fact only traffic on those waterways controlled by the British Waterways Board. There are no statistics available which cover the whole of the inland waterway system of Britain or the United Kingdom however this may be defined.

8.0.7. The need for a reappraisal of the statistics of the industry with particular emphasis on the limited coverage of the existing information was emphasized in *Barges or Juggernauts* [QRL 8]. This report includes a table showing for each of 20 river and canal systems the total tonnage of freight carried of all types, e.g. coastwise (see paragraph 2.1.9), foreign, special (see paragraph 2.1.8) and on non-sea-going vessels (see paragraph 2.1.13). These statistics, other than those of the British Waterways Board, were derived from National Ports Council port traffic statistics or from returns submitted to the group by the navigation authorities and independent waterway carriers. Since the publication of this report, discussions have been taking place between the Department of Transport, the British Waterways Board, the Independent Waterway Authorities and other interested parties with a view to agreeing the appropriate definitions and assessing the need and feasibility of collecting statistical information in addition to that supplied by the British Waterways Board and the ports.

8.0.8. There are two distinct forms of traffic which pass through inland waterways. The first is traffic in sea-going vessels (see paragraph 2.1.9) which loads or discharges at a port, dock or wharf situated on an inland waterway and the second is that carried on non-sea-going vessels (see paragraph 2.1.13), i.e. traffic passing between ports, docks or wharves situated on an inland waterway. Apart from the possibility of the restriction of the confidentiality rule on the availability of data, the first type of information is available from the port statistics. Complete information on a national basis is not available for the second type of traffic. A problem common to both types of statistic, however, is the definition of 'inland waterway'. There is, as yet, no agreement as to the correct definition of this term for statistical purposes. However, it has been proposed that the boundary between an inland waterway and the sea should be defined by the Winter Partially Smooth Water Limit (WPSWL). This limit is defined for each district in Great Britain and Northern Ireland in respect to rule 2 of the *Merchant Shipping (Life-Saving Appliances) Rules*, 1965 [B 16]. (The limits are set out in Schedule 1 of Cmnd. 1105.) Given this definition, it should be possible to measure the distance between the point at which a ship crosses the WPSWL and the wharf, dock or port at which the ship loaded or discharged. A statistic of tonne/kilometres could then be derived as a measure of the freight movement along the inland waterway section of the ship's voyage. Another possible definition is that given for 'controlled waters' in the Control of Pollution Act, 1974 [B 4]. 'Controlled Waters' are defined in Part II, Section 56 of [B 4] as 'the sea within three nautical miles from any point on the coast measured from low water mark of ordinary spring tides'. (See also paragraph 8.0.14.)

8.0.9. Given the definition of inland waterway, therefore, it should be comparatively simple to get statistics of freight (and passenger) movements on sea-going vessels, as much as of the information is already available. There is a grey area even here, however. The definition of a sea-going vessel is a vessel which goes to sea, and could exclude barges and lighters carried by LASH, BACAT, Seabee systems (see paragraph 2.1.13). Port statistics do not cover the movement of the lighter from the point at which it is loaded/discharged from the mother ship to the place at which its cargo is loaded/discharged.

8.0.10. As mentioned above, no statistics are collected regularly on a national basis of movements on inland waterways by ships which do not go to sea (internal maritime movements). In considering the sources of information which are available, it is convenient to note that the industry may be administratively regarded as having three distinct parts.

Firstly, the inland waterways operated by the British Waterways Board, secondly, the inland waterways operated privately and, thirdly, the river and estuarial waterways outside the canal systems.

8.0.11. As far as the canal systems are concerned, the British Waterways Board is the only organization which provides any regular and comprehensive statistical information about their activities (see paragraph 8.0.3 et seq.). The National Association of Inland Waterway Carriers, which is a trade association having a membership of 22 companies, operates craft on the inland waterways, both nationalized and private. The Association does collect information from its members annually but this is very limited. This information is not published. The following statistics are collected:

(1) Number of vessels in fleet.
(2) Carrying capacity of vessels.
(3) Number of 'Floating' employees.
(4) Number of 'Shore' employees.

8.0.12. The National Federation of Master Lightermen and Barge Owners is a federation of Associations located at London, Liverpool, Southampton, Hull and Bristol which include lightermen and barge owners operating on the river and estuarial systems in these areas. However, there is no central organizing body, the Associations being only very loosely federated. From the statistical point of view, the only active Association is that at London. The London Association of Master Lightermen and Barge Owners (AMLBO) has been collecting statistics from its members since they gave evidence to the Rochdale Committee [QRL 30]. Their annual statistical series goes back to 1963. Apart from adding a question about LASH/Seabee traffic, the questionnaire has been unchanged since that time.

8.0.13. The Association receives two annual returns from its members, one for tonnage carried and the other for the fleet of vessels. The returns cover only members of the Association. This means that interport movements of craft owned by the Port of London Authority are excluded but these are not significant. Again, only dumb barges are included in the survey so that, for instance, self-propelled tankers from the oil refineries to up-river distribution depots are excluded. The returns also exclude lighterage between the Thames and the Medway except that the number of LASH/Seabee units handled is recorded separately.

8.0.14. Apart from restrictions mentioned above, all movements are recorded which have an origin or a destination within the boundary of the Port of London Authority and which are on non-sea-going vessels (see paragraph 2.1.13). For the purpose of defining the latter, the Association has taken that in the Merchant Shipping (International Labour Convention) Act, 1925 [B 15], which relates to the employment of young persons. In effect this is their justification for using the boundaries of the Port of London Authority (PLA) (see also paragraph 8.0.8).

8.0.15. The AMLBO fleet returns record the following information:

(1) Number and carrying capacity by type of dumb barges owned.

(2) Number and BHP of craft towing tugs owned and whether equipped with radio-telephone.
(3) Number and NRT of dumb barges on yearly hire.
(4) Number and BHP of craft towing tugs on yearly hire.

8.0.16. The AMLBO tonnage return records the following information:

(a) Tonnage transhipped between ship and ship.
(b) Tonnage moved on canal and inland waterway.
(c) Tonnage lightered on river.

Each of the above classifications is broken down by commodity group, viz.:

(a) Coal.
(b) Refuse.
(c) Timber, plywood, etc.
(d) Oils and other liquids in bulk.
(e) Meat and refrigerated goods.
(f) General cargo.

General cargo is a residual balance. It includes, for instance, cement and grain because recording of these separately would reveal confidential information.

(g) LASH/Seabee or similar—number of units handled. (No tonnage is recorded of this traffic.)

The London Association of Master Lightermen and Barge Owners do not publish this information but tabulations prepared by the Association for its members are not confidential and copies are available on request from any serious enquirer. Other Associations of Master Lightermen and Barge Owners in the Federation do not collect statistics from their members.

CHAPTER 9

SHIPPING MOVEMENTS

9.0.0. Statistics of shipping movements have been collected and published for over 150 years. Tabulations of vessels employed in the foreign trade and vessels employed in the coasting trade were published monthly in the *Accounts Relating to the Trade and Navigation of the United Kingdom* (Board of Trade [QRL 2]). These figures were not given for the individual ports of the United Kingdom which is our concern in this review. This series ended in December 1974.

9.0.1. Statistics of movements at ports were published monthly in the *Board of Trade Journal* [QRL 9] up to the outbreak of the Second World War. Tabulations were given showing the number of vessels and their net tonnage in the foreign trades for British, Norwegian, German, Dutch, French, USA and Other Nationalities for the major British ports. Separate figures were given for arrivals with cargo and in ballast and departures with cargo and in ballast. In addition, figures were given for the coasting trade (see paragraph 2.1.9) by port showing arrivals with cargo and in ballast and departures with cargo and in ballast by numbers of vessels and their net tonnage.

9.0.2. The *Board of Trade Journal* [QRL 9] for 23 March 1946 referred to deficiencies in this series. 'The navigation statistics published hitherto have suffered from certain defects. As regards vessels recorded as entering or leaving with cargo, the figures included vessels loading or unloading mail only; vessels recorded as in ballast included those embarking or disembarking passengers only or entering for, or clearing with bunkers only as well as normal ballast movement. Movements in the totals might therefore conceal widely divergent movements as between these different classes of vessels and separate records of each have been kept as from 1st July, 1939.' Thereafter until April 1956, the *Board of Trade Journal* quoted only entrances and clearances.

9.0.3. The distinction between entrances and clearances on the one hand and arrivals and departures on the other should be noted. An entrance is recorded when a vessel arrives at a UK port from a foreign port of embarkation. Similarly a clearance is recorded when a vessel leaves a UK port for a foreign port of discharge. Shipping movement statistics specified as entrances and clearances would not record, for instance, the exit from a UK port of a vessel in the foreign trade which was calling at another UK port before proceeding overseas. Nor would an entry be recorded for this vessel at its second UK port of call. If the statistics record these inter-UK port movements of ships in the foreign trade they are defined as arrivals and departures.

9.0.4. From the issue of the *Board of Trade Journal* [QRL 9] of 14 April 1956, tabulations were published showing foreign trade arrivals and departures at principal ports, with cargo and in ballast and similar analyses for the coasting trade. From the issue of the *Board of Trade Journal* of 28 May 1965, figures were quoted of the number of vessels and their net tonnage entered and cleared for UK, Commonwealth and foreign flags with cargo and in ballast and by trading countries and area. Separate tables were also provided of foreign trade arrivals and departures at principal ports showing numbers of vessels and their net tonnage with cargo and in ballast. Similar details were also recorded for the coasting trades. The last figures of shipping movements published in the *Board of Trade Journal* were for the first quarter of 1970 in the *Journal* of 12 August 1970. From October 1970 the *Journal* was superseded by *Trade and Industry* [QRL 38] in which these statistics were continued up to 1971.

9.0.5. For the years 1963 and 1964, a special publication was issued by the Ministry of Transport entitled *Foreign Trade Shipping Movements at United Kingdom Ports* [QRL 18]. These publications gave statistics by ports and trading areas of arrivals and departures with cargo and in ballast by numbers of vessels and net tonnage, for tankers and other vessels. In addition summary tables were included showing for each port the numbers of arrivals and departures in total of tankers and other vessels for the following net tonnage classes:

0–1599 tons; 1600–3999 tons; 4000–9999 tons; 10,000 tons and over.

9.0.6. In 1965 the responsibility for the publication of the statistics of shipping movements at UK ports was taken over by the National Ports Council. Shipping movements statistics for 1965 were published in the *Digest of Port Statistics 1966* [QRL 14]. Publication continued annually until the *Digest of Port Statistics 1972* [QRL 14] which included a supplement on Shipping Movement Statistics for 1971. No national statistics of shipping movements at UK ports were published from 1972 until 1977.

9.0.7. The National Ports Council's *Digest of Port Statistics* [QRL 14] for the years 1966 to 1972 contained analyses by UK port of arrivals and departures by type of vessel, by trade route, by purpose of call (in ballast, etc.) for foreign and coastwise movements. The *Digest* for 1966 included annual series going back to 1956.

9.0.8. Until 1971 the movement statistics were compiled from returns of shipping submitted by HM Customs and Excise to the Ministry of Transport (Department of the Environment) in respect of the foreign trade and to the Board of Trade (Departments of Industry, Trade, and Prices and Consumer Protection) for coastwise trade. From 1 January 1971 the procedure was changed because the Department of the Environment had passed the responsibility of compiling and publishing these statistics to the National Ports Council and also because of the introduction of computer processing. From that date photocopies of arrival and sailing sheets (Forms C568 and C568A, see Appendix 13) were provided by HM Customs and Excise on a monthly basis to the Departments of Industry, Trade, and Prices and Consumer Protection and the National Ports Council. These arrival and sailing sheets were the source documents from which the National Ports Council compiled and published their tabulations. Tabulations of NRT of coastal vessels arrivals by port and by UK and foreign flag are prepared from these documents by the National Ports Council for the Departments of Industry, Trade, and Prices and Consumer Protection. Although no aggregations of data of foreign shipping movements were carried out until 1977, monthly raw data on the Customs arrival and sailing sheets are stored at the National Ports Council and are available on request for *ad hoc* analysis on payment of a fee.

9.0.9. The shipping movements statistics which have been published by the National Ports Council relate to voyages to and from ports in the United Kingdom made by sea-going vessels (i.e. vessels which actually go to sea, see paragraph 2.1.9). These movements exclude the following: vessels of war; pleasure yachts; tugs moving coastwise; vessels entering port for shelter, repair, embarkation/disembarkation of crew or passengers for medical attention; of crew, technicians or pilots; hovercraft and hydrofoils; vessels employed in cable laying, meteorological duties and servicing of oil rigs; fishing vessels of the UK flag; vessels employed within the limits of a port; vessels employed within estuarial limits or other limits wherein waterborne trade is not deemed to be by sea (see paragraph 2.1.13), unless they move between different ports; vessels whose entire cargo consists of goods for the armed services abroad, or goods shipped by a UK government department for the use of UK firms abroad.

9.0.10. Some of these exclusions follow from the fact that the movements are defined as foreign and coastwise (see paragraph 2.1.9). In addition it should be noted that ports are defined as Customs ports (see paragraph 2.1.3). However, not all the exclusions listed in paragraph 9.0.9 above are excluded from the basic source documents (forms C568 and C568A, see Appendix 13). For instance, data are included in these documents of movements of hovercraft and hydrofoils and of vessels employed in cable laying, meteorological duties and servicing oil rigs.

9.0.11. Movements 'with cargo' at any UK port relate to vessels which loaded or discharged cargo (excluding government stores, bunkers, ships' stores and passengers) at that port. Movements in ballast at any UK port relate to vessels which have not loaded or discharged cargo at that port. The classifications, therefore, relate to the purpose of the call, not the loaded or unloaded state of the vessel. For instance, a vessel recorded as in ballast may in fact have cargo on board. In ballast means that cargo was not loaded or unloaded at the port recording the arrival or departure.

9.0.12. Since January 1976, Lloyd's Register of Shipping, Shipping Information Services has collected information on shipping movements on computer file. These data are derived from information supplied by Lloyd's agents and correspondents. This Voyage History file contains statistics on arrivals and departures by port and the following details may be accessed on payment of a fee:

(1) ship name and former names,
(2) propulsion method,
(3) flag,
(4) year of build,
(5) tonnage,
(6) port.

The Voyage History file does not give a comprehensive coverage of movements at UK ports because it excludes

(1) coasters, yachts and fishing vessels,
(2) vessels of British and Continental Flag trading between the UK and ports between the Skaw and the Loire.

However, a separate computer file is maintained covering these exclusions.

9.1. Pilotage

9.1.0. Another source of information regarding shipping movements is the Returns of Pilotage submitted by pilotage authorities to the Marine Division of the Departments of Industry, Trade, and Prices and Consumer Protection. These returns have been made annually since 1946. These statistics are not comparable with the shipping-movement statistics derived from the arrival and sailing sheets of HM Customs and Excise (see paragraph 9.0.8) because the types of vessels excluded from the data are different. These exclusions, defined in the Pilotage Act, 1913 [B 17], are:

> Ships of the Royal Navy; pleasure yachts; all fishing vessels; ferry boats plying as such exclusively within the limits of a harbour authority; ships of less than 50 tons gross tonnage; ships exempted by by-law—a pilotage authority may by by-law exempt any of the following classes of ships, if not carrying passengers, up to any limit of gross tonnage: ships trading coastwise; home trade ships trading otherwise than coastwise and ships navigating within the seaward limits of a harbour authority. (Home trade is defined as UK trade routes between the Elbe and Brest.)

9.1.1. A summary of pilotage returns is prepared by the Marine Division of the Departments of Industry, Trade, and Prices and Consumer Protection. This summary gives the following information for each Pilotage District in the UK:

(a) Number of licensed pilots.
(b) Number of pilotage certificates in force.
(c) Number of ships piloted inwards or outwards, British and Foreign Flag separately.
(d) Total net tonnage of vessels piloted, inwards plus outwards, British and Foreign Flag separately.
(e) Pilotage revenue.
(f) Net earnings of First Class Pilot.

No data are available giving a breakdown by type of vessel or by trades similar to that of the shipping movements statistics derived from HM Customs and Excise. In addition, the number of ships piloted refers to the number of acts of pilotage. Multiple pilotage of the same shipping movement is not recorded. For a full description of the pilotage statistics and their relation to shipping movements statistics see *Economics and Marine Pilotage* by M. S. Bradbury, assisted by D. J. Lee, Department of Trade and Industry, 1973 [B 1].

CHAPTER 10

PORT FACILITIES

10.0.0. The Rochdale Report of 1962 [QRL 30] recorded that no comprehensive statistics were available about facilities at the ports in Great Britain at the time of that enquiry. The enquiry did gather together some very limited information. The Report includes a table showing the number of dry cargo berths by limiting depth of water of over 40 ft and for five class intervals below that depth. These figures were given for each of the 15 major ports in Great Britain. This information was brought up to date in *Port Development. An Interim Plan* published by the National Ports Council, July 1965 [QRL 24].

10.0.1. In 1968 the National Ports Council carried out the first comprehensive survey of facilities at the commercial ports in Great Britain. The results of this survey were published in the *Digest of Port Statistics, 1968* [QRL 14] and the following tabulations were given:

(a) Number of dry cargo berths by limiting depth of water of over 40 ft and for five class intervals below that depth; completed and under construction in July 1968, by port.
(b) Number of unit load berths by type of berth in operation and under construction and by date of completion by port.
(c) Number of unit-load berths in operation and under construction by maximum length by maximum beam and by maximum draught of vessel and by type of berth.
(d) Number of unit-load berths in operation and under construction by parking area allocated for unit-loads.
(e) Number of LO/LO berths by maximum lifting capacity of cranage available at the berth and by type of cranage.
(f) A schedule listing each unit transport berth and its characteristics as described in (a) to (e) above.
(g) A schedule of berths with abnormal load facilities available and under construction.

This survey was repeated in June 1969 and the results published in the *Digest of Port Statistics, 1969* [QRL 14]. The same tabulations were given in that issue but in addition similar statistics were given for Northern Ireland.

10.0.2. In 1974 the National Ports Council carried out a more detailed survey of port facilities which covered 46 of the major and medium-sized ports in Great Britain, the results of which were published in the *Annual Digest of Port Statistics, 1973, Volume II* [QRL 4]. (See Appendix 14 for copy of questionnaire.) The National Ports Council repeated this survey in 1976. The following tabulations were published in the 1973 *Digest* [QRL 4]:

(a) *Break bulk and specialized cargo berth facilities*
    This table lists for each port and berth the length of berth, its limiting depth of water,

the number of cranes by type and capacity and notes whether the berth is tidal or enclosed.
    (b) *Lock, harbour and dock entrance dimensions*
    For each berth or dock, the table shows the entrance dimensions by length and width and depth of water which define the maximum size of vessel that can reach the berth.
    (c) *Container and roll-on berths in operation and under construction*
    For each berth, the table gives its length, if it is a LO/LO berth, and limiting depth of water and the number of specialized cranes. It also notes whether the berth is tidal or in an enclosed dock.

10.0.3. The coverage of the break-bulk and specialized berths is not complete but the container and roll-on berth data cover all such berths completed and under construction as at August 1974. A container LO/LO berth is included in the table if it has, for ship working, a transporter crane, a Scotch derrick crane or a jib crane capable of lifting at least the smallest size of ISO container at suitable outreach. The RO/RO berths have an adjustable or fixed shore ramp with the load-bearing capacity required for commercial road or rail vehicles. Conventional berths which handle container traffic with mobile cranes or ships gear and RO/RO berths which can only carry light traffic, such as passenger cars, are excluded.

10.0.4. It will be noted that the information collected and published by the National Ports Council in 1974 does not cover facilities for bulk commodities of the traditional kind. Commodities such as iron ore and crude oil have traditionally been conveyed in large tonnages in specialized vessels operating to terminals where the equipment has been specifically designed for the rapid loading or unloading of the particular commodity. Generally these commodities are conveyed directly to the consuming industry located close to the importing terminal. The National Ports Council has been less concerned with the development of port facilities for these commodities because they are generally tied to the specialized local needs of a particular industry.

10.0.5. There is, however, a wider definition of bulk which could be applied which lays emphasis not on the specific nature of the demand for the bulk commodity but on the consignment of large tonnages from which economies of scale may be obtained throughout the transport flow. This means that a concept of 'bulk' which can be defined simply by naming certain commodities 'bulk', e.g. iron ore and crude oil, can no longer apply. There are a number of commodities which could be regarded as 'bulk' in the sense that they are moved in large tonnages in and across facilities specifically designed or operated for those commodities, although they may not necessarily be directly integrated into a particular local industrial process. For instance, forest products may be regarded as bulks in that they are transported in specialized vessels and are loaded at specialized facilities. Shipments, however, would not be tied to a particular terminal because of the local investment of a consuming industry nor is the economics such as to preclude completely the use of 'non-bulk' methods of transportation.

10.0.6. In the past, port traffic and port facilities have been categorized into 'bulk' and 'general cargo', the latter being subdivided into 'conventional break-bulk', LO/LO unit-load and RO/RO unit-load. Commodities have then been grouped as 'bulk', leaving the remainder to define 'general cargo'. The problem exemplified by forest products leads to the conclusion of the need for a further category which the National Ports Council has called 'specialized break-bulk'. Forest products can be carried in any of three ways: (a) conventional break-bulk, by which the timber is not pre-packed and is loaded and unloaded virtually plank by plank. This is, of course, now very unusual; (b) unit-load roll-on/roll-off services, by which the timber is transported by road vehicle or trailer on ferry services. This is quite a common feature of the Scandinavian traffic; (c) specialized vessels which carry packaged timber which can be loaded/unloaded at terminals specifically designed for forest products.

10.0.7. Accordingly in the survey of port facilities carried out in 1974 and 1976, the National Ports Council asked the port authorities for details of their specialized bulk traffics (see Appendix 14 for questionnaire). This questionnaire sought to classify those bulks which could be handled as bulks into three groups, viz.:

(a) conventional break-bulk general cargo;
(b) specialized bulk handling berth—that is a berth concentrating on a particular commodity and equipped with specialized handling facilities;
(c) industrial bulk handling berth—a berth associated with or owned by a particular industry and handling bulk commodities for that industry only.

CHAPTER 11

FINANCE

11.0.0. Financial statistics of the ports and inland waterways on an industry basis are very sparse. For 3 years only, 1971, 1972 and 1973, the National Ports Council published in *Port Financial Information* [QRL 25] detailed accounts of 11 major and 15 minor port undertakings. This publication ceased in 1973. A table is published in the *Annual Digest of Port Statistics, Volume II* [QRL 4] showing capital employed, revenue, expenditure and net surplus/deficit for each of 20 port authorities. All this information is a simple reproduction from the published annual accounts of port authorities.

11.0.1. Each year the Department of Transport receives a return from each of 36 port authorities, including the British Transport Docks Board, British Railways Board and British Waterways Board, recording capital expenditure. Aggregations of these expenditures, which yield reliable annual estimates for the total expenditures for the British ports industry, will be published in the *Annual Digest of Port Statistics, Volume II* [QRL 4] as from 1977. The capital expenditure return gives the following breakdown:

(1) Purchase of Land, Leases and Existing Buildings.
(2) New Building and Civil Engineering Works.
(3) Capital Dredging.
(4) Plant and Machinery.
(5) Vessels and Floating Plant.
(6) Vehicles.
(7) Professional Fees and Salaries.

11.0.2. Statistics of Gross Domestic Fixed Capital Formation and for Gross Capital Stock for MLH 706 are published by the Central Statistical Office in the *National Income and Expenditure* Blue Books [QRL 21]. Annual series are given for a 10-year run. Capital Formation is analysed by 'vehicles, ships and aircraft', 'plant and machinery' and 'new buildings and works'. The information is compiled from quarterly returns from a variety of sources, viz.:

Scottish Office Ports—HM Treasury.
Scottish Local Authority Ports—Scottish Office.
Local Authority Ports (England Wales)—Department of the Environment.
British Transport Docks Board ⎫
British Waterways Board ⎬ Returns submitted directly to CSO.
British Railways Board ⎪
Ten Public Trust Ports ⎭

(See Introduction, paragraph 2.1.0, for a description of the type of ownership and control of the ports industry.)

CHAPTER 12

CURRENT AND PROPOSED DEVELOPMENTS

12.0.0. The introduction of unit-load methods of cargo handling necessitated the construction of a completely new series of port transport statistics of traffic. These new series were started in 1965 and have over the years been improved and have been kept closely in line with technical progress in this sector of the industry. Prior to the arrival of unit-load methods in the UK, traffic statistics were based on analyses by commodity and trade route, with separate categories for foreign traffic, coastwise traffic and other traffic, called 'special'. These classifications were partly related to port charging structures but were derived mainly as a reflection of the different type of facilities required to handle different commodities. The emphasis at this time was particularly on the distinction between bulk commodities which were characterized by large tonnage flows carried in specialized single-commodity ships and discharged or loaded at berths designed for handling that particular commodity (bulks such as crude oil, iron ore and cereals are typical examples) and non-bulk commodities which were termed 'general cargo' and which were handled, prior to unitization, over conventional break-bulk berths. Unitization, whether LO/LO or RO/RO, introduced a new sub-set of general cargo, leaving a residual general-cargo traffic which was still handled by conventional means.

12.0.1. These classifications of traffic now need reappraisal. The distinction in port economic terms between bulks as defined in paragraph 12.0.0, which are typified by high tonnage, relatively low value per tonne raw materials and commodities of any description carried across berths specializing in that commodity, is very blurred. For instance, a berth specializing in the export of motor vehicles which are loaded on to car-carrier ships which themselves are specific to that trade have all the characteristics of the traditional bulk berths, viz. high throughput, and specific facilities. The difference is that whereas bulks such as iron ore would broadly speaking not be transported any other way but in bulk across such berths this is not true for other 'bulk' commodities such as cars. The latter, for instance, can economically equally be moved on RO/RO unit-load services. There is currently no regular collection of statistical information about this traffic which is handled at 'specialized' berths.

12.0.2. However, as mentioned in paragraph 12.0.0, these traffic classifications, including the considerations of the need for 'specialized' berth information, have all started from the standpoint of investment decision-making, that is they reflect the nature of port assets. In the context of medium/long-term planning, this is right. The question arises, however, as to what extent this emphasis on assets has not led to a situation in which the tonnage traffic statistics which are collected are out of balance with the revenue sources of the industry. If traffic statistics are to be used for assessing short-term trends in the ports industry then their relevance to revenue must be assured. A major difficulty is the lack of financial statistical information about the ports industry as a whole. Financial accounts are, of course, available for individual port authorities but these are not drawn up on a comparable basis. There are no price indices of output for the industry.

12.0.3. A major criticism of port statistics in the past has been the gap between publication and the date to which they refer. This is being met by the publication by the National Ports Council of a *Quarterly Bulletin of Port Statistics* [QRL 29] beginning with the first quarter 1976 data. This bulletin includes traffic statistics covering unit-loads and other traffic for the major and medium-size ports in Britain for foreign and coastwise. The *Bulletin* also contains tables supplied by HM Customs and Excise of traffic by Customs ports and trade routes. In addition, HM Customs and Excise launched a new quarterly bulletin, *Statistics of Trade through United Kingdom Ports* [QRL 33], in the autumn of 1976. Both these bulletins may eventually contain unit-load statistics but there is a difference in the definitions between those used by the National Ports Council and HM Customs and Excise which needs resolution. The Customs definition of a 'container' is much wider than that of the British Standards used by the National Ports Council. Similar differences exist between the definition of roll-on/roll-off. However, evidence so far suggest that shippers are having difficulty in providing the information required by Customs in respect to roll-on/roll-off traffic and it is unlikely that any data will be published.

12.0.4. There are no statistics of transhipment movements at UK ports derived from UK sources but it is expected that research recently initiated by government departments and the National Ports Council will enable sources for these data to be opened up. The basic Customs documents do include a box (see Appendix 9) for recording the port of loading or discharge which, if linked to the data on country of destination or origin, would yield a measure of transhipped traffic. The problem currently is that this entry is written and not coded so that it cannot be accessed by computer. Consideration is being given to finding a suitable coding system which could be accommodated on the forms at the same time preserving their alignment. There is also the possibility that some information on transhipment will be derived as a by-product of a separate exercise currently being undertaken by the National Ports Council and government departments on inland flow statistics (see below, paragraph 12.0.5.)

12.0.5. There are no statistics in the UK which measure the flows of international freight movements from the point of inland origin/destination to the port of loading/discharge. The inland point at which traffic is ultimately generated can play an important part in the determination of the location of port investment. In 1975 it was decided to carry out a pilot survey based on a sample of 1 month's Customs documents for both exports and imports which would not only yield some reliable national data of inland flows but also enable a decision to be made as to whether it would be feasible and worth while to carry out a survey of a whole year's data. The procedure is based on the specific Customs document relating to a consignment coupled with a questionnaire to the shipper signatory to the document. It follows a technique successfully carried out by the US Bureau of Customs [QRL 17]. The full survey based on a sample of documents taken for each month is being carried out during 1978. Results from this survey will be available in 1979, including estimates of the level of transhipment traffic. It will also be a check on the validity of the information in the port of loading/discharge box, from which to judge whether the rules and definitions governing the entry would need to be tightened up before the new codes are introduced.

12.0.6. A major part of the ports and inland waterways industry remains outside the statistical net because it falls between the ports themselves on the one hand and on the other the British Waterways Board. From the ports point of view, because the definition of traffic is traffic in vessels which actually go to sea, traffic within river estuaries (that is within the boundary of 'partially smooth water') is excluded from port statistics. These movements are not captured by the British Waterways Board partly because they themselves do not cover the whole of the canal system and partly because not all this traffic by any means passes along the canals. Some other organizations do collect information but they are local and there is as yet no co-ordinated national approach.

QUICK REFERENCE LIST—TABLE OF CONTENTS

Statistics of Port Enterprises	60
Foreign traffic by commodity	60
Coastwise traffic by commodity	60
Special traffic	60
Scheme and non-scheme port traffic	61
Container and roll-on traffic	61
Content of containers	61
Driver accompanied and unaccompanied road goods vehicles	61
Transhipment and Transit Movements	61
Fishery Traffic	62
Passenger Traffic	63
Accompanied cars	63
Statistics of Customs Ports	63
Foreign trade	63
Manpower	64
National Ports Council	64
Non-scheme ports	64
National Dock Labour Board	65
Department of Employment	65
Accident statistics	65
Inland Water Transport	66
Shipping Movements	66
Port Facilities	67
Finance	67
Current and Proposed Developments	67

QUICK REFERENCE LIST

Descriptive title	Breakdown	Area	Frequency	Publication (see QRL Key)	Text reference and remarks
STATISTICS OF PORT ENTERPRISES					
Imports/exports (million tons)	By major port	GB	1961	[QRL 30]	2.1.0, 2.1.1
Foreign and coastwise traffic (thousand tons)	By port, by commodity	GB	Annual	[QRL 14]	2.1.0
Imports/exports (thousand gross tonnes)	By port of Northern Ireland	GB	Annual	[QRL 39]	2.1.0, 2.2.6
Foreign traffic by commodity					
Exports/imports (thousand gross tonnes)	By port, by commodity	GB	Annual	[QRL 14] [QRL 4]	2.3.1 See para. 2.1.2 for distinction between statistics of port enterprises (foreign traffic) and statistics of Customs ports (foreign trade)
Coastwise traffic by commodity					
Inward/outward traffic (thousand gross tonnes)	By port, by commodity	GB	Annual	[QRL 14] [QRL 4]	2.4.1 See **Container and roll-on traffic** below for unit-load coastwise traffic
Coastal traffic (thousand millions tonne/kilometres)	—	GB	Annual	[QRL 3]	2.4.4
Coastal traffic in petroleum and petroleum products (thousand tonne/kilometres)	—	UK	Annual	[QRL 16]	2.4.4
Cross-channel traffic of Northern Ireland, inwards and outwards (thousand tonnes)	By commodity, by port of Northern Ireland	GB	Annual	[QRL 14]	2.4.6
Imports/exports to Northern Ireland (£'000)	By commodity By port of Northern Ireland	GB GB	Annual Annual	[QRL 4] [QRL 39]	2.4.6 2.4.6
Special traffic					
Special traffic (thousand tonnes)	By port/economic planning region, by type	GB	Annual	[QRL 4, 14]	2.5.1

QUICK REFERENCE LIST

Scheme and non-scheme port traffic					
Non-scheme traffic (thousand tons)	By commodity group by type of facility	GB	1971	[QRL 14, 37]	2.2.2
Scheme and non-scheme traffic (thousand tons)	By commodity group	GB	1971	[QRL 14]	2.2.2
Non-scheme 3rd party and own account traffic (thousand tons)	By economic region	GB	Annual	[QRL 37]	2.6.3 Time series for 1966–1971 only
Container and roll-on traffic					
Foreign traffic (thousand loaded units)	By port/economic planning region	GB	Annual	[QRL 4, 12]	2.7.0
Foreign and coastwise traffic (thousand loaded units)	By overseas country/ trading area	GB	Annual	[QRL 4, 12]	2.7.0
	By main trading area	GB	Annual	[QRL 27, 28]	2.7.0
	By type of unit	GB	Annual	[QRL 4, 12]	2.7.0
	By type of service and unit	GB	Annual	[QRL 4, 12]	2.7.0
Cross-channel unit-load traffic, inwards/outwards (number of loaded and empty units)	By category, by port of Northern Ireland	GB	Annual	[QRL 39]	2.7.8
Content of containers					
Foreign/coastwise unit transport traffic (thousand tons)	By commodity	GB	1970	[QRL 12]	2.8.0
Content of containers to/from North America (thousand net tons)	By commodity	GB	Annual	[QRL 12]	2.8.0 1969, 1970, 1971 only
Average weight of container (tons)	By size of container, by trade route	GB	Annual	[QRL 12]	2.8.2 1970, 1972 only
Driver accompanied and unaccompanied road goods vehicles					
Number of unaccompanied and accompanied road goods vehicles	By trade route	GB	Annual	[QRL 4, 12]	2.9.0
TRANSHIPMENT AND TRANSIT MOVEMENTS					
Number of loaded containers transhipped at London Customs port	By Customs port of entry by Customs port of exit	GB	1971	[QRL 12]	3.0.1

Descriptive title	Breakdown	Area	Frequency	Publication (see QRL Key)	Text reference and remarks
TRANSHIPMENT AND TRANSIT MOVEMENTS (*contd.*)					
Number of loaded containers transhipped at London Customs port (*contd.*)	By country of origin, by country of destination	GB	1971	[QRL 12]	3.0.1
UK imports transhipped at Rotterdam and Amsterdam (thousand tons)	By bulk commodity, by country of origin	UK	1967	[QRL 19]	3.0.3
Netherlands traffic (tons)	By Dutch port, by commodity, by country of origin/destination	Neth.	Monthly Annual	[QRL 34] [QRL 35]	3.0.3
	By Dutch port, by commodity by mode	Neth.	Monthly Annual	[QRL 34] [QRL 35]	3.0.3
UK imports and exports to Belgium (thousand tonnes)	By Belgian port	UK	Annual	[QRL 36]	3.0.3
US water-borne exports (shipping weight in millions of pounds)	By Customs district/port, by type of service	US	Annual	[QRL 40, 41]	3.0.4
	By trade area, by type of service	US	Annual	[QRL 40, 41]	3.0.4
US water-borne imports (shipping weight in millions of pounds)	By Customs district/port, by type of service	US	Annual	[QRL 40, 41]	3.0.4
	By trade area, by type of service	US	Annual	[QRL 40, 41]	3.0.4
FISHERY TRAFFIC					
Landings of fish (thousand tonnes)	By place of landing/economic planning region	GB	Annual	[QRL 4]	4.0.1
Landings of fish by British vessels (thousand cwt)	By type of fish, by UK country	UK	Annual	[QRL 31]	4.0.1
Landings of fish by British vessels (£'000)	By type of fish, by UK country	UK	Annual	[QRL 31]	4.0.1

QUICK REFERENCE LIST

PASSENGER TRAFFIC					
Number of pleasure cruises (thousands)	—		UK	Annual	[QRL 3]	5.0.1
Sea passenger movements (thousands)	By country of arrival and departure	UK	Quarterly	[QRL 9]	5.0.2 } pre-1964
	By port	UK	Quarterly	[QRL 9]	5.0.2
	By country of landing and embarkation	UK	Annual	[QRL 3, 20]	5.0.2 } post-1964
Passenger movements (thousands)	By port of arrival and departure, by route	UK	Annual	[QRL 3]	5.0.2
	By port	UK	Annual	[QRL 4, 14]	5.0.3
Accompanied cars					
Accompanied cars/buses—inward/outward movements (number of units)	By type of service, by trading area	GB	Annual	[QRL 12]	5.1.0
Accompanied cars (thousand vehicles)	By port/economic planning region, by type of service	GB	Annual	[QRL 4, 12]	5.1.0
Accompanied vehicles (thousand vehicles)	By country/trading area, by type of vehicle	GB	Annual	[QRL 4]	5.1.0
STATISTICS OF CUSTOMS PORTS					
Foreign trade					
Imports (tons and £'000)	By commodity, by country of consignment	UK	Annual	[QRL 22, 23]	6.1.0
Exports (tons and £'000)	By commodity, by country of destination	UK	Annual	[QRL 22, 23]	6.1.0
Imports/exports (quantity and value)	By port, by commodity	UK	Annual	[QRL 7]	6.1.0
		UK	Quarterly	[QRL 33]	6.1.0
Foreign trade (thousand tonnes)	By Customs port, by commodity, by trading area	UK	Annual	[QRL 4, 14]	6.1.1
Foreign trade (metric tons and £)	By commodity, by port	UK	Annual	[QRL 26]	6.1.2

Descriptive title	Breakdown	Area	Frequency	Publication (see QRL Key)	Text reference and remarks
MANPOWER					
National Ports Council					
Number of Port Transport employees	By occupational group, by port/economic planning region	GB	12 Jan. 1966	[QRL 14]	7.1.2
Number of dock workers	By specific occupation, by port/economic planning region, registered/unregistered	GB	12 Jan. 1966	[QRL 14]	7.1.2
Number of employees	By grade of employee, by port/economic planning region	GB	10 Jan. 1968 16 June 1975	[QRL 14] [QRL 4]	7.1.5 7.1.7
Number of management grades	By age, by port/economic planning region	GB	10 Jan. 1968 16 June 1975	[QRL 14] [QRL 4]	7.1.5 7.1.7
	By salary, by function, by age	GB	10 Jan. 1968 16 June 1975	[QRL 14] [QRL 4]	7.1.5 7.1.7
Number of supervisory grades	By age, by port/economic planning region	GB	10 Jan. 1968	[QRL 14]	7.1.5
	By category, by age	GB	10 Jan. 1968	[QRL 14]	7.1.5
Number of undertakings	By number of employees, by economic planning region	GB	10 Jan. 1968 10 June 1975	[QRL 14] [QRL 4]	7.1.5 7.1.5
Non-scheme ports					
Number of regular and casual workers	By type of facility	GB	1973	[QRL 37]	7.2.1

QUICK REFERENCE LIST

Number of employees	By type of facility, by basic hours, by basic wages	GB	1973	[QRL 37]	7.2.1
National Dock Labour Board					
Changes in workers register	By local board, by type of employee	GB	Annual	[QRL 6]	7.3.3
Labour requirements	By type of entrant, by type of removal	GB	Annual	[QRL 6]	7.3.3
	By local board, by workers register	GB	Annual	[QRL 6]	7.3.3
Number of workers register	By disposition	GB	Annual	[QRL 6]	7.3.3
		GB	Annual	[QRL 4]	
Weekly average wages per man on payroll	By quarter, by gross payments, by gross hours	GB	Quarterly	[QRL 6]	7.3.4
		GB	Quarterly	[QRL 4]	
Age distribution of workers register	By age group, by number of men	GB	Annual	[QRL 6]	7.3.5
	By local board, by age group	GB	Annual	[QRL 4]	7.3.5
Department of Employment					
Number of employees in port and inland water transport	By region, by sex	UK	Quarterly	[QRL 11, 13]	7.4.0
Percentage of insured workers unemployed	By sex	UK	Annual	[QRL 10]	7.4.0 Time series for 1948–1968 only
	By industry	UK	Annual	[QRL 1]	7.4.1 Time series for 1923–1939 only
Percentage unemployed	By age, by sex	GB	Six-monthly	[QRL 13]	7.4.1
Accident statistics					
Number of fatal accidents	By process	GB	Annual	[QRL 5]	7.5.0
	By incidence rate	GB	Quarterly	[QRL 13]	7.5.0
Number of accidents in port and inland water transport industry		GB	Annual	[QRL 5]	7.5.0
Industrial accidents in port and inland water transport industry (spells of incapacity)	By cause of accident, by age group	GB	Annual	[QRL 15]	7.5.4
Number of days incapacity	By cause of accident	GB	Annual	[QRL 15]	7.5.4
Number of days incapacity in transport and communications industry	By sex	GB	Annual	[QRL 32]	7.5.5

Descriptive title	Breakdown	Area	Frequency	Publication (see QRL Key)	Text reference and remarks
INLAND WATER TRANSPORT					
British waterways freight traffic (thousand tonnes)	By commodity group	GB	Monthly	[QRL 20]	8.0.3
British waterways freight traffic (tonne/kilometres)	—	GB	Monthly	[QRL 3]	8.0.6
					8.0.3
					8.0.6
Tonnage carried on UK inland waterways	By river and canal system	UK	1974	[QRL 8]	8.0.7
SHIPPING MOVEMENTS					
Foreign trade (tons)	By nationality of vessel	UK	Monthly	[QRL 2]	9.0.0
Coasting trade (tons)	By vessel	UK	Monthly	[QRL 2]	This series ended in 1974
Foreign trade (thousand net tons and number of vessels)	By port, by nationality of vessel	UK	Monthly	[QRL 9]	9.0.1 This series ended in 1939
Foreign trade (thousand net tons)	By port, by arrival and departure with cargo and in ballast	UK	Quarterly	[QRL 9]	9.0.4 This series commenced in April 1956
Coasting trade (thousand net tons)	By port, by arrival and departure with cargo and in ballast	UK	Quarterly	[QRL 9]	
Foreign trade with cargo (thousand net tons and number of vessels)	By nationality of vessel, by entrance and clearance	UK	Monthly	[QRL 9]	9.0.4 Time series from 1965–1970, 1971 only
		UK	Monthly	[QRL 38]	
Foreign trade (thousand net tons and number of vessels)	By port/trading area arrival and departure, with cargo and in ballast	UK	1963, 1964	[QRL 18]	9.0.5
Foreign movements (number of vessels)	By port/coastal group, by type of vessel	UK	Annual	[QRL 14]	9.0.7
	By port/coastal group, by purpose of call	UK	Annual	[QRL 14]	9.0.7

QUICK REFERENCE LIST

	By port/coastal group, by overseas trading area	UK	Annual	[QRL 14]	9.0.7

PORT FACILITIES

Number of dry cargo berths	By major port, by depth of water	GB GB	1962 1965	[QRL 30] [QRL 24]	10.0.0
Number of unit transport berths	By type, by port/economic planning region	GB GB	1968, 1969 1968, 1969	[QRL 14] [QRL 14]	10.0.1 10.0.1
Break bulk and specialized cargo berth facilities	By economic planning region/port/berth/facility	GB	1974	[QRL 4]	10.0.2
Lock, harbour and dock entrance dimensions (metres)	By economic planning region/port/berth	GB	1974	[QRL 4]	10.0.2
Container and roll-on berths in operation or under construction	By economic planning region/port/berth, by facility	GB	1974	[QRL 4]	10.0.2

FINANCE

Total capital employed (£'000)	By port undertaking, by type of capital	GB	Annual	[QRL 25]	11.0.0.0 1971, 1972, 1973 only
Capital employed, revenue, expenditure and net surplus/deficit (£'000)	By port undertaking	GB	Annual	[QRL 4]	11.0.0.0 Since 1974
Gross domestic fixed capital formation (£ million)	By private, public sector	UK	Annual	[QRL 21]	11.0.2

CURRENT AND PROPOSED DEVELOPMENTS

Foreign and coastwise traffic (thousand gross tonnes)	By port, by commodity group	GB	Quarterly	[QRL 29]	12.0.3
Imports/exports (tonnes and £)	By port/economic planning region, by commodity group	UK	Quarterly	[QRL 33]	12.0.3
Origin of exports and destination of imports in US (millions £)	By division and state, by form of transport	US	1970	[QRL 17]	12.0.5

QUICK REFERENCE LIST KEY TO PUBLICATIONS

Reference number	Author or organization responsible	Title	Publisher	Frequency or date of publication	Remarks
[QRL 1]	Mitchell, B. R. (with collaboration of Phyllis Deane)	Abstract of British Historical Statistics	Cambridge University Press	1962	
[QRL 2]	Board of Trade	Accounts Relating to the Trade and Navigation of the United Kingdom	HMSO, London	Monthly 1882–1964	Superseded by Overseas Trade Accounts of the UK [QRL 22]
[QRL 3]	Central Statistical Office	Annual Abstract of Statistics	HMSO, London	Annual	
[QRL 4]	National Ports Council	Annual Digest of Port Statistics	National Ports Council	Annual	Volumes I and II supersede [QRL 14]
[QRL 5]	Department of Employment	Annual Report of HM Chief Inspector of Factories	HMSO, London	Annual	
[QRL 6]	National Dock Labour Board	Annual Reports of the National Dock Labour Board	National Dock Labour Board	Annual	Publication ceased at beginning of 1978. See [QRL 33]
[QRL 7]	Commissioners of HM Customs and Excise	Annual Statement of the Overseas Trade of the United Kingdom	HMSO, London	Annual	
[QRL 8]	Inland Shipping Group of the Inland Waterways Association	Barges or Juggernauts	Inland Shipping Group	1974	
[QRL 9]	Board of Trade	Board of Trade Journal	HMSO	Weekly 1886–1970	In October 1970 it was superseded by Trade and Industry [QRL 38]
[QRL 10]	Department of Employment	British Labour Statistics: Historical Abstract 1886–1968	HMSO, London	1971	First published in 1969
[QRL 11]	Department of Employment	British Labour Statistics Yearbook	HMSO, London	Annual	
[QRL 12]	National Ports Council	Container and Roll-on Port Statistics, Great Britain	National Ports Council	Annual 1967–1973	Parts 1 and 2. Now incorporated in Annual Digest of Port Statistics [QRL 4]
[QRL 13]	Department of Employment	Department of Employment Gazette	HMSO, London	Monthly	Formerly Ministry of Labour Gazette

QUICK REFERENCE LIST

[QRL 14]	National Ports Council	Digest of Port Statistics	National Ports Council	Annual 1966–1972	No longer available. Superseded by Annual Digest of Port Statistics Volumes I and II [QRL 4]
[QRL 15]	Department of Health and Social Security	Digest of Statistics Analysing Certificates of Incapacity	Department of Health and Social Security	Annual 1951–1971	In 1972 it was superseded by Social Security Statistics [QRL 32]
[QRL 16]	Department of Energy	Digest of UK Energy Statistics	HMSO, London	Annual 1972	
[QRL 17]	Bureau of the Census, US Department of Commerce, Social and Economic Statistics Administration	Domestic and International Transportation of US Foreign Trade: 1970 General Cargo Commodities	US Department of Commerce		
[QRL 18]	Ministry of Transport	Foreign Trade Shipping Movements at UK Ports	Ministry of Transport	1963, 1964	No longer available
[QRL 19]	Management Services Ltd. for the National Ports Council	An Initial Study of the Likely Effect of Transhipment on Bulk Cargo Deep Sea Berth Requirements of the UK	Not published	1969	Available for consultation by appointment at the National Ports Council Library
[QRL 20]	Central Statistical Office	Monthly Digest of Statistics	HMSO, London	Monthly	
[QRL 21]	Central Statistical Office	National Income and Expenditure	HMSO, London	Annual	This publication is known as the 'Blue Book'
[QRL 22]	Board of Trade	Overseas Trade Accounts of the United Kingdom	HMSO, London	Monthly 1964–1970	Superseded by Overseas Trade Statistics of the United Kingdom [QRL 23]
[QRL 23]	Departments of Industry, Trades and Prices and Consumer Protection	Overseas Trade Statistics of the United Kingdom	HMSO, London	Monthly	From 1 Jan. 1970. Formerly Overseas Trade Accounts of the United Kingdom [QRL 22]
[QRL 24]	National Ports Council	Port Development. An Interim Plan	National Ports Council	1965	No longer available
[QRL 25]	National Ports Council	Port Financial Information	National Ports Council	1971, 1972, 1973	

Reference number	Author or organization responsible	Title	Publisher	Frequency or date of publication	Remarks
[QRL 26]	British Ports Association	*Port Statistics for the Foreign Trade of the United Kingdom*	British Ports Association	Annual	Parts I, II and III. British Ports Association was formerly Dock and Harbours Authorities Association
[QRL 27]	National Ports Council	*Port Traffic on Unit Transport Services, Great Britain, 1965 and 1966*	National Ports Council	1965, 1966	
[QRL 28]	National Ports Council	*Port Unit Transport Statistics, Great Britain*	National Ports Council	1968, 1969	
[QRL 29]	National Ports Council	*Quarterly Bulletin of Port Statistics*	National Ports Council	Quarterly	First publication was first quarter 1976
[QRL 30]	Ministry of Transport. Chairman: Lord Rochdale	*Report of the Committee of Inquiry into the Major Ports of Great Britain*	HMSO, London	1962	
[QRL 31]	Ministry of Agriculture, Fisheries and Food	*Sea Fisheries, Statistical Tables*	HMSO, London	Annual	
[QRL 32]	Department of Health and Social Security	*Social Security Statistics*	HMSO, London	Annual from 1972	Formerly *Digest of Statistics Analysing Certificates of Incapacity* [QRL 15]
[QRL 33]	HM Customs and Excise	*Statistics of Trade through United Kingdom Ports*	HMSO, London	Quarterly	First publication was first quarter 1976, see earlier [QRL 7]
[QRL 34]	Central Bureau voor de Statistiek	*Statistiek van het International Goendenvervoer in de Havens Rotterdam en Amsterdam*	Central Bureau voor de Statistiek, Netherlands	Annual	
[QRL 35]	Central Bureau voor de Statistiek	*Statistiek van het International Zeehavenvervoer*	Central Bureau voor de Statistiek	Monthly	
[QRL 36]	Ministère des Affaires Economiques	*Statistique annuelle du Traffic International des Ports*	Institut National de Statistique, Belgium	Annual	

QUICK REFERENCE LIST

[QRL 37]	National Ports Council	*Survey of Non-Scheme Ports and Wharves Preliminary Report, Final Report*	National Ports Council	1972 1973	
[QRL 38]	Departments of Industry, Trade, and Prices and Consumer Protection	*Trade and Industry*	HMSO, London	Weekly from Oct. 1970	Formerly *Board of Trade Journal* [QRL 9]
[QRL 39]	Department of Commerce, Northern Ireland	*The Trade of Northern Ireland*	Department of Commerce, Northern Ireland	Annual	Discontinued after 1974
[QRL 40]	US Department of Commerce	*US Waterborne Exports; Outbound in-transit Shipments, and Supplement–Department of Defense and Special Category Cargo*	US Department of Commerce	Annual	
[QRL 41]	US Department of Commerce	*US Waterborne General Imports and Inbound in-transit Shipments*	US Department of Commerce	Annual	

BIBLIOGRAPHY

[B 1] Bradbury, M. S., assisted by Lee, D. J. *Economics and Marine Pilotage* (Mimeo), Department of Trade and Industry, 1973.
[B 2] Eadie, W. T. *The Sampling of Mersey Docks and Harbours Company Ship Manifests* (Mimeo), National Ports Council, 1973.
[B 3] Hunter, E. *Ship Manifests as a Source of Statistical Information* (Mimeo), National Ports Council.
[B 4] UK Government. *Control of Pollution Act 1974*, Ch. 40, HMSO, London.
[B 5] UK Government, *Dock Workers (Regulation of Employment) Act 1946*, Ch. 22, HMSO, London.
[B 6] UK Government. *Dock Workers (Regulation of Employment) (Amendment) Order 1967*, HMSO, London.
[B 7] Health and Safety Executive, Factory Inspectorate. *Explanatory Note on Statistics of Accidents Notified under the Factories Act.*
[B 8] UK Government. *Factories Act 1961*, 9 and 10 Eliz. 2, Ch. 34, HMSO, London.
[B 9] US Department of Commerce. *Guide to Foreign Trade Statistics*, Washington.
[B 10] UK Government. *Harbours Act 1964*, Ch. 40, HMSO, London.
[B 11] Parliament of Northern Ireland. *Harbours Act (Northern Ireland) 1970*, Ch. 1, HMSO, Belfast.
[B 12] UK Government. *Health and Safety at Work Act 1974*, Ch. 37, HMSO, London.
[B 13] Peat, Marwick, Mitchell & Co. *Inspector's Report of Inquiry into Dues Charged by the British Transport Docks Board at Hull, Grimsby, Immingham, Goole and Rivers Humber and Ouse.* Appendix VII, 7 April 1975, Peat, Marwick, Mitchell & Co., London.
[B 14] UK Government. *Merchant Shipping Act 1906*, Ch. 48, HMSO, London.
[B 15] UK Government. *Merchant Shipping (International Labour Convention) Act 1925*, Ch. 42, HMSO, London.
[B 16] Board of Trade. *Merchant Shipping (Life-Saving Appliances) Rules 1965*, No. 1105, HMSO, London.
[B 17] UK Government, *Pilotage Act 1913*, 2 and 3 Geo. 5, Ch. 31, HMSO, London.
[B 18] Minister of Transport's Policy Statement on Nationalisation, *Ports Reorganisation*, July 1967, HMSO, London.
[B 19] Report of the Committee 1970–1972. *Safety and Health at Work*, Cmnd. 5034, HMSO, London.
[B 20] UK Government. *Sea Fishery Industry Act 1951*, Ch. 30, HMSO, London.
[B 21] UK Government. *Transport Act 1947*, Ch. 49, HMSO, London.
[B 22] UK Government. *Transport Act 1962*, Ch. 46, 10 and 11 Eliz. 2, HMSO, London.
[B 23] UK Government. *Transport Act 1968*, Ch. 73, HMSO, London.
[B 24] Report of an Inter-Departmental Working Party. *Unemployment Statistics*, November 1972, Cmnd. 5157, HMSO, London.
[B 25] British Waterways Board. *Report and Accounts*, Annual.

APPENDICES

Appendix 1   National Ports Council Forms P.S.3a and P.S.3b
Appendix 2   Commodity Classifications used by the National Ports Council
Appendix 3   National Ports Council Forms P.S.3c and P.S.3d
Appendix 4   HM Customs Form 'Transire'
Appendix 5   National Ports Council Form P.S.3e
Appendix 6   National Ports Council Questionnaire for the Survey of Non-scheme Ports and Wharves
Appendix 7   National Ports Council Forms P.S.48 (Revised), P.S.48 Annexes A, B, C
Appendix 8   Department of Transport Form for Collection of Statistics on (Driver) Accompanied and Unaccompanied Road Goods Vehicles, Trailers and Semi-trailers on Specialized Roll-on Services
Appendix 9   HM Customs Forms C10 (imports) and C273 (exports)
Appendix 10 National Ports Council Manpower Census Form
Appendix 11 National Dock Labour Board Form B50
Appendix 12 National Dock Labour Board Form B51
Appendix 13 HM Customs Forms C568 (arrival sheet); C568A (sailing sheet)
Appendix 14 National Ports Council Survey of Port Facilities Questionnaire

Appendix 1

NATIONAL PORTS COUNCIL P.S.3a

Foreign Traffic — Imports

Return from (Port Authority) ....

of imports through the Port of ....

during the year/quarter/ .... ended .... 197 ......

Commodity Code	Commodity	Logabax Code	For. Imports Tonnes	Commodity Code
1.11	Meat and meat preparations	11		1.11
1.12	Dairy products and eggs	12		1.12
1.131	Cereals, unmilled	13		1.131
1.132	Cereals, milled and preparations	14		1.132
1.14	Fruit and vegetables	15		1.14
1.15	Feeding stuffs for animals (excluding unmilled cereals)	16		1.15
1.2	Sugar and sugar preparations	17		1.2
1.3	Beverages	18		1.3
1.4	Other foodstuffs and tobacco (fish and fish preparations, tea, coffee, cocoa, lard, etc.)	19		1.4
2.1	Wood, lumber and cork	21		2.1
2.2	Pulp and waste paper	22		2.2
2.3	Textile fibres and their waste	23		2.3
2.4	Ores and scrap	24		2.4
2.51	Clay / Crude fertilisers and crude minerals other than clay	25		2.51
2.521	Oil seeds and nuts	26		2.521
2.522	Animal and vegetable oils and fats	27		2.522
2.523	Crude Rubber	28		2.523
2.524	Hides, skins, undressed furs and other basic materials (bonemeal, plants, esparto, lacs, etc.)	29		2.524
3.1	Coal, coke and briquettes	31		3.1
3.21	Crude petroleum	32		3.21
3.22	Petroleum products and natural and manufactured gas	33		3.22
4.11	Chemical fertilisers	34		4.11
4.12	Chemicals, other	35		4.12
4.2	Textile yarns, fabrics and made up articles	36		4.2
4.31	Cement	37		4.31
4.32	Non metallic mineral manufactures other than cement	38		4.32
4.4	Iron and steel	39		4.4
4.5	Non ferrous metals	41		4.5
4.6	Manufactures of metals	42		4.6
4.71	Machinery, non-electric	43		4.71
4.72	Machinery, electric	44		4.72
4.81	Road motor vehicles	45		4.81
4.82	Other road vehicles and other transport equipment	46		4.82
4.91	Wood and cork manufactures (excluding furniture)	47		4.91
4.92	Paper, paperboard and manufactures thereof	48		4.92
4.93	Other miscellaneous manufactured articles (building fixtures and fittings, furniture, travel goods, clothing, footwear, instruments, etc.)	49		4.93
5.1	Used packaging and empty returnable containers	51		5.1
5.2	Live animals	52		5.2
		53		
	Total			

SPECIMEN

APPENDICES

NATIONAL PORTS COUNCIL   P.S.3b

Foreign Traffic Exports

Return from (Port Authority) ....

of exports through the Port of ....

during the year/quarter/ .... ended .... 197 ....

Commodity Code	Commodity	Logabax Code	For. Exports Tonnes	Commodity Code
1.1	Meat and meat preparations Dairy products and eggs Cereals, unmilled [(1)......................tonnes] Cereals, milled and preparations Fruit and vegetables Feeding stuffs for animals (excluding unmilled cereals)	11	....	1.1
1.2	Sugar and sugar preparations	12	....	1.2
1.3	Beverages	13	....	1.3
1.4	Other foodstuffs and tobacco (fish and fish preparations, tea, coffee, cocoa, lard, etc.)	14	....	1.4
2.1	Wood, lumber and cork	21	....	2.1
2.2	Pulp and waste paper	22	....	2.2
2.3	Textile fibres and their waste	23	....	2.3
2.4	Ores and scrap	24	....	2.4
2.511	Clay	25	....	2.511
2.512	Crude fertilisers and crude minerals other than clay	26	....	2.512
2.52	Oil seeds and nuts Animal and vegetable oils and fats Crude rubber Hides, skins, undressed furs and other basic materials, (bonemeal, plants, copra, lacs, etc.)	27	....	2.52
3.1	Coal, coke and briquettes	31	....	3.1
3.21	Crude petroleum	32	....	3.21
3.22	Petroleum products and natural and manufactured gas	33	....	3.22
4.11	Chemical fertilisers	34	....	4.11
4.12	Chemicals, other	35	....	4.12
4.2	Textile yarns, fabrics and made-up articles	36	....	4.2
4.31	Cement	37	....	4.31
4.32	Non-metallic mineral manufactures other than cement	38	....	4.32
4.4	Iron and steel	39	....	4.4
4.5	Non-ferrous metals	41	....	4.5
4.6	Manufactures of metals	42	....	4.6
4.71	Machinery, non-electric	43	....	4.71
4.72	Machinery, electric	44	....	4.72
4.81	Road motor vehicles	45	....	4.81
4.82	Other road vehicles and other transport equipment	46	....	4.82
4.91	Wood and cork manufactures (excluding furniture)	47	....	4.91
4.92	Paper, paperboard and manufactures thereof	48	....	4.92
4.93	Other miscellaneous manufactured articles (building fixtures and fittings, furniture, travel. goods, clothing, footwear, instruments, etc.)	49	....	4.93
5.1	Used packaging and empty returnable containers	51	....	5.1
5.2	Live animals	52	....	5.2
		53		
	Total			

(1) Please enter here the tonnage, if any, of cereals, unmilled exported during the period, which are included in commodity code 1.1

Appendix 2

COMMODITY CLASSIFICATION FOR PORT STATISTICS

Commodity class	N.P.C. code	S.I.T.C. (Revised)
Foodstuffs, etc.		
Foodstuffs and tobacco		
Meat and meat preparations	1.11	01
Dairy products and eggs	1.12	02
Unmilled cereals	1.131	041 to 045
Milled cereals and cereal preparations	1.132	046 to 048
Fruit and vegetables	1.14	05
Animal feeding stuffs	1.15	08
Sugar and sugar preparations	1.2	06
Other foodstuffs and tobacco	1.4	03, 07, 09, 12
Beverages	1.3	11
Live animals	5.2	00, 941
Basic materials		
Wood, lumber and cork	2.1	24
Pulp and waste paper	2.2	25
Textile fibres and their waste	2.3	26
Ores and scrap	2.4	28
Crude fertilisers and crude minerals		
Clay	2.511	276.21
Other crude minerals	2.5	27 except 276.21
Oil seeds and nuts	5.21	22
Animal and vegetable oils and fats	5.22	41, 42, 43
Crude rubber	5.23	23
Other basic materials	2.524	21, 29
Manufactured goods		
Chemicals		
Fertilisers	4.11	56
Other chemicals	4.12	51 to 55, 57 to 59
Textile yarns, fabrics and made-up articles	4.2	65
Non-metallic mineral manufactures		
Cement	4.31	661.2
Other	4.32	66 except 661.2
Iron and steel	4.4	67
Non-ferrous metals	4.5	68
Manufactures of metals	4.6	69, 951, 961
Machinery		
Other than electric	4.71	71
Electric	4.72	72
Vehicles		
Road motor vehicles	4.81	732
Other vehicles	4.82	73 except 732
Wood and cork manufactures	4.91	63
Paper and manufactures thereof	4.92	64
Other manufactured goods	4.93	61, 62, 81 to 89, 911
Fuels		
Coal, coke and briquettes	3.1	32
Petroleum		
Crude	3.21	331
Petroleum products	3.22	332, 34

APPENDICES

Appendix 3

NATIONAL PORTS COUNCIL

P.S.3c

Coastwise Traffic – Inwards

Return from (Port Authority) ....

of coastwise cargo inwards through the Port of ....

during the year/quarter/ .... ended .... 197 ....

Commodity Code	Commodity	Logabax Code	Coast. In Tonnes	Commodity Code
1.11	Meat and meat preparations	11		1.11
1.12	Dairy products and eggs	12		1.12
1.131	Cereals, unmilled	13		1.131
1.132	Cereals, milled and preparations	14		1.132
1.14	Fruit and vegetables	15		1.14
1.15	Feeding stuffs for animals (excluding unmilled cereals)	16		1.15
1.2	Sugar and sugar preparations	17		1.2
1.3	Beverages	18		1.3
1.4	Other foodstuffs and tobacco (fish and fish preparations, tea, coffee, cocoa, lard, etc.)	19		1.4
2.1	Wood, lumber and cork	21		2.1
2.2	Pulp and waste paper	22		2.2
2.3	Textile fibres and their waste	23		2.3
2.4	Ores and scrap	24		2.4
2.511	Clay	25		2.511
2.512	Crude fertilisers and crude minerals other than clay	26		2.512
2.521	Oil seeds and nuts	27		2.521
2.522	Animals and vegetable oils and fats	28		2.522
2.523	Crude rubber	29		2.523
2.524	Hides, skins, undressed furs and other basic materials (bonemeal, plants, esparto, logs, etc.)	31		2.524
3.1	Coal, coke and briquettes	32		3.1
3.21	Crude petroleum	33		3.21
3.22	Petroleum products and natural and manufactured gas	34		3.22
4.11	Chemical fertilisers	41		4.11
4.12	Chemicals, other	42		4.12
4.2	Textile yarns, fabrics and made-up articles	43		4.2
4.31	Cement	44		4.31
4.32	Non-metallic mineral manufactures other than cement	45		4.32
4.4	Iron and steel	46		4.4
4.5	Non-ferrous metals	47		4.5
4.6	Manufactures of metals	48		4.6
4.71	Machinery, non-electric	49		4.71
4.72	Machinery, electric	51		4.72
4.81	Road motor vehicles	52		4.81
4.82	Other road vehicles and other transport equipment	53		4.82
4.91	Wood and cork manufactures (excluding furniture)	54		4.91
4.92	Paper, paperboard and manufactures thereof	55		4.92
4.93	Other miscellaneous manufactured articles (building fixtures and fittings, furniture, travel goods, clothing, footwear, instruments, etc.)	56		4.93
5.1	Used packaging and empty returnable containers	57		5.1
5.2	Live animals	58		5.2
		59		
	Total			

SPECIMEN

NATIONAL PORTS COUNCIL   P.S.3d

Coastwise Traffic – Outwards

Return from (Port Authority) ....

of coastwise cargo outwards through the Port of ....

during the year/quarter/ ....ended .... 197 ......

Commodity Code	Commodity	Logabax Code	Coast. Out Tonnes	Commodity Code
1.11	Meat and meat preparations	11	....	1.11
1.12	Dairy products and eggs	12	....	1.12
1.131	Cereals, unmilled	13	....	1.131
1.132	Cereals, milled and preparations	14	....	1.132
1.14	Fruit and vegetables	15	....	1.14
1.15	Feeding stuffs for animals (excluding unmilled cereals)	16	....	1.15
1.2	Sugar and sugar preparations	17	....	1.2
1.3	Beverages	18	....	1.3
1.4	Other foodstuffs and tobacco (fish and fish preparations, tea, coffee, cocoa, lard, etc.)	19	....	1.4
2.1	Wood, lumber and cork	21	....	2.1
2.2	Pulp and waste paper	22	....	2.2
2.3	Textile fibres and their waste	23	....	2.3
2.4	Ores and scrap	24	....	2.4
2.511	Clay	25	....	2.511
2.512	Crude fertilisers and crude minerals other than clay	26	....	2.512
2.521	Oil seeds and nuts	27	....	2.521
2.522	Animal and vegetable oils and fats	28	....	2.522
2.523	Crude rubber	29	....	2.523
2.524	Hides, skins, undressed furs and other basic materials (bonemeal, bristles, esparto, lacs, etc.)	31	....	2.524
3.1	Coal, coke and briquettes	32	....	3.1
3.21	Crude petroleum	33	....	3.21
3.22	Petroleum products and natural and manufactured gas	34	....	3.22
4.11	Chemical fertilisers	41	....	4.11
4.12	Chemicals, other	42	....	4.12
4.2	Textile yarns, fabrics and made-up articles	43	....	4.2
4.31	Cement	44	....	4.31
4.32	Non-metallic mineral manufactures other than cement	45	....	4.32
4.4	Iron and steel	46	....	4.4
4.5	Non-ferrous metals	47	....	4.5
4.6	Manufactures of metals	48	....	4.6
4.71	Machinery, non-electric	49	....	4.71
4.72	Machinery, electric	51	....	4.72
4.81	Road motor vehicles	52	....	4.81
4.82	Other road vehicles and other transport equipment	53	....	4.82
4.91	Wood and cork manufactures (excluding furniture)	54	....	4.91
4.92	Paper, paperboard and manufactures thereof	55	....	4.92
4.93	Other miscellaneous manufactured articles (building fixtures and fittings, furniture, travel goods, clothing, footwear, instruments, etc.)	56	....	4.93
5.1	Used packaging and empty returnable containers	57	....	5.1
5.2	Live animals	58	....	5.2
		59		
	Total			

SPECIMEN

Appendix 4

H.M. CUSTOMS AND EXCISE

TRANSIRE (ORIGINAL) **X.S. 18**

*Delete as necessary

PORT OF

*Sailing Vessel
*Steamer
*Motor Vessel

Official Number of Ship

Name of Ship	Net Tonnage	If British, Port of Registry / If Foreign, the Country	Master's Name	Whither Bound	Date of Sailing

I,   Master of the   do hereby declare the particulars stated on this form to be true, and that all the requirements of the Merchant Shipping Acts have been duly complied with.

Dated   19 .   Master

Cleared out   19 .   { Collector or other proper *Officer*

Agent..

Address..

This Document is to accompany the vessel and to be delivered at the Port of unlading with the name of the Wharf or place of discharge inserted on the back hereof.

(P.T.O.)

F 1965 (November 1970)

Further supplies of this form may be obtained from any Collector of Customs and Excise.

X.S. 18   528546 6M 7.77 E.P.

SPECIMEN

Foreign Goods, distinguishing Warehoused Goods removed under Bond	Goods liable to Excise Duty or entitled to Drawback thereof	Coal, including Culm, but excluding Manufactured Fuel	Other British goods
		Tons	

Shipped for use on board................................ ....tons of coal.

State whether carrying passengers

Last from   { Light / In Ballast / With Cargo

Vessel loading at

To be filled in at place of discharge

Date of Arrival........................

The above Cargo (or portion thereof, stating particulars) will be discharged at

*Insert Name of Dock, Wharf or Station.

* ....

Date..........................19   ....Master or Agent.

Agent........................   Address........................

Appendix 5

NATIONAL PORTS COUNCIL P.S. 3e

Special Traffic

Return from (Port Authority) ....

of special traffic through the Port of ....

during the year/quarter/ .... ended .... 197......

Commodity	Quantity	Unit
Bunkers: petroleum (quantity provided)		tonnes
Bunkers: coal (quantity provided)		tonnes
Dredged sand and gravel etc. landed for commercial purposes		tonnes
Fish, whales and natural produce of the sea landed direct		tonnes
Motor vehicles and trailers not for import or export: Inwards		number
Motor vehicles and trailers not for import or export: Outwards		number
Material shipped for dumping at sea:		tonnes
		tonnes
		tonnes
Traffic with off shore installations: Inwards		tonnes
Traffic with off shore installations: Outwards		tonnes

I enclose forms P.S. 3a, b, c and d, giving the returns for foreign, coastwise and special traffics for the period stated.

Signed for the Port Authority ....

Dated ....

To The National Ports Council, Commonwealth House, 1 19 New Oxford Street, London WC1A 1DZ

SPECIMEN

Notes for the completion of the form

1. Foreign traffic: traffic to and from destinations outside the United Kingdom [i.e. Great Britain, Northern Ireland, Isle of Man, Channel Islands and Continental Shelf (U.K. Parts)].
2. Coastwise traffic: Traffic between ports in the United Kingdom.
3. Special traffics: The following traffics should be excluded from the statistics of foreign and coastwise traffic and, if possible, recorded separately in the spaces provided: –
    (a) Bunkers: indicate the tonnage of (i) petroleum, (ii) coal bunkers.
    (b) Dredged sand and gravel: indicate the tonnage of sand, gravel, etc., landed at your port for commercial purposes after being dredged up.
    (c) Fish, whales, etc.: indicate the tonnage of fish, whales and natural produce of the sea landed direct from fishing vessels and fish carrier vessels.
    (d) Motor vehicles and trailers not for export or import. The numbers of motor vehicles and of trailers (e.g. tourist motor cars, roll-on/roll-off vehicles etc.) moving inwards and outwards through the port not being themselves for import or export should be given.
    (e) Material shipped for dumping at sea: Please indicate nature of material e.g. sewage, industrial waste. Dredged spoil dumped directly at sea without passing over quays should be excluded.
    (f) Traffic with off-shore installations: include all seaborne traffic with off-shore rigs and pipelines, whether construction and maintenance traffic or output from the rigs.
4. Weights: The weights given should be gross weights, inclusive of packing etc.
5. Periods covered: The statistics should relate to calendar years or quarters.
6. Ignore 'Logabax Code' column.
7. Insert " – " against any items in which there was no traffic.
8. Minor changes have been made to the layout and to the commodity descriptions, but these changes are intended only to simplify processing and clarify the codes. The changes do not amend in any way the classification of commodities as indicated in the Index to Commodity Classification for Port Statistics.

Appendix 6

NPC Survey of non-scheme ports, wharves, etc. 1972

NPC use only

Name and address of port operator/wharfinger ....

A. PORT FACILITIES AVAILABLE FOR CARGO HANDLING OPERATIONS

Question 1: Description of port, wharf, quay, jetty etc. (please provide details of each individual berth)

Name or number of berth, quay, wharf, jetty, etc.	Length of berth (ft)	Depth of water at MHWS (ft)	Land area used in conjunction with cargo handled (acres)	Whether loading/unloading by ship's or shore gear	Date(s) constructed
....	....	....	....	....	....
....	....	....	....	....	....
....	....	....	....	....	....
....	....	....	....	....	....

Please supply if possible a plan, drawing or illustration of these facilities

Question 2: What is the largest vessel (a) which has been accommodated? .... dwt
(b) which could at present be accommodated? .... dwt

Question 3: Are vessels using the facilities having to pay dues to any (other) harbour authority through whose area of jurisdiction for conservancy purposes they may pass? Yes/No (delete as applicable)
If "yes", which harbour authority? ....

SPECIMEN

NPC Survey of non-scheme ports (continued)

NPC use only

B. PORT TRAFFIC

Question 4: What type and quantity of cargo was loaded/unloaded during 1971 at the berth(s) listed in Question 1?

Main commodities loaded/unloaded	Quantity of cargo (tons)		
	Handled "on own account"*	Handled for third parties	Total cargo
(a) Petroleum	....	....	....
(b) Coal	....	....	....
(c) Grain	....	....	....
(d) Crude minerals/fertilisers	....	....	....
(e) Sand and gravel	....	....	....
(f) Other bulk commodities (please list)			
....	....	....	....
....	....	....	....
....	....	....	....
(g) All other commodities	....	....	....
Total quantity handled in 1971			
Total quantity in previous years { 1970	....	....	....
1969	....	....	....
1968	....	....	....
1967	....	....	....
1966	....	....	....

*"On own account" e.g. before or after industrial processing, including cargo for parent, subsidiary or other associated companies.

NPC Survey of non-scheme ports (continued)

MANPOWER AND CONDITIONS OF EMPLOYMENT

NPC use only

Question 5: Number of <u>men engaged on cargo handling operations</u> in the year ending 31st July 1972 at the berths listed under Question 1.

Basis of employment	Minimum Number	Maximum Number	Average Number
(a) Permanent/regular	....	....	....
(b) Casual	....	....	....

Question 6: Details of <u>pay and work</u> for the above men.

	Permanent/Regular men	Casual men if different when applicable
(i) Number of hours per man in basic week	.... hours	.... hours
(ii) Basic rate of pay per week	£...............	£...............
(iii) Overtime rates of pay	....	....
(iv) Other incentive payments if any (a) type	....	....
(b) rate	....	....
(v) Average gross earnings per week	£...............	£...............

SPECIMEN

NPC Survey of non-scheme ports (continued)

NPC use only

Question 7: Are there <u>Private Pension</u> arrangements?   Yes/No
If yes, please give brief details (e.g. employer/employee rates of contribution etc.)
....
....

Question 8: <u>Holiday</u> arrangements   (a) Number of weeks holiday ....
(excluding public holidays)   (b) Number of weeks paid holiday ....

Question 9: <u>Sick pay</u> arrangements, if any, in brief.
....
....

Question 10: Other <u>fringe benefits;</u> if any (e.g. subsidised meals/transport etc.)
....
....

Question 11: Are these men members of a <u>union</u>?   Yes/No
If yes, which union? ....

APPENDICES

NPC Survey of non-scheme ports (continued)

NPC use only

D. **FINANCIAL DATA**

(for the undertaking completing this questionnaire, in respect of port operations only)

Question 12: Summary Profit and Loss Account
Please complete.

	ACTUAL (year ended in)			ESTIMATE or Actual (year ended in)
	1971	1970	1969	1972
	£	£	£	£
Revenue				
Dues (ie. charges on ships and goods)	..	..	..	..
Cargo Handling	..	..	..	..
Warehousing/Storage	..	..	..	..
Other	.. ...	.. ...	.. ...	.. ...
Expenditure:				
Labour	..	..	..	..
Administration and general	.. ...	.. ...	.. ...	.. ...
Operating Surplus before depreciation	..	..	..	..
Depreciation	..	..	..	..
Operating Surplus/(Deficit) after depreciation	..	..	..	..
Interest Payable	..	..	..	..
Less Interest Receivable	..	..	..	..
Other items (eg. exceptional or non-recurring)				
.............................(give details)	..	..	..	..
.............................(give details)	..	..	..	..
Net Surplus / (Deficit)	...	...	...	...

SPECIMEN

NPC Survey of non-scheme ports (continued)

NPC use only

Question 13: Summary Balance Sheet
Please complete

	ACTUAL (year ended in)			ESTIMATE or Actual (year ended in)
	1971	1970	1969	1972
	£	£	£	£
Fixed Assets (gross)	..	..	..	..
Less: Accumulated Depreciation	..	..	..	..
Net Fixed Assets	..	..	..	..
Net Current Assets	..	..	..	..
Other Assets	..	..	..	..
Total Net Assets	...	...	...	...
Borrowings:-				
Bank Borrowings and short term loans	..	..	..	..
Loan Capital	..	..	..	..
Total Borrowings	..	..	..	..
Reserves and miscellaneous balances	..	..	..	..
Issued Share Capital	..	..	..	..
Total Sources of Capital	...	...	...	...

NPC Survey of non-scheme ports (continued) | NPC use only

Notes

(a) Please state basis of arriving at amount shown for Fixed Assets (gross) ....
(b) Please indicate basis of depreciation (i.e. on historic or replacement cost whether on all fixed assets other than freehold land) ....
(c) Please give particulars of Associated Companies and main ownership of own share capital (including name of parent company, if any) ....

Question 14 - Please provide details of <u>charges</u> (a) on ships (b) on goods (c) for cargo handling etc.
 (a) ....
 (b) ....
 (c) ....

L.   <u>SUPPLEMENTARY</u>

Question 15. As this standard questionnaire has to cover a wide variety of facilities and functions please indicate if there are any <u>special considerations</u> relating to your facilities which you wish to draw to the Council's attention.

....
....

<u>Signed for and on behalf of the undertaking</u> ....
Name (in Block Capitals) ....
Date   ....
Telephone Number   ....

SPECIMEN

APPENDICES

Appendix 7

N.P.C. Unit Transport Services Traffic, year ending 31st Dec. 19..... (PS48 Revised)

Port (Authority) ....

Country
(Please complete a separate return for each country)

Name of specialised Vessel Operator/Consortium

Special roll-on services ....

Special lift-on services
(If there is more than one operator of roll-on services please complete a separate return for each; similarly for lift-on services.)

Type of service and unit	Number of units				Tonnage (of goods traffic)	
	Loaded		Empty			
	In	Out	In	Out	In	Out
Roll-on/roll-off services*						
1. Railway wagons*						
2. Road goods vehicles, trailers*						
3. Lancashire flats*						
4. Bulk liquid containers*						
5. Other freight containers*						
of which 20′ or more ext. length	(........)	(........)	(........)	(........)	(........)	(........)
6. Other traffic						
(a) Import export vehicles*	XXX	XXX				
(b) Other goods traffic* (tons)	XXX	XXX	XXX	XXX		
(c) Accompanied cars (Nos.)			XXX	XXX	XXX	XXX
(d) Accompanied buses/coaches (Nos)			XXX	XXX	XXX	XXX
Special lift-on/lift-off services*						
7. Road goods vehicles/trailers*						
8. Lancashire flats						
9. Bulk liquid containers						
10. Other freight containers						
of which 20′ or more ext. length	(........)	(........)	(........)	(........)	(........)	(........)
All other (conventional) services						
11. Lancashire flats						
12. Bulk liquid containers						
13. Other freight containers						
of which 20′ or more ext. length	(........)	(........)	(........)	(........)	(........)	(........)

Notes on items asterisked above:—
  "**Roll-on roll-off services**" comprise **all** vessels with **ramp loading** via bow, stern or side doors (including those vessels with some lift-on/lift-off capacity).
  1. "Railway wagons"
  2 & 7. "Road goods vehicles/trailers" } include wagons and road goods vehicles carrying flats, containers, etc.

3, 4 & 5. Include flats, bulk liquid and other freight containers loaded by trailers limited to ship or to port use only.

  6a. "Import export vehicles" include cars, lorries, caravans, tractors, etc.
  6b. "Other goods traffic" includes all goods (not on road goods vehicles/trailers/flats, nor in bulk liquid or other freight containers) carried on roll-on/roll-off services, including goods carried on trailers limited to ship or to port use only.

  "**Special lift-on/lift-off services**" comprise specially constructed or adapted lift-on/lift-off vessels.

Signed for Port Authority .... date .... / ...... /19

NATIONAL PORTS COUNCIL

Unit Transport Services Traffic Return (PS48 Revised)

Notes on completing the return

1. Statistics for the year ending 31st December should be completed on a separate return for each country. The names of the specialised service operators, but not of the conventional service operators, should be given in order to determine the level of publication of national statistics without individual disclosure.

2. "Number of loaded units" should be given for all transport units except 6(a) import/export vehicles and 6(b) other goods traffic.

3. "Number of empty units" should be given for all transport units except 6(b) other goods and 6(c) accompanied cars and buses.

4. "Tonnage of goods traffic" should refer to the gross weight of the goods traffic inclusive of crate, internal wrapping and other packing but exclusive of the weight of the railway wagon, road goods vehicle, flat, bulk liquid or other container.

5. "Roll-on/roll-off services" comprise all vessels with ramp loading via bow, stern, or side doors, including those with some lift-on/lift-off capacity (*i.e.* excluding vessels with side doors for the transfer of goods between fork lift trucks on shore and fork lift trucks on board ship).

6. "Railway wagons", item 1, should comprise all railway wagons (including those carrying demountable Lancashire flats, bulk liquid containers and other freight containers) carried on train ferries.

7. "Road goods vehicles/trailers", items 2 and 7, should comprise all road goods vehicles and trailers, including those carrying demountable Lancashire flats, bulk liquid containers and other freight containers. Exclude dockside or ships trailers.

8. "Lancashire flats" (items 3, 8 and 11), "Bulk liquid containers" (items 4, 9 and 12) and "Other freight containers" (items 5, 10 and 13) should comprise all such units demounted; (*i.e.* should include those carried on dockside or ship trailers and should exclude those carried on railway wagons and road goods vehicles/trailers).

9. "Bulk liquid containers", should refer to tanks with a minimum capacity of 500 gallons.

10. A freight container is defined as:—
    "an article of equipment having an overall volume greater than 8 cubic metres (282 cubic feet), either rigid or collapsible, suitable for repeated use in the carriage of materials in bulk or package form and capable of transfer between one or more forms of transport". (British Standard 3951).

11. The very large freight containers, 20 feet (6 metres) or more external length, should be recorded again separately in brackets (*i.e.* in addition to being included in the total for all "other freight containers").

12. "Special lift-on/lift-off services" comprise specially constructed or adapted vessels with cellular design, or full width hatches and between deck beams, or equipment for underdeck/wing stowage of containers or flats (skates and channels).

13. Vessels of the following **mixed** types:—
    A. Mixed RoRo and LoLo should be included as RoRo service.
    B. Mixed LoLo and break bulk should be included as LoLo service.

14. Port authorities are invited where possible to give extra information especially on:—
    A. The commodities in unit transport traffic.
    B. The commodities carried in containers.
    C. The various sizes of containers: heights as well as lengths.

15. Where difficulty or exceptions are encountered, it would be helpful if these are noted together with any limitations to be placed upon the interpretation of the statistics.

Statistics Division
December, 1970.

APPENDICES

P.S. 48 Annex A

Number of Freight Containers by size, 19..

Port (Authority)...

Country ....

Specialised Operator ....

20ft. containers

	Inwards					Outwards				
	Height				All heights	Height				All heights
	8ft	4ft	8ft. 6in	4ft. 3in		8ft	4ft	8ft. 6in	4ft. 3in	
LOADED										
EMPTY										
TOTAL										

40ft. containers

	Inwards					Outwards				
	Height				All heights	Height				All heights
	8ft	4ft	8ft. 6in	4ft. 3in		8ft	4ft	8ft. 6in	4ft. 3in	
LOADED										
EMPTY										
TOTAL										

Other sizes (please specify) ....

	Inwards					Outwards				
	Height (please specify)				All heights	Height (please specify)				All heights
	...	...	....	....		...	...	....	....	
LOADED										
EMPTY										
TOTAL										

SPECIMEN

P.S. 48 Annex B

Number of loaded containers......ft. long by weight

Port (Authority) ....

Country ....

Specialised Operator ....

Weight group		Inwards *Gross weight (incl. container) *Net weight (excl. container)		Outwards *Gross weight (incl. container) *Net weight (excl. container)	
lb.	Tonnes		TOTAL		TOTAL
<2,200	<1	....	.....	....	.....
2,200+	1+	....	.....	....	.....
4,400+	2+	....	.....	....	.....
6,600+	3+	....	.....	....	.....
8,800+	4+	....	.....	....	.....
11,000+	5+	....	.....	....	.....
13,200+	6+	....	.....	....	.....
15,400+	7+	....	.....	....	.....
17,600+	8+	....	.....	....	.....
19,800+	9+	....	.....	....	.....
22,000+	10+	....	.....	....	.....
24,300+	11+	....	.....	....	.....
26,500+	12+	....	.....	....	.....
28,700+	13+	....	.....	....	.....
30,900+	14+	....	.....	....	.....
33,100+	15+	....	.....	....	.....
35,300+	16+	....	.....	....	.....
37,500+	17+	....	.....	....	.....
39,700+	18+	....	.....	....	.....
41,900+	19+	....	.....	....	.....
44,100+	20+	....	.....	....	.....
46,300+	21+	....	.....	....	.....
48,500+	22+	....	.....	....	.....
50,700+	23+	....	.....	....	.....
52,900+	24+				
55,100+	25+	....	.....	....	.....
57,300+	26+	....	.....	....	.....
59,500+	27+	....	.....	....	.....
61,700+	28+	....	.....	....	.....
63,900+	29+	....	.....	....	.....
66,120 & over	30 & over				
		All loaded containers		All loaded containers	

*Delete either Gross Weight or Net Weight

APPENDICES

P.S.48 Annex C

Number of restowage movements

Operator	Ship to Quay	Quay to Ship	Ship cell to Ship cell	Total

SPECIMEN

Definition of movements

Ship to Quay: lift of box from Ship to Quay to await subsequent lift back onto Ship.

Quay to Ship: lift of box from Quay to Ship after previous removal from the Ship.

Ship cell to Ship cell : lift of box from one cell and restowage directly into another cell.

Appendix 8

IN CONFIDENCE
ROLL ON-ROLL OFF GOODS VEHICLES

QUARTER 197_

NAME OF SHIPPING COMPANY _____ OPERATING BETWEEN _____ AND _____
(GB PORT)   (FOREIGN PORT)

COUNTRY OF REGISTRATION	POWERED VEHICLES		UNACCOMPANIED TRAILERS		ALL VEHICLES	
	Inward Disembarkation	Outward Embarkation	Inward Disembarkation	Outward Embarkation	Inward Disembarkation	Outward Embarkation
Austria						
Belgium						
Czechoslovakia						
Denmark						
France						
Germany, West (Federal Republic)						
Germany, East (Democratic Republic)						
Netherlands						
Spain						
Switzerland						
Great Britain						
Northern Ireland						
Others (Please specify)						
....						
....						
....						
TOTAL						

SPECIMEN

1. Powered vehicles include all vehicles of the following types, whether loaded or empty : a)Lorry: b)Lorry with trailer count as one vehicle; c)Articulated unit count as one vehicle; d)Van (if used for freight purposes).
2. Unaccompanied trailers are trailers and semi-trailers shipped without a tractive unit. Include both laded and unladen units

Directorate of Statistics   Please give name of person submitting this return _____ Tel ____ Ext ____
(LTG Division)
Department of the Environment   and if different from above name of firm _____
2 Marsham Street SW1P 3EB
01 212 8703

Appendix 10

NPC USE ONLY

National Ports Council
Commonwealth House
1-19 New Oxford Street
LONDON WC1A 1DZ

**MANAGEMENT CENSUS
AT 16th JUNE 1975**

GENERAL NOTES

1. Record only full-time permanent staff, and include all who spend more than half their working time on port or dock work. If for any special reason these numbers do not represent an average position of the numbers normally employed by your undertaking on port transport work, e.g. because you, as a normal feature of your operations, employ temporary or casual workers, please attach a separate note briefly explaining the position and indicating what the normal average numbers would be.

2. If your undertaking carries on operations at more than one location in the port covered, would you please either complete separate forms for each location or if you are unable to do this please supply the address of the location concerned so that forms can be sent to your undertaking at those locations. In this connection would you please note that in the case of major ports, e.g. London, we are anxious to have separate forms completed in respect of each major dock system. Should you require further copies of the form please contact Mr. Holt, Manpower Development Division (Tel.: 01-242 1200).

SECTION A

Name of undertaking

Address of undertaking to which the information relates

Nature of port transport operations carried out:

Please tick as appropriate

- Managing, maintaining, or operating harbour, wharf or jetty ... ☐
- Loading/unloading cargo ... ☐
- Embarking/disembarking passengers ... ☐
- Tallying, checking, sampling cargo ... ☐
- Warehousing, sorting, weighing, moving cargo ... ☐
- Lighterage of cargo ... ☐
- Towing ... ☐
- Berthing, mooring, rigging vessels ... ☐
- Other (please specify) ... ☐

Type of cargo handled

- Third party traffic ... ☐
- Own account traffic, including account of parent, subsidiary or associated company ... ☐
- Both third party and own account traffic ... ☐

Port to which the information relates ...

Signed for the undertaking ....

Telephone Number ....

Date ....

page 1

APPENDICES

C 273(1)(1977) ORIGINAL

1. Exporter (name and address)	2. Customs assigned number **CAN**		3. Tariff H'dng No. (first 4 digits)
	4. Airwaybill or Bill of Lading No.	5. Exporter's reference	
	6. House airwaybill No.	7. F/Agent's reference	

H M CUSTOMS AND EXCISE
*SPECIFICATION/PRE-SHIPMENT ENTRY FOR EXPORTS
THIS FORM MAY BE USED FOR ONE ITEM ONLY
For consignments of more than one item, attach a Form C 273 (Cont. Sheet) or use Form C 273 (4)

FOR OFFICIAL USE

7A. Forwarding Agent (name and address)	Insert codes here ▶	10.† COD	11. ICD	12. Cntnr.	13. Ro (a)	14. (b)	15. Flag	16. Port of Expt.
	†COD means Country of destination			17. Country of destination				

8. Date of Sailing/Flight etc.	9. Dock/Wharf/Station	**WARNING** There are heavy penalties for making false declarations	**NOTES** 1. Further instructions on the completion of this form will be found in the Customs and Excise Tariff and in Notice No. 276 and on its use in Notice No. 275.
18. Ship/Flight etc.	19. Port/Airport of export		
20. Port/Airport of discharge			

21. Marks and numbers	22. No. and kind of packages; description of goods	23. CAC	2. If return of the duplicate by post is required the address panel thereon should be completed.
		24. Tariff/Trade code number	3. Not to be used for goods on which UK duty relief is claimed (other than relief under the Import Duties Act 1958, section 7) or for goods for which an export licence (other than a CAP licence) is required.
		25. Quantity 2	27. Quantity 1 (net weight) / 28. Value (fob) (nearest £)
		26. Quantity 3	

SPECIMEN

30. For goods consigned to or via the EEC or to Greece or Turkey; insert X in appropriate box and complete or delete the items as appropriate	AG/ATR/CT Form type..........	attached to C 273 lodged—Customs No........	AG/ATR/CT form not required	29. Official use (Error analysis)
30A. For goods subject to CAP regulations				
IBAP Reg No.	CAP Form, *C1220/C1226 completed			

	31. Signatory's company and telephone No.
DECLARATION I, the undersigned, declare that; (a) all the particulars set forth above are correctly stated; (b) the exporter or agent is the holder of the Customs assigned number quoted; (c) the export of the goods specified does not contravene export control restrictions on account of the description, ultimate destination or any other reason.	32. Date
	33. Signature

830

C 273(1)(1977)   *Delete as necessary   F.3680 (Mar. 1977)   52-1057 2/77 GBR Ltd

GENERAL IMPORT ENTRY

C10 (1977) — HM Customs and Excise

For directions on the use and completion of this form see the Tariff and relevant Notices

1. Tariff Heading (1st 4 digits)
2. Consignor & Address (BLOCK CAPITALS)

FOR OFFICIAL USE

3. Importer's own Reference
4. Agent's own Reference
5. Importer & Address (BLOCK CAPITALS)
6. Importer's No.
7. CTC
8. Payment Code
9. Deferment Appl. No.
10. VAT acctg. Code
11. Agent & Address (BLOCK CAPITALS)
12. Agent's No.
13. Port of import
14. ICD
15. CWC
16. Type of Transport
17. Rate of Exchange
18. Date of Report
19. Flag
20. Vessel arr. Indicator
21. Container Identifier
22. Ship's name/aircraft flight No.
23. Port or place of foreign loading
24. Total amnt. due this entry — Deferred / Paid
25. Place of discharge (and examination if different)
26. B/L or AWB No.
27. Gen. Request Identifier
28. Valuation Declaration Identifier
29. No. of Tariff items this entry
30. Marks & Numbers Vehicle/Container Nos. packages etc.
31. Description of goods (ONE tariff item only)
32. Item No.
33. Tariff Trade Code
34. Tariff rate Identifier
35. Suspension rate Identifier
36. COO
37. Licence Identifier
38. Transit Identifier
39. Quota or Special Ceiling No.
40. Quantities as Tariff
41. Values this item
42. For VAT
43. Security Code
44. VAT rate Identifier
45. Document Identifier
46. Item Request

Error Codes
Add. chk. Reasons
Management Information Codes
Calculations checked | Rotation Number
Passed for: Payment £ ... Deferment £ ...
Signature ... Date
Approved for Deferment £
Deferment Officer ... Date
Payment accepted £
Cashier ... Date

Units 2 | Units 3 | Units

47. Value details, inc. freight and insurance
48. Rates of charge

	This item	B/Fwd	Total
Customs 49. Duty *Def./Paid	£	£	£
50. Levy *Def./Paid	£	£	£
Excise 51. Duty *Def./Paid	£	£	£
52. VAT *Def./Paid	£	£	£

53. VAT for postponed Acctg. £
54. Plus line
55. Other addresses (Warehouse, Exhibition, Local Officer etc.) (BLOCK CAPITALS)

56. **DECLARATION**
I, the undersigned, being the *importer/importer's authorised agent DECLARE that (i) the details shown on this entry *(including any continuation sheet(s)) are true and complete and the entry has been completed in accordance with the Commissioners' directions *(ii) that the General Valuation Statement referred to in Box 57 applies in relation to this entry.

57. Additional information

* NOTE
Delete words in italics when not applicable

Signatory's company & Telephone Number
Name and Status of signatory
Place and date of issue
Signature

WARNING — THERE ARE HEAVY PENALTIES FOR MAKING FALSE DECLARATIONS

58. Description, No. & date of Licence(s)
59. Post/Adj/Previous Prime entry No.

1.
2.

930 C10 (1977) F 2081 (Oct. 1977)

1

FOR OFFICIAL USE ONLY — C10 (1977) REVERSE OF COPY 1

Memoranda to:

Basis of value

Details of checks and/or examination:

PART 1 — ADJUSTMENT OF DEPOSIT/SECURITY

Authority £

Basis

Rates of duty

CONDITIONS OF REMOVAL: Taped, Sealed, Wired, Plombed, Crown locked, Gross weighed, Accompanied

Officer
C10X returned and attached | C10X request to amend allowed
Signature ... Date | Signature ... Date
OCN issued

Record of Interim Adjustments

Duty Code	£	£
Amount of Deposit		
Duty to Account		
Amount repaid		

Signature ... Date ... Operator ... Time
Clearance
Input: Date ... Time ... Initials ... Date
T Form Details
Status ... MCD £
Number ... No. and date
Date of Issue
Office of Departure

Record of Repayments

Post clearance

PART 2

Duty Code	£	£	£
Amount of Deposit			
Total duty to be charged			
Amount *payable/*to be repaid			

Written off on report item(s) number(s): —

All particulars agree except: —

*C147/C & E266A issued to
Initials ... Date

Deposit adjusted
*Delete as necessary
Initials ... Date

Initials

APPENDICES

SECTION B: MANAGEMENT GRADES (by salary, age and function)

1. Salary £7,000 and over p.a.

	Total	Age Group									
		20-24	25-29	30-34	35-39	40-44	45-49	50-54	55-59	60-64	65 and over
General[1]											
Financial											
Engineering											
Cargo handling											
Commercial/marketing											
Other[2]											
TOTAL											

2. Salary £4,500 - £6,999 p.a.

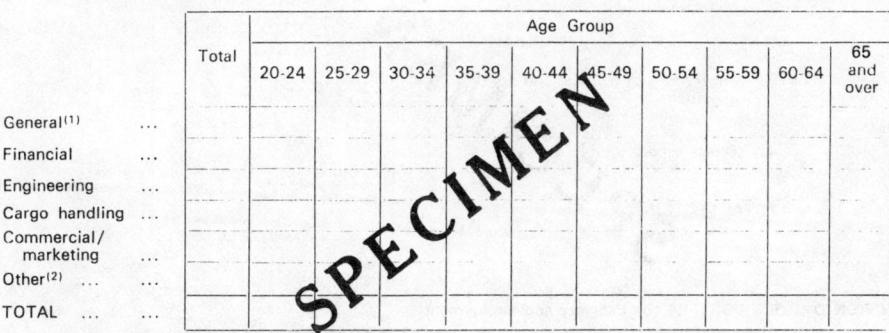

	Total	Age Group									
		20-24	25-29	30-34	35-39	40-44	45-49	50-54	55-59	60-64	65 and over
General[1]											
Financial											
Engineering											
Cargo handling											
Commercial/marketing											
Other[2]											
TOTAL											

3. Salary up to £4,499 p.a.

	Total	Age Group									
		20-24	25-29	30-34	35-39	40-44	45-49	50-54	55-59	60-64	65 and over
General[1]											
Financial											
Engineering											
Cargo handling											
Commercial/marketing											
Other[2]											
TOTAL											

| TOTAL SECTION B | | | | | | | | | | | |

Notes for Section B

[1] 'General': Managers concerned with controlling a range of activities embracing more than one specialist function and which includes the integration of these functions into the overall requirements of the organisation.

[2] 'Others': Those not covered under the specific categories set out within this section.

SECTION C: SUPERVISORY GRADES (by function)

Exclude all Registered Dock Workers from this Section and include them in Section D.

These grades cover a considerable range of duties which need to be distinguished from lower management where possible. Please include those who control a working group on a direct and frequent face to face basis. We interpret that the lowest level of supervision is that of chargehand, foreman, supervisor, office supervisors, etc., and may control several others of 'supervisory' status. Supervisors of dock workers, e.g. hatchbosses, gangers, ship foremen, should be excluded from this Section and included in Section D below.

1. Maintenance supervisors. This should include all those supervisors engaged in occupations for which a normal qualification of entry is a 5 year apprenticeship, e.g. plumbers, electricians, bricklayers and carpenters.
2. Clerical and office supervisors. Include all those in local and departmental offices as well as principal offices.
3. Supervisors of nautical and docking operations. Include all grades comparable to supervisors whose job is on the water (e.g. dredger) or assisting in the movement of vessels within the dock.
4. 'Other' supervisors. Include here all categories of supervisors not covered above.

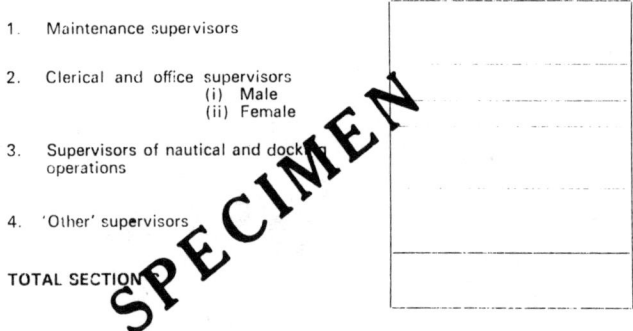

1. Maintenance supervisors
2. Clerical and office supervisors
   (i) Male
   (ii) Female
3. Supervisors of nautical and docking operations
4. 'Other' supervisors

TOTAL SECTION C

SECTION D: DOCKWORKERS (by category and deployment)

	TOTAL		Of Whom			
			Supervisory grades		Others	
	RDW's	Non RDW's	RDW's	Non RDW's	RDW's	Non RDW's
1. Bulk cargo berth						
2. Container berth						
3. Roll-on/Roll-off berth						
4. Other specialised berth						
5. Conventional berth						
6. Container groupage work						
7. Other work, e.g. receiving/delivering conventional cargo						
TOTAL SECTION D						

Notes on Section D

1. Record in "TOTAL" section all dockworkers under contract or employed by you.
2. Include as RDW's only Registered Dock Workers in Scheme ports. Employers of RDW's should show the total number of men under contract to them, including any men transferred out: men transferred in will be accounted for by the employer to whom they are under contract.
3. Please break down your "TOTAL SECTION D" figures, if possible, to indicate the normal deployment.

APPENDICES

SECTION E: ALL OTHER PERSONNEL EMPLOYED ON PORT TRANSPORT WORK
(excluding managers, supervisors and dockworkers already included above)

Skilled Tradesmen	
Office & Clerical workers	
All other e.g. unskilled, canteen workers	
TOTAL SECTION E	
TOTAL STAFF EMPLOYED IN PORT TRANSPORT WORK i.e. TOTAL OF SECTIONS B TO E	

SPECIMEN

Appendix 11

EMPLOYER'S WEEKLY RETURN N.D.L.B. FORM B50

DISPOSITION OF DOCK LABOUR FORCE

EMPLOYER { NAME.. PORT/SECTOR..................

REGN. No.................................... WEEK ENDED FRIDAY..................

TABLE A

Disposition—(Note 1)	Numbers of Men at Commencement of Each Working Shift—(Note 2)					
	Monday	Tuesday	Wednesday	Thursday	Friday	Totals
(1)	(2)	(3)	(4)	(5)	(6)	(7)
EMPLOYED (OWN REGISTER)						
1. Permanent Workers						
2. Supplementary Workers						
3. Sub-Totals						
EMPLOYED (TRANSFERRED IN)—(NOTE 3)						
4. Permanent Workers						
5. Supplementary Workers						
6. Temporarily Unattached Workers						
7. Sub-Totals						
8. TOTALS EMPLOYED (Lines 3 + 7)						
SURPLUS (TRANSFERRED OUT)						
9. Permanent Workers						
10. Supplementary Workers						
SURPLUS (OTHER)—(NOTE 4)						
11. Permanent Workers						
12. Supplementary Workers						
13. TOTALS SURPLUS (Lines 9 to 12)						
ABSENT (OWN REGISTER ONLY)						
14. Annual Holiday						
15. Public Holiday or in lieu						
16. Sick/Injured						
17. Other Authorised Absences (incl. Suspensions)						
18. *In Dispute—(Note 3)						
19. Other Unauthorised Absences						
20. TOTALS ABSENT (Lines 14 to 19)						
21. TOTAL STRENGTH–GROSS (Lines 8+13+20)						
22. NET (Line 21 — Line 7)						
NON-REGISTERED LABOUR EMPLOYED						
23. Listed Weekly Workers						
24. Allocated By Dock Labour Board						
25. LABOUR SHORTAGES						
26. *In Dispute—Men Trans. In Only (Note 3)						

* IN DISPUTE—Further details of disputes to be given overleaf in Table C.

TABLE B **CHANGES IN NET REGISTER (AS AT TUESDAY A.M.)—(NOTE 5)**

REGISTER	Net Register Last Week	Total Additions	REMOVALS									Net Register This Week
			Deaths		Retired	Left Industry	N.V.S.S. *		Summary Dismissal CL.14A(2)	Others	Totals	
			I.A.	Other			'A'	'B'				
(1)	(2)	(3)	(4)	(5)	(6)	(7)	(8)	(9)	(10)	(11)	(12)	(13)
1. Perm. Workers												
2. Supp. Workers												
3. TOTALS												†

† To correspond to figure on Line 22 (Tuesday) of Table A.
* National Voluntary Severance Scheme.

P.T.O.

N.D.L.B. FORM B50—(REVERSE)

DISPUTES—NEW AND CONTINUING (NOTE 6)

TABLE C.

Dispute Commenced		Work Resumed		Maximum No. of Men Involved This Week		Man/Days Lost This Week		Cause
Time	Date	Time	Date	Directly	In-directly	Directly	In-directly	
(1)	(2)	(3)	(4)	(5)	(6)	(7)	(8)	(9)

Any further disputes should be recorded on a supplementary sheet of paper with headings corresponding to those of Table C.

Signature ....

Date of Submission ....

SPECIMEN

NOTE 1 (Table A). Lines 1—22 relate to registered dock workers only. "Employed" figures to include men on non-dock work.

Lines 23 and 24 relate to other labour approved and/or allocated by the Dock Labour Board.

NOTE 2 (Table A). Cols. 2—7 are to record the disposition of men during normal days or shifts, the different workers on separate shifts being combined. Absentees must include permanent and supplementary workers from the date of their allocation to the employer until final termination, even if they have not yet started duty.

NOTE 3 (Table A). If men transferred in are in dispute at the commencement of a shift, they are to be shown separately on Line 26 of Table A (and also included in Table C). In all other circumstances, men transferred in are to be shown as employed on Lines 4, 5 or 6 of Table A.

NOTE 4 (Table A). Lines 11/12 relate to surplus labour which is to be paid in respect of under-employment and should not be duplicated by any authorised absence to be shown on Line 17.

NOTE 5 (Table B). I.A.—Deaths due to Industrial Accident.

Retired—to include all men aged 65 years and over who are compulsorily retired, or who voluntarily resign, whether with a pension or not.

Left Industry—to include all men under 65 years of age who voluntarily resign from the industry for reasons other than ill-health.

NOTE 6 (Table C). In computing man/days lost, hours of normal shifts (not overtime or week-end hours) during the current week only are to be assessed from the numbers of men in dispute and the period of dispute, to the nearest quarter of an hour, for each commonly involved group of workers, the resultant aggregate of hours being divided by 8 to give the required figure (to the nearest man/day).

Figures to be shown in Cols. 5 and 7 must relate to men and time lost by men directly participating in the stoppage of work.

Figures to be shown in Cols. 6 and 8 must relate to men and time lost by men unable to work but not directly participating in the stoppage.

For purposes of Cols. 5 to 8, account will only be taken of registered dock workers, including men transferred in, and of non-registered workers whose use had been approved by the Dock Labour Board.

NOTE 7 One copy of this return is to be submitted to the Local Dock Labour Board not later than three working days after the termination of the week to which the return relates.

S&O LTD. 12.70 90748

Appendix 12

N.D.L.B. **WEEKLY LABOUR RETURN** FORM B.51

PORT/AREA _____ WEEK _____

SPECIMEN

I. SUMMARY OF EMPLOYERS RETURNS (B50)

	DISPOSITION	AGGREGATE MAN/DAYS
	(1)	(2)
	EMPLOYED (OWN REGISTER)	
1.	Permanent Workers	
2.	Supplementary Workers	
3.	SUB-TOTAL	
	EMPLOYED (TRANSFERRED IN)	
4.	Permanent Workers	
5.	Supplementary Workers	
6.	Temporarily Unattached Workers	
7.	SUB-TOTAL	
8.	TOTAL EMPLOYED (LINES 3 + 7)	
	SURPLUS (TRANSFERRED OUT)	
9.	Permanent Workers	
10.	Supplementary Workers	
	SURPLUS (OTHER)	
11.	Permanent Workers	
12.	Supplementary Workers	
13.	TOTAL SURPLUS (Lines 9 to 12)	
	ABSENT (OWN REGISTER ONLY)	
14.	Annual Holiday	
15.	Public Holiday or in lieu	
16.	Sick/Injured	
17.	Other Authorised Absences (incl. Susp.)	
18.	In Dispute	
19.	Other Unauthorised Absences	
20.	TOTAL ABSENT (Lines 14 to 19)	
21.	TOTAL STRENGTH—GROSS (Lines 8 + 13 + 20)	
22.	NET (Line 21 − Line 7)	
	NON-REGISTERED LABOUR	
23.	Listed Weekly Workers	
24.	Allocated by Dock Labour Board	
25.	LABOUR SHORTAGES	
26.	IN DISPUTE—MEN TRANS. IN ONLY	

II. REGISTER OF TEMP. UNATTACHED WORKERS AS AT TUESDAY A.M.

	REGISTER	TOTAL	TOTAL LAST WEEK	NET CHANGE
	(1)	(2)	(3)	(4)
1.	Live – (Table VI) (Note 1)			
2.	Suspense – (Table VII) (Note 1)			
	DORMANT			
3.	Sick			
4.	Injured (Industrial only)			
	RELEASE			
5.	Temporary Release Schemes			
6.	Other Temporary Releases			
7.	Prolonged Sickness or Injury			
8.	H.M. Forces			
9.	TOTALS			

III. SUMMARY OF WORKERS' REGISTER AS AT TUESDAY A.M.

	REGISTER (NOTE 2)	TOTAL	TOTAL LAST WEEK	NET CHANGE
	(1)	(2)	(3)	(4)
1.	Permanent Workers			
2.	Supplementary Workers			
3.	Temporarily Unattached Workers			
4.	TOTALS			

IV. SUPPLEMENTARY INFORMATION AS AT TUESDAY A.M.

1.	Licensed Employers (Note 3) (Gross)		
2.	Registered Employers (Gross)		
3.	Listed Weekly Workers		
4.	Reserved Rights List		
5.			
6.			

V. CHANGES IN WORKERS' REGISTER—(NOTE 4)

REGISTERS	ADMITTED							REMOVED										Net Change	Rem'd to Res. Rts. List
	New Entrants		Readmitted		From Res. Rights List	From Other Regs.	TOTAL	Deceased		Disc. Action	Other Reasons						TOTAL		
	Sons	Others	After appeal	Other-wise				Ind. Acc	Other Causes		Retired	Left Ind.	N.V.S.S.* 'A'	N.V.S.S.* 'B'	Redundant	Ineffectives	To Other Regs.			
	(1)	(2)	(3)	(4)	(5)	(6)	(7)	(8)	(9)	(10)	(11)	(12)	(13)	(14)	(15)	(16)	(17)	(18)	(19)	(20)	(21)
1. Perms.																				
2. Supp.																				
3. T.U.W.																				
4. TOTALS																				

* National Voluntary Severance Scheme

P.T.O.

N.D.L.B.   FORM B.51 (REVERSE)

DISPOSITION OF TEMPORARILY UNATTACHED WORKERS

VI LIVE LOCAL REGISTER

	DISPOSITION	MON.	TUES.	WED.	THURS.	FRI.	TOTALS
	(1)	(2)	(3)	(4)	(5)	(6)	(7)
1.	EMPLOYED LOCALLY						
2.	TRANSFERRED TO OTHER PORTS/AREAS						
3.	AVAILABLE SURPLUS						
4.	EXCUSED						
5.	REFUSED EMPLOYMENT AS T.U.W's.						
6.	UNACCOUNTED						
7.	TOTALS						
8.	NON-REGD. (IN RESERVE)						

VII SUSPENSE REGISTER

	DISPOSITION	MON.	TUES.	WED.	THURS.	FRI.	TOTALS
	(1)	(2)	(3)	(4)	(5)	(6)	(7)
1.	Annual Holiday						
2.	Public Holiday or in lieu						
3.	Sick						
4.	Injured						
5.	Suspended						
6.	Dispute						
7.	Other Suspense						
8.	TOTALS						

VIII DISPUTES — NEW AND CONTINUING (Note 5)

DISPUTE COMMENCED		WORK RESUMED		MAXIMUM NO. OF MEN INVOLVED THIS WEEK		MAN/DAYS LOST THIS WEEK		CAUSE
Time	Date	Time	Date	DIRECTLY	INDIRECTLY	DIRECTLY	INDIRECTLY	
(1)	(2)	(3)	(4)	(5)	(6)	(7)	(8)	(9)

Date ....   Manager ....

NOTE 1 (Table II).   Totals of Col. (3) in Tables VI and VII respectively.

NOTE 2 (Table III).   Reconcile registers of permanent and supplementary workers with totals of net registers from Table B of Employers' Returns (B50).
Line 3 to correspond to Line 9 of Table II.

NOTE 3 (Table IV).   The number of Licensed Employers to include Licensing Authorities who have proposed to employ dock workers. The difference, if any, between the number of licensed employers and the number of registered employers should be the number of licensed employers who have not taken up registration or whose registration has been suspended by the National Board.

NOTE 4 (Table V).   Treat men summarily dismissed by employers under Clause 14A(2) as transfers between registers.

NOTE 5 (Table VIII).   Collate Table VIII from Tables C on Employers' Returns (B50), combining figures from different employers relating to any dispute with the same prime cause.

Appendix 13

H.M. Customs and Excise

C. 568

Account of the ARRIVAL of Vessels from Foreign and Coastwise since the last Return

*Port of .... Station .... Month of .... 197....

Date and time of arrival at dock or station	Name of vessel	Whence	Foreign or coastwise voyage (Insert "F" or "C")	† Arrival from London (insert "L")	† Nationality code	‡ Cargo code	** Net tonnage (to nearest ton)	** Number of arrivals	At which dock or station lying	Observations	For Long Room use — Date when and Port where inward Light Dues paid (If exempt insert "E", if not liable insert "N.L.")
(1)	(2)	(3)	(4)	(5)	(6)	(7)	(8)	(9)	(10)	(11)	(12)

SPECIMEN

Notes:
  * Insert additionally "N.I." for ports in Northern Ireland.
  ** For daily ferry traffic insert the net tonnage of the vessel multiplied by the number of daily voyages (col. 9.).
  † "1" for British
    "2" for other (including Irish Republican)

Code as follows:
  ‡ "1" for oil
    "2" for coal
    "3" for other cargo
    "B" in ballast or carrying passengers only.

Officer.................. Date..................

Sec. F. 2181 (June 1976)

Dd 449660 6/76 50M H.P.

APPENDICES

Account of the DEPARTURE of Vessels Foreign and Coastwise since the last Return

* Port of .... Station .... Month of .... 197...

Date and time of departure	Name of vessel	Where bound	Foreign or coastwise voyage (insert "F" or "C")	Departure for London (insert "L")	†Nationality code	‡Cargo code	**Net tonnage (to nearest ton)	**Number of departures	Date of arrival	Observations	For Long Room use — Date when and Port where outward Light Dues paid (if exempt insert "E"; if not liable insert "N.L.")
(1)	(2)	(3)	(4)	(5)	(6)	(7)	(8)	(9)	(10)	(11)	(12)

SPECIMEN

Notes: * Insert additionally "N.I." for ports in Northern Ireland:
** For daily ferry traffic insert in col. 8 multiple of net tonnage of vessel and number of daily voyages in col. 9
† "1" for British
  "2" for other (including Irish Republican)
‡ "1" for oil
  "2" for coal
  "3" for other cargo
  "B" in ballast or carrying passengers only

Officer .... Date ....

F 2182 (Apr. 1977)   Dd 566630 3/77 50M H.P.

C. 568A

Appendix 14

Notes on making the FACILITIES SURVEY

Column 4: 'Depth of water—limiting'. It is intended here that in the case of an impounded dock the depth quoted should be at normal impounded level, whereas for tidal berths it should be at MLWS. If however the berth depth is further limited by, for example, a shallower harbour entrance this further limiting depth should be quoted, and described in the 'Remarks' column.

Column 8: 'Leased to' should include names of companies to whom the berth is leased or for which there is some other long term commitment entitling them to *single use* of the berth.

Columns 10 and 11: 'Storage Accommodation and Area of Storage Accommodation' should specify separately both covered and open storage. The measurement units chosen should be those most appropriate to the type of storage and should be quoted,

> e.g. warehouses in thousand square metres useful floor space
> parking areas and open storage in hectares
> silos in tonnes capacity
> tanks in cubic metres or tonnes.

Open storage should not include roadways, railways and other parts of the area not normally used for holding cargoes. Storage remote from berths should be shown against each berth but the total area should be *given once and once only* allocated to the berth which utilizes the area most or in the case of equal use to the nearest berth. If insufficient space is available please attach separate sheets.

Column 'Remarks'. This should mainly be used to add points of additional importance that you feel are worth recording. In addition you are requested to expand on the characteristics of the RO/RO berths, viz.:

(1) Maximum width?
(2) Does it have a fixed ramp or an adjustable link span?
(3) Is there single or double access?

Indication should be given to those berths expected to be phased out by (a) 1980, (b) 1985.

ATTACHMENT A
PORT AUTHORITY:
Sheet No.

PARTICULARS OF PORT FACILITIES

NAME & TYPE OF WHARF/QUAY (1)	BERTH		DEPTH OF WATER (2)		OWNED BY	LEASED TO	PRINCIPAL TRAFFIC	STORAGE ACCOM.	AREA OF STORAGE ACCOM.	CRANES				REMARKS
	No.	LENGTH	LIMITING	ACTUAL	POTENTIAL						No.	TYPE (3)	CAPACITY	RADIUS OR OUTREACH	

(1) Container, Roll-on, etc.
(2) Limiting depth is in the case of impounded docks the depth at normal impounded level. In the case of tidal berths it is the depth at M.L.W.S.
(3) Illegible state single or twin lift.

SUBJECT INDEX

Accident Statistics Classifications, 7.5.0; 7.5.1
Accidents, 7.5
Accidents to registered dock workers, 7.5.2
Accompanied and unaccompanied road goods vehicles, 2.7.0; 2.9
Accompanied cars and buses, 2.7.7; 5.1.0
Age distribution of registered dock workers, 7.3.5
Age of port employees, 7.1.4; 7.1.5; 7.1.6
America, North, 2.8.0
AMLBO Commodity Classification, 8.0.16
AMLBO data availability, 8.0.16
AMLBO fleet data, 8.0.15
AMLBO tonnage data, 8.0.16
Amsterdam, transhipment via, 3.0.3
Antwerp, transhipment via, 1.0.4; 3.0.3
Areas of Customs ports, 2.1.3
Areas of port authorities, 2.1.3
Assets of the industry, 12.0.2
Availability of registered dock workers, 7.3.1

Barge aboard catamaran, 1.0.7; 2.1.13; 8.0.9
Bauxite, 3.0.3
Berths and docks, dimensions of entrances to, 10.0.2
Berths, container, 10.0.1; 10.0.2; 10.0.3
Berths, dry cargo, 10.0.0; 10.0.1
Berths, industry owned, 10.0.4; 10.0.5; 10.0.7
Berths, lift-on, lift-off, 10.0.1; 10.0.2, 10.0.3
Berths, specialized cargo, 10.0.2; 10.0.3; 10.0.4
Berths, unit-load, 10.0.1; 10.0.2; 10.0.3
Bill of entry service, 6.1.0; 6.2.3
Break-bulk facilities, 10.0.2; 10.0.3; 10.0.7; 12.0.0
Break-bulk products, specialized, 10.0.6; 10.0.7; 12.0.0; 12.0.1
British military supplies, 2.1.4
British ports association, 2.2.5; 6.1.2
British Railways Board, 11.0.1
British Transport Commission, 8.0.0
British Transport Docks Board, 11.0.1
British Waterways Board, 1.0.2; 1.0.7; 8; 11.0.1; 12.0.6
British Waterways Board, employment in, 8.0.5
British Waterways Board waterways, freight on, 8.0.3; 8.0.4; 8.0.6
Bulk commodities, 1.0.4; 12.0.0; 12.0.1
Bulk liquid containers, 2.7.2; 2.7.6
Bulk-load facilities, 10.0.4; 10.0.5; 10.0.6; 10.0.7; 12.0.1
Bulk products, transhipment of, 3.0.3
Buses, accompanied cars and, 2.7.7; 5.1.0

Cable-laying vessels, 9.0.9; 9.0.10
Caledonian and Crinan canals, 8.0.0
Capital investment, 1.0.4; 6.2.4; 11.0.0; 12.0.2
Capital stock, gross, 11.0.2
Car-carrier ships, 12.0.1
Cardiff, 2.1.3
Cars and buses, accompanied, 2.7.7; 5.1.0
Cars, tourist motor, 2.1.8; 5.1.0
Census of employment, 7.4.0
Certificates of Incapacity, 7.5.3
Channel Isles, Isle of Man and, 2.1.9; 2.2.0; 2.4.1
Classes of occupation, 7.1.1; 7.1.4
Clearances, definition of entrances and, 9.0.3
Coal for ships' use, petroleum and, 2.1.8
Coastal trade movements, 9.0.1; 9.0.4
Coastwise inwards and outwards movements balancing, 2.4.1
Coastwise inwards and outwards movement- 2.4.1; 2.4.2; 2.4.3
Coastwise traffic, 1.0.4; 2.1.9; 2.1.10; 2.1.11; 2.4; 8.0.7; 12.0.0
Coastwise traffic by commodity, 2.4
Coastwise traffic, dry cargo, 2.4.4
Coastwise traffic, petroleum, 2.4.4
Coastwise, tugs moving, 9.0.9
Coastwise unit-load traffic, 2.4.0
Coding of foreign ports, 3.0.2; 12.0.4
Commercial waterways, 8.0.1
Commodity classification, AMLBO, 8.0.16
Commodity classification, Customs, 6.1.3; 6.2.5
Commodity, coastwise traffic by, 2.4
Commodity Code, National Ports Council, 2.3.1; 2.3.5; 2.4.0; 2.4.6; 2.8.0; 6.2.5
Commodity content of containers, 2.8; 6.2.3; 6.2.4
Commodity data, Northern Ireland cross-Channel, 2.4.7
Commodity data, Northern Ireland foreign, 2.3.6
Commodity data, unit-load, 2.3.3; 2.3.4; 2.3.5; 2.4.0; 2.8; 6.2
Commodity, foreign traffic by, 2.3; 6.1
Commodity misclassification, 2.4.2
Commodity, special traffic by, 2.5.1
Container and roll-on traffic, 2.7; 6.2
Container berths, 10.0.1; 10.0.2; 10.0.3
Container contents, weight of, 2.8.2
Container, Customs definition of, 6.2.0; 12.0.3
Container, National Ports Council definition of, 2.7.1; 12.0.3
Containers, commodity content of, 2.8; 6.2.3; 6.2.4
Containers in transhipment and transit, 3.0.0; 3.0.1

Containers, size of, 2.7.7; 2.8.1; 2.8.2; 6.2.0
Continental Shelf traffic, 1.0.4
Control of Pollution Act, 1974, 8.0.8
Controlled water, 8.0.8
Conversion factors for units of measurement, 6.1.1; 6.1.3
Coverage of National Ports Council statistics, 2.2.1; 2.2.2; 2.6
Cranes, 10.0.2; 10.0.3
Crinan Canals, Caledonian and, 8.0.0
Crude oil, 1.0.4; 3.0.3; 10.0.4; 10.0.5; 12.0.0
Cruises, 5.0.1
Cruising waterways, 8.0.1
Customs and Excise, HM, 1.0.3; 1.0.6; 2.1.2; 2.1.3; 2.1.7; 2.1.16; 2.3.0; 2.3.1; 2.3.3; 2.3.6; 2.4.0; 2.7.3; 3.0.1; 3.0.2; 6; 9.0.8; 9.1.0; 9.1.1; 12.0.3; 12.0.5
Customs commodity classification, 6.2.5
Customs definition of container, 6.2.0; 12.0.3
Customs Port of London, 2.1.3; 3.0.1
Customs ports, areas of, 2.1.3

Deep sea, 2.7.4
Definition of dock worker, 7.1.0; 7.3.1
Definition of entrances and clearances, 9.0.3
Definition of inland waterway, 8.0.8
Definitions in unit-load statistics, 2.7.1; 2.7.2; 6.2.0
Department of Commerce, Northern Ireland, 2.1.0; 2.2.3; 2.2.6; 2.4.5; 2.4.6; 2.5.0
Department of Employment, 7.4
Department of Energy, 2.4.4
Department of Health and Social Security, 7.5.3; 7.5.5
Department of Manpower Services Northern Ireland, 7.4
Department of Transport, 1.0.1; 2.4.4; 2.7.0; 2.9.0; 8.0.3; 8.0.5; 8.0.7; 9.0.8; 11.0.1
Departments of Industry, Trade, Prices and Consumer Protection, 1.0.6; 2.4.4; 5.0.0; 5.0.1; 6.1.1; 9.0.8; 9.1.0; 9.1.1
Dimensions of entrances to berths and docks, 10.0.2
Dock and Harbours Act, 1966, 7.1.3
Dock Labour Scheme, 2.6.0; 7.3
Dock worker, definition of, 7.1.0; 7.3.1
Dock Workers (Regulation of Employment) Act, 1946, 7.1.0; 7.3.0; 7.3.1
Dock Workers, NDLB Annual Survey of, 7.3.5
Dock workers, registered, 7.1.1; 7.1.3; 7.3
Docks and Harbour Authorities Association, 6.1.2
Docks, dimensions of entrances to berths and, 10.0.2
Domestic traffic, 2.1.10; 2.1.11
Dredged sand and gravel, 2.1.8
Dry cargo berths, 10.0.0; 10.0.1
Dry cargo coastwise traffic, 2.4.4
Dumb barges, 8.0.13
Dumping at sea, material for, 2.1.8; 2.5.1

Earnings of Registered dock workers, 7.3.1
Effects of unit-load methods, 1.0.6; 12.0.0
Employed, numbers, 1.0.5; 7.1; 7.2; 7.3; 7.4

Employment at non-Scheme ports, 7.2
Employment at Scheme ports, 7.3
Employment, census of, 7.4.0
Employment in British Waterways Board, 8.0.5
Employment in Inland Water Transport, 7.4.0
Employment of dock workers, 1.0.0; 7
Entrances and clearances, definition of, 9.0.3
Entrances to berths and docks, dimensions of, 10.0.2
Estuaries, rivers and, 1.0.7; 2.1.9; 8.0.0; 8.0.10; 12.0.6
European Economic Community, 1.0.5; 2.1.10; 2.4.3; 6.1.3; 6.2.5
Expenditure, 11.0.0; 11.0.1

Facilities at ports, 10
Facilities, bulk load, 10.0.4; 10.0.5; 10.0.6; 10.0.7; 12.0.1
Facilities, National Ports Council surveys of, 10.0.1; 10.0.2
Factories Act, 1961, 7.5.0; 7.5.1; 7.5.6
Factory Inspectorate, 7.5.0; 7.5.1; 7.5.6
Felixstowe, 1.0.0; 2.7.4
Ferry boats, harbour, 9.1.0
Fertilizers, 1.0.4
Fish landings, 2.1.8; 4
Fishery harbours, 1.0.2; 2.2.0; 4
Fishery traffic, 4
Fishing vessels, 9.0.9; 9.0.12
Flag statistics, 6.1.1
Foreign trade, vessels employed in, 9.0.0; 9.0.1; 9.0.4
Foreign traffic, 2.1.7; 8.0.7; 12.0.0
Foreign traffic by commodity, 2.3; 6.1
Forest products, 10.0.5; 10.0.6
Freight on British Waterways Board waterways, 8.0.3; 8.0.4; 8.0.6

Gas pipelines, oil and, 2.1.7
General cargo, 10.0.6; 12.0.0
Goods Schedule Index, 2.4.6
Government-owned ports, 1.0.0
Grain, 1.0.4; 3.0.3; 12.0.0
Gravel, dredged sand and, 2.1.8
Great Britain traffic, Northern Ireland and, 2.4.5; 2.4.6; 2.4.7
Gross capital stock, 11.0.2
Gross domestic fixed capital formation, 11.0.2

Harbour ferry boats, 9.1.0
Harbours Act Northern Ireland, 1970, 2.2.3
Harbours Act, 1964, 1.0.1; 1.0.6; 2.1.0; 2.1.13; 2.2.0; 2.2.4; 7.1.0
Harwich, 2.7.4
Health and Safety at Work Act, 1974, 7.5.0
Health and Safety Commission, 7.5.0; 7.5.1
HM Customs and Excise, 1.0.3; 1.0.6; 2.1.2; 2.1.3; 2.1.7; 2.1.16; 2.3.0; 2.3.1; 2.3.3; 2.3.6; 2.4.0; 2.7.3; 3.0.1; 3.0.2; 6; 9.0.8; 9.1.0; 9.1.1; 12.0.3; 12.0.5
Hovercraft, 5.0.0; 5.1.0; 9.0.9; 9.0.10
Hydrofoils, 9.0.9; 9.0.10

SUBJECT INDEX

Independent Waterway Authorities, 8.0.7
Industry-owned berths, 10.0.4; 10.0.5; 10.0.7
Inland flow statistics, 2.1.11; 12.0.4; 12.0.5
Inland shipping group, 8.0.2
Inland Water Carriers, National Association of, 8.0.11
Inland Water Transport, employment in, 7.4.0
Inland waterway, definition of, 8.0.8
Inland waterways, 1.0.2; 1.0.7; 8
Inland Waterways Association, 8.0.2
Ipswich, 2.7.4
Iron ore, 1.0.4; 3.0.3; 10.0.4; 10.0.5; 12.0.0; 12.0.1
Isle of Man and Channel Isles, 2.1.9; 2.2.0; 2.4.1

Labour Scheme, Dock, 2.6.0; 7.3
Lancashire flats, 2.7.2; 2.7.6
Licences to employ registered dock workers, 7.1.3
Lift-on/lift-off berths, 10.0.1; 10.0.2; 10.0.3
Lighter aboard ship, 1.0.7; 2.1.13; 8.0.9; 8.0.12; 8.0.13; 8.0.16
List of British Waterways Board waterways, 8.0.0
List of ports, 2.2.4
List of Scheme ports, 7.3.0
Lloyds Register of Shipping, 9.0.12
Local authority ports, 1.0.0
Location of ports, 12.0.5
London Association of Master Lightermen and Barge Owners, 8.0.12; 8.0.15
London Authority, Port of, 2.1.3; 2.3.2; 7.1.3; 8.0.13; 8.0.14
London, Customs port of, 2.1.3; 3.0.1
Long tons, 2.1.2

Management Sciences Ltd., 3.0.3
Manchester Ship Canal Company, 1.0.0; 8.0.0
Manganese ore, 3.0.3
Manpower census, National Ports Council, 7.1.1; 7.1.3; 7.1.6; 7.1.7
Manpower data, National Ports Council, 7.1
Marine works in Scotland, 1.0.2; 2.2.0; 4
Material for dumping at sea, 2.1.8; 2.5.1
Measure of output, 2.1.5
Medway Ports Authority, 2.1.3; 8.0.13
Merchant Shipping Act, 1906, 5.0.0
Merchant Shipping Act, 1925, 8.0.14
Merchant Shipping Rules, 1965, 8.0.8
Mersey Docks and Harbour Company, 1.0.0; 2.3.4
Meteorological vessels, 9.0.9; 9.0.10
Military supplies, British, 2.1.4
Ministry of Agriculture, Fisheries and Food, 1.0.2; 2.2.0; 4.0.1
Motor cars, tourist, 2.1.8; 5.1.0
Motor vehicles, 2.1.8; 12.0.1
Movements at ports, 9.0.1

National Association of Inland Water Carriers, 8.0.11
National Association of Port Employers, 7.5.2
National Dock Labour Board, 1.0.1; 7.0.0; 7.2.0; 7.3
National Federation of Master Lightermen and Barge Owners, 8.0.12

National Joint Council of the Port Transport Industry, 1.0.1
National Ports Council Commodity Code, 2.3.1; 2.3.5; 2.4.0; 2.4.6; 2.8.0; 6.2.5
National Ports Council definition of container, 2.7.1; 12.0.3
National Ports Council Establishment, 1.0.1; 1.0.3; 2.1.0; 2.2.0; 6.1.1
National Ports Council manpower censuses, 7.1.1; 7.1.3; 7.1.6; 7.1.7
National Ports Council manpower data, 7.1
National Ports Council statistics, coverage of, 2.2.1; 2.2.2; 2.6
National Ports Council, statutory powers of, 1.0.6; 2.2.1; 2.2.4; 2.3.0; 2.4.0; 2.5.0; 7.1.0
National Ports Council surveys of facilities, 10.0.1; 10.0.2
National traffic, 2.1.10
Nationalization of waterways, 8.0.0
Nationalized ports, 1.0.0
Navigation statistics, 9.0.2
NDLB Annual Survey of Dock Workers, 7.3.5
Near sea, 2.7.4
Nimexe, 6.2.5
Non-foreign traffic, 2.1.10
Non-Scheme ports, employment at, 7.2
Non-Scheme ports, Scheme and, 2.2.2; 2.6; 7.2; 7.3
Non-sea-going vessels, 2.1.12; 8.0.7; 8.0.8; 8.0.14
Non-statutory companies, 1.0.0
North America, 2.8.0
Northern Ireland and Great Britain traffic, 2.4.5; 2.4.6; 2.4.7
Northern Ireland cross-Channel commodity data, 2.4.7
Northern Ireland Department of Commerce, 2.1.0; 2.2.3; 2.2.6; 2.4.5; 2.4.6; 2.5.0
Northern Ireland, Department of Manpower Services, 7.4
Northern Ireland foreign commodity data, 2.3.6
Northern Ireland traffic statistics, 2.2.3; 2.2.6; 2.3.6
Northern Ireland, transhipment from, 2.4.5
Northern Ireland unit-load statistics, 2.7.8
Northern Ireland, 1970, Harbours Act, 2.2.3
NSTR, 6.1.3; 6.2.5
Numbers employed, 1.0.5; 7.1; 7.2; 7.3; 7.4

Offshore installation traffic, 2.1.8; 2.5.1
Offshore oil, 1.0.4; 2.1.7
Oil and gas pipelines, 2.1.7
Oil, crude, 1.0.4; 3.0.3; 10.0.4; 10.0.5; 12.0.0
Oil jetty, 1.0.1
Oil, offshore, 1.0.4; 2.1.7
Oil-rigs, vessels servicing, 9.0.9; 9.0.10
Output, measure of, 2.1.5
Output, price indices of, 12.0.2
Ownership of ports, 1.0.0

Packaging, weight of, 2.1.2
Parkeston Quay, 2.7.4
Passenger traffic, 5
Petroleum and coal for ships' use, 2.1.8
Petroleum coastwise traffic, 2.4.4

Petroleum Industry Advisory Committee, 2.4.4
Phosphates, 3.0.3
Pilotage, 9.1
Pipelines, oil and gas, 2.1.7
Pleasure yachts, 9.0.9; 9.0.12
Port of London Authority, 2.1.3; 2.3.2; 7.1.3; 8.0.13; 8.0.14
Potassium, 3.0.3
Price indices of output, 12.0.2
Production unit, 2.1.5
Public trusts, 1.0.0

Quarterly ports data, 2.2.5; 6.2.3; 12.0.3

Railway wagons, 2.7.2; 2.7.6; 6.2.0; 6.2.1
Register of Shipping, Lloyds, 9.0.12
Registered dock workers, 7.1.1; 7.1.3; 7.3
Registered dock workers, accidents to, 7.5.2
Registered dock workers, age distribution of, 7.3.5
Registered dock workers, availability of, 7.3.1
Registered dock workers, earnings of, 7.3.1
Registered dock workers, licences to employ, 7.1.3
Restow movements, 2.1.15; 2.10
Revenue, 11.0.0; 12.0.2
River Thames, 7.1.3; 8.0.0; 8.0.13
Rivers and estuaries, 1.0.7; 2.1.9; 8.0.0; 8.0.10; 12.0.6
Road goods vehicles, 2.7.2; 2.7.6; 6.2.0; 6.2.1
Road goods vehicles, accompanied and unaccompanied, 2.7.0; 2.9
Rochdale Committee Report 1962, 1.0.6; 2.1.0; 2.1.1; 6.1.1; 7.5.0; 8.0.12; 10.0.0
Roll-on/roll-off vehicles, 2.1.8; 6.2.1
Roll-on traffic, container and, 2.7; 6.2
Rotterdam, transhipment via, 1.0.4; 3.0.3
Royal Navy ships, 9.1.0

Sand and gravel, dredged, 2.1.8
Scheme and non-Scheme ports, 2.2.2; 2.6; 7.2; 7.3
Scheme ports, employment at, 7.3
Scheme ports, list of, 7.3.0
Scotland, marine works in, 1.0.2; 2.2.0; 4
Sea Fishery Industry Act, 1951, 2.2.0
Sea-going vessels, 2.1.9; 2.1.11; 2.1.12; 2.1.13; 2.4.1; 8.0.8; 8.0.9
Seabee system, 8.0.9; 8.0.12; 8.0.13; 8.0.16
Self-propelled tankers, 8.0.13
Sheerness, 2.1.3
Shetland Islands, 2.1.9
Shipping, Lloyds Register of, 9.0.12
Shipping movements, 9
Ships' manifests, 2.3.4; 2.4.7; 2.8.0; 6.2.4
Short sea, 2.7.4
SITC(R), 2.3.1; 2.4.6; 3.0.3; 6.1.0; 6.1.2
Size of containers, 2.7.7; 2.8.1; 2.8.2; 6.2.0
Soya beans, 3.0.3
Special traffic, 2.1.8; 2.1.10; 2.1.11; 2.5; 8.0.7; 12.0.0
Special traffic by commodity, 2.5.1
Specialized break-bulk products, 10.0.6; 10.0.7; 12.0.0; 12.0.1
Specialized cargo berths, 10.0.2; 10.0.3; 10.0.4

Standardization of nomenclature for statistics, 2.1.10
Statutory companies, 1.0.0
Statutory Powers of National Ports Council, 1.0.6; 2.2.1; 2.2.4; 2.3.0; 2.4.0; 2.5.0; 7.1.0
Stoppages of work, 7.3.1; 7.4.2
Sulphur, 3.0.3
Survey of Dock Workers, NDLB Annual, 7.3.5
Surveys of facilities, National Ports Council, 10.0.1; 10.0.2

Thames, River, 7.1.3; 8.0.0; 8.0.13
Timber, 10.0.5; 10.0.6
Tonnes, 2.1.2
Tourist motor cars, 2.1.8; 5.1.0
Trailers and semi-trailers, 2.7.0; 2.9
Transhipment and transit, containers in, 3.0.0; 3.0.1
Transhipment bills, 3.0.1
Transhipment data for UK, United States, 3.0.4; 3.0.5
Transhipment from Northern Ireland, 2.4.5
Transhipment of bulk products, 3.0.3
Transhipment traffic, 1.0.4; 2.1.4; 2.1.16; 3; 12.0.4; 12.0.5
Transhipment via Amsterdam, 3.0.3
Transhipment via Antwerp, 1.0.4; 3.0.3
Transhipment via Rotterdam, 1.0.4; 3.0.3
Transire, 2.4.3
Transit traffic, 2.1.4; 2.1.16; 3
Transport Act, 1947, 8.0.0
Transport Act, 1962, 8.0.0
Transport Act, 1968, 8.0.1
Tugs moving coastwise, 9.0.9

Unemployed port workers, 7.4.1
Unit-load berths, 10.0.1; 10.0.2; 10.0.3
Unit-load commodity data, 2.3.3; 2.3.4; 2.3.5; 2.4.0; 2.8; 6.2
Unit-load device, weight of, 2.1.2
Unit-load methods, effects of, 1.0.6; 12.0.0
Unit-load statistics, definitions in, 2.7.1; 2.7.2; 6.2.0
Unit-load statistics, Northern Ireland, 2.7.8
Unit-load traffic, coastwise, 2.4.0
United States Bureau of Customs, 12.0.5
United States transhipment data for UK, 3.0.4; 3.0.5
Units of measurement, 2.1.2; 2.1.5; 2.1.14; 6.1.0; 6.1.1
Units of measurement, conversion factors for, 6.1.1; 6.1.3
Used packaging, 2.1.8; 2.5.0

Vessel size, 1.0.4
Vessels employed in foreign trade, 9.0.0; 9.0.1; 9.0.4
Vessels of war, 9.0.9
Vessels servicing oil-rigs, 9.0.9, 9.0.10

Waste material, 2.1.4
Waterway authorities, independent, 8.0.7

Waterway, definition of inland, 8.0.8
Waterways, commercial, 8.0.1
Waterways, cruising, 8.0.1
Waterways, nationalization of, 8.0.0
Weight of container contents, 2.8.2

Weight of packaging, 2.1.2
Weight of unit-load device, 2.1.2
Winter partially smooth water limit, 8.0.8; 12.0.6

Yachts, pleasure, 9.0.9; 9.0.12

18: CIVIL AVIATION

CELIA M. PHILLIPS
Lecturer in Statistics
London School of Economics

REFERENCE DATE OF SOURCES REVIEWED

This review is believed to represent the position, broadly speaking, as it obtained in September 1977. Later revisions have been inserted up to the proof-reading stage (October 1978), taking account, as far as possible, of any major changes in the situation.

LIST OF ABBREVIATIONS

AEA	Association of European Airlines
ATC	Air Traffic Control
ATLB	Air Transport Licensing Board
ATM	Air Traffic Movements
AUC	Airline Users Committee
BA	British Airways
BAA	British Airports Authority
BALPA	British Airline Pilots Association
BEA	British European Airways
BOAC	British Overseas Airways Corporation
BoT	Board of Trade
CAA	Civil Aviation Authority
CSO	Central Statistical Office
DoT	Department of Trade
DTI	Department of Trade and Industry
EARB	European Airlines Research Bureau
ECAC	European Civil Aviation Conference
EEC	European Economic Community
GLC	Greater London Council
IATA	International Air Transport Association
ICAO	International Civil Aviation Organization
IPS	International Passenger Survey
ITC	International Transport Carrier
NATS	National Air Traffic Services
NNI	Noise number index
OECD	Organization for Economic Co-operation and Development
OPCS	Office of Population Censuses and Surveys
SSRC	Social Science Research Council
UN	United Nations
WEAA	Western European Airports Association

ACKNOWLEDGEMENTS

I should like to thank everyone with whom I have discussed these data including the participants at the SSRC seminar and my old friends at Ifalpa.

At a time of frequent changes in the agency responsible for the collection of material one is very dependent upon the memories and co-operation of the individuals concerned. I am particularly grateful to S. Boxer, M. Ellis and A. White at the CAA, S. Maiden at the BAA, and J. Harris at the DoT. Throughout my work I have relied upon P. Scott at the CAA library to a great extent and I should like to thank him for the patience of himself and his colleagues.

I must also mention the secretaries at the Statistics Department here at the London School of Economics—Susan Coles, Susan Hayden, Valmai Lloyd Jones, Hazel Rice and Anne Usher, who had a nerve-racking summer dealing with various permutations of the Quick Reference List tables.

Finally, I should like to give a special thank you to Marie Louise de Villiers who worked as my research assistant over the summer, familiarized herself with the data and sources, and produced the Quick Reference List.

CONTENTS OF REVIEW 18

1.	**The Background to Figures on Civil Aviation**	117
1.1.	*Introduction*	117
1.2.	*Definitions and outline*	117
1.3.	*The general organization of civil aviation*	117
	1.3.1. The rise of the CAA and the BAA	117
	1.3.2. Airports	118
	1.3.3. Aircraft: commercial and general aviation	119
	1.3.4. Air traffic control	119
	1.3.5. Military aircraft	119
	1.3.6. The statistics generated	120
2.	**Statistical Returns: Basic Description**	121
2.1.	*Regular government and CAA sources*	121
	2.1.1. Introduction	121
	2.1.2. The summary of activity at aerodoromes and its sequels	122
	2.1.3. Operating and traffic statistics of UK airlines	123
	2.1.4. Origin and destination surveys	124
	2.1.5. The international passenger survey	125
	2.1.6. The survey of air freight demand	126
	2.1.7. Customs and Excise figures	126
	2.1.8. NATS work on air traffic	127
	2.1.9. NATS figures on accidents	129
	2.1.10. The noise surveys made by the OPCS and DTI (Civil Aviation)	129
	2.1.11. The general aviation study	130
	2.1.12. Financial results: United Kingdom airlines	131
	2.1.13. National income and balance of payments	131
	2.1.14. Employment	131
2.2.	*Sources from individual airport studies*	132
	2.2.1. The British Airports Authority	132
	2.2.2. Non-BAA airports, regional demand and in-flight surveys	134
2.3.	*International bodies*	135
	2.3.1. ICAO	136
	2.3.2. AEA (EARB) and ECAC	136
	2.3.3. WEAA	137
	2.3.4. IATA	137
	2.3.5. OECD, EEC and UN	137
2.4.	*Individual airline figures*	138

2.5. *The British Tourist Authority*	138
2.6. *The Airline Users Committee*	138
2.7. *Other individual studies*	139

3. Comments on Available Data — 141
3.1. *General aviation* — 141
3.2. *Air transport* — 141
    3.2.1. Passengers — 141
    3.2.2. Freight and mail — 142
    3.2.3. The aircraft — 143
    3.2.4. Accidents — 143
3.3. *Airports* — 144
    3.3.1. Transport facilities around airports — 144
    3.3.2. Noise — 145
    3.3.3. Employment — 146
3.4. *Personnel* — 146
3.5. *Financial statistics* — 146

4. Comments and Suggestions — 147
4.1. *The cataloguing and description of sources* — 147
4.2. *The coverage of sources* — 148
    4.2.1. Compatibility of measures — 148
    4.2.2. Insufficiencies in the data — 148
    4.2.3. Conclusion — 149

Addendum on Recent Developments — 150

Quick Reference List — 151
    Key to Publications — 264

Bibliography — 275

Coverage of Publications — 277

Useful Libraries and Bodies — 280

Appendix of Forms — 281
1. *Examples of monthly annual return of air traffic to CAA* — 282
2. *Flight information strip to NATS* — 289
3. *Examples of financial returns collected* — 294

Subject Index — 299

CHAPTER 1

THE BACKGROUND TO FIGURES ON CIVIL AVIATION

1.1. Introduction

This paper is primarily a review of the major statistical sources on civil aviation which are reasonably accessible to the general public. The main government and government agency material is discussed, as are data produced by bodies connected with the administration of different aspects of civil aviation management. In addition, unpublished sources—generally produced by consultants for government and official bodies—are also described where they are reasonably relevant to the main subject matter.

1.2. Definitions and Outline

The area covered by the term 'civil aviation' is difficult to define. Here it has been taken to include the people and machines involved in non-military flying and any measured side effects of such flying. The aircraft manufacturing industry, however, is not touched on.

Chapter 2 discusses the main censuses and surveys involved in the area and gives a general indication of their reliability. Chapter 3 covers the sources available on particular points. The general consistency of different measurements is discussed in the areas of general aviation, air transport, airport planning and airport and airline personnel. Finally, certain difficulties are elaborated upon and suggestions made about possible improvements in data production and availability.

Before studying the statistical sources in detail, a brief account of the general organization and management of civil aviation follows.

1.3. The General Organization of Civil Aviation

1.3.1. *The rise of the Civil Aviation Authority and the British Airports Authority*
Official figures on aircraft have existed in this country since 1919 when the Air Transport Licensing Board was set up. The basis of all the routine government statistics we will discuss was then established, but the interest of this review will focus on the experience of air traffic and private planes since 1955—the year in which air passengers carried across the Atlantic first exceeded sea travellers.

Civil aviation in this period is very different from the other forms of transport. In the first place, regional figures are not as important as airport figures; in fact regions are defined by their local airport. In the second place, a large proportion of air passengers and freight will go abroad and even private flights are likely to be to a foreign destination. Domestic traffic is not the sole concern of this paper.

The first difference means that figures on management are often given by airport or traffic control centre rather than region. The second difference means that foreign airlines and aircraft have to be considered in their flights to and from the UK, as do our national aircraft flights abroad. Economically speaking these flights are important to the country from the point of view of migration and the balance of payments so that any study of air traffic may find itself intimately involved in such questions.

At the same time the rapid growth of air traffic and airports since 1955 means that interest has been taken in the side effects of their expansion, and accidents, noise and the generation of traffic have been measured.

At the beginning of our period, different aspects of civil aviation came under different government departments. The immigration aspects came under the Home Office, while balance of payments were the interest of the Board of Trade. Aircraft and airport licensing and accidents were the concern of the Board of Trade also which owned many of the airports in the UK. Air navigation and air traffic were connected with the Ministry of Aviation or the Ministry of Defence.

The general complications of a system which had built up in response to rapid development in the use of aircraft are very lucidly described in the Edwards Report of 1969, *British Air Transport in the Seventies* [QRL 36], which recommended centralization in terms of both of departmental responsibility and air lines and charter organizations.

As a result, the Civil Aviation Authority (CAA) was set up in 1971. It took on all the functions outlined above except the first two—the Home Office remained responsible for immigration and kept an interest in international air movements and the Board of Trade (by then the Department of Trade and Industry) continued to look after the financial aspects of international air movements (Subsection 2.1.5).

Slightly earlier (in 1966) the British Airports Authority (BAA) was set up to take over the main commercial airports from the Board of Trade and this trend in change of ownership has continued.

The situation now is broadly speaking as follows—taking airports first.

1.3.2. *Airports*
All airports and airstrips for commercial use (including hiring out to private aircraft) have to be licensed by the CAA. The CAA publishes two major lists on all airports in the UK, *Air Pilot* [QRL 14] and *General Aviation Flight Guide* [QRL 69]. A handy and easily accessible quick reference book which covers most of the same points for airports is Robert Pooley's *United Kingdom and Ireland Air Touring Flight Guide* [QRL 7].

Airport ownership varies: Luton and Birmingham, for example, are local authority owned; Aberdeen and Prestwick come under the BAA and some smaller Scottish airports are run by the CAA. All have to come up to certain standards to carry particular types of traffic and all are subject to the CAA when any incidents, however minor, are reported. In addition they all have to make returns for the monthly survey of activity at airports in the UK and the Channel Islands and could be expected to co-operate in any reasonable study undertaken by Central Government. In fact, as Subsections 2.2.2 and Section 3.3 show, in many cases, local authority owners have been as concerned to study their airports as the CAA or BAA. Such studies have generally covered points of regional interest—travel to work areas, noise contours, traffic and the like, while Central Government surveys have also been interested in general Origin and Destination Surveys.

1.3.3. *Aircraft: commercial and general aviation*

So much for the airports, what about the aircraft which use them? All UK planes are registered (see [QRL 50, 76, 77 and 139]), and their weight, type, owner, etc., are given. Foreign planes are also registered on their own registers and the major users—foreign commercial airlines—are also known. Our knowledge of commercial airlines and their use of their craft is quite detailed. As with airports, they fill in monthly returns on their operating and traffic statistics to justify their commercial licence and the licensing authority, formerly the Air Transport Licensing Board (see [QRL 25]), now the CAA, publishes details.

However, the larger number of private planes, which occupy air space, are under no such compulsion and statistics on them are sparse. While individuals have been helpful when approached, a recent survey on General Aviation [QRL 126] (discussed in detail in Subsection 2.1.11) found that of 300 air clubs only 193 replied.

1.3.4. *Air traffic control*

A similar situation exists when we come to consider air traffic control. There are ATC centres at most airports. Each centre comes into one of three areas—London, Scotland and Shanwick which covers North Atlantic traffic. In the course of daily work, controllers make out flight strips for all traffic-controlled routes—covering all take-offs and landings and certain flight levels for civilian traffic. These flight strips are collected and collated by the National Air Traffic Services (NATS) and are readily available. In addition the controllers have co-operated with a detailed study of flying over their routes annually since 1966 (biennially since 1974). These figures cannot give an unbiased estimate of all flights because of uncontrolled traffic. This will be club and traffic due to the flight level involved. Censuses of all traffic made to supplement the controlled traffic figures have been discontinued largely because of the response bias suspected in air and gliding club returns.

1.3.5. *Military aircraft*

Military traffic does not come into the general area of this report, but it is worth noting that the military airports do perform some operations which might strictly speaking be regarded as 'civil' in scope. The study of General Aviation [QRL 126] studied all 29 military airfields to get some picture of this but we know that at the beginning of our period military personnel and their families would be carried regularly on international flights by transport planes either to duty or on 'indulgence' flights. Such travel is increasingly made from civil airports now. Numbers involved will be small relative to total passengers but will have gradually increased the figures for flights on 'military business', 'staff', or 'rejoining the family'. In addition, military traffic which comes under civil air traffic centre control is included in the civil figures under a separate head in recent publications of [QRL 22] (see Subsection 2.1.8).

1.3.6. *The statistics generated*

We thus have aircraft and airports which are directed to a high extent by government regulation on aspects such as registration, safety, technical standards, immigration and commercial flights. Their organization and administration leads to the production of extensive information on passengers, freight and flights. The same background means, however, that there are major difficulties if we are interested in manpower employed at airports or by airlines or any detail on the internal management of individual airports, although BAA airports are an ever improving exception to this rule. Uncontrolled traffic figures have been discontinued largely because of the bias suspected in the air and gliding club returns.

In all cases the airports, while responsible for standards of air operation, do not have much control over employees at the airport, only a small proportion of whom will actually be working for the airport itself. The majority of workers will be involved in catering, cleaning, ticket booking, etc., which are the responsibility of sub-contractors. Unless therefore the airport itself takes an interest in such staff, there is no record. So far only BAA [QRL 132 and 133] (1975) has carried out such a study on any scale. From the airlines' point of view, figures are generally given on the function of their staff, and whether they are air or ground staff, but a picture of their pay and conditions of work is generally available only from government legislation of a general nature.

The next chapter describes the main statistical sources which emerge from this framework. It will be seen that to a large extent their strengths and limitations stem from the structure.

CHAPTER 2

STATISTICAL RETURNS: BASIC DESCRIPTION

2.1. Regular Government and CAA Sources

2.1.1. *Introduction*

The major bulk of statistics on Civil Aviation, whether on aircraft, air passengers, the running of airports, accidents, or noise, is published by Central Government and the CAA. Basic annual figures are given by the expected abstracts published by the CSO, Department of the Environment and the Department of Transport [QRL 28, 104 and 137]. The situation for more detailed figures is somewhat confused—though the data produced are remarkably consistent—because of changes in departmental responsibilities over the 1960s and early 1970s. These changes are described in detail in the Edwards Report [QRL 36] (see Subsection 1.3.1) and the following outline may be helpful before each source is described in turn.

Taking first the situation for air passengers, freight and aircraft, there were two main annual published sources until 1967:

Summary of Activity at Aerodromes in the UK and Channel Islands, published by the Ministry of Aviation [QRL 127], and

Operating and Traffic Statistics of UK Airlines, published by the Board of Trade [QRL 98].

Each gave the results of a complete census: the first, of all airports in the UK and Channel Islands; the second, of airline companies operating in the area.

Between 1968 and 1972 the figures were published in one series of Business Monitors by the Department of Trade and Industry but in seven separate volumes, many of which contained elements of both sources and, in some cases, additional analyses [QRL 38–44].

In 1973, with the coming of the Civil Aviation Authority, all the statistics were recombined in one volume (in an annual and monthly version) [QRL 51 and 52] and are still produced in this way. Though strictly speaking the CAA is an independent agency, this chequered history means that in this volume we will consider statistics produced by the CAA with the government figures.

Repeated Origin and Destination surveys at different airports since 1965 have also been produced in a similar progression from Ministry of Aviation to BoT and DTI and now come under the CAA (Subsection 2.1.4).

Figures produced on accidents and air traffic control figures on aircraft movement collated by NATS, however, were the responsibility of the Board of Trade and the DTI and never came under aviation before their transfer to the CAA (see Subsections 2.1.8 and 2.1.9).

Noise measurement, however, and the international passenger survey still come under the auspices of the DoT (see Subsection 2.1.10).

Apart from these routine figures, additional work has been carried out on individual airports by the CAA and others. One obvious example is the work for the study of a third London airport. This will be discussed under Subsection 2.2.2 on individual airport statistics as a major part of the work is unpublished and produced by consultants.

A description of the main routine published sources for the Government and the CAA follows in the other subsections of Section 2.1.

2.1.2. *The summary of activity at aerodromes and its sequels*

The above publication [QRL 127] was produced monthly with annual summary with remarkable consistency over the period 1951–67. It gave the results of a continuous filling in of air transport details by all aerodromes on a compulsory basis. Figures collected cover those which an airport would be expected to collect for administrative purposes; numbers of aircraft handled and type, total passengers, and freight traffic. They cover the UK in detail, but figures for the Channel Islands generally only exist for 'all categories' of aircraft.

Arriving and departing aircraft are defined by 'type of movement'—basically commercial or non-commercial. The non-commercial category is a mixed bag—test and training, scheduled service positioning, aero club, official military, etc. For 'commercial' flights, however, we see the first attempts at differentiating between types of passenger and traffic —scheduled and charter category. In 1960 these were further subdivided to distinguish between corporation flights and others and the charter category separates inclusive tours and others. It is interesting to note that throughout the period take-offs and landings are counted separately. A further subdivision is given by nationality of operator.

Figures on passengers distinguish whether a passenger was terminal or transit and then give figures by the breakdowns for aircraft-movement type. Freight traffic is given by weight of cargo—short tons until 1966 and, from 1967 onwards, metric tons.

All figures are available monthly by individual airports in the CAA library but the main tables are presented annually in total with separate figures for London and some main airports.

In all the publication has five tables. Their coverage has been given in some detail because of their main failing—a lack of any published information about their origin or coverage.

Apart from brief notes covering questions like the change from short to metric tons in 1967 and the changes in category of scheduled flight, there is no other information on the basis of the figures or the method of collection.

It is worth noticing two points concerning the method of collecting the material, both connected with passengers.

In the first place 'passenger' means 'fare-paying and non-fare-paying passenger and crew'—the figures are concerned with the numbers coming through the airport, not merely fare-paying passengers.

Secondly, transit passengers are covered.

These two points make for discrepancies between passenger figures from this source and the other two sources on passengers—the origin and destination surveys and the DTI international passenger survey. This will be discussed in more detail under the subject heading in the next chapter.

In 1967 responsibility for the production of the figures moved from the Air Ministry to the DTI who published them from 1967 to 1972. There was no major change in the method and rationale of collection or the coverage but the figures are spread through a series of *Business Monitors*—C.A.1 to C.A.7 [QRL 38, 39, 40, 43, 44]—which also covered the earlier *Operating and Traffic Statistics of UK Airlines*.

There was no comment on any changes. The division into 'take off' and 'landing' was dropped and 'mail' was covered as well as 'freight'.

Since 1973 the figures have been presented monthly, quarterly and annually in the CAA monthly and annual statistics [QRL 51, 52]; see QRL for details of frequency for the different figures. The presentation is remarkably similar to that of earlier publications except for the absence of transit passengers and additional new information on international air passengers to and from UK airports. The notes on the figures are neither more nor less extensive than in the Air Ministry days and reference is only made to the DTI publications.

This means that the basic census of air transport and passenger and freight movements is undocumented. Judging by its presentation and general consistency it is a reliable source apart from this major limitation which would mean checking with the responsible authorities if the figures were to be used for research purposes.

2.1.3. *Operating and traffic statistics of UK airlines*

The concluding comment on airport statistics is also true for this 'census' of airlines [QRL 98]. Its history is also similar to that of [QRL 127] except that returns were made to the Board of Trade before 1968 and are given in [QRL 41 and 42] for 1968–72. The present notes by the compilers of the figures give the reasons for their collection: 'The system is designed to collect comprehensive statistics from which can be judged the course of the civil aviation industry and the impact of the CAA's decisions on it, and which will enable information to be supplied in fulfilment of international obligations' [QRL 51 and 52].

The figures collected have remained very consistent since the mid-1950s. They are concerned with flights rather than arrivals and departures and fare-paying passengers carried rather than numbers going through airports.

The present method of collection involves four forms: CAA No. Stats 200, 201, 202 and 205 (see Appendix of forms), the first is relevant to operators of scheduled and non-scheduled flights while the others cover scheduled and non-scheduled operators separately on a point-to-point basis, and the holders of Class 5 licences (licences which allow their holders to provide substitute charter flights).

Figures collected cover basic stocks and changes of stock in the type of aircraft owned by each operator, numbers of stage flights over the months by each, and numbers of fare-paying passengers and freight involved.

The main objective of the collection is the calculation of the performance of the airlines in terms of use of their facilities, and calculations of passenger loadings are given.

Figures on passengers are not readily comparable with those derived from [QRL 127] on airports. In the first place, only fare-paying passengers are given, so crew and complimentary passengers are not covered. Secondly, passengers on a flight are given regardless of whether the flight stage is the final one of the journey or not, i.e. passengers who will stay in the plane and not check out through the airport nor become transit passengers are given. For further discussion of the problem of counting passengers, see Subsection 3.2.1. Thus, although the figures are admirable in terms of their basic objective, they are difficult to use in conjunction with the other main traffic census.

2.1.4. *Origin and destination surveys*

The main source of information on passenger movements collected by the CAA is the series of surveys undertaken since 1965.

There is a full description of them all and a discussion of sampling techniques in CAP 363 (1975), *Origins and Destinations of Passengers at United Kingdom Airports* [QRL 99]. Besides this there is a fuller (unindexed) discussion of different aspects of the 1972 survey in *CAA Monthly Statistics* covering September 1973 to February 1974 [QRL 52].

The first survey—in 1965—was conducted by the Government Social Survey for the Ministry of Aviation [QRL 130]. It covered Heathrow and Gatwick airports and was effectively the result of adding questions to the International Passenger Survey for that year which ran from 19 June to 21 July. (For a general discussion of the IPS see Subsection 2.1.5 and L. J. Lickorish, Volume IV of this Review Series, Section 3.7.) The success of this survey led to an overall plan to cover all regions of the United Kingdom, and the next four surveys followed a roughly rotational design:

August–November 1968	BoT, survey covered Heathrow, Gatwick, Luton, Manston and Southampton [QRL 101].
June–October 1970	DTI survey covered the North West Scottish airports and Leeds Bradford [QRL 100].
June–October 1971	DTI survey covered Cardiff, Birmingham, East Midlands, Newcastle, Belfast and Bristol [QRL 103].
August–December 1972	DTI survey again covered the south-east: Heathrow, Gatwick, Luton, Southend and Stansted [QRL 84].
July–November 1975	CAA survey covered major airports in Scotland and Central England [QRL 102].

There was in addition a special survey undertaken in 1969 for the Roskill Commission which again dealt with Heathrow and Gatwick [QRL 53]. The survey designs are adequately described in CAP 363 and so will not be covered here.

All the surveys give figures on the original location or ultimate destination of passengers on journeys. In many (see Quick Reference List), methods of transport to and from the airport are also analysed.

This means that over the period there is a very clear picture of changes in air-passenger traffic in the London area and an estimated overall view for the UK in the early 1970s. Figures are compatible and have been grossed up to fit the 1972 totals. From the publications one can get a clear picture of the differences between airports in types of traffic and ease of access, and a breakdown of types of passengers. For most planning purposes the figures are admirable and the method of covering different planning areas at different times seems a reasonable economy.

There are two points to note about definitions, however, which make for difficulties of comparison with other data. The first covers the definition of 'passenger'. The survey covers all terminal passengers—fare paying and non-fare paying as for the airport statistics—but includes interline passengers—that is to say, passengers in transit for a domestic or international flight who because of the organization of the airport or the time of their next flight have to pass through Customs and Immigration before they can continue their air journey. At Heathrow, for example, almost all transferring passengers between international flights would not come into the figures. Those transferring to domestic routes would do so. From the point of view of comparing with other passenger estimates this adds to the difficulties. More seriously it means that the bigger airports have no real way of estimating the general pressure on transfer facilities at different times. In fact the BAA has estimated that around 2 million transit passengers are not covered by this method for Heathrow and a special survey was undertaken to examine them [QRL 131] (see Section 2.2).

The second point to note is the question of origin/destination. This is defined by initiated or completed journey. The figures combine the two. Anyone staying near the airport for longer than the overall journey might warrant is defined as having his origin or destination there. The visitor from Manchester who stays for the weekend with London friends before catching a plane to a business appointment in Frankfurt or the American tourist who goes to the London theatre before moving on to Windsor will both come under 'London' in the figures. Though this is realistic for traffic planners, it is likely that it will cause some bias in the results if consumer preferences are being studied. Such speculations cannot be tested, though certainly we know the figures for domestic business travel in London show the office as the place of origin/destination rather than the home.

Thus although the figures are generally useful in estimates of surface travel to airport, they do not entirely give the travel habits and requirements of people living in different areas of the country nor do they neceessarily provide a complete guide to tourist destinations.

2.1.5. *The international passenger survey*

There is another source of air passenger information in the results of the DTI's international passenger survey. This was introduced by the Government Social Survey under the auspices of the Board of Trade and first published during 1961 and 1962. It is still run by the OPCS. The main objective of the surveys, given in an outline in the *BoT Journal*, 23 August 1962 [B 49], is to provide information about the tourist industry and give a more secure basis for estimates of credits and debits in the account of 'travel' in the balance of payments.

Stratified random samples are taken in two surveys—one of international air passengers and the other on short sea routes. Specimen forms are shown in Volume IV of the Review Series, p. 99. Results are combined with Home Office immigration figures and published quarterly in the Business Monitor series *Overseas Travel and Tourism* (M.6) [QRL 46]. The background and techniques used by the survey are covered in an article in *Trade and Industry* (2 January 1976, 'Overseas travel and tourism 1974–75') [B 55]. The main interest of the figures focuses on the money aspect of travel but there are interesting figures over time on the balance between air and sea travel and a detailed breakdown of purpose of travel, area of residence, and destination or origin. In fact visits to the UK by foreigners are separated from journeys by British residents so there is a useful check against the international passengers in the origin and destination surveys. The definition of 'resident' as 'resident for 12 months or more' is similar for the two, except for the Home Office figures where 'nationality' is the relevant qualification, so the main figures are comparable.

Unlike the origin and destination surveys, the study continues over the year with varying sampling fractions for different airports and long and short air routes. About 80 per cent of possible traffic is surveyed overall for both air and sea passengers. The figures provide useful evidence of seasonal fluctuations in passengers both in total and from the point of view of country of origin and reason for travel. Methods have remained fairly constant since 1962 but sampling techniques are expected to change in the next year or so when they will be documented by OPCS.

2.1.6. *The survey of air freight demand*

June 1977 saw the publication by the CAA of the figures from the first detailed survey of air freight in the UK. *Air Freight Demand: a Survey of UK Shippers* [QRL 12] gives general estimates of reasons for using air, rather than sea, for freight, and breakdowns of load by type of commodity, size, weight, and urgency of customer demand.

The aims of the survey, outlined in the report, were

(i) to identify those factors which are relevant to the export mode decision,
(ii) to ascertain whether there is any connection between the size and urgency of air freight assignments,
(iii) to investigate the possible size of any potential demand for alternative, non-urgent, forms of scheduled air freight service.

The CAA used the results for forming proposed new regulations for the UK licensing of non-scheduled UK air freight services in December 1976.

A sampling frame of 9000 exporters was purchased from a commercial organization* and 3000 companies were drawn, leading to the sending out of 3098 forms when the firms' subsidiaries were taken into account. Two reminders were sent (the second with a further copy of the questionnaire) and the collection was closed after 11 weeks. The response rate was 31.8 per cent.

Although the low response means the figures should be treated with care, sensibly used they are valuable, and are certainly the first to answer the questions asked by the CAA. They will hopefully lead to further such studies.

2.1.7. *The Annual Statement of the Overseas Trade of the United Kingdom*

One additional original source on air freight—exports and imports only—is given by HMSO in Volume V of *Trade at Ports* [QRL 31] up to 1973 and, since then, in *Statistics of Trade through United Kingdom Ports* (1976 onwards). (For coverage of these figures see the companion review in this volume, Subsection 6.1.0.)

These annual import and export figures are produced by HM Customs and Excise. Tables give the quantity and value of the principal commodities for all sea ports and for the most important airports (from the point of view of freight) separately. Combined figures are also given for the remaining airports. They are a complete census of recorded declarations to HM Customs and Excise by importers and exporters or their agents. They do not, however, generally include goods in transit except for goods which are stored in bonded warehouses and afterwards exported.

In broad outline, then, they can serve as a useful point of comparison between air and sea figures for international freight and for overall estimates of exports.

---

*Incidentally showing the financial difficulties of not being in the same position as a Ministry or government department which would normally have free access to such information.

2.1.8. *NATS work on air traffic*

Turning away from the surveys which are mainly concerned with passenger and freight carried and money spent, we move to the area of traffic control. From the point of view of the measurement of air congestion and accident avoidance it is vitally necessary to have accurate knowledge of air traffic density over the United Kingdom. The United Kingdom is divided into three traffic control areas, London, Preston and Scottish,* with a fourth to cover Atlantic traffic with different centres each of which records individual flights coming within their control on documents called (see also Subsection 1.3.4 and the specimen in the Appendix) flight progress slips. Controlled aircraft have a set of routes within each segment that they may follow so that figures can be collected on movements along these limited tracks fairly easily from central information. National air traffic services provide two kinds of data on controlled aircraft.

There is a routine estimate every month based on a 7-day count which gives the number of flights for civil and military aircraft on each sector by route and direction along route. This gives a good running total where changes in frequency for different routes can be spotted very early—a kind of quality-control check. Type or size of aircraft or nature of flight is not given. These figures are for internal use and are not published but are available on request for research purposes in the CAA library.

The second analysis, made annually until 1974 but now on a biennial basis, is based on the same information—the flight progress strip—but the analysis of the results is much more detailed. A busy summer week is taken for all traffic control centres—generally the last week in July or the first in August but since 1976, the *first* week in July—and extensive computer analyses are made.† Results have been published, first under the Board of Trade (up to 1970), then the DTI (1971) and now the CAA [QRL 22].

Figures are given for all three (now two) areas separately and (since 1972) for Shanwick (the Atlantic control area). Each area is divided into sectors (e.g. Dover, Clacton, Lydd, etc. within the London area). For each of these sectors figures are given for each day by flight level, route, type of flight—civil, public, private or military, and category of aircraft—turbo jet, turbo prop or piston, nature of flight—take-off and landing, or over flight, and hour of the day. General figures are given for each individual route in the sector.

These are all important things to know from the point of view of air traffic control. The total daily figure broken down by nature of flight gives a basic idea of the capacity required by air traffic control. Frequency figures for hours of the day give an excellent check on how much lag there is in the system. Taken in conjunction with the monthly flight-check information, a detailed figure of traffic systems over the UK emerges.

To the individual who is not interested solely in air traffic control there are some difficulties. The figures are not really comparable over time as route structures have changed. Alterations, however, are carefully documented in the individual volumes. A more important point to note is that apart from data given in an introductory table the figures provide no overall estimate as, for the week concerned, all flights are counted in each sector so that there is considerable double counting. The longer the flight the more the double counting. A domestic routine flight from London to Aberdeen via Manchester will appear in each of the three areas and perhaps more than one route. A local private joy ride will probably stay

---

*This is true of most figures described, but from 1976 onwards 'Preston', now 'Manchester-Sub-Centre', is subsumed under the 'London' figures, although it can be analysed separately.

† The change in survey date is to phase collection of figures with the 2-yearly survey of Europe made by Eurocontrol with which the UK collection is now combined.

in one British area. This may give a fair indication of the relative distances covered by traffic, and the work done by air traffic control, but means that figures are not easily comparable with arrival and departure figures at the airports without considerable checking of detailed figures.

The accuracy of the results, after computer troubles in the early 1970s, has improved considerably. 'Informed guesswork' is still used to fill in details in a minority of cases— details not given. One per cent of flights are not covered in any way. A more difficult problem with the figures which will affect bias is the fact that the collection is made for 1 week only. In 1972 a pilots' strike invalidated one day of the week concerned, and a substitution to the equivalent day in the following week was required. More seriously, the 1974 survey coincided with the Cyprus air lift. Detailed study and comparisons with the monthly estimates can easily isolate the effects of such occurrences but they do make the figures more useful to the technical expert than a researcher looking for general trends in air traffic.

These figures, of course, only cover controlled air traffic and are likely, for reasons discussed in Subsection 1.3.4, to exclude much non-commercial traffic. From 1961 the Ministry of Aviation conducted four censuses of all air traffic (see [QRL 47]). These were continued by the Board of Trade in its 1967 study [QRL 48]. The last was made for the CAA in 1973 by Software Sciences [QRL 87] and there are no immediate plans to continue the operation. They provide the only 'snapshot' of all traffic in the air at a particular time.

The first two surveys were made in the winter months, but since then the NATS figures have been used for controlled aircraft and the same week chosen as for the NATS survey. The earlier censuses (1961–3) provide excellent guidance to the method of survey and the reliability of results. In 1961 complete enumeration was attempted over the week by asking pilots, including foreign pilots, to fill in cards with their route if they were airborne over the period, every hour on the hour. Response rates were 80 per cent for British registered aircraft and 90 per cent for gliders (response includes returning forms for the period of the survey with 'not in flight' written in). Checks against known figures for controlled traffic showed very few discrepancies so it was felt the method was generally successful. Later years followed the technique of the first census with a minor change—to allow for instruction hours at flying schools and clubs—of asking for information every hour on the half hour.

The figures presented give details of type of aircraft, business, and flight level which are not given by the controlled traffic figures and should be a useful supplement to them. They are also clearly explained and presented in a way compatible with the NATS survey. Later volumes are published by NATS.

There is one major problem with the survey which must be mentioned as it has led to its suppression. Although all the surveys up to and including the sixth (1967) are known to have a high response rate in terms of completed forms, only controlled traffic results can be checked for bias in behaviour. The two main groups of uncontrolled traffic, the military and air and glider clubs, cannot be checked in this way and figures of flight frequency over the period are felt to be inconsistent with general activity over the year. This is hinted at in the last reports and is a problem which leads to considerable— incalculable—bias. In fact little information is readily added to the data gained from the controlled-traffic survey.

Gradual awareness of this difficulty and a slowing down in the increase in traffic density (present air traffic control facilities are estimated until 1985) led to a gap after the 1967 survey for the BoT.

The latest survey, published by NATS in 1974, was performed by Software Sciences and shows a deterioration in the actual survey method. Instead of forms being issued to all owners of registered aircraft, in many cases they were left at central points like air clubs and airline offices and were unaddressed. This means that no response rate is known. In addition some replies were lost, so the general impression—despite beautifully presented tables—is one of less consistency in the results between the different sectors of air traffic than before.

For the time being then, there are no plans to mount another such survey. Accuracy, given the cost, is low, and there is a general lack of urgency since the pressure on air traffic has gone down in the recent economic crisis. This is unfortunate in the long run as the censuses were potentially the only true picture of general activity in the air but there is no immediate remedy for the inaccuracies described.

2.1.9. *NATS figures on accidents*

Figures on accidents have been presented annually for all aircraft on the British register since the beginning of the period [QRL 10]. Up to 1964 they were produced by the Ministry of Aviation and from 1965 to 1970 by the Board of Trade and the DTI. The CAA took over on its inception. From 1969 onwards figures on near misses have been included.

The general format is a complete enumeration of accidents by cause found including weather conditions, the crew, machinery, etc., and an analysis of passengers killed per revenue paying passenger and accidents per flight. Data are also given on stage of the flight—take off, landing, *en route*. Figures can be used in a general actuarial way.

Near-miss figures give all incidents reported by pilots and are annotated A or B—A being the situation where Airmiss Working Groups decided there was a significant risk of collision.

Considerable work has been done using these figures and unpublished surveys on individual routes on the lines of Subsection 2.1.6 to assess the cost and risk of *en route* accidents in different air traffic conditions (see Subsection 3.2.4).

The figures are comprehensive and any difficulty in their use mainly relates to actuarial difficulties with the infrequency of accidents and the difficulty of achieving flight details from published data. [QRL 1 and 2] give interesting summaries on figures on airmiss and collision risk in the UK and world wide and [B 1, 2, 3 and 9] are a good background to the theory. It is important to note that figures relate to British registered aircraft only and that for other aircraft accidents in the UK sources from the foreign governments have to be used. (See *World Airline Accidents: Summary* [QRL 140].) Also see Addendum for new summary of passenger accident statistics by the CAA.

2.1.10. *The noise surveys made by the OPCS and DTI (Civil Aviation)*

Unlike accident information hard figures on the disadvantages to those living near operating airports are rare though estimates are generally made for purposes of airport planning. Noise is the most common problem considered and many studies have been made of the noise level of particular aircraft and their take-off and landing patterns (see [B 11 and 21]). A study by Culver for the Board of Trade in 1969 analysed aircraft-noise complaints [QRL 3]. Two main enquiries have been made on the problems of aircraft noise and its effect on the general population and both provide useful figures.

The first was commissioned by the Wilson Committee on the Problem of Noise (1963) [QRL 92] and consists of two studies around London (Heathrow) Airport. The first results give aircraft noise in the vicinity of the airport near particular routes from the point of view of intensity and duration of sound. Such figures can then be used, given knowledge of routing systems, to make sound contours around any airport. There were 85 primary recording stations and 100 observations were made in each. Appendix L of McKennell (1963) [B 10] describes the study in more detail and the use of the results will be described in the next chapter of this review.

Having acquired a background knowledge of noise levels in the Heathrow area, a random sample of 1731 from the population was then interviewed within a 10-mile radius of the airport. A further 178 from a list of complainers were also questioned. In both cases the work was done over a short period to avoid knowledge of the reason for the survey being too widespread. The questionnaire itself was in two stages. The first asked general questions about local living conditions and the respondents' attitudes to them—the second concentrated on aircraft noise. The respondents' answers, coupled to their particular aircraft noise measures from the earlier survey, gave a clear picture of the general factors operating with respect to aircraft noise.

The two surveys are described in Appendix XI of the Wilson Report [QRL 92] as well as McKennell [B 10] and were carefully made. The results are clearly presented and analysis led to the setting up of the Noise Number Index—which will be discussed in Subsection 3.3.2.

The next enquiry, published in the *Second Survey of Aircraft Noise Annoyance round London (Heathrow) Airport* (1971), followed the same lines and is fully described in both the report and a DTI report (1971) [QRL 117] so a detailed description is not necessary. The sample design for the survey of individuals is interesting being pre-stratified in order to obtain a high proportion of individuals who suffer a large amount of noise infrequently, so that the noise index obtained earlier should be checked. Apart from this, the main difference between this and the earlier social survey is its larger coverage. The area covered was 15 miles east and west of the airport in addition to 10 miles north and south; 4700 people were interviewed in 162 'average' areas and a further 1575 were from the 39 'extreme' noise areas.

The most recent DTI publication, on night disturbance [QRL 90] (1977), uses known patterns of flights and results on people's sleeping patterns to estimate annoyance caused by night flying. Also see Addendum for the CAA Bibliography on this subject.

2.1.11. *The general aviation study*

Strictly speaking 'general aviation' does not come within the coverage of sources on civil aviation but as it is unlikely to be touched on in any other review in the series this brief note should be helpful.

The only source on the ownership and use of general aviation in this country, apart from aircraft registration and the census of air traffic (see Subsections 1.3.3 and 2.1.8), comes from surveys made in 1973 and published in *A Study of General Aviation in the South-east of England* (1974) [QRL 126]. Partly because it was difficult to define which craft were of direct relevance to SE England and partly because no such data were even available on a national basis all owners were covered. A 100 per cent sample of owners of the general aviation in the UK register was made. Private owners, clubs, commercial training and dealers were distinguished and approached in different ways. Most groups made a high response which covered 1431 owners and 2043 aircraft. Only clubs had a poorish response rate—107 did not reply from 300 names. So far as use of aircraft was concerned, the figures are also biased in the case of clubs because it is thought club secretaries—who could control who received questionnaires—tended to take the line of least resistance and handed them on to the keenest users. Nevertheless the survey as a whole is thought to give a reasonable picture of the use of air space by general aviation. The description of the study is also sound and helpful.

2.1.12. *Financial results: United Kingdom airlines*
The CAA, and earlier the DTI, have published annual financial results since 1968 for all UK airlines. In the earlier period estimates were made for the smaller airlines (covering 10 per cent of output) by referring to accounts filed at the companies' Registration Office and supplemented by some ICAO figures (see Subsection 2.3.1). Figures are given in [QRL 45 and 66] and from 1975 onwards have been incorporated in the *Annual Statistics* published by the CAA [QRL 51].

Since 1972 each company (including those which go out of business during the year) send in a quarterly and annual airline profit-and-loss statement, an annual appropriation account, and an annual balance sheet. The forms sent out are shown in [QRL 66]. The combined quarterly profit-and-loss statements, which are generally unaudited management accounts, are sometimes different from the annual summaries given. Perhaps more important to note, the figures given do not correspond with published company accounts since, where possible, the CAA has excluded companies' non-airline activities. This should make them a reasonable base for working out the profitability of different airline operations.

2.1.13. *National income and balance of payments*
Figures on the contribution of air travel to the National Income are given in the Blue Book [QRL 88] where consumers' expenditure on air travel is given annually (based on the Family Expenditure survey) and a treasury analysis of public expenditure and gross domestic fixed capital formation is given for air, rail and dock facilities combined.

Figures in the Pink Book on Balance of Payments [QRL 138] give invisible trade in civil aviation by UK and overseas airlines. Both these sources put civil aviation in the context of national expenditure and capital formation though it is disappointing that separate local authority and capital formation accounts are not available.

2.1.14. *Employment*
Annual figures on employment in air transport are published in *Transport Statistics Great Britain* [QRL 137] and give breakdowns by region, full-time or part-time work, and sex. The *Annual Abstract of Statistics* [QRL 28] gives overall employment and unemployment figures in the industry for Great Britain and the United Kingdom and the 1977 *Department of Employment Gazette* [QRL 54] gives the same unemployment figures classified by sex.

2.2. Sources from Individual Airport Studies

2.2.1. *The British Airports Authority*

The British Airports Authority was set up in 1966, initially covering 60 per cent of passenger movements and four airports—Heathrow, Gatwick, Stansted and Prestwick. By 1975 three more Scottish airports had been added—Edinburgh, Glasgow and Aberdeen—and 75 per cent of passenger movements were through the seven airports. Any statistics over and above those provided under a statutory provision for the CAA in some of the national publications covered in the first sections of Chapter 2 would therefore provide a valuable insight into the problems of the biggest commercial airports in the UK. The Authority does far more than provide statutory figures on its airports for the CAA, though there is close co-operation in statistical work undertaken.

Throughout the period there has been a continuous production of two series. Although these are not published they are readily available to the public on request so some account is given of them here in the hope that they will now form part of a recognized index.

Since 1969 the Authority has produced an annual report on patterns of traffic at British Airports Authorities airports [QRL 105]. The figures presented are collected routinely for the airport figures for the CAA (see Subsection 2.1.1) and some are published in the relevant sections of [QRL 51 and 52]. The emphasis in the BAA publication is on peak periods, and figures are generally taken from 13 weeks over the summer period. Terminal passenger and air transport movements are given for the peak month, peak day and peak hour during the period and the ratio of the peak to the annual average. Figures are given for each airport and Heathrow is divided into terminals. Busy hours are presented for the 30th and 100th busiest hours to give some idea of the overall distribution. The document is produced mainly for internal planning purposes but gives a very good picture for the general researcher of the pressure on airport facilities at the peak periods. As with figures in the *Summary of Activity at Aerodromes in the UK and Channel Islands* there is no figure for transit passengers but there is no other ambiguity in the figures.

Since 1968 there has also been a quarterly analysis of trends in passenger and aircraft movements [QRL 108]. This is in fact a reorganization of the figures already provided for the *Summary of Activity at Aerodromes* (Subsection 2.1.2). The classifications are similar. They are given for each of the BAA's airports and quarterly figures are compared with earlier years for seasonal trends.

The only continuous published material over the period, however, is contained in the annual reports of the BAA [QRL 35]. In addition to the general figures given in any company report on accounts and employees, there are generally additional figures on traffic and passengers similar to the two collections above, though not so extensive. It is clear that the reports are the only source on employees in airports which are not analysed in any other of the documents so far discussed. The 1976 report in particular gives a useful summary of the airports' working population over 1966–76 based on returns from airport employees.

The BAA has also been responsible for several one-off surveys giving useful figures for their airports. Since 1975 they have had a policy of publishing and selling such reports, but, before this, work is usually presented in a cyclostyled version for the BAA by consultants and can be seen at the BAA or CAA libraries.

The main surveys connected with the statistics department of the BAA in this way are on surface transport at Heathrow and Gatwick and were carried out in 1966 [QRL 80 and 81] and 1971 [QRL 128 and 129] by Freeman, Fox and Associates, and Jamieson and Mackay and prepared for the GLC and the Ministry of Transport as well as the BAA. They cover more details of transport to and from the airport than those usually gathered by the CAA origin and destination surveys.

Each had three main surveys, one in the departure lounge covering a weekday and a Sunday in a busy and slack period—4 days in all—and asked respondents how they had travelled to the airport; the second involved airport employers giving forms to all employees on travel to work. This had between 75 and 90 per cent response for all the studies; the third consisted of roadside interviews at points round the airports concerned aiming at finding the origin and destination of journeys in the neighbourhood. Additional studies were made of bus, coach and rail transport. The surveys are well presented and described and, as they are only peripherally concerned with civil aviation and passengers, will not be further discussed. It is interesting to note, however, that the survey on travel to work is the first on any aspect of airport employees to have been made in a readily available form.

Since 1972 road travel studies have been carried out annually and are available on application to the Operational Research Department of the BAA [QRL 113].

The BAA's recent published material is more relevant to our general area. It covers passengers and airport employees.

Origin and destination surveys were carried out for South-east airports [QRL 119] and Scottish airports [QRL 116] in 1975. In both cases, National Opinion Polls did the fieldwork but there is a difference between the two in methodology. For South-east airports—Heathrow, Gatwick and Luton—the BAA could aim at its main objective of measuring pressure on facilities in particular road transport at peak times. For Scottish airports figures were derived from part of the CAA origin and destination survey being carried out (see Subsection 2.1.4 and [QRL 102]).

The South-east study was made at each of the three airports in July/August, the latter being a peak period for departures from the UK and hence, it was hoped, for private transport to and from the airports. The usual questions on origin and destination, residence, reasons for journey and methods of land transport were asked. Sampling was made by the interviewer questioning the fifth person seen at the air terminals after completion of the last interview rather than on a time basis. The Scottish survey was carried out from July to November as part of the CAA programme and BAA abstracted results from the first 6 weeks, 21 July to 31 August. Sampling was then as for [QRL 102]. Questions were as for the South-east airports survey with an additional question covering business passengers in the oil industry and additional estimates of transfer passengers were made: 25 per cent for Aberdeen and Prestwick, 4 per cent for Glasgow and 2 per cent for Edinburgh.

This brings us to the report of a survey on transfer passengers in Heathrow for 1975 [QRL 131]. This is the first such published survey carried out for an airport where the problem has been supposed to cover approximately 2 million passengers who will not appear in the regular statistics.

Two weeks were chosen in 1975—4–10 August and 6–12 September. One-tenth of those leaving 'airside' departure lounges were briefly interviewed for 15 hours of the day (a 97 per cent coverage of the population). Using this technique, figures were obtained on 'airside' transferring passengers as well as the 'land-side' passengers—who already appear in the statistics of airports. The interview form was short—one side—and only involved one set of questions for those who had not arrived on another flight in the last 24 hours. Thus, for the first time, details of passengers changing flights without going through Customs facilities were extracted. (See Subsection 3.2.1 for a fuller discussion of the problems of estimating 'passengers'.)

The survey established that for the 1975 summer period, 44 per cent of transfer passengers would not be included in the normal airport count. Questions were also asked about length of time spent at the airport, baggage carried and size of party and a good picture of the facilities used by such passengers thus gained.

The other recently published material by the BAA is also innovatory and covers airport workers at seven of the BAA airports. Its results were published with a discussion of the methodology in 1975. Two main surveys were done. The first, at Heathrow, Gatwick and Stansted, covered the main South-east airports except Luton [QRL 132]. The second deals with the four Scottish airports analysed for the origin and destination survey [QRL 133].

Figures are given on numbers working, by job classification, length of service, place of residence, hours worked and time taken to get to work and transport used. A sample of employers was taken such that all organizations with a high number of employees were taken and others were selected with probability proportional to number of employees. The details varied between airports with the different target numbers arrived at but the method —block selection from lists of employees with a constant interval—was similar for all airports. The selected employers were then asked to distribute questionnaires to all employees and this was done by all except 2 employers (at Heathrow). The response rate was between 50 and 70 per cent.

The figures given then are the only data of any reliable basis on aspects of airport employees. Although they do not cover all airports, they give a good indication of general trends, covering as they do airports handling over three-quarters of air passengers.

One further publication, the 1976 *Heathrow Airport London Master Development Plan Report* [QRL 72], gives figures on employees and the use of road transport by air passengers, visitors and employees and combines information given by the last three surveys described.

2.2.2. *Non-BAA airports, regional demand and in-flight surveys*

A considerable number of cost-benefit studies were carried out in the 1960s and early 1970s by groups of consultants for the airport authorities—CAA, borough or private— responsible for the larger local centres. Main consultants at the beginning of the period were Alan Stratford and Associates, Atkins Planning, Sir Frederick Snow and Partners, with Software Sciences and Metra being more prominent in the 1970s. All the studies used the sources discussed so far but additional surveys were also generated on areas where official statistics were lacking. In particular the work by Alan Stratford and Partners (sometimes subcontracted from the others) led to surveys on passengers, noise and regional demand for airports.

Studies of Yorkshire and Humberside (1967) [QRL 20], Luton (1969) [QRL 85], Ballykelly (1970) [QRL 32] and Carlisle, Newcastle and Tees-side airports (1974) [QRL 96] all involved surveys aimed at about 50 per cent of local industry (stratified by size) and had a 70 per cent or more response rate when postal questionnaires were sent. Telephone surveys of travel agents were also used for some of these areas. These were all fairly small surveys but do provide the only source of information on specific holiday or business users apart from the general passenger.

With the setting up of the CAA such figures are reported in their publications as the main regional airports have been covered one by one on a consistent basis. The key, non-statistical, document, *Airport Planning: An Approach on a National Basis* [B 25], was published by the CAA in 1972 and describes the general coverage of airports. Two of the studies—on Central England [QRL 16] and the Northern Region, *Future Airport Development in the Northern Region* (1975) CAP 374, both published in 1975—use data collected by Alan Stratford and Metra of the type already described [QRL 49 and 96]. A detailed study of Wales and South-west England has also been made by the CAA [QRL 17]. A second, *Air Transport in the Scottish Highlands and Islands* [QRL 24], presents further work carried out by the authority. A summary is also given in the August issue of the 1973 CAA statistics [QRL 52]. In-flight passenger surveys were made for the CAA by all the main operators—Loganair, BEA, Scottish and Air Anglia. They were made in the first 2 weeks of April 1973. A formal industrial survey was not made but business passengers were asked whether they were connected with the oil industry. The response rate is not given and the general techniques are not adequately described. Since October 1977, a further study of the travel patterns of business passengers generated by the oil rigs has been made, see 'Sumburgh Airport: Passenger Survey 1977' in the Addendum.

In-flight surveys have generally not provided very good data. The major airlines make their own, and these will be discussed briefly in Section 2.4, but the main study made by an outside body was that of the Centre for Transport Studies at the University of Leeds under contract from the DTI, *Intercity Modal Split in Great Britain: Air v. Rail (1971)* [QRL 74]. This was a comparison of five intercity routes: London–Glasgow, London–Manchester, London–Liverpool, London–Birmingham and Glasgow–Manchester. Surveys were carried out on rail and air routes in 1968 and 1969.

Response rates to the air in-flight surveys were reasonable but not spectacular—65–75 per cent. Questions covered the usual material of the CAA Origin and Destination surveys with additional questions on income of passengers and travelling delays. The figures are interesting because of this additional information.

There is other material used for planning of individual and regional groups of airports. [QRL 4 and 5] deal with Birmingham, [QRL 33] with Bournemouth, [QRL 34] with Bristol, [QRL 57] with Norwich, [QRL 58] with Biggin Hill, [QRL 78] with Lee-on-Solent. Individual studies of Liverpool [QRL 56 and 79] and Gatwick [QRL 68 and 82] pay particular attention to the problem of aircraft noise while [QRL 73] gives the results of a survey made by Metra of Passengers and Baggage at Heathrow.

Regional surveys cover the North-west [QRL 15, 18, 19, 71 and 97], the North-east [QRL 23, 55, 89 and 95] and the Midlands [QRL 86]. Many have a small amount of hard information in them and may be focused on technical problems such as strength of the runway or design or cost of buildings. For a detailed analysis of their contents and availability see the Individual Studies section of the Quick Reference List.

2.3. International Bodies

In addition to national agencies which collect data about aviation, as might be expected, many international associations collect international material which includes UK or British airlines or airports. Some have extremely comprehensive statistics while others are limited by their memberships. All the bodies discussed here have their statistics indexed in the Quick Reference List and their coverage is also discussed in the Appendix.

2.3.1. *The International Civil Aviation Organization (ICAO)*
By far the most detailed and extensive statistics are produced by ICAO. Membership of ICAO involves the compulsory record filling by states and their airlines of internationally agreed data.

Although most figures produced are not more detailed than current CAA figures, in some respects, notably fleet personnel and finance, the historic series are better.

[B 50], the *Manual on the ICAO Statistical Programme* (1973), gives a very detailed account of methods of data collection and their coverage and limitations. Most figures have been collected since 1947.

The State is responsible for sending an annual report on aircraft accidents every calendar year (published in [QRL 11]), the civil aircraft on its register [QRL 50], and a quarterly airport Traffic Report [QRL 59]. This last only covers principal international airports so that those selected cover at least 80 per cent of international commercial traffic of all airports in the State—in the case of the UK this means Gatwick, Heathrow, Luton and Manchester, so airport figures from this source are not immediately comparable with either BAA or CAA figures.

International scheduled airlines send in the most material; a traffic report each month (published in [QRL 13]), a fleet and personnel report each calendar or fiscal year [QRL 61], the airline financial report each calendar or fiscal year [QRL 60], and, four times a year, a traffic flow report [QRL 62].

National and domestic scheduled airlines supply data for [QRL 13 and 61] but it may only emerge as a total amalgamated by the State. It is not obligatory to send the financial report [QRL 60] though UK airlines do so.

A monthly combined traffic summary is sent for all scheduled airlines.

Figures on non-schedule flights have only been produced since 1971. For international non-scheduled flights a similar range of data as for scheduled flights is collected, and non-financial statistics are published in [QRL 122]. The financial data are included in [QRL 60].

Only consolidated figures need be given for traffic fleet and personnel with domestic scheduled flights [QRL 122]. Financial details need not be given.

Both the Quick Reference List and details of coverage should make the figures clear. In general they are compatible with CAA figures and some of the financial and personnel figures published are more detailed.

There remain two isolated reports: [QRL 94] *North Atlantic Traffic Forecasts* (1966) gives figures on North Atlantic Air Traffic in the 1960s. Similar forecasts have continued run by NATS [QRL 93] (see Subsection 2.1.8).

[QRL 123] 1968—Statistical appraisal of non-scheduled commercial operations with large aircraft (1971) was the pilot for [QRL 122].

2.3.2. *The Association of European Airlines (AEA) (European Airlines Research Bureau) and the European Civil Aviation Conference (ECAC)*
Both the AEA and ECAC produce fairly specialized statistics. The AEA has published two 4-yearly reports in 1974 and 1977; [QRL 70] covers 1968–72 and [QRL 136] from 1973 onwards. These both give figures for the national airlines of the countries in the AEA—in the case of [QRL 70] only BOAC is given, more recently, figures cover BA and British Caledonian. Given this limitation there are interesting details of passenger, freight and mail traffic. Details such as number of take off and landings and length of flight are given.

[QRL 115] is a regular publication with monthly figures on scheduled intra-European passenger and cargo of member countries. Figures on passengers, freight and mail carried between these countries are given as shown in the Quick Reference List. The figures are more detailed than CAA published figures in some cases, but where this is not the case, they are comparable.

ECAC produces annual figures on non-scheduled traffic reported to member states [QRL 124]. It gives embarkations and arrivals of passengers at the UK by point of destination or origin and covers non-schedule flights only. It should make a valuable contribution to our knowledge of non-scheduled flights, but the data cannot readily be checked against other sources.

2.3.3. *The Western European Airports Association (WEAA)*
The WEAA produces monthly airport statistics. Entitled *Statistiques de traffic*, [QRL 125] covers Heathrow, Gatwick, Stansted, Glasgow/Prestwick and Edinburgh and deals with terminal and transit passengers, cargo uplifted and set down and aircraft movements by commercial/non-commercial. The figures are comparable with existing airport figures where they are published by the CAA [QRL 51 and 52].

2.3.4. *International Air Transport Association (IATA)*
[QRL 141] *World Air Transport Statistics* is another collection of airline statistics and gives annual figures for BA and British Caledonian, on passengers, freight and aircraft similar to those given by the CAA [QRL 51 and 52]. There are no new figures on the airlines so the main use of this material would be international comparison.

2.3.5. *The Organization for Economic Co-operation and Development (OECD), The European Economic Community (EEC), and the United Nations (UN)*
The three organizations in this group produce few detailed primary statistics but are included because they assemble their data from a particular point of view and for the sake of completeness.

Taking the OECD first, its publication *Tourism Policy and International Tourism in OECD Member Countries* [QRL 135] is mainly concerned with tourism. It has two tables involving civil aviation, one on terminal passengers by (international) airport and the other giving the shares of transport by foreign visitors between rail, sea and air for each OECD country.

The UN figures are given in the *Annual Bulletin of Transport Statistics for Europe* [QRL 29] and are entirely concerned with freight. They give goods entering and leaving each European country by merchandise group and split means of transport in the UK between road, sea and air. Each volume gives the figures for the last 2 years and the base year (1970).

The EEC publishes an annual compendium, *Basic Statistics of the Community* [QRL 65], which includes comparisons with other European countries, Canada, USA, Japan and the USSR and is mainly interesting because of the comparisons. The figures themselves come from IATA and ICAO and give the number of IATA member airlines in each country (i.e.

BA and British Caledonian in the UK) and for the scheduled services of these airlines, details on number of aircraft and passengers. Eurocontrol has also produced some statistics on aircraft movement but not on a regular basis. Anyone interested in their data should apply direct to them.

2.4. Individual Airline Figures

All airlines publish annual reports which, in addition to financial figures, generally give numbers of employees in a certain amount of detail. Without going through each UK airline report in detail it is worth discussing that of British Airways—the most comprehensive [QRL 37].

The 1976 report gives figures on operations, manpower and aircraft fleet over a 10-year period, including separate breakdowns for BEA and BOAC. The figures are complete but their extraction is not described. There is no list of published material although it is generally known that in-flight surveys are carried out regularly by the major airlines, for example [QRL 26], issued in 1967, gives such results for a BEA survey as does [QRL 75] (1968) for British United Airways.

One difficulty with the results is that it is not possible in most cases to marry the individual airline figures to 'UK' or 'non-UK' use and so strictly speaking data are not compatible with the other results discussed in this chapter. Balance sheets are also given which, for reasons discussed in Subsection 2.1.12, will not be exactly the same as those collected by the CAA.

2.5. The British Tourist Authority

Since 1969 the British Tourist Authority has published a *Digest of Tourist Statistics* (see *Review of United Kingdom Statistical Sources*, Vol. IV, Sections 2.2.2–2.2.5 for general comments). This mainly uses figures from the International Passenger Survey (Section 2.1.5) but the Authority makes two surveys of its own—the British Home Tourism Survey and the British National Travel Survey—which both give details of air transport within Britain. Analyses are by place of residence rather than immediate origin or destination and so form a useful supplement to the section on domestic passengers in the CAA origin and destination surveys.

2.6. The Airline Users Committee

The AUC is a consumer body set up to publish information to help the traveller. They produce free advisory booklets on air travel for the handicapped and the general use of airports which are obtainable from the CAA and at airports. It also acts as a receiver of complaints and in 1976 a document on European Air Fares was produced with interesting statistical details [QRL 64].

There has been an Annual Report since 1974 [QRL 30] which, in addition to a general description of airport developments which affect the consumer, gives an analysis of complaints received by the Committee each year, by type of service and nature of complaint (see Quick Reference List, 'Passengers: Miscellaneous' total figures). This is obviously not a statistical sample in any way but is our only source of figures on the type of things travellers find difficult at airways.

The document on Air Fares is more substantial. It is basically a collation of cost and fare data for Europe—figures such as airline staff productivity as a function of average passenger journey, and 'major items of operating costs' are given as well as fares operating on routes. Details are given in the 'Finance and Personnel': Miscellaneous sections of the Quick Reference List.

[QRL 112] (1975) on monitoring arrangements at the West London Terminal and Terminal 1 at Heathrow gives new material on passengers and their baggage. See 'Individual Studies: Individual Airports' in the Quick Reference List.

Future publications by the AUC should continue to have interesting figures and should certainly be consulted by any future researcher.

2.7. Other Individual Studies

Some useful figures come in reports which do not fit into our main categories. In particular are a few more studies on noise. In 1970 Morton-Williams and Berthoud carried out a survey of the attitudes to helicopter noise in Central London [QRL 6]. An experimental heliport was in operation during September 1970 near St. Catherine's Dock and those spending a reasonable amount of time in the area (either housewives, unemployed or local workers) during the day were questioned about the noise they heard due to the helicopters. There were 333 interviews and questions asked were similar to those asked for the Central London noise-annoyance survey [QRL 83] and the study of London Airport [QRL 92]. Schultz [QRL 8] (1972) gives figures on community noise ratings giving findings on the connection between noise heard and perceived in different circumstances.

The London Noise Survey [QRL 83] (1968) made by the Ministry of Public Building and Works compares aircraft noise with other noises in the environment as a cause of complaint in a detailed survey.

The CAA has made a detailed study [QRL 91] of noise caused by Concorde (1977) and presents complete noise, flight path, and complaints data gathered at Heathrow during the first year of scheduled Concorde operations. Complaints about particular flights are analysed by the distance of the complaints from the runway and the number of aircraft arrivals and departures at that time.

Details of findings from all four documents are given under 'Noise' in the Quick Reference List.

The Roskill Commission [QRL 53] (1971) has two appendices of statistical material some of which concern noise in particular places but it is listed under 'Individual Studies' in the Quick Reference List, containing as it does a plethora of information relating to particular places and a particular time. For those interested in the particular places covered, it is a useful source of information on data for the late 1960s.

Another government report with useful data, of a more general kind, is the Edwards report [QRL 36] (1969) (see Subsection 1.3.1) which gives planning and financial figures for the UK from 1958 (sometimes 1953) onwards. Details are also given under 'Individual Studies'.

The *Annual Abstract of Greater London Statistics* [QRL 27] gives aircraft movement freight and passenger figures for Heathrow, Gatwick, Luton, Southend, Stansted and

Westland Heliport of the type generally collected from airports but interesting because it gives all London figures together.

Two further documents relate to the London area. [QRL 111] (1967) on links for Heathrow Airport by the Transport Co-ordinating Council for London Interchanges gives figures on transport alternatives to and from Heathrow, from London and [QRL 114] (1973) by the London Chamber of Commerce and Industry gives interesting data on the business and social needs provided for by the London airports (for both see 'Airports' in the Quick Reference List).

Finally, and not least important, though unfortunately historical, in 1969 the National Board for prices and incomes issued [QRL 106] on the *Pay of Ground Staff at Aerodromes* which is the only detailed source of information on pay of all airport personnel (see 'Personnel: Airport workers and pay').

CHAPTER 3

COMMENTS ON AVAILABLE DATA

3.1. General Aviation

Figures on general aviation are more sparse than those on air transport, but numbers of non-commercial arrivals and departures at airports are given and separately analysed in the figures derived from the *Summary of Activity at Aerodromes*, [QRL 51 and 52 and predecessors] (see Subsection 2.1.1). Aircraft movements only are given but for earlier years (up to 1971) a breakdown of the airports used are given for this group. Figures are not available in detail for Channel Islands.*

The use of airports and frequency of flights by general aviation was also analysed in 1974 [QRL 126] (see Subsection 2.1.11). Here the emphasis is on aircraft; use of facilities, type of aircraft, and type of aircraft ownership, and numbers of passengers were not derived.

The censuses of traffic in non-controlled airspace [QRL 47, 48 and 87] (see Subsection 2.1.8) give a picture of air movements of many non-commercial flights which can be analysed separately. Some will also come in the figures gained from the surveys of traffic in controlled airspace [QRL 22]. Such figures, however, concentrate entirely on movements along air routes and give no idea of the number of passengers involved.

This combination of sources can give a monthly and annual estimate of use of airport facilities in the UK by non-commercial aircraft (but not the Channel Islands) and a series of pictures of their use of airspace. None of them gives any figures on the number of passengers involved or baggage carried.

3.2. Air Transport

There is a much greater body of statistics on commercial transport. Commercial airlines produce figures for themselves, government, and international agencies (see in particular Subsection 2.1.3 and Section 2.3) as do airports on most commercial flights (see Subsections 2.1.2, 2.2.1, 2.2.2 and Section 2.3).

3.2.1. *Passengers*

Figures on passengers come from two basic main sources—the airport and airline statistics (see Subsections 2.1.1 and 2.1.2) and the ATLB figures [QRL 25] for 1960–70. A third source—repeated origin and destination surveys—is primarily concerned with this area (see Subsection 2.1.4). The DTI international passenger survey is concerned with international passengers only (see Subsection 2.1.5). Differences in the coverage of these data reflect the method of their collection.

*Some, unpublished, figures are available on application to the BAA Statistics Department, see Appendix on Useful Libraries.

Airport statistics give the figures on all landside passengers, i.e. all those arriving at or leaving the airport except for those who change planes without going through Customs formalities. This includes non-fare-paying passengers and aircrew. The airline statistics—of passengers in their aircraft—gives all airside passengers, i.e. all passengers, including those who will change planes at the airport of origin or destination without going through the airport counting mechanism. It includes also those staying in their plane at the airport and continuing their journey. This definition only covers fare payers. A full discussion of the differences between these definitions is given in the Appendix to [QRL 99] (1975) on the origins and destination of passengers. The proportion of airside passengers will vary with the organization of the airport and its passport facilities for international flights. No airport will count passengers changing from domestic to domestic routes.

The BAA has got increasingly interested in this problem and in their Scottish origin and destination survey of 1975 [QRL 116] estimated the proportion of all passengers who were transferring at each airport on both air and land side (see Subsection 2.2.1). Their survey of transfer passengers at Heathrow airport [QRL 131] was aimed at finding out about transfer passengers and separate air side from land side. The results of this work have led to plans for a DTI survey covering a similar area.

The differences between revenue- and non-revenue-paying passengers and aircrew have not been analysed in such detail but providing they are allowed for when different figures are analysed should not lead to any great confusion.

The CAA origin and destination surveys (see Subsection 2.1.4) have a similar coverage to the airport statistics with much more detail on immediate destination and transport methods. A primary reason for them has been in connection with the planning of transport facilities around airports so they are discussed in more detail in Subsection 3.3.1.

The DTI International Passenger Survey, whose results are published in M.6 [QRL 46], is not concerned with domestic passengers and adds little from the point of view of a count of air passengers to the sources already described.

The British Tourist Authority gives figures on home air travel apart from Northern Ireland (see Section 2.5), but, again, these are basically concerned with tourism and add little to our knowledge of passenger movements. (A detailed description of the purposes and uses of the surveys mentioned in this paragraph is given in Volume IV of this series, *Tourism*, by L. J. Lickorish.)

The surveys by consultants (see Subsection 2.2.2) give general estimates of passenger traffic gleaned from government sources but in some cases studies have been made of local employers and tourist agents which gives a picture of business and tourist traffic. (See in particular [QRL 20, 32, 85 and 96].)

Passenger baggage is covered in all the BAA surveys on air passengers and some of the consultants' reports and is particularly dealt with in [QRL 73].

Other QRLs relevant to this section are [QRL 4, 5, 15, 17, 18, 19, 21, 23, 24, 25, 26, 28, 30, 34, 36 and 37] on individual airports and [QRL 13] the ICAO figures on airline traffic. (See Subsection 2.3.1.)

3.2.2. *Freight and mail*

As for air passengers, the main sources are *Summary of Activity at Aerodromes* and *Operating and Traffic Statistics of UK Airlines* (see Subsections 2.1.2 and 2.1.3). The results of both are now published in the CAA statistics (both monthly and annual) [QRL 51 and 52]. Figures derived from the former give figures for the weight of cargo taken up and set down by tonne. Between 1968 and 1972 figures on mail were also included but these are now given by the relevant postal department. Company stores, excess baggage and diplomatic bags are also excluded as is cargo in transit. The airline statistics on the other hand cover mail handled by postal administrations and include troops' mail, vehicles carried, excess baggage and diplomatic bags.

Both lots of figures have been collected in a consistent way over our period and are amenable to analysis. One measure of airline productivity given in the CAA volumes is 'tonne-kilometre', a composite measure including passengers and freight.

The only minor detail to watch is the change in ton to tonne between 1969 and 1970. Up to this date the imperial ton was used, then the short ton for 1 year, followed by the metric tonne from 1970 onwards.

Freight figures are not generally given by BAA or consultant documents on airports though 'baggage handled' is sometimes quantified (see Quick Reference List, 'Individual Studies').

The value of freight carried on terminal international flights is given by Customs and Excise figures [QRL 31] (see Subsection 2.1.7).

A main recent source on Freight has been that given by the CAA study of air-freight demand [QRL 12], see Subsection 2.1.6.

3.2.3. *The aircraft*

As described in Chapter 1, there are lists of all licensed aircraft and their owners by type of craft and licence and additional figures on commercial aircraft [QRL 25].

Figures on their movements are available from the *Summary of Activity at Aerodromes* by aircraft type, business and airline [QRL 51 and 52]. The airline statistics also give more details for each company of aircraft type on particular routes.

Data on aircraft movements are provided by the ATC surveys of air traffic (described in Subsection 2.1.8).

Each of these sources gives adequate statistics on traffic involved in air transport from their particular points of view but cannot be expected to be compatible. The airport statistics are concerned with movement of aircraft to and from the airport, airline statistics have an interest in type of craft using particular routes, while the concern of ATC is traffic density on different air routes.

3.2.4. *Accidents*

Air accident figures are given by NATS (see Subsection 2.1.9) and ICAO (see Subsection 2.3.1). In addition to published figures on accidents, both at take off and landing and *en route* by cause, and a special section on *en route* collisions and near misses (since 1971) the CAA has a considerable literature on the effects of air-route structure on the probability of air accidents and air misses. [QRL 1] relates the two and [B 2] and [B 3] describe the methodological problems involved.

A main difficulty with the accident figures is not their coverage, but their meaning. Risks may be analysed in terms of aircraft miles, air passenger miles, air passenger or aircraft flights, or aircraft stage of flight (landing and take off carry more risk than *en route* flying however long or densely populated the route).

The figures have, however, been collected over a long period and enable studies to be made over time of accident risks by aircraft type, airline and airports with different Air Traffic Control facilities.

3.3. Airports

In recent years there has been an increasing interest in the planning and management of airports especially from the point of view of their effect on the environment. The Roskill Commission on the placing of a third London airport was one of many studies made on individual airports or potential sites by the CAA and consultants in the late 1960s and early 1970s (see Subsection 2.2.2 and Section 2.7). Such studies tended to use material already published and described elsewhere in this chapter, but extra work was also done in some cases to enable cost-benefit studies to be made. Although the CAA documents, commenting on the studies *Airport Development in the Central England Area* (1975) [QRL 16] and a similar work on Wales and South-West England (1976) [QRL 67] were critical of some of their conclusions—based on the weightings of results—the basic statistics collected were not queried.

The main area of interest covered by such studies and other material on airports covers transport facilities around airports, aircraft noise and employment.

3.3.1. *Transport facilities around airports*

As mentioned earlier on passengers (Subsection 3.2.1), both the CAA and earlier DTI origin and destination surveys ask questions about the most recent origin and immediate destination of passengers in an attempt to see which basic routes will be most used in the immediate vicinity of the airports studied. The DTI international passenger survey [QRL 46] also uses this system (see Subsection 2.1.5). This means that there is a series of views of immediate airport-generated journey patterns in the vicinity of the major airports coupled with quarterly figures for journeys of international passengers. Methods of ground transport are also known. Heathrow and Gatwick in particular are very well covered by the figures, having been studied in three of the main origin and destination surveys undertaken by the DTI (see Subsection 2.1.4) [QRL 84, 101, 102].

The BAA airports have had additional figures collected on them, from both the point of view of passenger travel and general traffic generated (see Subsection 2.2.1) [QRL 80, 81, 128, 129, 116, 119]. All their airports have had passenger-movement studies made on them in conjunction with the CAA, and additional work has been carried out on the movements of airport personnel and general ground traffic.

General traffic flows for Heathrow, Stansted and Gatwick have been measured by a series of surveys, and mechanical counts are also made of important routes around the airports at peak traffic times [QRL 113]. The surveys of airport employees give additional figures on background travelling habits around the airports [QRL 132 and 133].

Some of the consultant studies on airports also look at this area. The section 'Transport to and from the Airport' in the Quick Reference List gives the detailed references.

3.3.2. *Noise*

The measurement of aircraft noise and its effects is complicated by its context. Physical measures can be made of the noise levels produced by different types of aircraft at different points of flight operation and these are carefully made when aircraft prototypes are produced and in subsequent retests of models and routine checks by the airlines. Such figures are specified for each aircraft type with limits and listed by the DTI as described in the Noise Advisory Council document (1974) *Aircraft Engine Noise Research* [B 19]. The noise foot prints produced by an individual aircraft are also given in [QRL 90, 91 and 92].

The actual annoyance or physical distress caused by such noise levels is much more difficult to measure, depending as it does on the configuration of flight paths and stage of flight reached in relation to the surrounding population and the density of that population.

We also know that figures are to some extent modified by the respondent's knowledge of what he is hearing. Appendix X of the Wilson Report [QRL 92] gives the results of a test made at the National Physical Laboratory in Farnborough. Sixty people were asked to judge the annoyance value of different sounds. In general aircraft noise was perceived as 'very noisy' when 93 decibels were reached compared with 80 for motor vehicles. In the same way when a scale of annoyance was used, noise heard outside was considered 'annoying' at 105 decibels while that heard inside a building was disliked to the same extent at 87 decibels.

Two major surveys of aircraft noise have been made in this country—both in the Heathrow area [QRL 92 and 117] (see Subsection 2.1.10). They are similar in approach though the methodology of the second is more complicated. Both attempt to connect the physical noise level in particular areas—measured in loudness and duration of flights and their frequency—and the attitudes of the inhabitants of the areas. Particular attention is paid to any conditioning effect where residents have lived in the zone for some time. Night flying is analysed separately as are the figures for old people and different social groups. (See Subsection 2.1.10 for details of the DTI noise surveys and Section 2.7 for some other studies.)

In both major surveys an attempt was made to form a scale of noise annoyance and produce sound contours on the Heathrow area using the objective figures on sound level as a base. The first survey derived a scale that combined noise level and frequency (the Wilson index). Contours using this index are given in DTI (1973) *Action against Aircraft Noise: Progress Report* [B 17] and such contours are used for some of the airport-planning documents described in Subsection 2.2.2. See [QRL 9, 15, 16, 17, 18, 19, 21, 33, 34, 53, 56, 68, 82, 86, 96 and 120].

The second survey found a threshold effect in noise toleration in that frequency of flights was seen by the population to be less annoying than the noise level after a certain level of noise had been reached. This threw some doubt on the original index. A research subcommittee of the Noise Advisory Council considered this problem in 1972 and no change was made despite the fact that most measures in other countries are less dependent on the number of aircraft movements than our own.

An idea of the general annoyance from aircraft noise in the London area can also be gained from a survey carried out by the same agents as the first airport survey for the Building Research Station of the Ministry of Public Building and Works (1968) [QRL 83]. In most areas of Central London, where the Noise Number Index can be quite high, other sounds are more generally mentioned by respondents to the questionnaire.

None of these surveys studies the effects on health of the general population as opposed to their subjective reaction. The Wilson Committee mentioned the possibility but decided that even if it were possible to isolate the effects of aircraft noise, extreme effects would be too rare for analysis.

The problem of weighing the social annoyance of noise against the safety problem in aircraft control of noise abatement measures is described in a 1971 Noise Abatement Council document [B 20], *Flight Routing near Airports*, which has technical comments from the pilot's point of view by BALPA.

3.3.3. *Employment*

Perhaps the most deficient area in the whole field of civil aviation is that of employment in the airport and around its area although the situation is improving. The BAA have made their surveys of airport workers [QRL 132 and 133] at seven of their airports (see Subsection 2.2.1) and the annual report also gives background figures for all BAA airport workers [QRL 35]. The *Annual Abstract of Statistics* also gives annual figures on airport workers [QRL 28] as does *Transport Statistics Great Britain* [QRL 137]. For figures on the pay and conditions of airport workers in 1969 see [QRL 106] (described in Section 2.7).

When it comes to estimates of regional employment generated by the airport, there are results in individual consultants' reports (see Subsection 2.2.2). In particular [QRL 19, 20, 21, 33, 49, 89, 107, 116, 118 and 137] all contain some figures on local employment or airport employment. See the Quick Reference List, 'Individual Studies', for details.

3.4. Personnel

Figures on airline personnel are more cut and dried but hardly more full and are given in airlines annual reports and by ICAO [QRL 61] by type of work. As far as pilots are concerned, we have a list of commercial and general aviation pilots granted licences to fly. In the case of commercial pilots, tests are stringent, so a general standard of health can be assumed though no other information is generally available about pilots and navigators.

3.5. Financial Statistics

The main sources of financial statistics on airlines are given in Subsections 2.1.12 and 2.3.1. CAA sources are not always compatible with ICAO or company accounts because they remove income and expenditure not connected with Civil Aviation.

When studies of individual airports have been made (see Subsection 2.2.2) there have been frequent attempts at cost-benefit analysis or assessment, at least of costs of new building. These studies can be found under 'Individual Studies' in the Quick Reference List, but [QRL 5, 15, 16, 17, 18, 19, 20, 21, 32, 33 and 53] especially should be noted.

CHAPTER 4

COMMENTS AND SUGGESTIONS

4.1. The Cataloguing and Description of Sources

As would only be expected in such a new area, the main national figures on Civil Aviation covered in this volume are collected by central government and its agencies. The main problems with the statistics produced stem from one main source—the rapid change in government departmental responsibility for different aspects of Civil Aviation since the war.

The main changes were outlined in Chapter 1 and permeate all discussion of sources as statistics on passengers moved from Ministry of Aviation to Board of Trade and DTI and then to CAA. At each change, no record is made of the earlier source. The CAA, for example, in its first presentation of annual statistics only refers back to relevant DTI publications and not to early (pre-1968) sources. This is true also where surveys such as the Origin and Destination surveys (Subsection 2.1.4) or the NATS surveys of controlled aircraft (see Subsection 2.1.8) are concerned. In such situations one is in greater difficulty as it is often hard to find out when the first survey was conducted. As until recently descriptions of survey design and methodology are often confined to the first such study of a series, this makes the situation doubly irritating. Generally speaking, for many of the surveys and detailed figures routinely collected, the only sources on methodology are direct communication with the individuals concerned in the work. Although in all cases workers in the area were extremely helpful, it does seem rather an inefficient way of producing material.

Even the new CAA monthly statistics began in 1973 with added articles each month covering subjects from new results in the Origin and Destination survey, air transport in the Highlands, balance of payments, and charter flights. This additional section was discontinued in June 1974 and is unindexed. Interesting articles are referred to in this text.

On the other hand, the monthly civil aviation statistics represent considerable overpublication. Every month the figures from airports and airlines (see Subsection 2.1.1) are produced in many varied breakdowns over a long retrospective period with the addition of the one new monthly figure or, in the case of quarterly figures, with no new figures at all. It would seem that a basic annual production with published figures added in monthly or quarterly would be more economic and would free resources for a list of earlier publications of such figures, the method of their collection and an amplification of the key to material. This last in most cases is still as brief as in the earliest cyclostyled documents of the early 1950s.

It is easy to criticize such details, especially when an agency is new like the CAA, and it is only fair to say that even in the year while this review has been revised many new developments have been seen. Judging by recent publications on survey work particularly it seems that CAA is aware of the difficulties of assessing their data and is gradually filling the gap in reference material. [QRL 99], for example, is an extremely useful summary of the Origin and Destination surveys and recent surveys, such as [QRL 12] on air-freight users, give a careful and thorough description of their methodology.

Other producers of statistics are not guiltless in this area either. The BAA, for example, has only had a publication policy since 1975. It does, however, in any current document give the reference and results of earlier work which can be extracted from the relevant statistical branch but still produces routine work, available on request, which is not catalogued or available in the BAA library and therefore involves contact with BAA statistical and Operations Research staff to establish its existence.

On the positive side, however, this situation is rapidly changing and should mean that by the 1980s comprehensive catalogues and descriptions of surveys should make the work of the researcher in the field very much easier in its early stages.

4.2. The Coverage of Sources

As far as the coverage of sources is concerned there are two main areas of interest: the compatibility of statistics given and the scarcity of figures in certain areas.

4.2.1. *Compatibility of measures*

In Chapter 3 major differences between the main measures in each data area were discussed. While they might lead to exasperation when different sources are being combined, they could not mislead any but the careless as they are always carefully noted (however briefly). This means that in any area where two or more sources are to be used footnotes and appendices must be scoured, but the difficulties are no greater than is usual in such a situation.

Differences in definition reflect administrative differences between collectors and differences in interest between the primary analysers. They do mean, however, that it would be unwise to use origin and destination surveys to estimate the propensity of residents in different parts of London or regions of England to fly, for example, or try to estimate the number of planes flying in the busy season directly from NATS data. In both these cases, however, the primary purpose of the data collected is of such importance that one could hardly fault survey designers for not trying to fulfil secondary requirements.

4.2.2. *Insufficiencies in the data*

There are two major areas where statistics are insufficient for some purposes: general aviation and airport facilities.

(i) *General aviation*. The situation for figures on general aviation is outlined in Section 3.1. While figures of aircraft movement between airports are adequate, nothing is known of the numbers of people involved in such flights as passengers.

The one-off study of general aviation made in 1974 [QRL 126] covered such questions and gives the best picture we have of non-commercial aircraft activity.

Figures produced by the NATS censuses which have used a similar method of data collection have proved to be so biased and expensive to produce that the work has been discontinued and it is difficult not to think that the general aviation study will not have the same bias—in activity level over the period of the survey.

The only cure for this would be compulsory recording of flights over a longer period but in less detail so that activity levels come back to normal as the survey became accepted as more commonplace. This would involve legislation in the first place and considerable expense and hardly seems practicable at the moment. It does, however, mean that the 3292 planes run by business and private individuals and clubs have little known about them compared with the 578 commercial planes on the British register at the end of 1975. From many points of view this comparison is irrelevant. The passengers and freight covered and size of the aircraft concerned (almost all commercial craft are over 5700 kilogrammes while other craft are mainly below 2730 kilogrammes) mean that commercial airlines are our major concern in this area. In addition they are more generally in air-controlled airspace.

The disproportionate number of accidents involving privately owned small aircraft, however, means that this lack in data will continue to be a worry for planners.

(ii) *Airport facilities*. New work by the BAA (see Subsection 2.2.1) indicates that prospects in this area are less gloomy.

The internal organization of airports and the differences in their ownership make it difficult and perhaps irrelevant for a national scale survey to be organized. However, as airports become a large factor in the local environment as employers, destinations for traffic, and contributors of noise to the environment studies will increasingly be needed on the lines of BAA work. A paper presented by the 1972 President of the BAA at the Quiet Aircraft Symposium [B 7] discusses the social aspects of major airports and is a useful background for ideas on future work.

Certainly more needs to be known about employment conditions and prospects in the main airports. Continuing work is likely on ground traffic in their areas. So far as noise measurement is concerned, the difficulty here is choice of measure and the complexity and expense of the repeated social surveys necessary if changes in public attitudes are to be taken into account by planners.

4.2.3. *Conclusion*

The last few years have seen a dramatic improvement in the availability and presentation of the national statistics on Civil Aviation by the agencies responsible. Both the BAA and the CAA give lists of their new publications which indicate their coverage, and the CAA is increasingly issuing its own bibliographies and summaries and analyses of general material (see Addendum, [QRL 2] and [B 1]). ICAO, the other main generator of statistics in this area, in [B 50] also gives a clear account of the coverage of all their collected statistics.

The only quibble one might have with the current position is the tendency to overpublish described in Section 4.1 and the lack of indexing of volumes [QRL 51 and 52]. One new development which, if followed too often, might lead to difficulties for the researcher could arise from the publication of a survey such as that on Sumburgh Airport (see Addendum) which is not listed because it is not for sale. Perhaps, if the policy of producing specialized non-confidential documents for limited publications is to continue, they could be listed with new publications as 'shelved at the CAA library'.

If these details of listing and indexing volumes of statistics were followed it might well be that a document such as this written in 1995 referring back to 1970 onwards could take the form of a brief paper. References to the main sources and bibliographies would be given but the writer could concentrate on problems of conceptualization and measurement in different areas.

ADDENDUM ON RECENT DEVELOPMENTS

Since September 1977, CAA work on air accidents and noise annoyance has continued. In both these fields, documents have concentrated on analysing and collating the extensive figures which already exist (see Subsections 3.2.4 and 3.3.2).

The three CAA papers dealing with accident figures are:

CAA Paper 77008: *Analysis of Bird Strikes Reported by European Airlines 1972–5* (October 1977)

CAA Paper 78007: *Analysis of Bird Strikes to U.K. Registered Aircraft 1976* (May 1978)

both by J. Thorpe of the Safety Data Unit and, continuing the analyses of long-term trends in the accident figures,

CAA Paper 77027: *Fatal Accident Statistics for Passenger Air Transport Services 1960–1976* (January 1978) by S. J. Devon.

The paper on noise, produced by the CAA on behalf of the DT in June 1978, is DORA Research Paper 7812: *Noise and Sleep: A Survey of the Literature on Sleep Disturbance by Noise*. It concentrates on sources of noise due to overflying aircraft.

A selective bibliography on heliports has also appeared—CAA Paper 78005—by D. K. Sharp (April 1978), but the main new statistical work to appear has been that on the passenger traffic at Sumburgh Airport (see footnote to p. 135). This is worth describing in outline as, although printed and published and available to readers at the CAA library, *Sumburgh Airport: Passenger Survey 1977* (June 1978) is not for sale and, therefore, not in their list of new publications.

The study was made against the background of a sharp rise in users of the airport—59,000 passengers in 1972 to 397,000 in 1977—and looks at peak busy times on different routes, and average waits of passengers and operators at the airport. The figures collected are closely linked with immediate planning decisions on the running of the airport and the detailed connection between use of the airport and occupation of traveller. Figures cover a one-in-five sample for helicopter passengers and a one-in-sixteen for aircraft for 10–23 November. The methodology is clearly described as in all the recent CAA publications and the questionnaire printed. All in all, a specialized survey, but well worth examination by anyone interested in this particular area.

QUICK REFERENCE LIST—TABLE OF CONTENTS

General Aviation 154

Passengers 154
  Scheduled services 154
    All services 154
    International services 156
    Domestic services 158
  Non-scheduled services 160
    All services 160
    International services 161
    Domestic services 162
    Inclusive tours 162
    Other separate fare and ABCs 164
  Miscellaneous total figures 165
  Terminal passengers 167
  Transit passengers 170
  Origin and destination 171
    Ultimate passenger origin and destination 171
    Overnight stop 173
    Experience of air travel 174
    Passengers by income, sex, age, family structure 174
    Passengers being met/seen off 175
    Booking patterns 175
    Business passengers 175
    Miscellaneous figures 176
  Tourism 177
  By aircraft type 177
  By licence operations 178
    International, domestic, all 178

Cargo 179
  Scheduled services 179
    All services 179
    International services 182
    Domestic services 185
  Non-scheduled services 188
    All services 188

International services	190
Domestic services	191
Inclusive tours	192
Other separate fare and ABCs and other charters	192
Miscellaneous total figures	193
Licence operations	196
Aircraft type and utilization	196
Air-freight users	197
Aircraft	197
Scheduled services	197
All services	197
International services	199
Domestic services	201
Non-scheduled services	203
All services	203
International services	205
Domestic services	206
Inclusive tours	207
Other separate fare, and ABC	208
Miscellaneous totals	208
By licence operations	209
Aircraft type and utilization	209
Aircraft movements	212
Air traffic control figures	217
Air traffic census figures	218
Accidents	221
To aircraft engaged on public transport	221
To aircraft not engaged on public transport	223
Air misses	223
Mid-air collisions	224
General	225
Airports	225
General	225
Transport to and from the airport	227
By mode of transport	227
Travel to work	228
Roadside interview survey	229
Rail passenger survey	231
London Transport bus survey	231
Survey of parked cars	231
Survey of movements associated with air freight	232
Coach survey	233
Taxi survey	233
Miscellaneous	233

QUICK REFERENCE LIST

Traffic-flow figures	234
Passengers: origin and destination	236

Noise 236
    General 236
    Night operations 240
    Complaints 240

Personnel 241
    Number 241
    Expenditure 243
        Pilots and co-pilots 243
        Other cockpit personnel 243
        Cabin attendants 243
    Airport workers 244
    Pay 246
    Miscellaneous 247

Finance 247

Individual Studies 249
    Individual airports 249
    Airports by region 254
    Airlines 260
    Miscellaneous 261

QUICK REFERENCE LIST

Descriptive title	Breakdown	Frequency	Publication (see QRL Key)	Text reference and remarks
GENERAL AVIATION	See **Aircraft movements** (p. 213) and **INDIVIDUAL STUDIES** (p. 250)			
Individual airports	Birmingham			
Regional airports	Bristol			
	Lancashire			
	Midlands			
	North			
	South-east airports			
	Yorkshire			
PASSENGERS				
Scheduled services				
All services				
Seat km available	Total for UK airlines	Annual & Monthly	[QRL 51, 52]	2.1.3, 3.2.1
	By individual airline	Annual & Monthly	[QRL 51, 52]	2.1.3, 3.2.1
	By individual international scheduled airline	Annual	[QRL 13]	2.3.1, 3.2.1, 4.2.1
	By individual airline	Annual	[QRL 136]	2.3.2, 3.2.1
	By individual airline	Annual	[QRL 141]	2.3.4, 3.2.1
(Available seat miles)	By airline + total + per cent increase on previous year	Monthly	[QRL 41, 98]	2.1.3, 3.2.1
	By airline	Monthly	[QRL 42, 98]	2.1.3, 3.2.1
(Available seat miles)	Total for UK airlines	Annual & Monthly	[QRL 51, 52, 28]	2.1.3, 3.2.1, 1.3.6
Seat km used	By individual airline	Annual & Monthly	[QRL 51, 52]	2.1.3, 3.2.1
(Passenger km performed)	By individual international scheduled airline	Annual	[QRL 13]	2.3.1, 3.2.1, 4.2.1
(Revenue passenger km)	By individual airline	Annual	[QRL 136]	2.3.2, 3.2.1
(Passenger km flown)	By individual airline	Annual	[QRL 141]	2.3.4, 3.2.1
(Passenger km flown)	Total UK private companies	Annual	[QRL 28]	1.3.6, 3.2.1
Seat km used as percentage of available	Total for UK airlines	Annual & Monthly	[QRL 51, 52]	2.1.3, 3.2.1
	By airline	Annual & Monthly	[QRL 51, 52]	2.1.3, 3.2.1

QUICK REFERENCE LIST

Passenger tonne km used	Total for UK airlines (by airline)	Annual & Monthly	[QRL 51, 52, 28]	2.1.3, 3.2.1, 1.3.6
	By international scheduled airline	Annual	[QRL 13]	2.3.1, 3.2.1, 4.2.1
	By airline (including baggage)	Annual	[QRL 141]	2.3.4, 2.3.6, 3.2.1
	Total UK private companies	Annual	[QRL 28]	1.3.6, 3.2.1
(Passenger load short ton miles)	By airline + total + percentage increase on previous year	Monthly	[QRL 41]	2.1.3, 3.2.1
	By airline	Monthly	[QRL 98]	
(Passenger load short ton miles)	Total for UK airlines	Monthly	[QRL 42]	2.1.3, 3.2.1
		Annual	[QRL 137]	1.3.6, 3.2.1
No. of passengers uplifted (Passengers carried)	By airline, and total for UK airlines	Monthly & Annual	[QRL 52, 51]	2.1.3, 3.2.1
	By international scheduled airline	Annual	[QRL 13]	2.3.1, 3.2.1, 4.2.1
	Total for UK airways	Annual	[QRL 28]	
	Total for UK private companies	Annual	[QRL 28]	
	By airline for IATA North Atlantic traffic	Annual	[QRL 136]	2.3.2, 3.2.1
(Revenue passengers)	By airline	Annual	[QRL 136]	2.3.2, 3.2.1
	By airline	Annual	[QRL 141]	2.3.4, 3.2.1
	By airline + total + percentage increase on previous year	Annual	[QRL 141]	2.3.4, 3.2.1
	By airline	Monthly	[QRL 42]	2.1.3, 3.2.1
		Monthly	[QRL 98]	2.1.3, 3.2.1
	Total for UK airways	Annual	[QRL 137]	1.3.6, 3.2.1
	Percentage against chartered passengers by airport 1972		[QRL 99]	2.1.4, 3.2.1
(Passengers carried)	Between UK and abroad, aircraft registered in UK and abroad separately	Annual	[QRL 28]	1.3.6, 3.2.1
Passenger load factor (Per cent)	By individual international scheduled airline	Annual	[QRL 13, 65*]	2.3.1, 3.2.1, 4.2.1
	By individual airline for IATA North Atlantic traffic	Annual	[QRL 136]	2.3.2, 3.2.1
(Revenue passenger load factor)	By airline	Annual	[QRL 136]	2.3.2, 3.2.1
	By airline	Monthly	[QRL 141]	2.3.4, 3.2.1
	By airline + total percentage increase on previous year	Monthly	[QRL 41]	2.1.3, 3.2.1
	By airline	Monthly	[QRL 98]	2.1.3, 3.2.1
Passenger revenue US $	By airline	Annual	[QRL 136]	2.3.2, 3.2.1
Passenger revenue per passenger km US ¢	By airline	Annual	[QRL 136]	2.3.2, 3.2.1

*[QRL 65]—UK IATA airlines only.

Descriptive title	Breakdown	Frequency	Publication (see QRL Key)	Text reference and remarks
PASSENGERS (*contd.*)				
Scheduled services (*contd.*)				
All services (*contd.*)				
Percentage change in no. of passengers	By airline	Annual	[QRL 141]	2.3.4, 3.2.1
Available seats per aircraft	By airline: passenger services	Annual	[QRL 136]	2.3.2, 3.2.1
Revenue passenger per aircraft	By airline: passenger services	Annual	[QRL 136]	2.3.2, 3.2.1
International services				
Seat km available	Total for UK airlines	Annual & Monthly	[QRL 51, 65*, 52]	2.1.3, 3.2.1
	By airline	Annual & Monthly	[QRL 51, 65*, 52]	2.1.3, 3.2.1
	By international scheduled airline	Annual & Monthly	[QRL 51, 52]	2.1.3, 3.2.1
	By airline, Local Europe, Intra Europe, Intercontinental	Annual	[QRL 136]	2.3.2, 3.2.1
	By airline	Annual	[QRL 141]	2.3.4, 3.2.1
(Available seat miles)	By airline	Monthly	[QRL 41]	2.1.3, 3.2.1
		Monthly	[QRL 42]	
		Monthly	[QRL 98]	
Seat km used	Total for UK airlines by year	Annual & Monthly	[QRL 51, 65*, 52]	2.1.3, 3.2.1, 1.3.6
	By airline	Annual	[QRL 28]	
		Annual & Monthly	[QRL 51, 52]	2.1.3, 3.2.1
(Passenger km performed)	By international scheduled airline	Annual & Monthly	[QRL 13]	2.3.1, 3.2.1, 4.2.1
(Revenue passenger km)	By individual airline, Local Europe, Intra Europe, Intercontinental	Annual	[QRL 136]	2.3.2, 3.2.1
(Passenger miles flown)	By airline	Annual	[QRL 141]	2.3.4, 3.2.1
	By airline	Monthly	[QRL 41]	2.1.3, 3.2.1
		Monthly	[QRL 42]	
		Monthly	[QRL 98]	
(Passenger km flown)	Total for UK airlines	Annual	[QRL 137]	1.3.6, 3.2.1
	Total for UK private companies	Annual	[QRL 28]	1.3.6

QUICK REFERENCE LIST

Seat km used as percentage of available	Total for UK airlines	Annual & Monthly	[QRL 51, 52]	2.1.3, 3.2.1
	By airline	Annual & Monthly	[QRL 51, 52]	2.1.3, 3.2.1
Passenger tonne km used	Total for UK airlines	Annual & Monthly	[QRL 51, 52]	2.1.3, 3.2.1, 1.3.6
		Annual	[QRL 28]	2.1.3, 3.2.1
	By airline	Annual & Monthly	[QRL 51, 52]	2.1.3, 3.2.1
	By international scheduled airline (including baggage)	Annual & Monthly	[QRL 13]	2.3.1, 3.2.1, 4.2.1
(Passenger load short ton miles)	By airline	Annual	[QRL 141]	2.3.4, 3.2.1
	By airline	Monthly	[QRL 41]	2.1.3, 3.2.1
		Monthly	[QRL 42]	
		Monthly	[QRL 98]	
No. of passengers uplifted	Total for UK airlines	Annual	[QRL 137]	1.3.6, 3.2.1
	Total for UK private companies	Annual	[QRL 28]	1.3.6, 3.2.1
	By individual airline	Annual & Monthly	[QRL 51, 52]	2.1.3, 3.2.1
(Passengers carried)	By international scheduled airline	Annual & Monthly	[QRL 13]	2.3.1, 3.2.1, 4.2.1
(Revenue passengers)	By airline, Local Europe, Intra Europe, Intercontinental	Annual	[QRL 136]	2.3.2, 3.2.1
(Passengers carried)	By individual airline	Annual	[QRL 141]	2.3.4, 3.2.1
	By airline	Monthly	[QRL 41, 42, 98]	1.1.3, 2.1.3, 3.2.1
	Total for UK airlines	Annual	[QRL 137]	1.3.6, 3.2.1
	By airline and flight stage	Monthly	[QRL 62]	2.3.1, 3.2.1
	By airport	Annual & Monthly	[QRL 59]	2.3.1, 3.2.1
	By flight stage and airline	Monthly	[QRL 62]	2.3.1, 3.2.1
	Intra European traffic. By two countries	Monthly	[QRL 115]	2.3.2, 3.2.1, 4.2.1
	North Atlantic traffic. BOAC only	1968–72	[QRL 70]	2.3.2, 3.2.1
(Passengers carried)	Total for UK airways and UK private companies separately	Annual	[QRL 28]	1.3.6, 3.2.1
Air passenger traffic	By UK and foreign airports and by year	Annual	[QRL 31]	2.1.2, 3.2.1
No. of seats available per aircraft	By international scheduled airlines	Annual	[QRL 61]	2.3.1, 3.2.1
	Local Europe, Intra Europe and Intercontinental and overseas traffic separately. Passenger services. By airline	Annual	[QRL 136]	2.3.2, 3.2.1

*[QRL 65]—UK IATA airlines only.

Descriptive title	Breakdown	Frequency	Publication (see QRL Key)	Text reference and remarks
PASSENGERS (contd.)				
Scheduled services (contd.)				
International services (contd.)				
No. of passengers per aircraft (Revenue passenger per aircraft)	By airlines	Annual	[QRL 61]	2.3.1, 3.2.1
	Local Europe, Intra Europe and Intercontinental overseas traffic separately. Passenger services, By airline	Annual	[QRL 136]	2.3.2, 3.2.1
Passenger load factor	By airline	Annual	[QRL 61]	2.3.1, 3.2.1
	By individual international scheduled airline	Annual & Monthly	[QRL 13]	2.3.1, 3.2.1, 4.2.1
	By airline, Local Europe, Intra Europe, Intercontinental	Annual	[QRL 136]	2.3.2, 3.2.1
	By airline	Annual	[QRL 141]	2.3.4, 3.2.1
	By airline	Monthly	[QRL 41]	1.1.3, 2.1.3, 3.2.1
		Monthly	[QRL 42]	
		Monthly	[QRL 98]	
	By airline and flight stage	Monthly	[QRL 62]	2.3.1, 3.2.1
	By flight stage and airline	Monthly	[QRL 62]	2.3.1, 3.2.1
	North Atlantic traffic. BOAC only	1968–72	[QRL 70]	2.3.2, 3.2.1
Passenger load (kg)	By airline	Annual	[QRL 61]	2.3.1, 3.2.1
Passenger revenue US $	By individual airline, Local Europe, Intra Europe, Intercontinental	Annual	[QRL 136]	2.3.2, 3.2.1
Passenger revenue per passenger km US ¢	By airline, Local Europe, Intra Europe, Intercontinental	Annual	[QRL 136]	2.3.2, 3.2.1
International air passenger traffic	By routes: UK airport and foreign airport	Quarterly	[QRL 44]	2.1.2, 3.2.1
Passengers embarked and disembarked (separately.)	By airport	Annual & Monthly	[QRL 59]	2.3.1, 3.2.1
Direct transit	By airport	Annual & Monthly	[QRL 39]	2.3.1, 3.2.1
Passenger seats available	By airline and flight stage	Monthly	[QRL 62]	2.3.1, 3.2.1
	By flight stage and airline	Monthly	[QRL 62]	2.3.1, 3.2.1
	North Atlantic traffic. BOAC only		[QRL 70]	2.3.2, 3.2.1
Domestic services				
Seat km available	By airline	Annual	[QRL 51]	2.1.3, 3.2.1

QUICK REFERENCE LIST

	By airline	Monthly	[QRL 52]	2.1.3, 3.2.1
	By international scheduled airline		[QRL 13]	2.3.1, 3.2.1, 4.2.1
	By domestic airline	Annual & Monthly		
	By airline	Annual	[QRL 13]	2.3.1, 3.2.1, 4.2.1
	By airline	Annual	[QRL 136]	2.3.2, 3.2.1
	By airline	Annual	[QRL 141]	2.3.4, 3.2.1
(Available seat miles)	By airline	Annual & Monthly	[QRL 41, 42, 98]	1.1.3, 2.1.2, 3.2.1
Seat km used	Total for UK airlines	Annual & Monthly	[QRL 51, 52]	2.1.3, 3.2.1
	By airline		[QRL 51, 52]	2.1.3, 3.2.1
(Passenger km performed)	By international scheduled airline	Annual & Monthly	[QRL 13]	2.3.1, 3.2.1
	By domestic scheduled airline	Annual	[QRL 13]	2.3.1, 3.2.1
(Revenue passenger km)	By airline	Annual	[QRL 136]	2.3.2, 3.2.1
(Passenger km flown)	By airline	Annual	[QRL 141]	2.3.4, 3.2.1
(Passenger km flown)	Total for UK airlines	Annual	[QRL 137]	1.3.6, 3.2.1
(Passenger miles flown)	Total for domestic scheduled air services	Annual	[QRL 137]	1.3.6, 3.2.1
(Passenger km flown)	Total for Great Britain, domestic scheduled airlines	Annual	[QRL 28]	1.3.6, 3.2.1
(Passenger km flown)	Total for UK airways	Annual	[QRL 28]	1.3.6, 3.2.1
(Passenger km flown)	Total for UK private companies	Annual	[QRL 28]	1.3.6, 3.2.1
Seat km used as percentage of available	Total for UK airlines	Annual & Monthly	[QRL 51, 52]	2.1.2, 3.2.1
	By individual airline	Annual & Monthly	[QRL 51, 52, 28]	2.1.3, 3.2.1
Passenger tonne km used	Total for UK airlines	Annual & Monthly	[QRL 51, 52]	2.1.3, 3.2.1
	By airline	Annual & Monthly	[QRL 51, 52]	2.1.3, 3.2.1
	By international scheduled airline	Annual & Monthly	[QRL 13]	2.3.1, 3.2.1
	By domestic scheduled airline	Annual	[QRL 13]	2.3.1, 3.2.1
	By airline (including baggage)	Annual	[QRL 141]	2.3.4, 3.2.1
(Passenger load short ton miles)	By airline	Monthly	[QRL 41, 42, 98]	2.1.2, 3.2.1
	Total for UK airlines	Annual	[QRL 137]	1.3.6, 3.2.1
	Total for UK private companies	Annual	[QRL 28]	1.3.6, 3.2.1
No. of passengers uplifted	By individual airline	Annual & Monthly	[QRL 51, 52]	2.1.3, 3.2.1

160   CIVIL AVIATION

Descriptive title	Breakdown	Frequency	Publication (see QRL Key)	Text reference and remarks
PASSENGERS (contd.) **Scheduled services** (contd.) *Domestic services* (contd.)				
(Passengers carried)	By international scheduled airline	Annual & Monthly	[QRL 13]	2.3.1, 3.2.1
	By domestic scheduled airline	Annual & Monthly	[QRL 13]	2.3.1, 3.2.1
(Revenue passengers)	By airline	Annual	[QRL 136]	2.3.2, 3.2.1
	By airline	Annual	[QRL 141]	2.3.4, 3.2.1
	Total for UK airlines	Annual	[QRL 137]	1.3.6, 3.2.1
	Total for domestic scheduled air services	Annual	[QRL 104]	2.1.1, 3.2.1
	Total for UK airways and UK private companies separately	Annual	[QRL 28]	1.3.6, 3.2.1
No. of seats available per aircraft	By domestic scheduled airlines	Annual	[QRL 61]	2.3.1, 3.2.1
	By airline. Passenger services	Annual	[QRL 136]	2.3.2, 3.2.1
No. of passengers per aircraft	By airline	Annual	[QRL 61]	2.3.1, 3.2.1
(Revenue passengers per aircraft)	By airline. Passenger services	Annual	[QRL 136]	2.3.2, 3.2.1
Passengers load factor	By airline	Annual	[QRL 61]	2.3.1, 3.2.1
	By international airline	Annual & Monthly	[QRL 13]	2.3.1, 3.2.1
(Per cent)	By domestic airline	Annual	[QRL 13]	2.3.1, 3.2.1
	By domestic airline	Annual	[QRL 136]	2.3.2, 3.2.1
	By airline	Monthly	[QRL 41, 42, 98]	2.1.3, 3.2.1
Passenger load (kg)	By airline	Annual	[QRL 61]	2.3.1, 3.2.1
Passenger revenue US $	By individual airline	Annual	[QRL 136]	2.3.2, 3.2.1
Passenger revenue per passenger km US ¢	By individual airline	Annual	[QRL 136]	2.3.1, 3.2.1
Non-scheduled services* *All services*				
Seat km available	By airline	Annual & Monthly	[QRL 51, 52]	2.1.3, 3.2.1
Seat km used	By airline	Annual & Monthly	[QRL 51, 52]	2.1.3, 3.2.1
(Passenger km)	By non-scheduled operating airlines	Annual	[QRL 122]	2.3.1, 3.2.1

*See also **Terminal passengers** and **Transit passengers**, pp. 167–71.

(Passenger km)	By scheduled airlines	Annual	[QRL 122]	2.3.1, 3.2.1
(Passenger km)	By international airline	Annual & Monthly	[QRL 13]	2.3.1, 3.2.1
(Passenger km)	By airline	Annual	[QRL 141]	2.3.4, 3.2.1
Seat km used as percentage available	By airline	Annual & Monthly	[QRL 51, 52]	2.1.3, 3.2.1
Passenger tonne km used	By individual airline	Annual & Monthly	[QRL 51, 52]	2.1.3, 3.2.1
No. of passengers uplifted	By individual airlines	Annual & Monthly	[QRL 51, 52]	2.1.3, 3.2.1
(Passengers carried)	By airline + total + percentage increase on previous year	Monthly	[QRL 41, 98]	2.1.3, 3.2.1
	Between UK and abroad. Aircraft registered in UK and abroad separately	Annual	[QRL 28]	1.3.6, 3.2.1
Average passengers carried per aircraft	By non-scheduled operating airlines	Annual	[QRL 122]	2.3.1, 3.2.1
International air passenger traffic	By routes: UK airport and foreign airports	Monthly average	[QRL 52]	2.1.3, 3.2.1
International services				
Seat km available	By individual airlines	Annual & Monthly	[QRL 51, 52]	2.1.3, 3.2.1
Seat km used	By individual airlines	Annual & Monthly	[QRL 51, 52]	2.1.3, 3.2.1
(Passenger km)	By non-scheduled operating airlines	Annual & Monthly	[QRL 122]	2.3.1, 3.2.1
(Passenger km)	By scheduled airlines. Non-scheduled revenue traffic	Annual	[QRL 122]	2.3.1, 3.2.1
(Passenger km)	By international scheduled airline	Annual & Monthly	[QRL 13]	2.3.1, 3.2.1
(Passenger km)	By individual airline	Annual	[QRL 141]	2.3.4, 3.2.1
Seat km used as percentage available	By airlines	Annual & Monthly	[QRL 51, 52]	2.1.3, 3.2.1
Passenger tonne km used	By individual airlines	Annual & Monthly	[QRL 51, 52]	2.1.3, 3.2.1
No. of passengers uplifted	By individual airlines	Annual & Monthly	[QRL 51, 52]	2.1.3, 3.2.1
(Per cent)	Charter (v. scheduled) by airport	Annual & Monthly	[QRL 59]	2.3.1, 3.2.1
	By airport			

162 CIVIL AVIATION

Descriptive title	Breakdown	Frequency	Publication (see QRL Key)	Text reference and remarks
PASSENGERS (contd.)				
Non-scheduled services* (contd.)				
International services (contd.)				
Air passenger traffic by charter	By UK and foreign airports	Annual	[QRL 52]	2.1.2, 3.2.1
International air passenger traffic	By routes: UK airport and foreign airport	Quarterly	[QRL 44]	2.1.2, 3.2.1
Passengers embarked and disembarked separately	By airport	Annual & Monthly	[QRL 59]	2.3.1, 3.2.1
Passengers direct transit	By airport	Annual & Monthly	[QRL 59]	2.3.1, 3.2.1
Domestic services				
Seat km available	By airlines	Annual & Monthly	[QRL 51, 52]	2.1.2, 3.2.1
Seat km used	By airlines	Annual & Monthly	[QRL 51, 52]	2.1.2, 3.2.1
(Passenger km)	By non-scheduled operating airlines	Annual	[QRL 122]	2.3.1, 3.2.1
(Passenger km performed)	By international scheduled airline	Annual & Monthly	[QRL 13]	2.3.1, 3.2.1
(Passenger km performed)	By domestic scheduled airline	Annual	[QRL 13]	2.3.1, 3.2.1
(Passenger km flown)	By airline	Annual	[QRL 141]	2.3.4, 3.2.1
Seat km used as percentage available	By individual airlines	Annual & Monthly	[QRL 51, 52]	2.1.2, 3.2.1
Passenger tonne km used	By individual airlines	Annual & Monthly	[QRL 51, 52]	2.1.2, 3.2.1
No. of passengers uplifted	By individual airlines	Annual & Monthly	[QRL 51, 52]	2.1.2, 3.2.1
Inclusive tours				
Seat km available	Total for UK airlines	Annual & Monthly	[QRL 51, 52]	2.1.2, 3.2.1
(Available seat miles)	By airline: international, domestic, and total ITCs	Monthly	[QRL 42, 98]	2.1.3, 3.2.1
Seat km used	Total for UK airlines	Annual	[QRL 28]	1.3.6, 3.2.1
	Total for UK airlines by year	Annual & Monthly	[QRL 51, 52]	2.1.2, 3.2.1

*See also **Terminal passengers** and **Transit passengers**, pp. 167–71.

QUICK REFERENCE LIST

(Passenger km)	By non-scheduled operating airlines, international traffic	Annual	[QRL 122]	2.3.1, 3.2.1
(Passenger km)	By non-scheduled operating airlines, international traffic	Annual & Monthly	[QRL 122]	2.3.1, 3.2.1
(Passenger km)	By non-scheduled operating airlines: international and domestic	Annual	[QRL 122]	2.3.1, 3.2.1
(Passenger miles)	By airline: international domestic and total ITCs	Monthly	[QRL 42, 98]	2.1.3, 3.2.1
(Passenger km)	By individual airlines for international traffic as percentage of total	Annual	[QRL 122]	2.3.1, 3.2.1
Seat km used as percentage available	Total for UK airlines	Annual	[QRL 28]	1.3.6, 3.2.1
	Total for UK airlines	Annual & Monthly	[QRL 51, 52]	2.1.2, 3.2.1
Passengers carried	Total for UK airlines	Annual	[QRL 28]	1.3.6, 3.2.1
	Total for UK airlines	Annual & Monthly	[QRL 51, 52]	2.1.2, 3.2.1
	By airline: international, domestic and total ITCs	Monthly	[QRL 42, 98]	2.1.3, 3.2.1
	Intra ECAC traffic: for UK	Monthly	[QRL 124]	2.3.2, 3.2.1
	On AEA airlines between ECAC member states, by season	Annual	[QRL 124]	2.3.2, 3.2.1
	All UK and foreign airlines. Outward passengers no. & percentage change over previous year	Annual	[QRL 25]	1.3.6, 3.2.1
Average distance per passenger	Total for UK airways	Annual	[QRL 28]	1.3.6, 3.2.1
	Total for UK airlines	Annual & Monthly	[QRL 51, 52]	2.1.2, 3.2.1
Passengers departing from UK airports on ITC flights	Total for UK airlines	Annual	[QRL 28]	1.3.6, 3.2.1
	By season, by airline totals, origin of traffic and destination	Annual	[QRL 51]	2.1.2, 3.2.1
Passenger load factor	By airline for international domestic, total ITCs	Monthly	[QRL 42, 98]	2.1.3, 3.2.1
Passengers embarked from UK	For destinations in other ECAC member states two seasons winter/summer	Annual	[QRL 124]	2.3.2, 3.2.1
	For destinations in non-ECAC states in Europe, Mediterranean, Middle East and North Africa, two seasons	Annual	[QRL 124]	2.3.2, 3.2.1
	For intercontinental destinations, and seasons	Annual	[QRL 124]	2.3.2, 3.2.1
	To Spain and Portugal (by area by seasons)	Annual	[QRL 124]	2.3.2, 3.2.1

164　　CIVIL AVIATION

Descriptive title	Breakdown	Frequency	Publication (see QRL Key)	Text reference and remarks
PASSENGERS (contd.)				
Non-scheduled services* (contd.)				
Inclusive tours (contd.)				
(On outbound portions of ITCs)	For destinations in other ECAC member states	Annual	[QRL 124]	2.3.2, 3.2.1
(On outbound portions of ITCs)	For destinations in non-ECAC states in Europe, Mediterranean, Middle East and North Africa	Annual	[QRL 124]	2.3.2, 3.2.1
(On outbound portions of ITCs)	For intercontinental destinations	Annual	[QRL 124]	2.3.2, 3.2.1
Passengers arriving in UK	From North America, year and seasons	Annual	[QRL 124]	2.3.2, 3.2.1
Other separate fare and ABCs				
Seat km available	Total for UK airlines	Annual & Monthly	[QRL 51, 52, 28]	2.1.2, 3.2.1, 1.3.6
(Available seat miles)	By airline, international, domestic and total, other separate fare services	Monthly	[QRL 42, 98]	2.1.3, 3.2.1
Seat km used	Total for UK airlines	Annual & Monthly	[QRL 51, 52, 28]	2.1.2, 3.2.1, 1.3.6
(Passenger km)	By individual non-scheduled operating airlines, international, domestic and total	Annual	[QRL 122]	2.3.1, 3.2.1
(Passenger miles)	By airline, international, domestic and total other separate fare services	Monthly	[QRL 42, 98]	2.1.3, 3.2.1
	By individual non-scheduled operating airlines, other flights	Annual	[QRL 122]	2.3.1, 3.2.1
	By individual non-scheduled operating airlines, other flights	Monthly	[QRL 122]	2.3.1, 3.2.1
Seat km used as percentage available	Total for UK airlines	Annual & Monthly	[QRL 51, 52, 28]	2.1.2, 3.2.1, 1.3.6
Passengers carried	Total for UK airlines	Monthly	[QRL 42, 98]	2.1.2, 3.2.1, 1.3.6
	By airline, international, domestic and total other separate fare services			
	Between ECAC member states, by country, year and season	Annual	[QRL 124]	2.3.2, 3.2.1
	Between UK and abroad	Annual	[QRL 28]	1.3.6, 3.2.1

*See also **Terminal passengers** and **Transit passengers**, pp. 167–71.

QUICK REFERENCE LIST

Average distance per passenger	Total for UK airlines	Annual & Monthly	[QRL 51, 52]	2.1.2, 3.2.1
Passenger load factor	By airline, international, domestic and total other separate fare services	Monthly	[QRL 42, 98]	2.1.3, 3.2.1
Passengers embarked in UK	For destinations in non-ECAC states in Europe, Mediterranean, Middle East and North Africa, by season	Annual	[QRL 124]	2.3.2, 3.2.1
Passengers arriving in UK	For intercontinental destinations by season	Annual	[QRL 124]	2.3.2, 3.2.1
	From North America by season	Annual	[QRL 124]	2.3.2, 3.2.1
Miscellaneous total figures				
Air passenger traffic	By UK and foreign airports	Annual & Monthly	[QRL 51, 52]	2.1.2, 3.2.1
(International)	By routes: UK airport and foreign airport	Quarterly	[QRL 44]	2.1.2, 3.2.1
Air passenger traffic per cent change	By UK and foreign airports	Annual & Monthly	[QRL 51, 52]	2.1.2, 3.2.1
	By route: UK airport and foreign airport	Quarterly	[QRL 44]	2.1.2, 3.2.1
(Passengers carried)	By airline, major European air charter carrier	For 1969 & 1971	[QRL 70]	2.3.2, 3.2.1
Passengers (terminal and transit) at UK airports (and seaports) (international)	By airport	Annual	[QRL 51]	2.1.2, 3.2.1
(Terminal only)	By international airport	Annual	[QRL 135]	2.3.5, 3.2.1
Passengers at UK airports percentage change	By airport (and seaport): all and international only	Annual	[QRL 51]	2.1.2, 3.2.1
Domestic passengers by main routes	By the two airports	Annual & Monthly	[QRL 51, 52]	2.1.2, 3.2.1
(Percentage change on last year)	By the two airports	Annual	[QRL 52]	2.1.2, 3.2.1
Passenger movements between planning regions and airports	By planning region and airport	1975	[QRL 51]	2.1.2, 3.2.1
	By planning region and airport		[QRL 28]	2.1.4,
Total passengers	By airport	Annual & Monthly	[QRL 51, 52, 38, 127]	2.1.2, 3.2.1
(Terminal and transit passengers)	By airport (BAA airports)	Quarterly	[QRL 108]	2.2.1, 3.2.1
	AEA per cent of total intercontinental traffic BOAC	1974	[QRL 70]	3.3.2, 3.2.1
	By airline, major European air charter carriers	1974	[QRL 70]	2.3.2, 3.2.1
	By airport	Annual & Monthly	[QRL 125]	2.3.3, 3.2.1

Descriptive title	Breakdown	Frequency	Publication (see QRL Key)	Text reference and remarks
PASSENGERS (contd.) Miscellaneous total figures (contd.) Total passengers (Terminal and transit passengers)				
	By airport and total commercial air transport	Annual & Monthly	[QRL 59]	2.3.1, 3.2.1
	By airport and total international air transport	Annual & Monthly	[QRL 59]	2.3.1, 3.2.1
	By airport and total domestic air transport	Annual & Monthly	[QRL 59]	2.3.1, 3.2.1
	By airport ranked in order of no. of passengers	Annual & Monthly	[QRL 125]	2.3.3, 3.2.1
	Total passengers handled at UK, civil aerodromes	Annual	[QRL 28]	1.3.6, 3.2.1
Passengers embarked and disembarked	By airport and total commercial air transport	Annual & Monthly	[QRL 59]	2.3.1, 3.2.1
	By airport and total international air transport	Annual & Monthly	[QRL 59]	2.3.1, 3.2.1
	By airport and total domestic air transport	Annual & Monthly	[QRL 59]	2.3.1, 3.2.1
Passenger km performed	By international scheduled airline: international, domestic and total	Annual & Monthly	[QRL 59]	2.3.1, 3.2.1
	By domestic scheduled airline, 5 years: international, domestic, total	Annual & Monthly	[QRL 59]	2.3.1, 3.2.1
	By country	Annual	[QRL 65]	2.3.5, 3.2.1
	AEA carriers per cent share of total intercontinental traffic, BOAC only	1974	[QRL 70]	2.3.2, 3.2.1
International passenger tonne km (All services)	By individual airline	Annual	[QRL 141]	2.3.4, 3.2.1
Passengers per aircraft	By airport, average load of commercial aircraft	Annual & Monthly	[QRL 125]	2.3.3, 3.2.1
	By airport, average load of combined aircraft	Annual	[QRL 125]	2.3.3, 3.2.1
Passenger transport: consumer cost indices	Expenditure on air transport and others	Annual	[QRL 137]	1.3.6, 3.2.1
All passenger transport: by mode	Per cent of passenger km by mode of transport	Annual	[QRL 137, 104]	1.3.6, 3.2.1

QUICK REFERENCE LIST

Business and leisure passengers	Per cent by airport	1972	[QRL 99]	2.1.4, 3.2.1
Foreign and UK passengers	Per cent by airport	1972	[QRL 99]	2.1.4, 3.2.1
Types of passengers using airports	Six types by five London airports	1972	[QRL 99]	2.1.4, 3.2.1
Interline passengers	Scottish airports and NW airports	1970	[QRL 100]	2.1.4, 3.2.1
	Scottish and Central England airports by airport	1975	[QRL 102]	2.1.4, 3.2.1
Per cent of passengers UK or non-UK	Total Scottish airports	1975	[QRL 116]	2.2.1, 3.2.1
	By Scottish airport	1975	[QRL 116]	2.2.1, 3.2.1
	Total SE airports	1975	[QRL 119]	2.2.1, 3.2.1
	By SE airport	1975	[QRL 119]	2.2.1, 3.2.1
	Heathrow and Gatwick	1966 1971, 1975	[QRL 119]	2.2.1, 3.2.1
Passenger complaints	By type of service	Annual	[QRL 30]	2.6, 3.2.1
	By nature of complaint	Annual	[QRL 30]	2.6, 3.2.1
Available seat km	By country	Annual	[QRL 65]	2.3.5, 3.2.1
Passenger load factor	By country	Annual	[QRL 65]	2.3.5, 3.2.1
Comparison of air and rail travel	By fare (US $) and time. By route 5 years	Annual	[QRL 135]	2.3.5, 3.2.1
Share of transport by foreign visitors	By type of transport	Annual	[QRL 135]	2.3.5, 3.2.1
Terminal passengers				
Terminal passengers	By airport	Annual	[QRL 125]	2.1.2, 3.2.1, 2.3.3
	By airport	Quarterly	[QRL 44, 43]	2.1.2, 3.2.1
	By airport	Annual & Monthly	[QRL 51, 52, 38, 127]	2.1.2, 3.2.1
(Total traffic)	By airport	Annual	[QRL 135]	2.3.5, 3.2.1
	Total for UK airports	Annual & Monthly	[QRL 51, 52]	2.1.2, 3.2.1
	Total for UK civil aerodromes	Annual	[QRL 28]	1.3.6, 3.2.1
	By airport	1975	[QRL 100]	2.1.4, 3.2.1
	Scotland and London area airports	1968	[QRL 100]	2.1.4, 3.2.1
Percentage of terminal passengers at all UK airports	By airport	Annual	[QRL 51, 52]	2.1.2, 3.2.1
Percentage of all UK terminal passengers at airports this size and smaller	By airport	Annual	[QRL 51, 52]	2.1.2, 3.2.1
UK operators: scheduled terminal passengers	Total for UK airports	Annual & Monthly	[QRL 51, 52]	2.1.2, 3.2.1

Descriptive title	Breakdown	Frequency	Publication (see QRL Key)	Text reference and remarks
PASSENGERS (contd.)				
Terminal passengers (contd.)				
(BA and others separate)	By airports	Annual & Monthly	[QRL 51, 52]	2.1.2, 3.2.1
(Corporations and others)	By airports	Monthly	[QRL 38, 127]	2.1.2, 3.2.1
UK operators: non-scheduled terminal	Total for UK airports	Annual & Monthly	[QRL 51, 52]	2.1.2, 3.2.1
Passengers	By airport	Annual & Monthly	[QRL 51, 52]	2.1.2, 3.2.1
(Charter BA and others separate)				
(Charter corporations and others)	By airport	Monthly	[QRL 38, 98]	2.1.3, 3.2.1
Foreign operators: scheduled terminal passengers	Total for UK airports	Annual & Monthly	[QRL 51, 52]	2.1.2, 3.2.1
	By airport	Annual & Monthly	[QRL 51, 52]	2.1.2, 3.2.1
Foreign operators: non-scheduled terminal passengers (Charter)	By airport	Monthly	[QRL 42, 38]	2.1.3, 3.2.1
	Total for UK airports	Annual & Monthly	[QRL 51, 52]	2.1.2, 3.2.1
	By airport	Annual & Monthly	[QRL 51, 52, 38, 98]	2.1.2, 3.2.1
Terminal passengers: mean percentage for last 5 years	By airport	Annual	[QRL 51]	2.1.2, 3.2.1
	By airport	1964-8 & 1969-73	[QRL 99]	2.1.4, 3.2.1
Terminal passengers: percentage change on last year	By airport and year	Annual & Monthly	[QRL 51, 52]	2.1.2, 3.2.1
	By airport for total, international, domestic terminal passengers	Annual	[QRL 51, 52]	2.1.2, 3.2.1
	By airport	Annual	[QRL 135]	2.3.5, 3.2.1
	By airport	Monthly	[QRL 38, 127]	2.1.2, 3.2.1
	By airport	Quarterly	[QRL 44]	2.1.2, 3.2.1
Terminal passengers: percentage growth on previous year	Total for UK airports	Annual	[QRL 51, 52]	2.1.2, 3.2.1
International terminal passengers	By airport	Annual & Monthly	[QRL 51, 52]	2.1.2, 3.2.1
(International air traffic)	By airport	Annual	[QRL 135]	2.3.5, 3.2.1
(Per cent)	By airport	Annual	[QRL 125]	2.3.3, 3.2.1

QUICK REFERENCE LIST 169

	By airport and area of the world	Annual	[QRL 125]	2.3.3, 3.2.1
	By airport	Quarterly	[QRL 43]	2.1.2, 3.2.1
	By airport	Quarterly	[QRL 44]	2.1.2, 3.2.1
(Percentage change on last year)	By airport	Annual	[QRL 52]	2.1.2, 3.2.1
(Terminating no. and per cent)	By airport	1975	[QRL 99]	2.1.2, 3.2.1
	NW and Scottish airports, terminal and terminating	1970	[QRL 100]	2.1.4, 3.2.1
	By airport. Scotland and Central England	1975	[QRL 102]	2.1.4, 3.2.1
	London airports. Terminating and interline	1968	[QRL 101]	2.1.4, 3.2.1
	London area airports. Terminating and interline	1968	[QRL 101]	2.1.4, 3.2.1
Domestic terminal passengers	By airport	Annual & Monthly	[QRL 51, 52]	2.1.2, 3.2.1
(Domestic air traffic)	By airport for 3 years	Annual	[QRL 52]	2.1.2, 3.2.1
(Per cent)	By airport for 2 years	Annual & Monthly	[QRL 135]	2.3.5, 3.2.1
	By airport	Quarterly	[QRL 125]	2.3.3, 3.2.1
	By airport	Quarterly	[QRL 43]	2.1.2, 3.2.1
	By airport 2 years	Annual	[QRL 44]	2.1.2, 3.2.1
(Percentage change on last year)	By airport	1975	[QRL 51, 52]	2.1.2, 3.2.1
(Terminating no. and per cent)	By airport	1970	[QRL 99]	2.1.4, 3.2.1
	NW and Scottish airports, terminal and terminatory		[QRL 100]	2.1.4, 3.2.1
	By airport	Annual & Monthly	[QRL 125]	2.3.3, 3.2.1
	By airport. Scotland and Central England terminating and interline	1975	[QRL 102]	2.1.4, 3.2.1
Scheduled terminal passengers	By airport	Annual & Monthly	[QRL 125]	2.3.3, 3.2.1
Non-scheduled terminal passengers	By BAA airport	Quarterly	[QRL 108]	2.2.1, 3.2.1
(Charter)	By airport	Monthly	[QRL 125]	2.3.3, 3.2.1
	By BAA airport	Quarterly	[QRL 108]	2.2.1, 3.2.1
Composition by passenger type	International, domestic, leisure, business, UK, foreign per cent Heathrow	1968 & 1972	[QRL 99]	2.1.4, 3,2.1
(Terminating)	Total London airport	1968 & 1972	[QRL 99]	2.1.4, 3.2.1
(Terminating)	International and domestic business and leisure, NW and Scottish airports	1970	[QRL 100]	2.1.4, 3.2.1
(Terminating)	International and domestic, business and leisure, by survey airports	1971	[QRL 103]	2.1.4, 3.2.1

170 CIVIL AVIATION

Descriptive title	Breakdown	Frequency	Publication (see QRL Key)	Text reference and remarks
PASSENGERS (contd.)				
Terminal passengers (contd.)				
(Terminal)	International and domestic, business and leisure, UK and foreign charter and scheduled. For survey airports 1975	1975	[QRL 102]	2.1.4, 3.2.1
	International and domestic, business and leisure per cent, Scottish and Central England airports	1970 & 1975	[QRL 102]	2.1.4, 3.2.1
Hourly traffic flows	By airport: arrival, departure, two-way, peak hour, 30th value, 100th value, 5 per cent busy hour value	Quarterly	[QRL 105]	2.2.1, 3.2.1
Comparative standard busy route (SBR) flows	By BAA airport: arrival, departure, two-way, 9 years	Quarterly	[QRL 105]	2.2.1, 3.2.1
Ratio SBR to annual traffic ($\times 10^{-6}$)	By BAA airport: arrival, departure, two-way, 9 years	Annual	[QRL 105]	2.2.1, 3.2.1
Percentage of annual terminal passengers handled per month	By BAA airport	Annual	[QRL 105]	2.2.1, 3.2.1
Daily pattern of traffic over peak week	By BAA airport	Annual	[QRL 105]	2.2.1, 3.2.1
Percentage of arrival passenger traffic handled in each hour of an average busy day	By BAA airport	Annual	[QRL 105]	2.2.1, 3.2.1
Percentage of departure passenger traffic handled in each hour of an average busy day	By BAA airport	Annual	[QRL 105]	2.2.1, 3.2.1
Percentage of two-way passenger traffic handled in each hour of average busy day	By BAA airport	Annual	[QRL 105]	2.2.1, 3.2.1
Transit passengers				
Transit passengers	By airport	Annual & Monthly	[QRL 51, 52] [QRL 125] [QRL 38, 127]	2.1.2, 3.2.1, 2.3.3
	By airport, international scheduled, international non-scheduled, total international, total domestic flights	Annual & Monthly	[QRL 59]	2.3.1, 3.2.1

QUICK REFERENCE LIST

By airport, total commercial air transport	Annual & Monthly	[QRL 51, 52]	2.1.2, 3.2.1
By BAA airport	Quarterly	[QRL 108]	2.2.1, 3.2.1
Total for UK civil aerodromes	Annual	[QRL 28]	1.3.6, 3.2.1
By airport	Annual & Monthly	[QRL 51, 52]	2.1.2, 3.2.1
UK operators: (scheduled services) (BA and others)			
By airport	Monthly	[QRL 38, 127]	2.1.2, 3.2.1
UK operators (non-scheduled services) (BA and other charter)			
By airport	Annual & Monthly	[QRL 51, 52]	2.1.2, 3.2.1
Overseas operators (scheduled services)			
By airport	Monthly	[QRL 38, 127]	2.1.2, 3.2.1
By airport	Annual & Monthly	[QRL 51, 52]	2.1.2, 3.2.1
Overseas operators: charter flights (non-scheduled)			
By airport	Annual & Monthly	[QRL 38, 127]	2.1.2, 3.2.1
By hour of arrival/departure	1976	[QRL 131]	2.2.1, 3.2.1
Daily passenger flow by Heathrow terminal	1976	[QRL 131]	2.2.1, 3.2.1
Daily transfer passenger flow as percentage of total departing passenger flow, Heathrow			
Daily transfer passenger flow	1976	[QRL 131]	2.2.1, 3.2.1
Terminal of arrival, terminal of departure, Heathrow			
By destination as percentage of terminal passenger flow, Heathrow	1976	[QRL 131]	2.2.1, 3.2.1
Time spent between flights	1976	[QRL 131]	2.2.1, 3.2.1
Per cent by terminal of arrivals, departure period, Heathrow			
No. leaving the airport during their stay	1976	[QRL 131]	2.2.1, 3.2.1
By reason for doing so, Heathrow			
Bags to passenger ratio	1976	[QRL 131]	2.2.1, 3.2.1
By arrival or departure terminal, Heathrow			
Origin and destination			
Ultimate passenger origin and destination			
Total for each London Airport	1975	[QRL 99]	2.1.4, 3.2.1
(See journey purpose by air destination)			
By type of passenger			
Business passengers (UK and foreign residents) and leisure passengers (UK and foreign residents)			

CIVIL AVIATION

Descriptive title	Breakdown	Frequency	Publication (see QRL Key)	Text reference and remarks
PASSENGERS (contd.) **Origin and destination** (contd.) *Ultimate passenger origin and destination* (contd.)				
	Comparison of 1968 and 1972 international passengers Heathrow	1975	[QRL 99]	2.1.4, 3.2.1
	Percentage (total London airports) origin/destination from Central London	1975	[QRL 99]	2.1.4, 3.2.1
	NW and Scottish airports (by airport)	1972	[QRL 100]	2.1.4, 3.2.1
	By airports	1972	[QRL 100]	2.1.4, 3.2.1
	Per cent between Scottish and Central airports, 1975	1975	[QRL 102]	2.1.4, 3.2.1
	By airport. Scottish and Central England airports, 1975	1975	[QRL 102]	2.1.4, 3.2.1
(Surface origin and destination)	International and domestic passengers Heathrow and other UK airports 1968, origin/destination in UK, and South-east and GLC	1968	[QRL 101]	2.1.4, 3.2.1
(Business, inclusive tour holiday, other leisure, percentage)	By individual Scottish airports	1975	[QRL 116]	2.2.1, 3.2.1
(Business and leisure, percentage)	By individual South-east airports	1975	[QRL 119]	2.2.1, 3.2.1
International and domestic passengers and total	By London airports 1972	1975	[QRL 99]	2.1.4, 3.2.1
(Per cent)	Total London airports (origin/destination from Central London)	1975	[QRL 99]	2.1.4, 3.2.1
	Airports NW and Scottish 1970 (by airport)	1972	[QRL 100]	2.1.4, 3.2.1
	By airports	1972	[QRL 100]	2.1.4, 3.2.1
	Scottish and Central England airports 1970–5	1970	[QRL 100]	2.1.4, 3.2.1
Scheduled and charter (Per cent)	London Airports (origin and destination) from Central London	1975	[QRL 99]	2.1.4. 3.2.1
UK and non-UK	Areas in Scotland and rest of UK, Scottish airports total (BAA airports)	1975	[QRL 116]	2.2.1, 3.2.1
(Per cent)	By individual Scottish airport (BAA airports)	1975	[QRL 116]	2.2.1, 3.2.1
(Terminal)	By areas in Scotland, by Scottish airport (BAA airports)	1975	[QRL 116]	2.2.1, 3.2.1

QUICK REFERENCE LIST

(Surface origin)	Per cent by areas in SE and rest of UK, total SE airports (BAA airports)	1975	[QRL 119]	2.2.1, 3.2.1
(Surface origin)	Per cent by areas in SE and rest of UK, by individual SE airports (BAA airports)	1975	[QRL 119]	2.2.1, 3.2.1
All passengers	Heathrow and Gatwick 1971 and 1975. By origin	1975	[QRL 119]	2.2.1, 3.2.1
	By country of embarkation. Inward passenger flow Heathrow	Annual	[QRL 28]	1.3.6, 3.2.1
	By country of larding. UK outward passenger movement	Annual	[QRL 28]	1.3.6, 3.2.1
Terminal and transfer (by destination)	Average daily flow Heathrow	1976	[QRL 131]	2.2.1, 3.2.1
(Origin/destination)	Daily transfer passenger flow	1976	[QRL 131]	2.2.1, 3.2.1
	Daily non-business transfer passenger flow Heathrow	1976	[QRL 131]	2.2.1, 3.2.1
(Terminal)	By airport	Quarterly	[QRL 108]	2.2.1, 3.2.1
(Terminating)	By airport of origin and destination for domestic passengers	1968	[QRL 101]	2.1.4, 3.2.1
	For Heathrow and other airports. International passengers	1968	[QRL 101]	2.1.4, 3.2.1
Terminal and transfer: (interline)	Domestic international and domestic Channel Islands interline passengers through Heathrow and Gatwick 1968	1968	[QRL 101]	2.1.4, 3.2.1
(Terminal)	International and domestic passengers at London area airports 1968. UK origin and destination	1968	[QRL 101]	2.1.4, 3.2.1
Ultimate origin/destination by immediate origin/destination	For areas in UK London airports, passengers 1968	1968	[QRL 101]	2.1.4, 3.2.1
Expected travel time	Percentage of passengers from regions of O/D in time groups by airport	1972	[QRL 100]	2.1.4, 3.2.1
Overnight stop				
	Passengers departing from Heathrow and Gatwick. By origin in UK	1965	[QRL 130]	2.1.4, 3.2.1
Number stopping overnight	Passengers arriving at Heathrow and Gatwick from overseas, by destination in UK	1965	[QRL 130]	2.1.4, 3.2.1
	Passengers departing from Heathrow and Gatwick, by origin in UK	1965	[QRL 130]	2.1.4, 3.2.1
Reason for overnight stop	Passengers arriving at Heathrow and Gatwick for overseas, by destination in UK	1965	[QRL 130]	2.1.4, 3.2.1

Descriptive title	Breakdown	Frequency	Publication (see QRL Key)	Text reference and remarks
PASSENGERS (*contd.*)				
Origin and destination (*contd.*)				
Experience of air travel				
Number of times flown before	Per cent Scottish and Central England airports (two totals)	1975	[QRL 100]	2.1.4, 3.2.1
	By household income. Scottish and Central England airports (two totals)	1975	[QRL 100]	2.1.4, 3.2.1
Passengers by income, sex, age, family structure				
By income: by types of passenger	International and domestic total London airports	Annual	[QRL 99]	2.1.4, 3.2.1
	Business and leisure, total London airports	Annual	[QRL 99]	2.1.4, 3.2.1
	UK and foreign, total London airports	Annual	[QRL 99]	2.1.4, 3.2.1
	Charter and scheduled, total London airports	Annual	[QRL 99]	2.1.4, 3.2.1
	O/D in/out South-east, total London airports	Annual	[QRL 99]	2.1.4, 3.2.1
	Business, leisure total NW and Scottish airports 1970	1972	[QRL 100]	2.1.4, 3.2.1
	Business, leisure scheduled, charter, by airports	1972	[QRL 100]	2.1.4, 3.2.1
	Business, leisure, UK, foreign, domestic, International, Scottish and Central England airports 1970 (two totals)	1972	[QRL 100]	2.1.4, 3.2.1
By sex: by journey reason (Per cent)	Central England and Scottish airports (two totals) 1975	1975	[QRL 102]	2.1.4, 3.2.1
By age: by type of passenger (Per cent)	International (UK and foreign), domestic (UK and foreign), all terminating Scottish and Central England airports (two totals) 1975	1975	[QRL 102]	2.1.4, 3.2.1
By age: by route (Per cent)	Scheduled and charter, leisure passengers	1975	[QRL 99]	2.1.4, 3.2.1
By family structure: by type of passenger (Per cent)	Leisure (UK, foreign, all) total London airports	1975	[QRL 99]	2.1.4, 3.2.1
	Leisure passengers. Scottish and Central England airports (two totals) 1970	1972	[QRL 100]	2.1.4, 3.2.1

QUICK REFERENCE LIST

Passengers being met/seen off
Passengers travelling alone
  (Per cent)   By type of passenger, total London airports   1975   [QRL 99]   2.1.4, 3.2.1
  (Per cent)   By no. of people meeting (seeing off) passengers, total London airports   1975   [QRL 99]   2.1.4, 3.2.1
  (Per cent)   By five London airports and planning region, of O/D   1975   [QRL 99]   2.1.4, 3.2.1
  (Per cent)   By primary mode of transport and airport   1975   [QRL 99]   2.1.4, 3.2.1

Passengers not being met or seen off
  (Per cent)   By type of passenger, total London airports   1975   [QRL 99]   2.1.4, 3.2.1
  (Per cent)   By no. of people travelling with passenger, total London airports   1975   [QRL 99]   2.1.4, 3.2.1
  (Per cent)   By five London airports and planning region, of O/D   1975   [QRL 99]   2.1.4, 3.2.1

Percentage travelling with 0–5+ passengers
   By primary mode of transport and airport   1975   [QRL 99]   2.1.4, 3.2.1
   By number and type of passengers, total London airports   1975   [QRL 99]   2.1.4, 3.2.1

Percentage meeting or seeing off 0–5+ passengers
   By number and type of passenger, total London airports   1975   [QRL 99]   2.1.4, 3.2.1

Booking patterns
By length of time ticket booked
  (Per cent)   All passengers, total London airports   1975   [QRL 99]   2.1.4, 3.2.1
  (Per cent)   Scheduled and charter UK and foreign, international and domestic, business leisure passengers   1975   [QRL 99]   2.1.4, 3.2.1
  (Per cent)   Scheduled passengers by route 1972   1975   [QRL 99]   2.1.4, 3.2.1
   UK and foreign, scheduled and charter for business, leisure. Central England and Scottish airports 1975   1975   [QRL 102]   2.1.4, 3.2.1

Business passengers
By type of firm and by type of passenger
  (Per cent)   International (UK and foreign), domestic (UK and foreign), all: total London airports   1975   [QRL 99]   2.1.4, 3.2.1
   As above for Scottish, Central England airports (two totals)   1975   [QRL 102]   2.1.4, 3.2.1

By business of firm and by permanent residence   Parts of the world, and total, total London airports   1975   [QRL 99]   2.1.4, 3.2.1

By country of residence
  (Per cent)   No. of passengers   1975   [QRL 99]   2.1.4, 3.2.1

176   CIVIL AVIATION

Descriptive title	Breakdown	Frequency	Publication (see QRL Key)	Text reference and remarks
PASSENGERS (*contd.*)				
Origin and destination (*contd.*)				
Business passengers (*contd.*)				
Business passengers connected with oil industry (Per cent)	By individual Scottish airports, BAA airports	1975	[QRL 116]	2.2.1, 3.2.1
	Total for Scottish airports by business of firm	1975	[QRL 102]	2.1.4, 3.2.1
Daily business transfer passenger flow	Heathrow	1976	[QRL 131]	2.2.1, 3.2.1
Business passengers (Per cent)	International and domestic Scottish and Central England airports (two totals)	1975	[QRL 102]	2.2.1, 3.2.1
Miscellaneous figures	By aircraft type and aircraft origin and destination. London airports	1968	[QRL 101]	2.1.4, 3.2.1
	Totals by year for various countries, by country of landing and embarkation	Annual & Monthly	[QRL 51, 52]	2.1.2, 3.2.1
	By airport and region of origin and destination	Annual	[QRL 125]	2.3.3, 3.2.1
	By airports of origin and destination in UK (i.e. domestic O/D) (number of passengers and percentage increase)	Quarterly	[QRL 43]	2.1.2, 3.2.1
	International air passenger transport to and from UK airports (by foreign airport of origin)	Annual	[QRL 44]	2.3.5, 3.2.1
	Passenger movements between planning regions and airports: by planning region and airport	Annual	[QRL 51, 99, 102]	2.1.2, 2.1.4, 3.2.1
	Passengers carried by US airlines on routes between UK and rest of Europe, total	1975	[QRL 99]	2.1.3, 3.2.1
	Traffic flow between individual ECAC member states, no. and per cent	1974	[QRL 70]	2.3.2, 3.2.1
	Passengers departing from Heathrow and Gatwick by country of destination	1968	[QRL 130]	2.1.4, 3.2.1
	Passengers arriving at Heathrow and by country of origin	1968	[QRL 130]	2.1.4, 3.2.1

QUICK REFERENCE LIST

Tourism

Overseas visitors to the UK				
By mode of travel and country of residence	Number of visits	Annual	[QRL 63]	2.5, 3.2.1
By mode of travel, country of residence and purpose of visit		Annual	[QRL 137, 63]	1.3.6, 3.2.1, 2.5
Overseas visitors by individual country of origin	By mode of transport and percentage using each mode	Quarterly Annual	[QRL 46] [QRL 63]	2.1.5, 3.2.1 2.1.5, 3.2.1
Visits abroad by UK residents	By mode of travel and country visited	Quarterly	[QRL 46]	2.1.5, 3.2.1
	No. of visits a year	Annual	[QRL 63]	2.5, 3.2.1
	By mode of travel, countries visited and purpose of visit	Quarterly	[QRL 46]	2.1.5, 3.2.1
Total figures: visits to and from the UK	By mode of transport	Annual	[QRL 137]	1.3.6, 3.2.1
Relative shares of the main forms of transport (arrivals by sea, air, road, rail) used by foreign visitors	By country	Annual	[QRL 135]	2.3.5, 3.2.1
Journey purpose by nationality (UK and foreign)	By purpose of journey, type of flight (scheduled or charter), NW and Scottish airports	1972	[QRL 100]	2.1.4, 3.2.1
(UK, non-UK, total) (per cent)	Scottish airports separately and total (BAA airports)	1975	[QRL 116]	2.2.1, 3.2.1
(UK, non-UK, total)	Per cent SE airports separately and total (BAA airports)	1975	[QRL 119]	2.2.1, 3.2.1
Journey purpose by air destination	Per cent by SE airports (BAA airports)	1975	[QRL 119]	2.2.1, 3.2.1
	Destination and origin, daily transfer passenger flow, Heathrow	1976	[QRL 131]	2.2.1, 3.2.1
Journey purpose: business and leisure	Per cent Heathrow and Gatwick 1966, 1971, 1975	1975	[QRL 119]	2.2.1, 3.2.1
European tourist arrivals	By country and mode of transport	1974	[QRL 70]	2.3.2, 3.2.1

By aircraft type

Passenger stage flights	All airlines	Annual & Monthly	[QRL 51, 52]	2.1.2, 3.2.1
	By individual airline	Annual & Monthly	[QRL 51, 52] [QRL 42]	2.1.2, 3.2.1 2.1.3, 3.2.1
Passenger aircraft hours	All airlines	Annual & Monthly	[QRL 51, 52] [QRL 42]	2.1.2, 3.2.1 2.1.3, 3.2.1

177

Descriptive title	Breakdown	Frequency	Publication (see QRL Key)	Text reference and remarks
PASSENGERS (*contd.*)				
By aircraft type (*contd.*)				
	By airline	Annual & Monthly	[QRL 51, 52] [QRL 42]	2.1.2, 3.2.1 2.1.3, 3.2.1
Passengers carried	All airlines	Annual & Monthly	[QRL 51, 52] [QRL 42]	2.1.2, 3.2.1 2.1.3, 3.2.1
	By airline	Annual & Monthly	[QRL 51, 52] [QRL 42]	2.1.2, 3.2.1 2.1.3, 3.2.1
Passenger km (miles before 1971)	All airlines	Annual & Monthly	[QRL 51, 52] [QRL 42]	2.1.2, 3.2.1 2.1.3, 3.2.1
	By airline	Annual & Monthly	[QRL 51, 52] [QRL 42]	2.1.2, 3.2.1 2.1.3, 3.2.1
By licence operations				
International, domestic, all				
(CAA figures by airline)				
No. of passengers uplifted (total)	For class 3, 7, and exempt: international and domestic; class 5: UK and non-UK operators; class 2: advanced booking charter and other; and class 4: international and domestic, inclusive tour or other	Annual & Monthly	[QRL 51, 52] [QRL 42]	2.1.2, 3.2.1 2.1.3, 3.2.1
Seat km available: used and used as per cent available	For class 2; classes 3, 4, 7 and exempt: international, domestic; class 5: UK non-UK operator	Annual & Monthly	[QRL 51, 52] [QRL 42]	2.1.2, 3.2.1 2.1.3, 3.2.1
Variable licence charges for airline operations	By airline and year and class of licence	Annual	[QRL 51]	2.1.2, 3.2.1
No. of inclusive tour passengers uplifted	Class 2 and class 4, class 3: international and domestic	Annual & Monthly	[QRL 51, 52] [QRL 42]	2.1.2, 3.2.1 2.1.3, 3.2.1
Passenger tonne km used	Class 7 and exempt: international and domestic; class 5: UK and non-UK operators	Annual & Monthly	[QRL 51, 52] [QRL 42]	2.1.2, 3.2.1 2.1.3, 3.2.1
(By own aircraft operations and nonchargeable operations) Passenger analysis by type of licence and fare category	Operations subject to variable charge by type of licence	Annual & Monthly Monthly	[QRL 51, 52] [QRL 42] [QRL 52]	2.1.2, 3.2.1 2.1.3, 3.2.1 2.1.3, 3.2.1

QUICK REFERENCE LIST

CARGO				
Scheduled services				
All services				
Tonne km used: total	Total for UK airlines	Annual	[QRL 28, 51]	1.3.6, 2.1.3, 3.2.2
	Total for UK airlines	Monthly	[QRL 52]	2.1.3, 3.2.2
	By UK airline: passenger and cargo services	Annual & Monthly	[QRL 51, 52]	2.1.3, 3.2.2
	By international scheduled airline	Annual & Monthly	[QRL 13]	2.3.1, 3.2.2
	By all freight services	Annual & Monthly	[QRL 13]	2.3.1, 3.2.2
Short ton miles	By airline	Annual	[QRL 141]	2.3.4, 3.2.2
	By airline: all freight services	Annual	[QRL 141]	2.3.4, 3.2.2
	By airline	Monthly	[QRL 42, 98]	2.1.3, 3.2.2
	By airline: passenger, freighter, all services	Annual	[QRL 136]	2.3.2, 3.2.2
	Total UK private companies	Annual	[QRL 28]	1.3.6, 3.2.2
Tonne km used: freight	Total for UK airlines	Annual	[QRL 51, 28]	1.3.6, 2.1.3, 3.2.2
	Total for UK airlines	Monthly	[QRL 52]	2.1.3, 3.2.2
	By airline: passenger and cargo services	Annual	[QRL 51]	2.1.3, 3.2.2
	By individual airline: passenger and cargo services	Monthly	[QRL 52]	2.1.3, 3.2.2
Short ton miles	By airline	Monthly	[QRL 41]	2.1.3, 3.2.2
	By airline: passenger and freight services	Monthly	[QRL 42]	2.1.3, 3.2.2
	By international scheduled airline	Annual & Monthly	[QRL 13]	2.3.1, 3.2.2
	By all freight services	Annual & Monthly	[QRL 13]	2.3.1, 3.2.2
	By airline	Annual	[QRL 141]	2.3.4, 3.2.2
	By airline: all freight services	Monthly	[QRL 42]	2.1.3, 3.2.2
	By airline: passenger freight and all services	Annual	[QRL 136]	2.3.2, 3.2.2
Tonne km used: mail	Total for UK airlines	Annual & Monthly	[QRL 51, 52]	2.1.2, 3.2.2
	By airline: passenger and cargo services	Annual & Monthly	[QRL 51, 52]	2.1.2, 3.2.2
Short ton miles	By airline	Monthly	[QRL 41]	2.1.3, 3.2.2
	By airline: passenger and freight services	Monthly	[QRL 42]	2.1.3, 3.2.2
	By international scheduled airline	Annual & Monthly	[QRL 13]	2.3.1, 3.2.2

Descriptive title	Breakdown	Frequency	Publication (see QRL Key)	Text reference and remarks
CARGO (*contd.*) **Scheduled services** (*contd.*)* *All services* (*contd.*)				
Short ton miles	By all freight services	Annual & Monthly	[QRL 13]	2.3.1, 3.2.2
	By airline	Annual	[QRL 141]	2.3.4, 3.2.2
	By airline: passenger freighter and all services	Annual	[QRL 136]	2.3.2, 3.2.2
Total available tonne km	Total UK private companies	Annual & Monthly since 1946	[QRL 28]	1.3.6, 3.2.2
	Total UK airlines	Annual	[QRL 51, 52]	2.1.2, 3.2.2
	Total for individual UK airlines	Annual	[QRL 51]	2.1.2, 3.2.2
	By UK airlines: passenger and cargo services	Annual & Monthly	[QRL 51, 52]	2.1.2, 3.2.2, 2.1.3
Capacity short ton miles	By airline	Monthly	[QRL 41]	2.1.3, 3.2.2
	By airline: passenger and freight services	Monthly	[QRL 42]	2.1.3, 3.2.2
	By international scheduled airlines	Annual & Monthly	[QRL 13]	2.1.3, 3.2.2
	By all freight services	Annual & Monthly	[QRL 13]	2.1.3, 3.2.2
	By airline	Annual & Monthly	[QRL 141]	2.3.4, 3.2.2
	By airline: all freight services	Annual	[QRL 141]	2.3.4, 3.2.2
	By airline: passenger and freighter and all services	Annual	[QRL 136]	2.3.2, 3.2.2
	Total UK airlines, plus percentage growth on last year	Annual	[QRL 28]	1.3.6, 3.2.2
Cargo uplifted tonnes	By individual airline: passenger and cargo services	Annual & Monthly	[QRL 51, 52]	2.1.2, 3.2.2, 2.1.3
	Cargo load kg, mail load kg separately, scheduled airline: domestic and international	Annual	[QRL 61]	2.3.1, 3.2.2

*See also **Non-scheduled services**, *All services*, pp. 189, 190.

QUICK REFERENCE LIST

Freight tonnes carried	By international scheduled airline	Annual & Monthly	[QRL 13]	2.3.1, 3.2.2
	By all freight services	Annual & Monthly	[QRL 13]	2.3.1, 3.2.2
	By airline	Annual & Monthly	[QRL 141]	2.3.4, 3.2.2
Freight	By airport	Monthly	[QRL 125]	2.3.3, 3.2.2
	Total UK airways and UK private companies separately	Annual	[QRL 28]	1.3.6, 3.2.2
Freight	By airport	Monthly	[QRL 125]	2.3.3, 3.2.2
Short tons	By airline: freight and mail separately	Monthly	[QRL 41]	2.1.3, 3.2.2
	By airline: passenger and freight services: vehicles carried and rest of cargo	Monthly	[QRL 42]	2.1.3, 3.2.2
	By airport and type of operation. All mixed all cargo (BAA airports)	Quarterly	[QRL 103]	2.2.1, 3.2.2
	Freight and mail separately by airline, on passenger and freighter services	Annual	[QRL 136]	2.3.2, 3.2.2
Per cent growth on tonne kilometres available on previous year	Total for UK airlines	Annual 1946 onwards	[QRL 51]	2.1.2, 3.2.2
	By airline	Annual	[QRL 141]	2.3.4, 3.2.2
Tonne km used as percentage of tonne kilometres available	Total for UK airlines	Annual & Monthly	[QRL 51, 52]	2.1.2, 3.2.2, 2.1.3
	By airline: passenger and cargo services	Annual & Monthly	[QRL 51, 52]	2.1.3, 3.2.2
	By airline	Annual & Monthly	[QRL 52, 42]	2.1.3, 3.2.2, 2.1.2
Per cent change in tonne km used	By airline	Annual	[QRL 41]	2.1.3, 3.2.2
	By airline	Annual	[QRL 141]	2.3.4, 3.2.2
Tonne km used vehicles included in cargo (Short ton miles)	By airline: passenger and freight services	Monthly	[QRL 42]	2.1.3, 3.2.2
Freight revenue US $	By airline: passenger and freighter and all services	Annual	[QRL 136]	2.3.2, 3.2.2
Freight revenue per freight tonne km US $	By airline: passenger, freighter and all services	Annual	[QRL 136]	2.3.2, 3.2.2
Mail revenue US $	By airline	Annual	[QRL 136]	2.3.2, 3.2.2
Mail revenue per freight tonne—km US $	By airline: passenger, freighter and all services	Annual	[QRL 136]	2.3.2, 3.2.2

CIVIL AVIATION

Descriptive title	Breakdown	Frequency	Publication (see QRL Key)	Text reference and remarks
CARGO (contd.) **Scheduled services** (contd.) *International services*				
Tonne km used: total	Total for UK airlines	Annual & Monthly	[QRL 51, 52]	2.1.2, 3.2.2, 2.1.2
	By airline: passenger and cargo services	Annual & Monthly	[QRL 51, 52]	2.1.2, 3.2.2, 2.1.2
	By airline: freighter services	Annual	[QRL 136]	2.3.2, 3.2.2
Cargo scheduled. All available payload per aircraft. Tonnes carried per aircraft	By airline: freighter services	Annual	[QRL 136]	2.3.2, 3.2.2
	By international scheduled airline	Annual & Monthly	[QRL 59]	2.3.1, 3.2.2
	By all freight services	Annual & Monthly	[QRL 59]	2.3.1, 3.2.2
	By airline	Annual	[QRL 141]	2.3.4, 3.2.2
	By airline: all freight services	Annual	[QRL 141]	2.3.4, 3.2.2
	By airline: passenger and freight services	Monthly	[QRL 42]	2.1.2, 3.2.2
	By airline: passenger, freighter and all services: local Europe traffic, Intra European traffic and Intercontinental and overseas traffic	Annual	[QRL 136]	2.3.2, 3.2.2
Short ton miles	Total UK private companies	Annual	[QRL 28]	1.3.6, 3.2.2
Tonne km used: freight	Total for UK airlines	Annual	[QRL 28]	1.3.6, 3.2.2
	Total for UK airlines	Annual & Monthly	[QRL 51, 52]	2.1.2, 3.2.2, 2.1. 3.
	By individual airline: passenger and cargo services	Annual & Monthly	[QRL 51]	2.1.1, 3.2.1
Short ton miles	By airline	Monthly	[QRL 41]	2.1.3, 3.2.2
	By airline: passenger and freight services	Monthly	[QRL 42]	2.1.3, 3.2.2
	Vehicles included in cargo: by airline, passenger and freight service	Monthly	[QRL 42]	2.1.3, 3.2.2
	By international scheduled airline	Annual & Monthly	[QRL 13]	2.3.1, 3.2.2

QUICK REFERENCE LIST

	By all freight services	Annual & Monthly	[QRL 13]	2.3.1, 3.2.2
	By airline	Annual	[QRL 141]	2.3.4, 3.2.2
	By airline: all freight services	Annual	[QRL 141]	2.3.4, 3.2.2
	By airline: passenger, freighter and all services: local Europe traffic, Intra continental and overseas traffic	Annual	[QRL 136]	2.3.2, 3.2.2
Tonne km used: mail	Total UK private companies	Annual	[QRL 28]	1.3.6, 3.2.2
	Total for UK airlines	Annual	[QRL 28]	1.3.6, 3.2.2
	Total for UK airlines	Annual & Monthly	[QRL 51, 52]	2.1.2, 3.2.2, 2.1.3
	By airline: passenger and cargo services	Annual & Monthly	[QRL 51, 52]	2.1.2, 3.2.2, 2.1.3
Short ton miles	By airline	Monthly	[QRL 41]	2.1.3, 3.2.2
	By airline: passenger and freight services	Monthly	[QRL 42]	2.1.2, 3.2.2
	By international scheduled airlines	Annual & Monthly	[QRL 13]	2.3.1, 3.2.2
	By all freight services	Annual & Monthly	[QRL 13]	2.3.1, 3.2.2
	By airline	Annual	[QRL 141]	2.3.4, 3.2.2
	By airline: all freight services	Annual	[QRL 141]	2.3.4, 3.2.2
	By airline: passenger, freighter, all services; local Europe, inter-European, Intercontinental and overseas	Annual	[QRL 136]	2.3.2, 3.2.2
Total available tonne km	Total UK private companies	Annual	[QRL 28]	1.3.6, 3.2.2
	Total for UK airlines	Annual & Monthly	[QRL 51, 52]	2.1.2, 3.2.2, 2.1.3
	By airline: passenger and cargo services	Annual & Monthly	[QRL 51, 52]	2.1.2, 3.2.2, 2.1.3
Capacity short ton miles	By airline	Monthly	[QRL 41]	2.1.3, 3.2.2
	By airline: passenger and freight services	Monthly	[QRL 42]	2.1.2, 3.2.2
	By international scheduled airline	Annual & Monthly	[QRL 59]	2.3.1, 3.2.2
	By all freight services	Annual & Monthly	[QRL 13]	2.3.1, 3.2.2
Local Europe traffic	By airline	Annual	[QRL 141]	2.3.4, 3.2.2
	By airline: all freight services	Annual	[QRL 141]	2.3.4, 3.2.2
	By airline: passenger, freighter, all services: local Europe, Intra European, Intercontinental and overseas	Annual	[QRL 136]	2.3.2, 3.2.2

184 CIVIL AVIATION

Descriptive title	Breakdown	Frequency	Publication (see QRL Key)	Text reference and remarks
CARGO (contd.) **Scheduled services** (contd.) *International services* (contd.)				
Tonne km used as percentage of tonne kilometres available	Total for UK airlines	Annual & Monthly	[QRL 51, 52]	2.1.2, 3.2.2, 2.1.3
	By individual airlines: passenger and cargo services	Annual & Monthly	[QRL 51, 52]	2.1.2, 3.2.2, 2.1.3
Cargo uplifted tonnes	By individual airline: passenger and cargo services	Annual & Monthly	[QRL 51, 52]	2.1.2, 3.2.2, 2.1.3
(Short tons)	Freight: by airline	Monthly	[QRL 41]	2.1.3, 3.2.2
	Mail: by airline	Monthly	[QRL 41]	2.1.3, 3.2.2
	By airline: passenger and freight services: cargo including vehicles separately	Monthly	[QRL 42]	2.1.3, 3.2.2
	Freight: by individual airport	Annual & Monthly	[QRL 59]	2.3.1, 3.2.2
	Mail: by individual airport	Annual & Monthly	[QRL 59]	2.3.1, 3.2.2
	By individual international scheduled airline	Annual & Monthly	[QRL 13]	2.3.1, 3.2.2
	By all freight services	Annual & Monthly	[QRL 13]	2.3.1, 3.2.2
	By individual airline	Annual	[QRL 141]	2.3.4, 3.2.2
	By airline: all freight services	Annual	[QRL 141]	2.3.4, 3.2.2
	Freight tonnes: Intra European traffic. By two countries. Passenger and freight services separately	Annual	[QRL 115]	2.3.2, 3.2.2
	Mail tonnes: Intra European traffic. By two countries. Passenger and freight services separate	Monthly	[QRL 115]	2.3.2, 3.2.2
	Cargo only by airport	Monthly	[QRL 52]	2.1.3, 3.2.2
	Freight and mail: by airline and flight stage: separate and all	Monthly (for certain months each year)	[QRL 62]	2.3.1, 3.2.2
Freight	IATA North Atlantic traffic: by airline	Annual	[QRL 136]	2.3.2, 3.2.2

Freight (Local/Europe): by airline: freighter services	Annual	[QRL 136]	2.3.2, 3.2.2
By airline: passenger, freighter services: local Europe, Intra European, Intercontinental and overseas: freight and mail separately	Annual	[QRL 136]	2.3.2, 3.2.2
Freight and mail: loaded and unloaded	Annual	[QRL 28]	1.3.6, 3.2.2
Weight load factor, per cent			
By airport: freight and mail separately	Annual & Monthly	[QRL 59]	2.3.1, 3.2.2
By individual international scheduled airline	Annual & Monthly	[QRL 13]	2.3.1, 3.2.2
By all freight services	Annual & Monthly	[QRL 13]	2.3.1, 3.2.2
By airline	Annual	[QRL 141]	2.3.4, 3.2.2
By airline: all freight services	Annual	[QRL 141]	2.3.4, 3.2.2
By airline	Monthly	[QRL 41]	2.1.3, 3.2.2
By airline: passenger and freight services	Monthly	[QRL 42]	2.1.3, 3.2.2
By airline: passenger, freighter and all services: local Europe, Intra European, Intercontinental and overseas traffic	Annual	[QRL 136]	2.3.2, 3.2.2
Total payload capacity (tonnes)			
By airline and flight stage	Monthly (for certain months each year)	[QRL 62]	2.3.1, 3.2.2
By flight stage and airline	Monthly (for certain months each year)	[QRL 62]	2.3.1, 3.2.2

Domestic services

Tonne km used: total			
Total for UK airlines	Annual	[QRL 28]	1.3.6, 3.2.2
Total for UK airlines	Annual & Monthly	[QRL 51, 52]	2.1.2, 3.2.2, 2.1.2
By airline: passenger and cargo services	Annual & Monthly	[QRL 51, 52]	2.1.2, 3.2.2, 2.1.2
By individual international scheduled airline	Annual & Monthly	[QRL 13]	2.3.1, 3.2.2
By domestic scheduled airline	Annual	[QRL 13]	2.3.1, 3.2.2

Descriptive title	Breakdown	Frequency	Publication (see QRL Key)	Text reference and remarks
CARGO (contd.) **Scheduled services** (contd.) *Domestic services* (contd.)				
	By all freight services	Annual & Monthly	[QRL 13]	2.3.1, 3.2.2
	By airline	Annual	[QRL 141]	2.3.4, 3.2.2
	By airline: all freight services	Annual	[QRL 141]	2.3.4, 3.2.2
Short ton miles	Total UK private companies	Annual	[QRL 28]	1.3.6, 3.2.2
Available payload per aircraft, tonnes carried per aircraft	By airline	Annual	[QRL 136]	2.3.2, 3.2.2
	Local Europe, Intra-European, Inter-continental and overseas	Annual	[QRL 136]	2.3.2, 3.2.2
	By airline: Local Europe, Intra-European, Intercontinental and overseas	Annual	[QRL 136]	2.3.2, 3.2.2
	By airline: passenger and all services	Annual	[QRL 136]	2.3.2, 3.2.2
Tonne km used: Mail	Total for UK airlines	Annual	[QRL 28]	1.3.6, 3.2.2
	Total for UK airlines	Annual & Monthly	[QRL 51, 52]	2.1.2, 3.2.2, 2.1.3
	By airline: passenger and cargo services	Annual & Monthly	[QRL 51, 52]	2.1.2, 3.2.2, 2.1.3
Short ton miles	By airline	Monthly	[QRL 41]	2.1.3, 3.2.2
	By airline: passenger and freight services	Monthly	[QRL 42]	2.1.3, 3.2.2
	By individual domestic scheduled airline	Annual & Monthly	[QRL 13]	2.3.1, 3.2.2
	By individual international scheduled airline	Annual & Monthly	[QRL 13]	2.3.1, 3.2.2
	By all freight services	Annual & Monthly	[QRL 13]	2.3.1, 3.2.2
	By airline	Annual	[QRL 141]	2.3.4, 3.2.2
	By airline: all freight services	Annual	[QRL 141]	2.3.4, 3.2.2
	By airline: passenger and all services	Annual	[QRL 136]	2.3.2, 3.2.2
Tonne km used: freight	Total for UK airlines	Annual	[QRL 28]	1.3.3, 3.2.2
	Total for UK airlines	Annual & Monthly	[QRL 51, 52]	2.1.2, 3.2.2, 2.1.3
	By airline. Passenger and cargo services	Annual & Monthly	[QRL 51, 52]	2.1.2, 3.2.2
(Short ton miles)	By airline	Monthly	[QRL 41, 98]	2.1.3, 3.2.2

QUICK REFERENCE LIST

(Short ton miles)	By airline. Passenger and freight services	Monthly	[QRL 42, 98]	2.1.3, 3.2.2
	By domestic scheduled airline	Annual	[QRL 13]	2.3.1, 3.2.2
	By international scheduled airline	Annual & Monthly	[QRL 13]	2.3.1, 3.2.2
	By all freight services	Annual & Monthly	[QRL 13]	2.3.1, 3.2.2
	By airline	Annual	[QRL 141]	2.3.4, 3.2.2
	By airline. All freight services	Annual	[QRL 141]	2.3.4, 3.2.2
	By airline. Passenger and all services	Annual	[QRL 136]	2.3.2, 3.2.2
	By airline. All services	Annual	[QRL 136]	2.3.2, 3.2.2
(Percentage on passenger services)	Total UK private companies	Annual	[QRL 28]	1.3.6, 3.2.2
Total available tonne km	Total for UK airlines	Annual & Monthly	[QRL 51, 52]	2.1.2, 3.2.2
	By airline. Passenger and cargo services	Annual & Monthly	[QRL 51, 52]	2.1.2, 3.2.2
(Capacity short ton miles)	By airline	Monthly	[QRL 41, 98]	2.1.3, 3.2.2
(Capacity short ton miles)	By airline. Passenger and freight services	Monthly	[QRL 42, 98]	2.1.2, 3.2.2
	By international scheduled airline	Annual & Monthly	[QRL 13]	2.3.1, 3.2.2
	By all freight services	Annual & Monthly	[QRL 13]	2.3.1, 3.2.2
	By domestic scheduled airline	Annual	[QRL 13]	2.3.1, 3.2.2
	By airline	Annual	[QRL 141]	2.3.4, 3.2.2
	By airline. All freight services	Annual	[QRL 141]	2.3.4, 3.2.2
	By airline. Passenger and all services	Annual	[QRL 136]	2.3.2, 3.2.2
Tonne km used as per cent of TK available	Total for UK airlines	Annual & Monthly	[QRL 51, 52]	2.1.2, 3.2.2
	By individual airline	Annual & Monthly	[QRL 51, 52]	2.1.2, 3.2.2
Cargo uplifted tonnes	By individual airline. Passenger and cargo services	Annual & Monthly	[QRL 51, 52]	2.1.2, 3.2.2
Freight tonnes carried				
(Cargo only)	By airport	Monthly	[QRL 52]	2.1.2, 3.2.2
	Freight and mail separately	Monthly	[QRL 41, 98]	2.1.2, 3.2.2
(Short tons carried)	By airline. Passengers and freight services: freight and vehicles separately	Monthly	[QRL 42, 98]	2.1.2, 3.2.2
(Short tons)	By domestic scheduled airline	Annual	[QRL 59]	2.3.1, 3.2.2
	By international scheduled airline	Annual & Monthly	[QRL 59]	2.3.1, 3.2.2

CIVIL AVIATION

Descriptive title	Breakdown	Frequency	Publication (see QRL Key)	Text reference and remarks
CARGO (contd.) **Scheduled services** (contd.) *Domestic services* (contd.)	By all-freight services	Annual & Monthly	[QRL 59]	2.3.1, 3.2.2
(Freight tonnes carried)	By airline	Annual	[QRL 141]	2.3.4, 3.2.2
	By airline. All-freight services	Annual	[QRL 141]	2.3.4, 3.2.2
	By airline. Passenger services: freight and mail separately	Annual	[QRL 136]	2.3.2, 3.2.2
	Total UK airways and UK private companies separately	Annual	[QRL 28]	1.3.6, 3.2.2
Weight load factor, per cent	By airline	Monthly	[QRL 41, 98]	2.1.3, 3.2.2
	By airline. Passenger and freight services	Monthly	[QRL 42, 98]	2.1.2, 3.2.2
	By individual domestic scheduled airline	Annual	[QRL 13]	2.3.1, 3.2.2
	By all freight services	Annual	[QRL 13]	2.3.1, 3.2.2
	By international scheduled airline	Annual & Monthly	[QRL 13]	2.3.1, 3.2.2
	By airline	Annual	[QRL 141]	2.3.4, 3.2.2
	By airline. All-freight services	Annual	[QRL 141]	2.3.4, 3.2.2
	By airline. Passenger and all services	Annual	[QRL 136]	2.3.2, 3.2.2
Freight and mail revenue US $	By airline. Passenger and all services, freight and mail separately and total	Annual	[QRL 136]	2.3.2, 3.2.2
Freight and mail revenue per freight tonne km US ¢	By airline. Passenger and all services, freight and mail separately	Annual	[QRL 136]	2.3.2, 3.2.2
Non-scheduled services *All services* Tonne km used: total	By individual airline	Annual & Monthly	[QRL 51, 52]	2.1.2, 3.2.2
(Performed)	By airline. Revenue traffic	Annual	[QRL 122]	2.3.1, 3.2.2
	By airline. Revenue transport services	Annual	[QRL 122]	2.3.1, 3.2.2
	By airline. Revenue transport services All-freight/mail services	Annual	[QRL 122]	2.3.1, 3.2.2
(All freight/mail)	By airline	Annual	[QRL 122]	2.3.1, 3.2.2
	By airline	Annual	[QRL 122]	2.3.1, 3.2.2
	By airline. Revenue traffic	Annual	[QRL 122]	2.3.1, 3.2.2

QUICK REFERENCE LIST

	By scheduled airline. All freight traffic	Annual	[QRL 122]	2.3.1, 3.2.2
	By international scheduled airline	Annual & Monthly	[QRL 13]	2.3.1, 3.2.2
	By domestic scheduled airline	Annual	[QRL 13]	2.3.1, 3.2.2
	By all freight services	Annual & Monthly	[QRL 13]	2.3.1, 3.2.2
Tonne km used: freight and mail	By airline	Annual	[QRL 141]	2.3.1, 3.2.2
	By individual airline. Freight and mail separately	Annual & Monthly	[QRL 51, 52]	2.1.2, 3.2.2
Total available tonne km	Total for UK airlines	Annual	[QRL 28]	1.3.6, 3.2.2
	Total for UK airlines	Annual & Monthly	[QRL 51, 52]	2.1.2, 3.2.2
	By airline	Annual & Monthly	[QRL 51, 52]	2.1.2, 3.2.2
(Capacity short ton miles)	By airline	Monthly	[QRL 41, 98]	2.1.3, 3.2.2
(Capacity short ton miles)	By airline	Monthly	[QRL 42, 98]	2.1.3, 3.2.2
	By airline. Revenue transport services	Annual	[QRL 59]	2.3.1, 3.2.2
	By airline. Revenue traffic	Annual	[QRL 122]	2.3.1, 3.2.2
	By scheduled airline. All freight traffic	Annual	[QRL 122]	2.3.1, 3.2.2
	By international scheduled airline	Annual & Monthly	[QRL 13]	2.3.1, 3.2.2
	By domestic scheduled airline	Annual	[QRL 13]	2.3.1, 3.2.2
	By all freight services	Annual	[QRL 13]	2.3.1, 3.2.2
	By airline	Annual	[QRL 141]	2.3.4, 3.2.2
	Total for UK airlines, plus percentage growth on last year	Annual	[QRL 28]	1.3.6, 3.2.2
Per cent growth of available TK on previous year	Total for UK airlines	Annual since 1946	[QRL 52]	2.1.3, 3.2.2
	By airline	Annual & Monthly	[QRL 51, 52]	2.1.3, 3.2.2
Cargo uplifted tonnes	By airline	Annual & Monthly	[QRL 51, 52]	2.1.3, 3.2.2
(Freight)	By airport	Annual & Monthly	[QRL 125]	2.3.3, 3.2.2
(Charter)	By airport and type of operation: total mixed and all cargo: BAA airports	Quarterly	[QRL 103]	2.2.1, 3.2.2
Cargo tonnes picked up: UK operators (BA and others) (charter)*	By airport	Annual & Monthly	[QRL 51, 52]	2.1.2, 2.1.3, 3.2.2

*See overleaf.

CIVIL AVIATION

Descriptive title	Breakdown	Frequency	Publication (see QRL Key)	Text reference and remarks
CARGO (contd.)				
Non-scheduled services (contd.)				
All services (contd.)				
(Corporations and others)*	By airport	Annual & Monthly	[QRL 40]	2.1.2, 3.2.2
Cargo tonnes set down: UK operators*				
(BA and others) (charter)*	By airport	Annual & Monthly	[QRL 51, 52]	2.1.2, 2.1.3, 3.2.2
(Corporations and others)	By airport	Annual & Monthly	[QRL 40]	2.1.2, 3.2.2
Cargo tonnes picked up/set down: overseas operators* (Charter)*	By airport	Annual & Monthly	[QRL 51, 52]	2.1.2, 2.1.3, 3.2.2
Per cent TKs performed on aircraft	By airline. For large and small aircraft separately	Annual	[QRL 122]	2.3.1, 3.2.2
Annual per cent in TKs performed	By airline	Annual	[QRL 122]	2.3.1, 3.2.2
Weight load factor per cent: average per aircraft	By airline	Annual	[QRL 122]	2.3.1, 3.2.2
	By airline. Revenue traffic	Annual	[QRL 122]	2.3.1, 3.2.2
	By scheduled airline. All freight traffic	Annual	[QRL 122]	2.3.1, 3.2.2
Average payload carried per aircraft	By airline	Annual	[QRL 122]	2.3.1, 3.2.2
International services				
Tonne km used: total	By airline	Annual & Monthly	[QRL 122] [QRL 51, 52]	2.3.1, 3.2.2, 2.1.2
	By airline. Freight, mail services and revenue traffic	Annual	[QRL 122]	2.3.1, 3.2.2
	By scheduled airline. All freight traffic	Annual	[QRL 122]	2.3.1, 3.2.2
	By international scheduled airline	Annual & Monthly	[QRL 13]	2.3.1, 3.2.2
	By individual domestic scheduled airline	Annual	[QRL 13]	2.3.1, 3.2.2

*Also available for **Scheduled services**, *All services*, see p. 180.

QUICK REFERENCE LIST

By all freight services	Annual & Monthly	[QRL 13]	2.3.1, 3.2.2
By airline	Annual	[QRL 141]	2.3.4, 3.2.2
Tonne km used: freight and mail			
By airline	Annual & Monthly	[QRL 51, 52]	2.1.2, 2.1.3, 3.2.2
Total available tonnes km			
By airline	Annual & Monthly	[QRL 51, 52] [QRL 59]	2.1.2, 2.1.3, 3.2.2, 2.3.1
(Capacity short ton miles)	Monthly	[QRL 41, 98]	2.1.3, 3.2.2
(Capacity short ton miles)	Monthly	[QRL 42, 98]	2.1.2, 3.2.2
By airline. Revenue traffic	Annual	[QRL 122]	2.3.1, 3.2.2
By scheduled airline. All freight traffic	Annual	[QRL 122]	2.3.1, 3.2.2
By international scheduled airline	Annual & Monthly	[QRL 13]	2.3.1, 3.2.2
By domestic scheduled airline	Annual	[QRL 13]	2.3.1, 3.2.2
By all freight services	Annual & Monthly	[QRL 13]	2.3.1, 3.2.2
Cargo uplifted tonnes			
By airline	Annual	[QRL 141]	2.3.4, 3.2.2
By airline	Annual & Monthly	[QRL 51, 52]	2.1.2, 2.1.3, 3.2.2
Charter cargo only			
By airport	Monthly	[QRL 52]	2.1.2, 2.1.3, 3.2.2
By airport. Freight and mail separately	Annual & Monthly	[QRL 59]	2.3.1, 3.2.2
TKs used as percentage TKs available			
By airline	Annual & Monthly	[QRL 51, 52]	2.1.2, 3.2.2, 2.1.3

Domestic services

Tonne km used: total			
By airline	Annual & Monthly	[QRL 51, 52]	2.1.2, 2.1.3, 3.2.2
By international scheduled airline	Annual	[QRL 13]	2.3.1, 3.2.2
By domestic scheduled airline	Annual	[QRL 13]	2.3.1, 3.2.2
By all freight services	Annual & Monthly	[QRL 13]	2.3.1, 3.2.2
Tonne km used: freight and mail			
By airline	Annual	[QRL 141]	2.3.4, 3.2.2
By airline. Freight and mail separately	Annual & Monthly	[QRL 51, 52]	2.1.2, 2.1.3, 3.2.2
Total available tonne km			
By airline	Annual & Monthly	[QRL 51, 52]	2.1.2, 2.1.3, 3.2.2
(Capacity short ton miles)	Monthly	[QRL 41, 98]	2.1.3, 3.2.2
(Capacity short ton miles)	Monthly	[QRL 42, 98]	2.1.2, 3.2.2

Descriptive title	Breakdown	Frequency	Publication (see QRL Key)	Text reference and remarks
CARGO (*contd.*)				
Non-scheduled services (*contd.*)				
Domestic services (*contd.*)				
	By international scheduled airline	Annual & Monthly	[QRL 13]	2.3.1, 3.2.2
	By domestic scheduled airline	Annual	[QRL 13]	2.3.1, 3.2.2
	By all freight services	Annual & Monthly	[QRL 13]	2.3.1, 3.2.2
Cargo uplifted tonnes	By airline	Annual	[QRL 141]	2.3.4, 3.2.2
	By airline	Annual & Monthly	[QRL 51, 52]	2.1.2, 2.1.3, 3.2.2
(Charter cargo only)	By airport	Monthly	[QRL 52]	2.1.2, 2.1.3, 3.2.2
TKs used as per cent available	By airline	Annual & Monthly	[QRL 51, 52]	2.1.2, 2.1.3, 3.2.2
Weight load factor per cent	By airline. Revenue traffic	Annual	[QRL 122]	2.3.1, 3.2.2
	By scheduled airline. All freight traffic	Annual	[QRL 122]	2.3.1, 3.2.2
Freight and mail; loaded and unloaded	By airport. Freight and mail separately	Annual & Monthly	[QRL 59]	2.3.1, 3.2.2
Per cent of TKs performed on large aircraft	By airline	Annual	[QRL 122]	2.3.1, 3.2.2
Inclusive tours				
Tonne km available	Total for UK airlines	Annual	[QRL 28]	1.3.6, 3.2.2
	Total for UK airlines and by airline	Annual & Monthly	[QRL 51, 52]	2.1.2, 2.1.3, 3.2.2
(Capacity short ton miles)	By airline. All international and domestic	Monthly	[QRL 42, 98]	2.1.2, 2.1.3, 3.2.2
Other separate fare and ABCs and other charters				
Tonne km available	Total for UK airlines	Annual	[QRL 28]	1.3.6, 3.2.2
	Total for UK airlines	Annual & Monthly	[QRL 51, 52]	2.1.2, 2.1.3, 3.2.2
(Other charters)	Total for UK airlines	Annual	[QRL 28]	1.3.6, 3.2.2
	Total for UK airlines	Annual & Monthly	[QRL 51, 52]	2.1.2, 2.1.3, 3.2.2

QUICK REFERENCE LIST

(Other separate fare charters: short ton miles)	By airlines. All, international and domestic	Monthly	[QRL 42, 98]	2.1.2, 2.1.3, 3.2.2
(All exempt services and sub-charters: short ton miles)	By airline. All, international and domestic	Monthly	[QRL 42, 98]	2.1.2, 2.1.3, 3.2.2
Miscellaneous total figures				
Output in available tonne km	By individual UK airline	Annual	[QRL 51, 52]	2.1.2, 2.1.3, 3.2.2
	Total for UK airlines, plus percentage increase on last year	Annual	[QRL 28]	1.3.5, 3.2.2
Percentage of all UK tonne km performed	By individual UK airline	Annual	[QRL 51, 52]	2.1.2, 2.1.3, 3.2.2
Per cent of available UK tonne km of UK airlines this size and smaller	By UK airlines	Annual	[QRL 51, 52]	2.1.2, 2.1.3, 3.2.2
Total available tonne km	Total UK airlines	Annual since 1946	[QRL 51, 52]	2.1.2, 2.1.3, 3.2.2
	Per cent growth on previous year. Total UK airlines	Annual since 1946	[QRL 51, 52]	2.1.2, 2.1.3, 3.2.2
(Scheduled and non-scheduled)	By international scheduled airline. All international and domestic	Annual & Monthly	[QRL 13]	2.3.1, 3.2.2
(Scheduled and non-scheduled)	By domestic scheduled airlines. All international and domestic	Annual	[QRL 13]	2.3.1, 3.2.2
Cargo loaded and unloaded	Freight and mail by airport, total commercial air transport	Annual & Monthly	[QRL 59]	2.3.1, 3.2.2
	Freight and mail total international air transport: by airport	Annual & Monthly	[QRL 59]	2.3.1, 3.2.2
	Freight and mail total domestic by airport	Annual	[QRL 59]	2.3.1, 3.2.2
	Commercial freight and mail (separately) picked up and set down at UK civil aerodromes	Annual	[QRL 28]	1.3.6, 3.2.2
Cargo tonnes: domestic	Freight and mail separately by airport	Annual & Monthly	[QRL 59]	2.3.1, 3.2.2
	Cargo total UK airways, scheduled services	Annual	[QRL 137]	1.3.6, 3.2.2
	By airport and type of flight: total, mixed, and all cargo, BAA airports	Quarterly	[QRL 103]	2.2.1, 3.2.2
Cargo tonnes: international	By airport	Annual	[QRL 51, 52]	2.1.2, 2.1.3, 3.2.2
	Freight and mail. By airport	Annual & Monthly	[QRL 59]	2.3.1, 3.2.2
	Cargo. Total UK airways scheduled services	Monthly	[QRL 137]	1.3.6, 3.2.2

CIVIL AVIATION

Descriptive title	Breakdown	Frequency	Publication (see QRL Key)	Text reference and remarks
CARGO (*contd.*)				
Miscellaneous total figures (*contd.*)				
Cargo tonnes: Total	By airport and type of flight: total, mixed, all cargo, BAA airports	Quarterly	[QRL 103]	2.1.2, 2.3.2
	By airport	Annual & Monthly	[QRL 51, 52]	2.1.2, 2.1.3, 3.2.2
	Freight by airport	Monthly	[QRL 40]	2.1.2, 3.2.2
	Cargo only. By airport	Monthly	[QRL 52]	2.1.2, 2.1.3, 3.2.2
(Freight)	By airport. Total commercial air transport	Annual & Monthly	[QRL 59]	2.3.1, 3.2.2
(Mail)	By airport	Annual & Monthly	[QRL 59]	2.3.1, 3.2.2
	By airport and traffic of cargo and mail aircraft	Annual	[QRL 125]	2.3.3, 3.2.2
	Freight and mail by airport	Annual & Monthly	[QRL 125]	2.3.3, 3.2.2
	Terminal freight aircraft. By airport: combined and cargo aircraft	Annual	[QRL 125]	2.3.3, 3.2.2
	North Atlantic cargo traffic BOAC (+ per cent total)	Monthly	[QRL 115]	2.3.2, 3.2.2
	Total UK airways. Scheduled services	Annual	[QRL 137]	1.3.6, 3.2.2
	By airport (BAA airport)	Quarterly	[QRL 103]	2.2.1, 3.2.2
	By airport and type of flight: total, mixed, all cargo (BAA airport)	Quarterly	[QRL 103]	2.2.1, 3.2.2
	Commercial freight and mail separately, handled at UK civil aerodromes (total figures)	Annual	[QRL 28]	1.3.6, 3.2.2
Cargo tonnes: per cent change on last year	Cargo tonnes: mean per cent change in past 5 years	Annual & Monthly	[QRL 51, 52]	2.1.2, 2.1.3, 3.2.2
	By airport. On international air services	Annual	[QRL 51, 52]	2.1.2, 2.1.3, 3.2.2
	By airport and on all international air services	Annual	[QRL 51]	
	By airport	Monthly	[QRL 52, 40]	2.1.2, 2.1.3, 3.2.2
	By airport. Terminal freight and mail separately	Annual	[QRL 125]	2.3.3, 3.2.2

QUICK REFERENCE LIST

Tonne km performed: total (Scheduled and non-scheduled)	By international scheduled airline (all domestic and international)	Annual & Monthly	[QRL 13]	2.3.1, 3.2.2
(Scheduled and non-scheduled)	By domestic scheduled airline. All domestic and international	Annual	[QRL 13]	2.3.1, 3.2.2
(Scheduled)	Freight and mail separate. Total for UK airlines: international domestic and all totals	Annual	[QRL 137]	1.3.6, 3.2.2
Airports ranked by amount of freight and mail	By airport. Freight and mail separately	Annual	[QRL 125]	2.3.3, 3.2.2
Weight load factor: per cent	By airport and traffic of cargo and mail aircraft	Annual	[QRL 125]	2.3.3, 3.2.2
Average tonnage by cargo aircraft	By airport and traffic of cargo and mail aircraft	Annual	[QRL 125]	2.3.3, 3.2.2
Terminal freight traffic by region of origin and destination	By airport and region of the world	Annual	[QRL 125]	2.3.3, 3.2.2
(Percentage)	Per cent by airport and region of the world	Annual	[QRL 125]	2.3.3, 3.2.2
(Cargo handled by area of O/D)	By airport	Quarterly	[QRL 103]	2.2.1, 3.2.2
(Goods entering and leaving the UK)	By merchandise group and whether by road, sea or air	Annual	[QRL 29]	2.3.5, 3.2.2
Import and export	By airport, commodity and value and quantity	Annual	[QRL 31]	2.1.7, 3.2.2
International goods transport by various modes of transport	By country: including transit, and excluding transit separately	Annual	[QRL 29]	2.3.5, 3.2.2
International goods transport by various modes of transport and commodity group	By country: goods entered and goods left the country separately	Annual	[QRL 29]	2.3.5, 3.2.2
Cargo tonnes: between countries	UK and Europe. All and freighter services. 2 years. Per cent change	Monthly	[QRL 115]	2.3.2, 3.2.2
Between airports (London and Manchester and European cities)	Freighter services	Monthly	[QRL 115]	2.3.2, 3.2.2
Ratio of sea freight to air freight by weight	UK including oil, excluding oil	Monthly	[QRL 115]	2.3.2, 3.2.2
Indices of average value per unit weight of freight	UK 3 years	Monthly	[QRL 115]	2.3.2, 3.2.2
Weight distribution of air freight	No. of consignments per cent by weight and area of world	Annual & Monthly	[QRL 51, 52]	2.1.2, 2.1.3, 3.2.2
	Tonnes per cent by weight and area of world	Annual & Monthly	[QRL 51, 52]	2.1.2, 2.1.3, 3.2.2

Descriptive title	Breakdown	Frequency	Publication (see QRL Key)	Text reference and remarks
CARGO (*contd.*)				
Licence operations				
Tonne km available	Classes 2 and 3; class 4, 6 and 7 and exempt: all, international and domestic; class 5: UK and non-UK operators	Annual & Monthly	[QRL 51, 52]	2.1.2, 2.1.3, 3.2.2
	Operators, subject to variable charge, by type of licence	Annual & Monthly	[QRL 51, 52]	2.1.2, 2.1.3, 3.2.2
(Capacity tonne kilometres available)	By type of licence and ownership of aircraft	Annual & Monthly	[QRL 51, 52]	2.1.2, 2.1.3, 3.2.2
(Capacity ton miles available)	By licence type and type of services. Total UK airlines	Monthly	[QRL 42, 98]	2.1.2, 3.2.2
Tonne km used	Classes 2 and 3; Classes 4, 6, 7 and exempt: all, international, domestic, class 5: UK and non-UK operators	Annual & Monthly	[QRL 51, 52]	2.1.2, 2.1.3, 3.2.2
	Operators subject to variable charge by type of licence	Annual & Monthly	[QRL 51, 52]	2.1.2, 2.1.3, 3.2.2
(Ton miles)	By licence type and type of service. Total UK airlines	Monthly	[QRL 42, 98]	2.1.2, 3.2.2
Tonne km used: freight and mail	Class 7 and exempt: all, international domestic; class 5, UK and non-UK operators	Annual & Monthly	[QRL 51, 52]	2.1.2, 2.1.3, 3.2.2
	Operations subject to variable charge by type of licence	Annual & Monthly	[QRL 51, 52]	2.1.2, 2.1.3, 3.2.2
TKs used as per cent available	Classes 2 and 3; Classes 4, 6, 7 and exempt: class 5: UK, and non-UK operators	Annual & Monthly	[QRL 51, 52]	2.1.2, 2.1.3, 3.2.2
	Operations subject to variable charge by type of licence	Annual & Monthly	[QRL 51, 52]	2.1.2, 2.1.3, 3.2.2
Cargo uplifted tonnes	Class 6, 7 and exempt: all, international, domestic; class 5: UK, non-UK operators	Annual & Monthly	[QRL 51, 52]	2.1.2, 2.1.3, 3.2.2
Aircraft type and utilization				
Stage flights: cargo	All airlines by type of plane	Annual & Monthly	[QRL 42, 51, 52, 98]	2.1.2, 3.2.2
	By airline and type of plane	Annual & Monthly	[QRL 42, 51, 52, 98]	2.1.2, 3.2.2

QUICK REFERENCE LIST

Aircraft hours: cargo	All airlines by type of plane	Annual & Monthly	[QRL 51, 52, 42, 98]	2.1.2, 2.1.3, 3.2.2
	By airline and type of plane	Annual & Monthly	[QRL 51, 52, 42, 98]	2.1.2, 2.1.3, 3.2.2
Air freight users				
Mode of transport used for exports	By mode of transport and no. of companies using it	June & July 1976	[QRL 12]	2.1.6, 3.2.2, 4.1
	By air freight users, mode and percentage of total exports by weight	June & July 1976	[QRL 12]	2.1.6, 3.2.2, 4.1
Party normally deciding mode of transport	By air freight users only	June & July 1976	[QRL 12]	2.1.6, 3.2.2, 4.1
Reasons for using air freight	Reasons ranked	June & July 1976	[QRL 12]	2.1.6, 3.2.2, 4.1
Reasons for not using air freight		June & July 1976	[QRL 12]	2.1.6, 3.2.2, 4.1
Urgency of air freight consignments	By weight and type of service. By weight and transport mode decision taken	June & July 1976	[QRL 12]	2.1.6, 3.2.2, 4.1
The demand for various types of air freight service	By proportion of consignments, weight and type of service	June & July 1976	[QRL 12]	2.1.6, 3.2.2, 4.1
Proportion of air freight users total export tonnage consigned by air		June & July 1976	[QRL 12]	2.1.6, 3.2.2, 4.1
Export tonnages of air freight users by geographical destination		June & July 1976	[QRL 12]	2.1.6, 3.2.2, 4.1
Commodity classification of exports by air		June & July 1976	[QRL 12]	2.1.6, 3.2.2, 4.1
Urgency and consignment sizes of air freight exports	By weight, type of service and part of world	June & July 1976	[QRL 12]	2.1.6, 3.2.2, 4.1
AIRCRAFT				
Scheduled services				
All services				
Aircraft km	By airline. Passenger and cargo services separately	Annual	[QRL 51]	2.1.2, 3.2.3, 2.1.3
	By airline. Passenger and cargo services separately	Monthly	[QRL 52]	2.1.2, 3.2.3, 2.1.3
(Miles)	By airline	Annual & Monthly	[QRL 41, 98]	2.1.3, 3.2.3
(Percentage increase in last year) (Miles)	By airline. Passenger and freight services separately	Annual & Monthly	[QRL 42, 98]	2.1.3, 3.2.3

CIVIL AVIATION

Descriptive title	Breakdown	Frequency	Publication (see QRL Key)	Text reference and remarks
AIRCRAFT (contd.) **Scheduled services** (contd.) *All services* (contd.)				
	By airline. International scheduled airline	Annual & Monthly	[QRL 13]	2.3.1, 3.2.3
	By airline, scheduled, all freight services	Annual & Monthly	[QRL 13]	2.3.1, 3.2.3
	By airline. Passenger and freighter services separately	Annual	[QRL 136]	2.3.2, 3.2.3
	By airline. Scheduled, all freight services	Annual	[QRL 141]	2.3.4, 3.2.3
	Total UK airways	Annual	[QRL 137]	1.3.6, 3.2.3
	Total UK airways	Annual	[QRL 28]	1.3.6, 3.2.3
	Total UK private companies	Annual	[QRL 28]	1.3.6, 3.2.3
Distance per hour flown	By international scheduled airline	Annual	[QRL 61]	2.3.1, 3.2.3
	By domestic scheduled airline	Annual	[QRL 61]	2.3.2, 3.2.3
Number of revenue landings	By airline, passenger and freighter services separately	Annual	[QRL 136]	2.3.2, 3.2.3
Average stage distance	By airline. Passenger and freighter services separately	Annual	[QRL 136]	2.3.2, 3.2.3
(Stage flights—average length)	Total UK airways	Annual	[QRL 28]	1.3.6, 3.2.3
(Stage flights—average length)	Total UK private companies	Annual	[QRL 28]	1.3.6, 3.2.3
Stage flights	By airline. Passenger and cargo services separately	Annual	[QRL 51]	2.1.2, 3.2.3, 2.1.3
	By airline. Passenger and cargo services separately	Monthly	[QRL 52]	2.1.2, 3.2.3, 2.1.3
	By airline. Passenger and freight services separately	Annual & Monthly	[QRL 42, 98]	2.1.3, 3.2.3
	Total UK airways	Annual	[QRL 28]	1.3.6, 3.2.3
	Total UK private companies	Annual	[QRL 28]	1.3.6, 3.2.3
	By airline. Passenger and cargo services separately	Annual	[QRL 51]	2.1.2, 3.2.3, 2.1.3
Aircraft hours	By airline. Passenger and cargo services separately	Monthly	[QRL 52]	2.1.2, 3.2.3, 2.1.3
	By airline. Passenger and freight services separately	Annual & Monthly	[QRL 42, 98]	2.1.3, 3.2.3
	By airline. International scheduled airline	Annual & Monthly	[QRL 13]	2.3.1, 3.2.3

QUICK REFERENCE LIST 199

By airline. Scheduled all freight services	Annual & Monthly	[QRL 13]	2.3.1, 3.2.3
By airline. Passenger and freighter services separately	Annual	[QRL 136]	2.3.2, 3.2.3
By airline	Annual & Monthly	[QRL 59]	2.3.1, 3.2.3
By airline. Scheduled all freight services	Annual	[QRL 141]	2.3.4, 3.2.3
By airline. International scheduled airlines	Annual & Monthly	[QRL 13]	2.3.1, 3.2.3

Aircraft departures

By airline. Scheduled all freight services	Annual & Monthly	[QRL 13]	2.3.1, 3.2.3
By airline	Annual	[QRL 141]	2.3.4, 3.2.3
By airline. Scheduled all freight services	Annual	[QRL 141]	2.3.4, 3.2.3
By airline. Passenger and freighter services separately	Annual	[QRL 36]	2.3.2, 3.2.3

Unduplicated route km

By airline	Annual	[QRL 141]	2.3.4, 3.2.3

(Length of scheduled route network)

International services
Aircraft km

By airline. Passenger and cargo services separately	Annual	[QRL 51]	2.1.2, 3.2.3, 2.1.3
By airline. Passenger and cargo services separately	Monthly	[QRL 52]	2.1.2, 3.2.3, 2.1.3

(Miles)

By airline	Monthly	[QRL 41, 98]	2.1.3, 3.2.3
By airline. Passenger and freight services separately	Monthly	[QRL 42, 98]	2.1.3, 3.2.3
By airline. International scheduled airline	Annual	[QRL 13]	2.3.1, 3.2.3
By airline. International scheduled airline	Monthly	[QRL 13]	2.3.1, 3.2.3
By airline. Scheduled all freight services	Annual & Monthly	[QRL 13]	2.3.1, 3.2.3
By airline. Local Europe traffic. Passenger and freight services separately	Annual	[QRL 136]	2.3.2, 3.2.3
By airline. Intra European traffic. Passenger and freighter services separately	Annual	[QRL 136]	2.3.2, 3.2.3
By airline. Intercontinental and overseas traffic passenger and freighter services separately	Annual	[QRL 136]	2.3.2, 3.2.3

200 CIVIL AVIATION

Descriptive title	Breakdown	Frequency	Publication (see QRL Key)	Text reference and remarks
AIRCRAFT *(contd.)*				
Scheduled services *(contd.)*				
International services (contd.)	By airline. Total and all freight services separately	Annual	[QRL 141]	2.3.4, 3.2.3
	Total UK airways	Annual	[QRL 137]	1.3.6, 3.2.3
	Total UK airways	Annual	[QRL 28]	1.3.6, 3.2.3
	Total UK private companies	Annual	[QRL 28]	1.3.6, 3.2.3
Aircraft movements	By airport	Monthly	[QRL 59]	2.3.1, 3.2.3
Average number of flights per day	IATA North Atlantic traffic. By airline	Annual	[QRL 136]	2.3.2, 3.2.3
Stage flights	By airline. Passenger and cargo services separately	Annual	[QRL 51]	2.1.2, 3.2.3, 2.1.3
	By airline. Passenger and cargo services separately	Monthly	[QRL 52]	2.1.2, 3.2.3, 2.1.3
	By airline. Passenger and freight services separately	Monthly	[QRL 42, 98]	2.1.3, 3.2.3
	Total UK airways	Annual	[QRL 28]	1.3.6, 3.2.3
	Total UK private companies	Annual	[QRL 28]	1.3.6, 3.2.3
Aircraft hours	By airline. Passenger and cargo services separately	Annual	[QRL 51]	2.1.2, 3.2.3, 2.1.3
	By airline. Passenger and cargo services separately	Monthly	[QRL 52]	2.1.2, 3.2.3, 2.1.3
	By airline. Passenger and freight services separately	Monthly	[QRL 42, 98]	2.1.3, 3.2.2
	By airline. International scheduled airline	Annual & Monthly	[QRL 13]	2.3.1, 3.2.3
	By airline. Scheduled, all freight services	Annual & Monthly	[QRL 13]	2.3.1, 3.2.3
(Aircraft block hours flown)	By airline. Local Europe traffic. Passenger and freight services separately	Annual	[QRL 136]	2.3.2, 3.2.3
(Aircraft block hours flown)	By airline. Local Europe traffic. Intra European traffic. Passenger and freight services separately	Annual	[QRL 136]	2.3.3, 3.2.3
(Aircraft block hours flown)	By airline. Intercontinental and overseas traffic, passenger and freighter services separately	Annual	[QRL 136]	2.3.2, 3.2.3

QUICK REFERENCE LIST

Aircraft departures	By airline. Total and all freight services separately	[QRL 141]	Annual	2.3.4, 3.2.3
	By airline. International scheduled airline	[QRL 13]	Annual & Monthly	2.3.1, 3.2.3
	By airline. Scheduled, all-freight services	[QRL 13]	Annual & Monthly	2.3.1, 3.2.3
	By airline. Total, all freight services	[QRL 141]	Annual	2.3.4, 3.2.3
Number of revenue landings	By airline. Local Europe traffic. Passenger and freight services separately	[QRL 136]	Annual	2.3.2, 3.2.3
	By airline. Intra European traffic. Passenger and freight services separately	[QRL 136]	Annual	2.3.2, 3.2.3
	By airline. Intercontinental and overseas traffic. Passenger and freighter services separately	[QRL 136]	Annual	2.3.2, 3.2.3
Average stage distance	By airline. Local Europe traffic. Passenger and freighter services separately	[QRL 136]	Annual	2.3.2, 3.2.3
	By airline. Intra European traffic. Passenger and freighter services separately	[QRL 136]	Annual	2.3.2, 3.2.3
	By airline. Intercontinental and overseas traffic, passenger and freighter services separately	[QRL 136]	Annual	2.3.2, 3.2.3
(Stage flights—average length)	Total UK airways	[QRL 28]	Annual	1.3.6, 3.2.3
(Stage flights—average length)	Total UK private companies	[QRL 28]	Annual	1.3.6, 3.2.3
Unduplicated route km	By airline. Local Europe traffic. Passenger and freighter separately	[QRL 136]	Annual	2.3.2, 3.2.3
	By airline. Intra-European traffic. Passenger and freighter services separately	[QRL 136]	Annual	2.3.2, 3.2.3
	By airline. Intercontinental and overseas traffic. Passenger and freighter services separately	[QRL 136]	Annual	2.3.2, 3.2.3
(Length of scheduled route network)	By freighter services	[QRL 136]	Annual	2.3.2, 3.2.3
(Length of scheduled route network)	By airline	[QRL 141]	Annual	2.3.4, 3.2.3
Aircraft flights (between UK and abroad)	Aircraft registered in UK and abroad separately. Total	[QRL 28]	Annual	1.3.6, 3.2.3
Domestic services				
Aircraft km	By airline. Passenger and cargo services separately	[QRL 51]	Annual	2.1.2, 3.2.3, 2.1.3

201

CIVIL AVIATION

Descriptive title		Breakdown	Frequency	Publication (see QRL Key)	Text reference and remarks
AIRCRAFT (contd.)					
Scheduled services (contd.)					
Domestic services (contd.)					
		By airline. Passenger and cargo services separately	Monthly	[QRL 52]	2.1.2, 3.2.3, 2.1.3
(Miles)		By airline	Monthly	[QRL 41, 98]	2.1.3, 3.2.3
(Miles)		By airline. Passenger and freighter services separately	Monthly	[QRL 42, 98]	2.1.3, 3.2.3
		By airline. International scheduled airline	Annual & Monthly	[QRL 13]	2.3.1, 3.2.3
		By domestic scheduled airline	Annual & Monthly	[QRL 13]	2.3.1, 3.2.3
		By airline. Scheduled all freight services	Annual & Monthly	[QRL 13]	2.3.1, 3.2.3
		By airline. Passenger services	Annual	[QRL 136]	2.3.2, 3.2.3
		By airline. Total and all freight services separately	Annual	[QRL 141]	2.3.4, 3.2.3
		Total UK airways	Annual	[QRL 137, 28]	1.3.6, 3.2.3
		Total UK private companies	Annual	[QRL 28]	1.3.6, 3.2.3
Aircraft departures		By international scheduled airline	Annual & Monthly	[QRL 13]	2.3.1, 3.2.3
		By domestic scheduled airline	Annual & Monthly	[QRL 13]	2.3.1, 3.2.3
		By airline. Scheduled. All-freight services	Annual & Monthly	[QRL 13]	2.3.1, 3.2.3
		By airline. Total and all freight services separately	Annual	[QRL 141]	2.3.4, 3.2.3
Average stage distance		By airline. Passenger services	Annual	[QRL 136]	2.3.2, 3.2.3
(Stage flights—average length)		Total UK airways	Annual	[QRL 28]	1.3.6, 3.2.3
(Stage flights—average length)		Total UK private companies	Annual	[QRL 28]	1.3.6, 3.2.3
Stage flights		By airline. Passenger and cargo services separately	Annual	[QRL 51]	1.3.2, 3.2.3
		By airline. Passenger and cargo services separately	Monthly	[QRL 52]	1.3.2, 3.2.3
		By airline. Passenger and freight services separately	Monthly	[QRL 42, 98]	2.1.3, 3.2.3

QUICK REFERENCE LIST

Category	Frequency	Reference	Sections
Total UK airways	Annual	[QRL 28]	1.3.6, 3.2.3
Total UK private companies	Annual	[QRL 28]	1.3.6, 3.2.3
By airline. Passenger services	Annual	[QRL 136]	2.3.2, 3.2.3
By airline	Annual	[QRL 141]	2.3.4, 3.2.3
Unduplicated route km (Length of scheduled route network)			
Aircraft hours			
By airline. Passenger and cargo services separately	Annual	[QRL 51]	2.1.2, 3.2.3, 2.1.3
By airline. Passenger and cargo services separately	Monthly	[QRL 52]	2.1.2, 3.2.3, 2.1.3
By airline. Passenger and freight services separately	Monthly	[QRL 42, 98]	2.1.3, 3.2.3
By airline. International scheduled airlines	Annual & Monthly	[QRL 13]	2.3.1, 3.2.3
By airline. Domestic scheduled airline	Annual	[QRL 13]	2.3.1, 3.2.3
By airline. Scheduled all freight services	Annual & Monthly	[QRL 13]	2.3.1, 3.3.2
By airline. Passenger services	Annual	[QRL 136]	2.3.2, 3.2.3
By airline. Total and all freight services separately	Annual	[QRL 141]	2.3.4, 3.2.3
No. of revenue landings			
By airline. Passenger services	Annual	[QRL 136]	2.3.2, 3.2.3
Non-scheduled services			
All services			
Aircraft km			
By airline. Passenger and cargo services separately	Annual & Monthly	[QRL 51, 52]	2.1.2, 3.2.3, 2.1.3
By airline (Miles)	Monthly	[QRL 41, 98]	2.1.3, 3.2.3
By airline (Percentage increase on last year)	Monthly	[QRL 41, 98]	2.1.3, 3.2.3
By airline	Monthly	[QRL 42, 98]	2.1.3, 3.2.3
By airline. Non-scheduled operators	Annual	[QRL 122]	2.3.1, 3.2.3
By airline. Scheduled airlines	Annual	[QRL 122]	2.3.1, 3.2.3
By scheduled airline. All freight traffic	Annual	[QRL 122]	2.3.1, 3.2.3
By international scheduled airline	Annual & Monthly	[QRL 13]	2.3.1, 3.2.3
By domestic scheduled airline	Annual & Monthly	[QRL 13]	2.3.1, 3.2.3
By airline. All freight services	Annual & Monthly	[QRL 13]	2.3.1, 3.2.3
Aircraft departures			
By airline	Annual	[QRL 141]	2.3.4, 3.2.3
By airline. Non-scheduled operators	Annual	[QRL 122]	2.3.1, 3.2.3

CIVIL AVIATION

Descriptive title	Breakdown	Frequency	Publication (see QRL Key)	Text reference and remarks
AIRCRAFT (contd.) Non-scheduled services (contd.) All services (contd.)				
	By scheduled airline	Annual	[QRL 122]	2.3.1, 3.2.3
	By scheduled airline. All freight traffic	Annual	[QRL 122]	2.3.1, 3.2.3
	By international scheduled airline	Annual & Monthly	[QRL 13]	2.3.1, 3.2.3
	By domestic scheduled airline	Annual & Monthly	[QRL 13]	2.3.1, 3.2.3
	By airline. All freight services	Annual & Monthly	[QRL 13]	2.3.1, 3.2.3
Average stage distance per aircraft	By airline	Annual	[QRL 141]	2.3.4, 3.2.3
	By airline. Non-scheduled operators	Annual	[QRL 122]	2.3.1, 3.2.3
Stage flights	By airline. Passenger and cargo services separately	Annual	[QRL 51]	2.1.2, 3.2.3, 2.1.3
	By airline. Passenger and cargo services separately	Monthly	[QRL 52]	2.1.2, 3.2.3, 2.1.3
	By airline	Monthly	[QRL 42, 98]	2.1.3, 3.2.3
	By airline. Passenger and cargo services separately	Annual	[QRL 51]	2.1.2, 3.2.3, 2.1.3
Aircraft hours	By airline. Passenger and cargo services separately	Monthly	[QRL 52]	2.1.2, 3.2.3, 2.1.3
	By airline	Monthly	[QRL 42, 98]	2.1.3, 3.2.3
	By airline. Non-scheduled operators. Revenue transport services	Annual	[QRL 122]	2.3.1, 3.2.3
	By airline. Non-scheduled operators—aerial work and non-revenue separately	Annual	[QRL 122]	2.3.1, 3.2.3
	By scheduled airline	Annual	[QRL 122]	2.3.1, 3.2.3
	By scheduled airline. Non-revenue	Annual	[QRL 122]	2.3.1, 3.2.3
	By scheduled airline. All freight traffic	Annual	[QRL 122]	2.3.1, 3.2.3
	By scheduled airline. Non-revenue. All freight traffic	Annual	[QRL 122]	2.3.1, 3.2.3
	By international scheduled airline	Annual & Monthly	[QRL 13]	2.3.1, 3.2.3
	By domestic scheduled airline	Annual & Monthly	[QRL 13]	2.3.1, 3.2.3

QUICK REFERENCE LIST

	By airline. All freight services	Annual & Monthly	[QRL 13]	2.3.1, 3.2.3
	By airline	Annual	[QRL 141]	2.3.4, 3.2.3
International services				
Aircraft km	By airline. Passenger and cargo services separately	Annual	[QRL 51]	2.1.2, 3.2.3, 2.1.3
	By airline. Passenger and cargo services separately	Monthly	[QRL 52]	2.1.2, 3.2.3, 2.1.3
(Miles)	By airline	Annual	[QRL 41, 98]	2.1.3, 3.2.3
(Miles)	By airline	Monthly	[QRL 42, 98]	2.1.3, 3.2.3
	By airline. Non-scheduled operators	Annual	[QRL 122]	2.3.1, 3.2.3
	By scheduled airline	Annual	[QRL 122]	2.3.1, 3.2.3
	By scheduled airline. All freight traffic	Annual	[QRL 122]	2.3.1, 3.2.3
	By international scheduled airline	Annual & Monthly	[QRL 13]	2.3.1, 3.2.3
	By domestic scheduled airline	Annual & Monthly	[QRL 13]	2.3.1, 3.2.3
	By scheduled airline. All freight services	Annual & Monthly	[QRL 13]	2.3.1, 3.2.3
Aircraft movements	By airline	Annual	[QRL 141]	2.3.4, 3.2.3
Aircraft departures	By airport	Annual	[QRL 59]	2.3.1, 3.2.3
	By airline. Non-scheduled operators	Annual	[QRL 122]	2.3.1, 3.2.3
	By scheduled airline	Annual	[QRL 122]	2.3.1, 3.2.3
	By scheduled airline. All freight traffic	Annual	[QRL 122]	2.3.1, 3.2.3
	By international scheduled airline	Annual & Monthly	[QRL 13]	2.3.1, 3.2.3
	By domestic scheduled airline	Annual & Monthly	[QRL 13]	2.3.1, 3.2.3
	By airline. All freight services	Annual & Monthly	[QRL 13]	2.3.1, 3.2.3
Stage km	By airline	Annual	[QRL 141]	2.3.4, 3.2.3
	By airline. Passenger and cargo services separately	Annual	[QRL 51]	2.1.2, 3.2.3, 2.1.3
	By airline. Passenger and cargo services separately	Monthly	[QRL 52]	2.1.2, 3.2.3, 2.1.3
Aircraft hours	By airline	Monthly	[QRL 42, 98]	2.1.3, 3.2.3
	By airline. Passenger and cargo services separately	Annual	[QRL 51]	2.1.2, 3.2.3, 2.1.3
	By airline. Passenger and cargo services separately	Monthly	[QRL 52]	2.1.2, 3.2.3, 2.1.3
	By airline	Monthly	[QRL 42, 98]	2.1.3, 3.2.3

206   CIVIL AVIATION

Descriptive title	Breakdown	Frequency	Publication (see QRL Key)	Text reference and remarks
AIRCRAFT (*contd.*)				
Non-scheduled services (*contd.*)				
International services (*contd.*)				
	By airline. Non-scheduled operators	Annual	[QRL 122]	2.3.1, 3.2.3
	By airline. Scheduled airlines	Annual	[QRL 122]	2.3.1, 3.2.3
	By scheduled airline. Non-revenue	Annual	[QRL 122]	2.3.1, 3.2.3
	By scheduled airline. All freight traffic	Annual	[QRL 122]	2.3.1, 3.2.3
	By scheduled airline. All freight services. Non-revenue	Annual	[QRL 122]	2.3.1, 3.2.3
	By international scheduled airline	Annual & Monthly	[QRL 13]	2.3.1, 3.2.3
	By domestic scheduled airline	Annual & Monthly	[QRL 13]	2.3.1, 3.2.3
	By airline. All freight services	Annual & Monthly	[QRL 13]	2.3.1, 3.2.3
	By airline	Annual	[QRL 141]	2.3.4, 3.2.3
Aircraft flights (Between UK and abroad)	Aircraft registered in UK and abroad separately. Total	Annual	[QRL 28]	1.3.6, 3.2.3
Domestic services				
Aircraft km	By airline. Passenger and cargo services separately	Annual	[QRL 51]	2.1.2, 3.2.3, 2.1.3
	By airline. Passenger and cargo services separately	Monthly	[QRL 52]	2.1.2, 3.2.3, 2.1.3
(Miles)	By airline	Annual & Monthly	[QRL 41, 98]	2.1.3, 3.2.3
	By airline. Non-scheduled operators	Annual	[QRL 122]	2.3.1, 3.2.3
	By international scheduled airline	Annual & Monthly	[QRL 13]	2.3.1, 3.2.3
(Miles)	By domestic scheduled airline	Annual & Monthly	[QRL 13]	2.3.1, 3.2.3
	By airline. Scheduled airline. All freight services	Annual & Monthly	[QRL 13]	2.3.1, 3.2.3
Aircraft departures	By airline	Annual	[QRL 141]	2.3.4, 3.2.3
	By airline. Non-scheduled operators	Annual	[QRL 122]	2.3.1, 3.2.3
	By international scheduled airline	Annual & Monthly	[QRL 13]	2.3.1, 3.2.3

QUICK REFERENCE LIST

	By domestic scheduled airline	Annual & Monthly	[QRL 13]	2.3.1, 3.2.3
	By scheduled airline. All freight services	Annual & Monthly	[QRL 13]	2.3.1, 3.2.3
Stage flights	By airline. Passenger and cargo services separately	Annual	[QRL 51]	2.1.2, 3.2.3, 2.1.3
	By airline. Passenger and cargo services separately	Monthly	[QRL 52]	2.1.2, 3.2.3, 2.1.3
Aircraft hours	By airline	Monthly	[QRL 42, 98]	2.1.3, 3.2.3
	By airline. Passenger and cargo services separately	Annual	[QRL 51]	2.1.2, 3.2.3, 2.1.3
	By airline. Passenger and cargo services separately	Monthly	[QRL 52]	2.1.2, 3.2.3, 2.1.3
	By airline	Monthly	[QRL 42, 98]	2.1.3, 3.2.3
	By airline. Non-scheduled operators	Annual	[QRL 122]	2.3.1, 3.2.3
	By international scheduled airline	Annual & Monthly	[QRL 14]	2.3.1, 3.2.3
	By international scheduled airline	Annual & Monthly	[QRL 13]	2.3.1, 3.2.3
	By domestic scheduled airline	Monthly	[QRL 13]	2.3.1, 3.2.3
	By scheduled airline. All freight services	Annual & Monthly	[QRL 13]	2.3.1, 3.2.3
	By airline	Annual	[QRL 141]	2.3.4, 3.2.3
Inclusive tours				
Aircraft km	Total UK airlines	Annual	[QRL 51]	2.1.2, 3.2.3, 2.1.3
	Total UK airlines	Monthly	[QRL 52]	2.1.2, 3.2.3, 2.1.3
	By airline. All, international, domestic, inclusive tour charters	Monthly	[QRL 42, 98]	2.1.3, 3.2.3
Aircraft hours	Total UK airways	Annual	[QRL 28]	1.3.6, 3.2.3
	By airline. All, domestic, international inclusive tour charters	Monthly	[QRL 42, 98]	2.1.3, 3.2.3
Stage flights (number)	Total UK airlines	Annual	[QRL 51]	2.1.2, 3.2.3, 2.1.3
	Total UK airlines	Annual	[QRL 52]	2.1.2, 3.2.3, 2.1.3
	By airline. All, international, domestic inclusive tour charters	Monthly	[QRL 42, 98]	2.1.3, 3.2.3
Stage flights average distance	Total UK airlines	Annual	[QRL 28]	1.3.6, 3.2.3
	Total UK airlines	Annual	[QRL 51]	2.1.2, 3.2.3, 2.1.3
	Total UK airlines	Monthly	[QRL 52]	2.1.2, 3.2.3, 2.1.3
	Total UK airlines	Annual	[QRL 28]	1.3.6, 3.2.3

208   CIVIL AVIATION

Descriptive title	Breakdown	Frequency	Publication (see QRL Key)	Text reference and remarks
AIRCRAFT (*contd.*)				
Non-scheduled services (*contd.*)				
Domestic services (*contd.*)				
Other separate fare, and ABC				
Aircraft km	Total for UK airlines	Annual	[QRL 51]	2.1.2, 3.2.3, 2.1.3
	Total for UK airlines	Monthly	[QRL 52]	2.1.2, 3.2.3, 2.1.3
	By airline. Other separate fare charters, all, domestic, international	Monthly	[QRL 42, 98]	2.1.3, 3.2.3
(Miles)	By airline. All exempt services and sub-charters, all, domestic, international	Monthly	[QRL 42, 98]	2.1.3, 3.2.3
Aircraft hours	Total UK airlines	Annual	[QRL 28]	1.3.6, 3.2.3
	By airline. Other separate fare charters. All domestic, international	Monthly	[QRL 42, 98]	2.1.3, 3.2.3
	By airline. All exempt services and sub-charters, all domestic and international	Monthly	[QRL 42, 98]	2.1.3, 3.2.3
Stage flights	Total UK airlines	Annual & Monthly	[QRL 51, 52]	2.1.2, 2.1.3, 3.2.3
	By airline. Other separate fare charters, all, domestic, international	Monthly	[QRL 42, 98]	2.1.3, 3.2.3
	By airline. All exempt services sub-charters. All, domestic and international	Monthly	[QRL 42, 98]	2.1.3, 3.2.3
Stage flights average distance	Total UK airlines	Annual	[QRL 28]	1.3.6, 3.2.3
	Total for UK airlines	Annual & Monthly	[QRL 51, 52]	2.1.2, 2.1.3, 3.2.3
	Total for UK airlines	Annual	[QRL 28]	1.3.6, 3.2.3
Miscellaneous totals				
Aircraft km and hours flown	By type of service: international and domestic routes separately	Annual	[QRL 61]	2.3.1, 3.2.3
Aircraft hours non-revenue	By international scheduled airline. International, domestic and all	Annual & Monthly	[QRL 13]	2.3.1, 3.2.3
	By international scheduled airline. International and domestic	Annual & Monthly	[QRL 13]	2.3.1, 3.2.3
	By international scheduled airline. Domestic	Annual & Monthly	[QRL 13]	2.3.1, 3.2.3
	By domestic scheduled airline. International domestic and all	Annual	[QRL 13]	2.3.1, 3.2.3

QUICK REFERENCE LIST

Aircraft flights	By airline. All freight services—international domestic and all	Annual & Monthly	[QRL 13]	2.3.1, 3.2.3
	By airline	Annual	[QRL 141]	2.3.4, 3.2.3
	Air traffic between UK and abroad	Annual	[QRL 28]	1.3.6, 3.2.3
By licence operations				
Licence applications	By type of application and result of application	Annual 1960–70	[QRL 25]	1.3.6, 3.2.3
Aircraft km	Classes 2, 3, 4, 6, 7 and exempt: international and domestic and class 5: UK and non-UK	Annual & Monthly	[QRL 51, 52]	2.1.2, 2.1.3, 3.2.3
Stage flights	Classes 2, 3, 4, 6, 7 and exempt: international and domestic and class 5: UK and non-UK	Annual & Monthly	[QRL 51, 52]	2.1.2, 2.1.3, 3.2.3
Aircraft hours	Classes 2, 3, 4, 6, 7 and exempt: international and domestic and class 5: UK and non-UK	Annual & Monthly	[QRL 51, 52]	2.1.2, 2.1.3, 3.2.3
Aircraft type and utilization				
Aircraft type and manufacturer	Details about each type of aircraft	Annual	[QRL 77]	1.3.3, 3.2.3
Aircraft km	All UK airlines. By aircraft type	Annual & Monthly	[QRL 51, 52]	2.1.2, 2.1.3, 3.2.3
	By airline. By aircraft type	Annual & Monthly	[QRL 51, 52]	2.2.1, 2.1.3, 3.2.3
Stage flights: passenger and cargo separately	By airline. By aircraft type	Annual	[QRL 42, 98]	2.1.3, 3.2.3
	By airline. By aircraft type	Annual & Monthly	[QRL 51, 52]	2.1.2, 2.1.3, 3.2.3
	All airlines. By aircraft type	Annual & Monthly	[QRL 51, 52]	2.1.2, 2.1.3, 3.2.3
Aircraft hours				
(Passenger and cargo separately)	By UK airlines. By aircraft type	Monthly	[QRL 42, 98]	2.1.3, 3.2.3
(Passenger and cargo separately)	All UK airlines. By aircraft type	Annual & Monthly	[QRL 51, 52]	2.1.2, 2.1.3, 3.2.3
(Passenger and cargo separately)	By airline. By aircraft type	Annual & Monthly	[QRL 51, 52]	2.1.2, 2.1.3, 3.2.3
(Total and revenue)	By scheduled airline. Aircraft type, manufacturer, model and weight	Annual	[QRL 61]	2.3.1, 3.2.3
(Total and revenue)	By scheduled airline, aircraft type, manufacturer, model and domestic/international airline	Annual	[QRL 61]	2.3.1, 3.2.3
(Total and revenue)	By non-scheduled operator, manufacturer, model and weight	Annual	[QRL 122]	2.3.1, 3.2.3

210   CIVIL AVIATION

Descriptive title	Breakdown	Frequency	Publication (see QRL Key)	Text reference and remarks
AIRCRAFT (contd.)				
Aircraft type and utilization (contd.)				
Aircraft in service				
(At end of year or quarter)	All UK airlines. By aircraft type	Annual & Quarterly	[QRL 51, 52] [QRL 42, 98]	2.1.2, 2.1.3, 3.2.3
(At end of year or quarter)	By airline. By aircraft type	Annual & Quarterly	[QRL 51, 52]	2.1.2, 2.1.3, 3.2.3
(At end of month)	By airline. By aircraft type	Monthly	[QRL 42, 98]	2.1.3, 3.2.3
	By airline. International scheduled airlines	Monthly	[QRL 42, 98]	2.1.3, 3.2.3
	By scheduled airline. Aircraft type, manufacturer, model and weight	Annual	[QRL 61]	2.3.1, 3.2.3
	By scheduled airline. Aircraft type, manufactuter, model and domestic/international airline	Annual	[QRL 61]	2.3.1, 3.2.3
	Domestic scheduled airlines. By airline and manufacturer and model	Annual	[QRL 61]	2.3.1, 3.2.3
(Fleet)	By airline. Non-scheduled operators	Annual	[QRL 122]	2.3.1, 3.2.3
Daily utilization per aircraft	All UK airlines. By aircraft type	Annual & Quarterly	[QRL 51, 52]	2.1.2, 2.1.3, 3.2.3
	By airline. By aircraft type	Annual & Quarterly	[QRL 51, 52]	2.1.2, 2.1.3, 3.2.3
(Average daily revenue hours)	Fixed-wing turbo jet aircraft 9000 kg and over. By airline, manufacturer and model	Annual	[QRL 61]	2.3.1, 3.2.3
(Average daily revenue hours)	International scheduled airlines. By airline, manufacturer and model	Annual	[QRL 61]	2.3.1, 3.2.3
(Average daily revenue hours)	Domestic schedule airlines. By airline, manufacturer and model	Annual	[QRL 61]	2.3.1, 3.2.3
(Average daily utilization)	By aircraft type and airline	Annual	[QRL 141]	2.3.4, 3.2.3
Average annual utilization per aircraft (hours)	All UK airlines	Annual	[QRL 42, 51, 98]	2.1.3, 3.2.3
(Annual utilization total)	By airline	Annual	[QRL 42, 51, 98]	2.1.3, 3.2.3
	By airline—short/medium haul and long haul separately	Annual	[QRL 136]	2.3.2, 3.2.3
	By scheduled airline. Aircraft type, manufacturer, model and weight	Annual	[QRL 61]	2.3.1, 3.2.3

QUICK REFERENCE LIST

	By scheduled airline. Aircraft type, manufacturer, model and domestic/international airline	Annual	[QRL 61]	2.3.1, 3.2.3
	By non-scheduled operator. Manufacturer, model and weight	Annual	[QRL 122]	2.3.1, 3.2.3
Civil aircraft on register (Commercial air transport operators)	By country. Aircraft type, weight, manufacturer and model	Annual & Monthly	[QRL 50]	2.3.1, 3.2.3
Civil aircraft on register (Other operators)	By country and aircraft type. Weight, manufacturer and model	Annual & Monthly	[QRL 50]	2.3.1, 3.2.3
Civil aircraft on register (Total)	By country and aircraft type. Weight, manufacturer and model	Annual & Monthly	[QRL 50]	2.3.1, 3.2.3
	By aircraft registration marks. Supply no., owner, type, constructor's number, year of construction, engine, maximum weight lb/kg, certificate of airworthiness, category and date of expiry, remarks	Annual	[QRL 76]	1.3.3, 3.2.3
	By registration number, manufacturer, serial number, make, model, year manufactured, owner and owner's address. For aircraft on US Civil Aircraft register	Annual	[QRL 76]	1.3.3, 3.2.3
Average maximum take-off weights	By airline. Aircraft type, manufacturer, model and weight	Annual	[QRL 61]	2.3.1, 3.2.3
	By scheduled airline. Manufacturer, model and domestic/international airline	Annual	[QRL 61]	2.3.1, 3.2.3
Total tonnes of maximum take-off weights	By non-scheduled operator. Manufacturer, model and weight	Annual	[QRL 122]	2.3.1, 3.2.3
Utilization: no. of departures: total and renewal	By scheduled airline. Aircraft type, manufacturer, model and weight	Annual	[QRL 61]	2.3.1, 3.2.3
	By scheduled airline. Aircraft type, manufacturer, model and domestic/international airline	Annual	[QRL 61]	2.3.1, 3.2.3
	By non-scheduled operator, manufacturer, model and weight	Annual	[QRL 122]	2.3.1, 3.2.3
Aircraft in service at the end of the year	By non-scheduled owner/operator. Manufacturer, model and weight	Annual	[QRL 122]	2.3.1, 3.2.3
(No. of aircraft)	By airline	Annual	[QRL 136]	2.3.2, 3.2.3
(No. of aircraft)	By aircraft type and airline. Own operations and total operations, separately	Annual	[QRL 136]	2.3.2, 3.2.3

212 CIVIL AVIATION

Descriptive title	Breakdown	Frequency	Publication (see QRL Key)	Text reference and remarks
AIRCRAFT (*contd.*)				
Aircraft type and utilization (*contd.*)				
(Operating fleet)	By aircraft type and airline	Annual	[QRL 141]	2.3.4, 3.2.3
Flight stage	By airline. Type of aircraft and no. of flights	Monthly	[QRL 62]	2.3.1, 3.2.3
	By station pair, airlines, type of aircraft and no. of flights	Monthly	[QRL 62]	2.3.1, 3.2.3
Aircraft revenue hours per aircraft	By aircraft type and airline. Own and total operations separately	Annual	[QRL 136]	2.3.2, 3.2.3
Average stage distance	By aircraft type and airline. Own and total operations separately	Annual	[QRL 136]	2.3.2, 3.2.3
All up weight	By aircraft type	Annual	[QRL 69]	1.3.2, 3.2.3
Tyre pressure	By aircraft type	Annual	[QRL 69]	1.3.2, 3.2.3
Load classification	By aircraft type	Annual	[QRL 69]	1.3.2, 3.2.3
Aircraft movements				
Total movements	Total for UK airports and percentage change over time	Annual	[QRL 51]	2.1.2, 2.1.3, 3.2.3
	By airport over time	Annual	[QRL 51]	2.1.2, 2.1.3, 3.2.3
	By airport	Annual & Monthly	[QRL 51, 52]	2.1.2, 2.1.3, 3.2.3
		Annual (except where quarterly)	[QRL 38, 127]	2.1.2, 3.2.2
	Total—all airports and London area airports quarterly	Annual (except where quarterly)	[QRL 38, 127]	2.1.2, 3.2.3
	By airport for Commercial Air Transport	Annual & Monthly	[QRL 59]	2.3.1, 3.2.3
	By airport for total international air transport	Annual & Monthly	[QRL 59]	2.3.1, 3.2.3
	By airport for domestic air transport	Annual & Monthly	[QRL 59]	2.3.1, 3.2.3
	By airport all other	Annual & Monthly	[QRL 59]	2.3.1, 3.2.3
	By airport	Annual & Monthly	[QRL 125]	2.3.3, 3.2.3
	By airport	Quarterly	[QRL 108]	2.2.1, 3.2.3

QUICK REFERENCE LIST

Commercial movements	Total for UK airports over time	Annual & Monthly	[QRL 51, 52]	2.1.2, 2.1.3, 3.2.3
	By airport. Per cent of total movement	Annual	[QRL 125]	2.3.3, 3.2.3
	Civil aircraft. Total activity at civil aerodromes	Annual	[QRL 28]	1.3.6, 3.2.3
Commercial movements other than air transport	Total for UK airports over time	Annual & Monthly	[QRL 51, 52]	2.1.2, 2.1.3, 3.2.3
Commercial movements other than air transport movements, local pleasure and empty charter positioning	Total activity at civil aerodromes	Annual	[QRL 28]	1.3.6, 3.2.3
	By airport	Annual (except where quarterly)	[QRL 38, 127]	2.1.2, 3.2.3
	By airport	Annual & Monthly	[QRL 51, 52]	2.1.2, 2.1.3, 3.2.3
Non-commercial movements other than aero club and private, test and training	Total for UK airports, by airport	Annual	[QRL 51]	2.1.2, 2.1.3, 3.2.3
Non-commercial movements other than general aviation	By airport. Per cent of total	Annual	[QRL 125]	2.3.3, 3.2.3
Air transport movements	Total for UK airports and annual percentage change over time	Annual	[QRL 51]	2.1.2, 2.1.3, 3.2.3
	Total for UK airports	Annual & Monthly	[QRL 51, 52]	2.1.2, 2.1.3, 3.2.3
	By airport and annual per cent change over time	Annual	[QRL 51, 52]	2.1.2, 2.1.3, 3.2.3
	By airport	Annual (except where quarterly)	[QRL 38, 127]	2.1.2, 3.2.3
	Total for all airports, London area airport	Annual (except where quarterly)	[QRL 38, 127]	2.1.2, 3.2.3
	By airports, airports ranked	Annual & Monthly	[QRL 125]	2.3.3, 3.2.3
	By airport	Annual & Monthly	[QRL 125]	2.3.3, 3.2.3
	By airport and per cent	Annual & Monthly	[QRL 125]	2.3.3, 3.2.3
Cargo and mail aircraft	By airport	Annual	[QRL 137]	1.3.6, 3.2.3
	By airport and type of flight. All mixed and all cargo, BAA airports	Quarterly	[QRL 108]	2.2.1, 3.2.3

Descriptive title	Breakdown	Frequency	Publication (see QRL Key)	Text reference and remarks
AIRCRAFT (*contd.*)				
Aircraft movements (*contd.*)				
	By airport. Combined aircraft	Monthly	[QRL 125]	2.3.3, 3.2.3
	By airport. BAA airports	Quarterly	[QRL 108]	2.2.1, 3.2.3
	By civil aircraft. Total activity of civil aerodromes	Annual	[QRL 28]	1.3.6, 3.2.3
Non-commercial movements	Total for UK airports over time	Annual	[QRL 51, 52]	2.1.2, 2.1.3, 3.2.3
	By airport per cent of total	Annual & Monthly	[QRL 125]	2.3.3, 3.2.3
	Civil aircraft. Total activity at civil aerodromes	Annual	[QRL 28]	1.3.6, 3.2.3
Non-commercial movements: aero club and private (separately)	Total for UK airports	Annual since 1961	[QRL 51, 52]	2.1.2, 2.1.3, 3.2.3
	By airport	Annual & Monthly	[QRL 51, 52] [QRL 38, 127]	2.1.2, 2.1.3, 3.2.3
Non-commercial movements: test and training	Total for UK airports	Annual & Monthly	[QRL 51, 52]	2.1.2, 3.2.3, 2.1.3
	By airport	Annual & Monthly	[QRL 51, 52, 38, 137]	2.1.2, 3.2.3, 2.1.3
Non-commercial movements: general aviation	By airport	Quarterly	[QRL 108]	2.2.1, 3.2.3
	By airport, per cent of total	Annual & Monthly	[QRL 125]	2.3.3, 3.2.3
	By airport	Annual & Monthly	[QRL 125]	2.3.3, 3.2.3
Commercial movements: local pleasure	By airport	Quarterly	[QRL 108]	2.2.1, 3.2.3
	By airport	Annual & Monthly	[QRL 51, 52] [QRL 38, 137]	2.1.2, 3.2.3, 2.1.3
Commercial movements: empty charter positioning	By airport	Annual & Monthly	[QRL 51, 52] [QRL 38, 137]	2.1.2, 3.2.3, 2.1.3
Non-commercial: other flights by air transport operators	By airport	Annual & Monthly	[QRL 51, 52] [QRL 38, 137]	2.1.2, 3.2.3, 2.1.3
Non-commercial: private	By airport	Annual & Monthly	[QRL 51, 52] [QRL 38, 137]	2.1.2, 3.2.3, 2.1.3
Non-commercial: official	By airport	Annual & Monthly	[QRL 51, 52] [QRL 38, 137]	2.2.2, 3.2.3, 2.1.3
Air-transport movements: average increase over previous 5 years	Total for all airports and London area airports	Annual	[QRL 38, 127] [QRL 69]	2.1.2, 3.2.3, 2.1.3 1.3.2, 3.2.3

QUICK REFERENCE LIST

(Average annual growth rate over 5 years)	Total for all airports, London area airports separately (quarterly)	Annual	[QRL 38, 127]	2.1.2, 3.2.3
Total movements: mean percentage change (last 5 years)	By airport over time	Annual	[QRL 51]	2.1.2, 3.2.3, 2.1.3
(Average annual growth rate over 5 years)	Total for all airports, London area airports separately (quarterly)	Annual	[QRL 38, 127]	2.1.2, 3.2.3
Non-commercial: military	By airport	Annual & Monthly	[QRL 51, 52]	2.1.2, 3.2.3, 2.1.3
	By airport	Quarterly	[QRL 38, 127]	
			[QRL 108]	2.2.1, 3.2.3
Air transport movements: scheduled services: UK operators (BA and others)	By airport	Annual & Monthly	[QRL 51, 52]	2.1.2, 3.2.3, 2.1.3
			[QRL 38, 127]	
	Total UK airports	Annual & Monthly	[QRL 51, 52]	2.1.2, 3.2.3, 2.1.3
(Corporation and others) (BA and others)	By airport	Annual	[QRL 137]	1.3.6, 3.2.3
Air transport movements: Scheduled services: overseas operators	By airport	Annual & Monthly	[QRL 51, 52]	2.1.2, 3.2.3, 2.1.3
			[QRL 38, 127]	
	Total UK airports	Annual & Monthly	[QRL 51, 52]	2.1.2, 3.2.3, 2.1.3
Air transport movements: charter services: overseas operators (Non-scheduled)	By airport	Annual	[QRL 137]	1.3.6, 3.2.3
	By airport	Annual & Monthly	[QRL 51, 52]	2.1.2, 3.2.3, 2.1.3
			[QRL 38, 127]	
	Total UK airports	Annual & Monthly	[QRL 51, 52]	2.1.2, 3.2.3, 2.1.3
			[QRL 38, 127]	
Air transport movements: charter services: UK operators (BA and others)	By airport	Annual	[QRL 137]	1.3.6, 3.2.3
	By airport	Annual & Monthly	[QRL 51, 52]	2.1.2, 3.2.3, 2.1.3
			[QRL 38, 127]	
(Corporation and others) (BA and others)	Total UK airports	Annual & Monthly	[QRL 51, 52]	2.1.2, 3.2.3, 2.1.3
	By airport	Annual	[QRL 137]	1.3.6, 3.2.3
International air transport movements	By airport,	Annual & Monthly	[QRL 51, 52]	2.1.2, 3.2.3, 2.1.3
(+ per cent change on last year)	By airport	Annual & Monthly	[QRL 125]	2.3.3, 3.2.3

Descriptive title	Breakdown	Frequency	Publication (see QRL Key)	Text reference and remarks
AIRCRAFT (*contd.*)				
Aircraft movements (*contd.*)				
	By airport and type of flight. All mixed, all cargo	Quarterly	[QRL 108]	2.1.2, 3.2.3
Domestic air transport movement	By airport	Annual & Monthly	[QRL 125]	2.3.3, 3.2.3
	By airport and type of flight. All mixed, all cargo	Quarterly	[QRL 108]	2.2.1, 3.2.3
Air transport landings diverted	No. and rate by airport of intended landing	Annual & Monthly	[QRL 51, 52]	2.1.2, 3.2.3, 2.1.3
	By UK airports of actual and intended landings	Annual & Monthly	[QRL 51, 52]	2.1.2, 3.2.3, 2.1.3
	By UK airports of actual and intended landings and date of diversion	Monthly	[QRL 52]	2.1.2, 3.2.3, 2.1.3
	By airport of actual and intended landing and date of diversion	Annual	[QRL 38, 127]	2.1.2, 3.2.3
Air transport movements	Peak month and peak day by BAA airport	Annual	[QRL 105]	2.2.1, 3.2.3
	Ratio peak to average month by BAA airport 10 years	Annual & Monthly	[QRL 105]	2.2.1, 3.2.3
	Hourly traffic flows by BAA airport—arrival, departure, two-way	Annual & Monthly	[QRL 105]	2.2.1, 3.2.3
	Comparative Standard Busy Rate (SBR) flows: by BAA airport—arrival, departure, two-way	Annual	[QRL 105]	2.2.1, 3.2.3
	Ratio of SBR to annual traffic ($\times 10^{-6}$) by BAA airport—arrival, departure, two-way	Annual	[QRL 105]	2.2.1, 3.2.3
	Percentage handled per month by BAA airport	Annual	[QRL 105]	2.2.1, 3.2.3
	Daily pattern of traffic over a peak week by BAA airport	Annual	[QRL 105]	2.2.1, 3.2.3
	Percentage of arrival ATM traffic handled in each hour of an average busy day by BAA airport	Annual	[QRL 105]	2.2.1, 3.2.3
	Percentage of two-way ATM traffic handled in each hour of an average busy day by BAA airport	Annual	[QRL 105]	2.2.1, 3.2.3
Air transport movements	Percentage increase on last year	Annual	[QRL 51]	2.1.2, 3.2.3, 2.1.3

	Total for all airports, London area airports separate	Quarterly	[QRL 38, 127]	2.1.2, 3.2.3
	By passenger and cargo aircraft	Monthly	[QRL 52]	2.1.2, 3.2.3
	By airport	Annual	[QRL 38, 127]	2.1.2, 3.2.3
	Percentage increase on last year	Annual	[QRL 51]	2.1.2, 3.2.3, 2.1.3
Total movements	Total all airports. London area airports separate	Quarterly	[QRL 38, 127]	2.1.2, 3.2.3
Air traffic control figures				
Total movements: by day and UK overflights, ATCC overflights and others	By air traffic control centre	Annual	[QRL 22]	2.1.8, 3.2.3
Total flights	By sector	Annual*	[QRL 22]*	2.1.8, 3.2.3
	Middle air space service, London ATCC	Annual	[QRL 22]	2.1.8, 3.2.3
	By sector	Annual	[QRL 22]	2.1.8, 3.2.3
	All flights by day, hour and sector middle air space service, London ATCC	Annual	[QRL 22]	2.1.8, 3.2.3
	Peak values	Annual	[QRL 22]	2.1.8, 3.2.3
	By air traffic control centre	Annual	[QRL 22]	2.1.8, 3.2.3
	Middle air space services, London ATCC	Annual	[QRL 22]	2.1.8, 3.2.3
	By airway/upper air routes by day and sector	Annual	[QRL 22]	2.1.8, 3.2.3
	Hourly distribution, day, hour and type of flight traffic control area north/south	Annual	[QRL 22]	2.1.8, 3.2.3
Total movements	By day and type of flight. By air traffic control centre	Annual	[QRL 22]	2.1.8, 3.2.3
	By day and type of aircraft. By air traffic control centre	Annual	[QRL 22]	2.1.8, 3.2.3
	Hourly entry rate. All flights by hour and day. By air traffic control centre	Annual	[QRL 22]	2.1.8, 3.2.3
	By day and flight level	Annual	[QRL 22]	2.1.8, 3.2.3
	By air-traffic control centre	Annual	[QRL 22]	2.1.8, 3.2.3
	Busiest hour and busiest minute. By day and sector	Annual	[QRL 22]	2.1.8, 3.2.3
Daily movements at selected airports	By airport and day	Annual	[QRL 22]	2.1.8, 3.2.3
Peak hourly movement rate at selected airports	By airport, day, rate and peak hour	Annual	[QRL 22]	2.1.8, 3.2.3

*All [QRL 22] in this section have data annually from 1965 until 1974 and biennially from 1974 onwards.

CIVIL AVIATION

Descriptive title	Breakdown	Frequency	Publication (see QRL Key)	Text reference and remarks
AIRCRAFT (*contd.*)				
Air traffic control figures (*contd.*)				
Route distribution by airports	By route, segment weekly total, + per cent of arrivals/departures London flight information region	Annual	[QRL 22]	2.1.8, 3.2.3
Air traffic census figures				
Total activity: by area, aircraft type	Uncontrolled traffic (military and civil)	1974	[QRL 87]	2.1.8, 3.2.3, 4.2.2
	Uncontrolled traffic	1967	[QRL 48]	2.1.8, 3.2.3, 4.2.2
	Controlled traffic	1967	[QRL 48]	2.1.8, 3.2.3, 4.2.2
Total activity: by area and height band	Uncontrolled traffic, military and civil. Powered fixed-wing aircraft	1974	[QRL 87]	2.1.8, 3.2.3, 4.2.2
	Uncontrolled and controlled traffic separately	1967	[QRL 48]	2.1.8, 3.2.3, 4.2.2
Total activity by area and flight category	Uncontrolled traffic (military and civil)	1974	[QRL 87]	2.1.8, 3.2.3, 4.2.2
	Uncontrolled traffic	1961–3	[QRL 47]	2.1.8, 3.2.3, 4.2.2
Total activity by use of airspace, and flight category	Uncontrolled traffic (military and civil: powered fixed-wing aircraft	1974	[QRL 87]	2.1.8, 3.2.3, 4.2.2
	Uncontrolled traffic (military and civil: helicopters)	1974	[QRL 87]	2.1.8, 3.2.3, 4.2.2
	Gliders and helicopters, separately	1961–3	[QRL 47]	2.1.8, 3.2.3, 4.2.2
Total activity by flight category	Uncontrolled traffic (military and civil: gliders)	1974	[QRL 87]	2.1.8, 3.2.3, 4.2.2
Total activity by height band and use of airspace	Uncontrolled traffic (military and civil: powered fixed-wing aircraft)	1974	[QRL 87]	2.1.8, 3.2.3, 4.2.2
	Uncontrolled traffic (military and civil: gliders)	1974	[QRL 87]	2.1.8, 3.2.3, 4.2.2
Total activity by height band, type of equipment and use of airspace	Uncontrolled traffic (military and civil: powered fixed-wing aircraft	1974	[QRL 87]	2.1.8, 3.2.3, 4.2.2
	Uncontrolled traffic (military and civil: helicopters)	1974	[QRL 87]	2.1.8, 3.2.3, 4.2.2
Total activity by type of flight plan filed	Uncontrolled *en route* traffic (military and civil)	1974	[QRL 87]	2.1.8, 3.2.3, 4.2.2
Total activity by day and period of time	Uncontrolled and controlled traffic separately	1961–3	[QRL 47]	2.1.8, 3.2.3, 4.2.2
	Uncontrolled powered fixed-wing aircraft and controlled traffic separately	1967	[QRL 48]	2.1.8, 3.2.3, 4.2.2

QUICK REFERENCE LIST

Total activity by area and day	Uncontrolled and controlled traffic separately	1961–3	[QRL 47]	2.1.8, 3.2.3, 4.2.2
	Uncontrolled powered fixed-wing aircraft and controlled traffic separately	1967	[QRL 48]	2.1.8, 3.2.3, 4.2.2
Total activity by flight category and height band	Uncontrolled traffic	1961–3	[QRL 47]	2.1.8, 3.2.3, 4.2.2
Total activity by flight category and period of time	Uncontrolled traffic	1961–3	[QRL 47]	2.1.8, 3.2.3, 4.2.2
Total activity by flight category, day and period of time	Uncontrolled traffic 2 days	1961–3	[QRL 47]	2.1.8, 3.2.3, 4.2.2
Total activity by type of aircraft	Controlled and uncontrolled traffic separately	1961–3	[QRL 47]	2.1.8, 3.2.3, 4.2.2
Total activity by area	Gliders and helicopters separately	1961–3	[QRL 47]	2.1.8, 3.2.3, 4.2.2
Total activity by height	Gliders and helicopters separately	1961–3	[QRL 47]	2.1.8, 3.2.3, 4.2.2
	Gliders and helicopters separately	1967	[QRL 48]	2.1.8, 3.2.3, 4.2.2
Total activity by day	Gliders and helicopters separately	1961–3	[QRL 47]	2.1.8, 3.2.3, 4.2.2
Total activity by height band, day and hour	Civil traffic. 2 days	1961–3	[QRL 47]	2.1.8, 3.2.3, 4.2.2
Daily totals of flights: by day and use of airspace	Uncontrolled traffic (military and civil: powered fixed-wing aircraft)	1974	[QRL 87]	2.1.8, 3.2.3, 4.2.2
	Uncontrolled traffic (military and civil: helicopters)	1974	[QRL 87]	2.1.8, 3.2.3, 4.2.2
	Uncontrolled traffic (military and civil: gliders)	1974	[QRL 87]	2.1.8, 3.2.3, 4.2.2
Peak hourly totals of flights	By day, type of aircraft, no. of aircraft in busiest hour, uncontrolled traffic and military and civil	1974	[QRL 87]	2.1.8, 3.2.3, 4.2.2
Daily total activity, by use of airspace	Uncontrolled traffic (military and civil: powered fixed-wing aircraft)	1974	[QRL 87]	2.1.8, 3.2.3, 4.2.2
	Uncontrolled traffic (military and civil: helicopters)	1974	[QRL 87]	2.1.8, 3.2.3, 4.2.2
	Uncontrolled traffic (military and civil: gliders)	1974	[QRL 87]	2.1.8, 3.2.3, 4.2.2
	Uncontrolled aircraft (powered fixed-wing aircraft)	1967	[QRL 48]	2.1.8, 3.2.3, 4.2.2
Daily total activity: selected peak days	By area, day (military and civil: powered fixed-wing aircraft)	1974	[QRL 87]	2.1.8, 3.2.3, 4.2.2
Daily total activity by flight category	By day (military and civil: uncontrolled traffic: powered fixed-wing aircraft)	1974	[QRL 87]	2.1.8, 3.2.3, 4.2.2
	Uncontrolled traffic	1961–3	[QRL 47]	2.1.8, 3.2.3, 4.2.2
	Uncontrolled traffic	1967	[QRL 48]	2.1.8, 3.2.3, 4.2.2
Daily total activity	By day and flight information region. Controlled traffic (military and civil)	1974	[QRL 87]	2.1.8, 3.2.3, 4.2.2

220　　　　　　　　　　　　　　　CIVIL AVIATION

Descriptive title	Breakdown	Frequency	Publication (see QRL Key)	Text reference and remarks
AIRCRAFT (*contd.*)				
Air traffic census figures (*contd.*)				
Peak activity for each day	By aircraft type, day time of peak and peak activity. Uncontrolled traffic (military and civil)	1974	[QRL 87]	2.1.8, 3.2.3, 4.2.2
(Daily peak activity)	By day, time of peak, peak activity and flight information region. Controlled traffic (military and civil)	1974	[QRL 87]	2.1.8, 3.2.3, 4.2.2
	By area maxima of hourly counts. Uncontrolled and controlled traffic separately	1967	[QRL 48]	2.1.8, 3.2.3, 4.2.2
Peak activity for busy weekday	By aircraft type, area, time of peak and peak activity. Uncontrolled traffic (military and civil)	1974	[QRL 87]	2.1.8, 3.2.3, 4.2.2
	By area and height band. Maxima of hourly counts, Monday to Friday. Controlled and uncontrolled traffic separately	1961–3	[QRL 47]	2.1.8, 3.2.3, 4.2.2
	By flight category and area. Maxima of hourly counts. Monday to Friday. Uncontrolled traffic	1961–3	[QRL 47]	2.1.8, 3.2.3, 4.2.2
(Peak activity for weekday)	By flight category and height. Maxima of hourly counts. Monday to Friday. Uncontrolled traffic	1961–3	[QRL 47]	2.1.8, 3.2.3, 4.2.2
Peak activity for busy weekend day	By aircraft type, area, time of peak and peak activity. Uncontrolled traffic (military and civil)	1974	[QRL 87]	2.1.8, 3.2.3, 4.2.2
	By area and height band, maxima of hourly counts Saturday and Sunday. Controlled and uncontrolled separately	1961–3	[QRL 47]	2.1.8, 3.2.3, 4.2.2
(Peak activity for weekday)	By flight category and area. Maxima of hourly counts. Saturday and Sunday. Uncontrolled traffic	1961–3	[QRL 47]	2.1.8, 3.2.3, 4.2.2
	By flight category and height. Maxima of hourly counts. Saturday and Sunday. Uncontrolled traffic	1961–3	[QRL 47]	2.1.8, 3.2.3, 4.2.2

QUICK REFERENCE LIST

Hourly counts for days 3 and 7	By time and flight information region.	1974	[QRL 87]	2.1.8, 3.2.3, 4.2.2
	Uncontrolled traffic (military and civil: by powered fixed-wing aircraft, helicopter or glider)			
	By time and flight information region and type of aircraft. Controlled traffic (military and civil)	1974	[QRL 87]	2.1.8, 3.2.3, 4.2.2
	By time and flight information. Controlled traffic. All aircraft (military and civil separately)	1974	[QRL 87]	2.1.8, 3.2.3, 4.2.2
No. of aircraft filing flight plans	By day and type of aircraft	1967	[QRL 48]	2.1.8, 3.2.3, 4.2.2
No. of aircraft communicating with air traffic services	By day and type of aircraft	1967	[QRL 48]	2.1.8, 3.2.3, 4.2.2

ACCIDENTS
To aircraft engaged on public transport

Scheduled passenger operations	Serial no., date, aircraft, registration no., operator, location, injury to occupants, damage to aircraft, nature of accident	Annual	[QRL 10]	2.1.8, 3.2.4
(Domestic air flights)	By year and no. of deaths and injuries	Annual 1964 onwards	[QRL 137]	1.3.6, 3.2.4
	Notifiable accidents. Total and fatal separately. Passengers killed, crew killed	Annual	[QRL 51]	2.1.8, 3.2.4
	Number of fatal accidents	Annual	[QRL 28]	2.1.8, 3.2.4
	Passenger casualties: killed and seriously injured separately	Annual	[QRL 28]	2.1.8, 3.2.4
	Crew casualties: killed and seriously injured separately	Annual	[QRL 28]	2.1.8, 3.2.4
	Aircraft stage flights per fatal accident	Annual	[QRL 28]	2.1.8, 3.2.4
	Aircraft miles flown per fatal accident	Annual	[QRL 28]	2.1.8, 3.2.4
	Passengers carried per passengers killed	Annual	[QRL 28]	2.1.8, 3.2.4
	Passenger miles flown per passenger killed	Annual	[QRL 28]	2.1.8, 3.2.4
	Fatal accidents: by aircraft stage miles and separately	Annual	[QRL 28]	2.1.8, 3.2.4
	Passengers killed by passengers miles flown	Annual	[QRL 28]	2.1.8, 3.2.4
Non-scheduled passenger operations	Serial no., date, aircraft, registration no., operator, location, injury to occupants, damage to aircraft, nature of accident	Annual	[QRL 10]	2.1.8, 3.2.4

CIVIL AVIATION

Descriptive title	Breakdown	Frequency	Publication (see QRL Key)	Text reference and remarks
ACCIDENTS (contd.)				
To aircraft engaged on public transport (contd.)				
	Notifiable accident—total and fatal separately. Passengers killed, crew killed	Annual	[QRL 51]	2.1.8, 3.2.4
Non-scheduled cargo operations	Serial no., date, aircraft, registration no., operator, location, injury to occupants, damage to aircraft, nature of accident	1966 onwards Annual	[QRL 28]	2.1.8, 3.2.4
All passenger services	By notifiable accidents—total and fatal separately. Passengers killed, crew killed	Annual 1966 onwards	[QRL 51]	2.1.8, 3.2.4
All scheduled services (Passenger and freight)	By notifiable accidents—total and fatal separately	Annual 1966 onwards	[QRL 51]	2.1.8, 3.2.4
All non-scheduled services (Passenger and freight)	By notifiable accidents—total and fatal separately	Annual 1966 onwards	[QRL 51]	2.1.8, 3.2.4
All services (Passenger and freight)	By notifiable accidents—total and fatal separately	Annual 1966 onwards	[QRL 51]	2.1.8, 3.2.4
Fixed-wing aircraft over 2300 kg: scheduled services				
(Passenger and freight together)	By no. of accidents and fatal accidents	Annual	[QRL 10]	2.1.8, 3.2.4
(Passenger services)	By no. of accidents, fatal accidents, passengers killed, crew killed	Annual	[QRL 10]	2.1.8, 3.2.4
Non-scheduled services				
(Passenger and freight together)	By no. of accidents and fatal accidents	Annual	[QRL 10]	2.1.8, 3.2.4
(Passenger services)	By no. of accidents, fatal accidents, passengers and crew killed	Annual	[QRL 10]	2.1.8, 3.2.4
All services				
(Passenger and freight together)	By no. of accidents and fatal accidents	Annual	[QRL 10]	2.1.8, 3.2.4
(Passenger services)	By no. of accidents, number of fatal accidents, passengers and crew	Annual	[QRL 10]	2.1.8, 3.2.4
Accidents by no. of stage flights	By type of services	Annual	[QRL 10]	2.1.8, 3.2.4
Accidents by no. of aircraft: km flown	By type of service	Annual	[QRL 10]	2.1.8, 3.2.4
Accidents by aircraft hours flown	By type of service	Annual	[QRL 10]	2.1.8, 3.2.4
Passenger fatality rates by passenger km flown	By type of service	Annual	[QRL 10]	2.1.8, 3.2.4
Passenger fatality rates by no. of passengers carried	By type of service	Annual	[QRL 10]	2.1.8, 3.2.4

QUICK REFERENCE LIST

Rotary-wing aircraft over 2300 kg: all services	By no. of accidents. no. of fatal accidents, passengers and crew killed	Annual	[QRL 10]	2.1.8, 3.2.4
Accidents by stage flights		Annual	[QRL 10]	2.1.8, 3.2.4
Accidents by hours flown		Annual	[QRL 10]	2.1.8, 3.2.4
Passenger fatalities by no. of passengers carried		Annual	[QRL 10]	2.1.8, 3.2.4
To aircraft not engaged on public transport				
Aircraft by weight	Series no., date, aircraft, registration no., operator, location, injury to occupants, damage to aircraft, nature of accident	Annual	[QRL 10]	2.1.8, 3.2.4
Air misses				
Number of reported air-miss incidents	Civil aircraft in UK airspace. By class of aircraft. Air transport and other civil	Annual	[QRL 10]	2.1.8, 3.2.4
Number of air misses	By height and type of airspace	Combined 1966–71	[QRL 1]	2.1.8, 3.2.4
	By type of traffic and type of airspace	Combined 1966–71	[QRL 1]	2.1.8, 3.2.4
	By quality of radar: for each of the two aircraft	Combined 1966–71	[QRL 1]	2.1.8, 3.2.4
	By combinations of classes of aircraft	Combined 1966–71	[QRL 1]	2.1.8, 3.2.4
	By risk category	Monthly 1966–71	[QRL 1]	2.1.8, 3.2.4
	By risk category: all categories A and B together and category A	Annual 1954–66	[QRL 1]	2.1.8, 3.2.4
Causes	By cause and type of air miss	Combined figures 1966–71	[QRL 1]	2.1.8, 3.2.4
	By annual frequency	Annual 1966–71	[QRL 1]	2.1.8, 3.2.4
Air misses over the UK involving public transport's serious risk of collision	By no. of air misses and public transport movements	Annual 1966–71	[QRL 1]	2.1.8, 3.2.4
Ratio of no. of air misses to no. of collisions		Annual 1966–71	[QRL 1]	2.1.8, 3.2.4
Data held on air-miss computer	Situation, aircraft/controller, and causal data. No figures		[QRL 1]	2.1.8, 3.2.4

Descriptive title	Breakdown	Frequency	Publication (see QRL Key)	Text reference and remarks
ACCIDENTS (*contd.*)				
Mid-air collisions				
Fatal accidents	By type of aircraft, giving no. of aircraft involved		[QRL 2]	2.1.8, 3.2.4
	Total occupants in fatal and all accidents separately	Combined figures 1946–75	[QRL 2]	2.1.8, 3.2.4
	Fatality rate per cent fatal accidents and all accidents separately	1946–75	[QRL 2]	2.1.8, 3.2.4
	Fatalities by phase of flight		[QRL 2]	2.1.8, 3.2.4
	No. of passenger aircraft		[QRL 2]	2.1.8, 3.2.4
	No. of fatalities, no. of survivors	Time periods within 1946–75	[QRL 2]	2.1.8, 3.2.4
	No. of deaths per fatal accident		[QRL 2]	2.1.8, 3.2.4
	Fatality rate		[QRL 2]	2.1.8, 3.2.4
Fatal aircraft accident rate	By no. of fatal aircraft accidents, no. of mid-air collisions and percentage	Time periods within 1946–75	[QRL 2]	2.1.8, 3.2.4
Causes	By type, no. and percentage	Time periods within 1946–75	[QRL 2]	2.1.8, 3.2.4
Degree of damage	By phase of flight and no. of aircraft and degree of damage	Time periods within 1946–75	[QRL 2]	2.1.8, 3.2.4
Purpose of flight	By purpose, no. of aircraft and percentage	Time periods within 1946–75	[QRL 2]	2.1.8, 3.2.4
Combination of categories of aircraft in collision involving passenger aircraft	No. of collisions		[QRL 2]	2.1.8, 3.2.4
	No. of passenger aircraft involved		[QRL 2]	2.1.8, 3.2.4
	No. of passenger aircraft incurring fatal accidents	Time periods within 1946–75	[QRL 2]	2.1.8, 3.2.4
	Proportion of passenger aircraft incurring fatal accidents as percentage		[QRL 2]	2.1.8, 3.2.4
Geographical location	By region, no. of collisions and no. of aircraft—jet and non-jet separately	Time periods within 1946–75	[QRL 2]	2.1.8, 3.2.4

QUICK REFERENCE LIST

Engine categories	By engine category and percentage jet and non-jet separately	Time periods within 1946–75	[QRL 2]	2.1.8, 3.2.4
Mid-air collisions involving civil aircraft	Giving date, aircraft, engine category, operator, location, purpose of flight, occupants—crew and passengers separately. Fatalities—crew and passengers separately, collision height, phase of flight	1946–75	[QRL 2]	2.1.8, 3.2.4
General				
Accidents to helicopters and gyro planes	Serial no., date, aircraft, registration no., location, injury to occupants, damage to aircraft, nature of accident	Annual	[QRL 10]	2.1.8, 3.2.4
Accidents to balloons	Serial no., date, aircraft, registration no., location, injury to occupants, damage to aircraft, nature of accident	Annual	[QRL 10]	2.1.8, 3.2.4
Aircraft involved in accidents	By type of accident and nature of flight	Annual	[QRL 10]	2.1.8, 3.2.4
	By 26 types of accident date, registration no., operator, location		[QRL 11]	2.1.8, 3.2.4
	Per cent by type of accident	1946–75	[QRL 2]	2.1.8, 3.2.4
	By apparent cause and nature of flight	Annual	[QRL 10]	2.1.8, 3.2.4
	By 73 types of aircraft. Date, registration no., operator, location	1946–75		2.1.8, 3.2.4
	By date of accident. Date, registration no., operator, location	1946–75	[QRL 2]	2.1.8, 3.2.4
	Date, aircraft, registration no., operator, location, nature of flight, total aboard, injury to occupants, damage to aircraft, nature of accidents	1946–75	[QRL 2]	2.1.8, 3.2.4
Nature of flight and degree of injury sustained	No. of accidents, no. of fatal accidents, rate of accidents, by flying hours	Annual	[QRL 10]	2.1.8, 3.2.4
General aviation: fixed- and rotary-wing aircraft under 2300 kg		Annual	[QRL 10]	2.1.8, 3.2.4
Analysis of individual accidents		Annual	[QRL 11]	2.3.1, 3.2.4
AIRPORTS				
General				
Information by civil aerodrome	Position, operating hours, lighting, met. office, hangarage, maintenance, restaurant, landing fee, code, remarks, car hire, radio, fuel, tel. no. UK and Ireland	Annual	[QRL 7]	1.3.2, 3.3

Descriptive title	Breakdown	Frequency	Publication (see QRL Key)	Text reference and remarks
ACCIDENTS (contd.) General (contd.)				
(By aerodrome for use by international commercial air transport)	Position, ref. termp., magnetic variation, operations hours, operator, tel. no. and address hotels and restaurants, medical facilities, transport, cargo-handling facilities, fuel, hangarage, repair facilities, fire and rescue equipment, seasonal availability, local flying restrictions and remarks, pre-flight altimeter check points, meteorological data, surface elevations, physical characteristics, movement areas, visual ground aids, lighting aids, marking, safety altitudes, obstructions	Annual	[QRL 69, 14]	1.3.2, 3.3
Information by military aerodrome	Position operating hours, lighting, remarks, radio, tel. no. code	Annual	[QRL 7]	1.3.2, 3.3
Information by private airfield and landing field	Position, remarks, fuel, tel. no., operating hours, radio	Annual	[QRL 7]	1.3.2, 3.3
Information by helipads:				
(By heliport)	Position, remarks, fuel, tel. no.	Annual	[QRL 7]	1.3.2, 3.3
(By heliport)	Position, classification, operating hours, air traffic control, manoeuvring area, day marking, lighting, safety altitude, refuelling, repair facilities, hangarage, elevation, variation charges, obstructions, holding points, local restrictions	Annual	[QRL 14, 69]	1.3.2, 3.3
Additional information	Air-traffic control and frequencies	Annual	[QRL 7]	1.3.2, 3.3
	Navigational aids—by airport	Annual	[QRL 7]	1.3.2, 3.3
	Rate penetration service—by airport	Annual	[QRL 7]	1.3.2, 3.3
	Lower airspace trial radar service—by airport	Annual	[QRL 7]	1.3.2, 3.3
	Aeronautical light beacons—by airport	Annual	[QRL 7]	1.3.2, 3.3
	Special restrictions, instructions, warnings, by airport	Annual	[QRL 14, 69]	1.3.2, 3.3
	Aerodrome obstructions and safety altitudes, by airport	Annual	[QRL 14, 69]	1.3.2, 3.3
	Aeronautical ground lights, by airport	Annual	[QRL 14, 69]	1.3.2, 3.3
	Identification letters, by airport	Annual	[QRL 14, 69]	1.3.2, 3.3

Information by non-custom aerodromes and air stations which are available for use by civil aircraft	Aerodrome temperature data, by airport Position, elevation, magnetic variation, runway, declared distances, surface elevations, lighting, ground services, operator, tel. no., remarks	Annual Annual	[QRL 14, 69] [QRL 14, 69]	1.3.2, 3.3 1.3.2, 3.3

Transport to and from the airport
By mode of transport

By trip purpose	Non-transfer passengers. By detailed mode of transport. Heathrow and Gatwick	1967	[QRL 80, 81]	2.2.1, 3.3
	Non-transfer passengers. Heathrow and Gatwick	1967	[QRL 80, 81]	2.2.1, 3.3
	Air passengers (excluding transfer passengers)	Annual 1966–71	[QRL 128]	2.2.1, 3.3
	Home-based air passengers. Sunday and weekday. Gatwick	August 1971	[QRL 128]	2.2.1, 3.3
	Non-home-based ron-UK and UK air passengers. Sunday and weekday. Gatwick	August 1971	[QRL 128]	2.2.1, 3.3
By residency	By car ownership, by land use at origin. Heathrow and Gatwick	1967	[QRL 80, 81]	2.2.1, 3.3
(UK and non-UK)	By day for non-home-based air passenger journeys. Gatwick	August 1971	[QRL 128]	2.2.1, 3.3
By origin area	Non-transfer passengers. Heathrow and Gatwick	1967	[QRL 80, 81]	2.2.1, 3.3
By type of flight	Non-transfer passengers. Gatwick	1967	[QRL 80]	2.2.1, 3.3
Passenger using rail service from Victoria	By origin area and mode to Victoria. Gatwick	1967	[QRL 80]	2.2.1, 3.3
By terminal building	Non-transfer passengers, Heathrow	1967	[QRL 81]	2.2.1, 3.3
	As a percentage all passengers, Heathrow	1971	[QRL 129]	2.2.1, 3.3
By trip purpose and residency	Passengers starting from central London, Gatwick	1967	[QRL 80]	2.2.1, 3.3
Passenger starting from central London using public transport	By trip purpose and residency	1967	[QRL 80]	2.2.1, 3.3
By day	Saturday and Sunday	1971	[QRL 129]	2.2.1, 3.3
	All air passengers excluding air transfer passengers. Weekday and Sunday, number and percentage. Gatwick	1967	[QRL 80]	2.2.1, 3.3
	Weekday and Sunday, all air passengers, excluding air transfer passengers. Gatwick	1966–71	[QRL 128]	2.2.1, 3.3
By car ownership	Home-based air passenger journeys, day and year and mode to airport. Gatwick	1966–71	[QRL 128]	2.2.1, 3.3

Descriptive title	Breakdown	Frequency	Publication (see QRL Key)	Text reference and remarks
AIRPORTS (contd.) **Transport to and from the airport** (contd.) *By mode of Transport* (contd.) *Travel to work* By mode of transport	By car/non-car owning household, by sex, by origin and car/non-car-owning household, by origin near the airport, by trips to each airport area. Gatwick	1967	[QRL 80]	2.2.1, 3.3
	By car/non-car-owning household, by sex, by origins and car/non-car-owning household, by origin near the airport, by trips to each airport area. Heathrow	1967	[QRL 81]	2.2.1, 3.3
	By household car ownership and sex for before and after Piccadilly line extension. Heathrow	1967	[QRL 81]	2.2.1, 3.3
By last mode of transport	By household car ownership and sex	1967	[QRL 80, 81]	2.2.1, 3.3
	By sex. Heathrow and Gatwick	1967	[QRL 80]	2.2.1, 3.3
By employment categories	By trips to each airport area. Heathrow	1967	[QRL 80, 81]	2.2.1, 3.3
By arrival time	By airport, area. Heathrow and Gatwick	1967	[QRL 81]	2.2.1, 3.3
	By percentages for each hour by mode and sex. Heathrow	1967		2.2.1, 3.3
Work journeys	By mode, day	1966 and 1971	[QRL 128]	2.2.1, 3.3
Using underground or British Rail	By alighting station. Heathrow	1967	[QRL 81]	2.2.1, 3.3
By last bus route used	By major airport area. Heathrow	1967	[QRL 81]	2.2.1, 3.3
Car drivers' trips to work	By access point and major access area. Heathrow	1967	[QRL 81]	2.2.1, 3.3
Proportions of cars used for work trips, which are used to leave the airport during meal breaks	By major airport area. Heathrow	1967	[QRL 81]	2.2.1, 3.3
Inbound and outbound work person journeys in 24 hours	By type of public transport and area of origin weekday and Sunday. Gatwick	1971	[QRL 128]	2.2.1, 3.3
	By mode and area non-car-owning households, weekday. Gatwick	1971	[QRL 128]	2.2.1, 3.3
Inbound and outbound home-based work person journeys in 24 hours	By mode and area—car-owning households, weekday. Gatwick	1971	[QRL 128]	2.2.1, 3.3

QUICK REFERENCE LIST

Roadside interview survey

Inbound traffic	Hourly variation by vehicle type, origin by vehicle type, hourly variation by vehicle type and destination in airport. Heathrow and Gatwick	1967	[QRL 80, 81]	2.2.1, 3.3
Inbound trips	Vehicle trips by district vehicle type, vehicle trips by origin zone close to the airport, car driver trips by purpose and destination in airport, car driver and car passenger trips by purpose and destination in airport. Heathrow and Gatwick	1967	[QRL 80, 81]	2.2.1, 3.3
	Car occupancy of inbound trips: by driver purpose and destination in airport. Heathrow	1967	[QRL 81]	2.2.1, 3.3
Inbound trips to main entrance and public car park	By vehicle type, cars by hour, cars by main origin, areas, cars by driver purpose, car driver and car passenger trips by purpose. Gatwick	1967	[QRL 80]	2.2.1, 3.3
(Entering central terminal area)	Cars by driver purpose, average car occupancy by driver purpose, car drivers, and car passengers, by purpose. Heathrow	1967	[QRL 81]	2.2.1, 3.3
Vehicles stopping at the main entrance	Hourly variation, by vehicle type, by type of car movement and number of car trips by driver purpose. Gatwick	1967	[QRL 80]	2.2.1, 3.3
Seasonal variation in traffic flow	Entering the central terminal area, by month and day. Heathrow	1967	[QRL 81]	2.2.1, 3.3
	Entering and leaving the airport at Hatton Cross, by month and day. Heathrow	1967	[QRL 81]	2.2.1, 3.3
Inbound trips: by light goods vehicles	By driver purpose and destination in airport. Heathrow	1967	[QRL 81]	2.2.1, 3.3
Inbound trips: number of inbound cars carrying air passengers	By number per car, and airport terminal. Heathrow	1967	[QRL 81]	2.2.1, 3.3
24-hour volumes of traffic entering central terminal	By vehicle type. Heathrow	1967	[QRL 81]	2.2.1, 3.3
16-hour volumes of traffic entering central terminal area	By vehicle type, inbound and internal trips. Heathrow	1967	[QRL 81]	2.2.1, 3.3
Hourly traffic using central terminal access tunnel	By hour and type of traffic. Heathrow	1967	[QRL 81]	2.2.1, 3.3
Origins of inbound vehicles entering central terminal area	By origin area and type of traffic. Heathrow	1967	[QRL 81]	2.2.1, 3.3

230   CIVIL AVIATION

Descriptive title	Breakdown	Frequency	Publication (see QRL Key)	Text reference and remarks
AIRPORTS (*contd.*)				
Transport to and from the airport (*contd.*)				
Roadside interview survey (*contd.*)				
Total cordon vehicle movement	06.00 to 20.00 hours by direction and day. Heathrow	1971	[QRL 129]	2.2.1, 3.3
	06.00 to 20.00 hours by direction, day and per cent cars. Heathrow	1971	[QRL 129]	2.2.1, 3.3
Total vehicle movement roundabout	By mode, location, 06.00–20.00, weekday inbound and outbound. Heathrow	1971	[QRL 129]	2.2.1, 3.3
Classified volumetric counts	06.00–20.00: by station number, location, recorded flows, corrected flow, through traffic (all excluding coaches). Heathrow	1971	[QRL 129]	2.2.1, 3.3
Corrected vehicle flows	Vehicles 06.00–20.00 by area of airport origin. Heathrow	1971	[QRL 129]	2.2.1, 3.3
Airport origin	Private vehicle users in 24 hours. By trip purpose. Gatwick	1971	[QRL 128]	2.2.1, 3.3
Trip purpose	By vehicle type, trip purpose and per cent 06.00–20.00. Inbound and outbound traffic and 4-spur roundabout Sunday. Heathrow and Gatwick	1971	[QRL 129]	2.2.1, 3.3
Work journeys	Vehicle and person movement by station. Gatwick	1971	[QRL 128]	2.2.1, 3.3
Number of vehicles entering– leaving the airport	By entry point. 16-hour period. Gatwick	1971	[QRL 128]	2.2.1, 3.3
	By vehicle type. 24 hours. Gatwick	1971	[QRL 128]	2.2.1, 3.3
	Hourly variation by vehicle type. Gatwick	1971	[QRL 128]	2.2.1, 3.3
Use of goods vehicles entering the airport	By use, weekday and Sunday. 24 hours. Gatwick	1971	[QRL 128]	2.2.1, 3.3
Average private vehicle occupancy	By vehicle type and journey purpose. Gatwick	1971	[QRL 128]	2.2.1, 3.3
Average number of air passengers per inbound private vehicle	By vehicle type and journey purpose. Gatwick	1971	[QRL 128]	2.2.1, 3.3
Number of private vehicles	By journey purpose, their origin at the airport. Weekday and Sunday. Outbound journeys. Gatwick	1971	[QRL 128]	2.2.1, 3.3
	By journey purpose and the car park which they use. Weekday and Sunday. Outbound journeys. Gatwick	1971	[QRL 128]	2.2.1, 3.3

QUICK REFERENCE LIST 231

Number of forecourt users whose outbound journey originated at the terminal building	By journey purpose. Weekday and Sunday. Gatwick	1971	[QRL 128]	2.2.1, 3.3
Inbound and outbound work person journeys in 24 hours by private vehicle transport	By area of origin. Weekday and Sunday. Gatwick	1971	[QRL 128]	2.2.1, 3.3
Rail passenger survey				
Rail passengers arriving and alighting at Gatwick	By origin of rail trip, from Victoria Station, Gatwick	1967	[QRL 80]	2.2.1, 3.3
Rail passenger journeys to and from the airport	By journeys purpose and origin or destination district. Weekdays and Sunday. Gatwick	1971	[QRL 128]	2.2.1, 3.3
London Transport bus survey				
Passengers alighting from and boarding London Transport buses	By hour. Heathrow	1967	[QRL 81]	2.2.1, 3.3
Bus passengers to and from central terminal	By hour of day. Heathrow	1967	[QRL 81]	2.2.1, 3.3
Bus passengers to and from the airport	By journey purpose and district of origin or destination. Weekday and Sunday, Heathrow	1971	[QRL 129]	2.2.1, 3.3
Departing bus passengers	By final destination. Heathrow	1967	[QRL 81]	2.2.1, 3.3
	By purpose in central terminal area. Heathrow	1967	[QRL 81]	2.2.1, 3.3
	By route and proportion changing to other transport after alighting. Heathrow	1967	[QRL 81]	2.2.1, 3.3
	Changing to other transport after alighting by continuation mode. Heathrow	1967	[QRL 81]	2.2.1, 3.3
Bus passengers	By trip purpose, weekday and Sunday. Heathrow	1971	[QRL 129]	2.2.1, 3.3
Perimeter bus passenger counts	By location, direction and two peak periods. Heathrow	1971	[QRL 129]	2.2.1, 3.3
Survey of parked cars				
Hourly arrival and departure patterns of vehicles using public car parks	Hourly pattern and departure patterns of vehicles. Gatwick	1967	[QRL 80]	2.2.1, 3.3
Duration of stay of vehicles using public car parks	Gatwick	1967	[QRL 80]	2.2.1, 3.3
Number of vehicles parked in the public car parks	By hour of day. Gatwick	1967	[QRL 80]	2.2.1, 3.3
Location of parked cars	Gatwick	1967	[QRL 80]	2.2.1, 3.3

Descriptive title	Breakdown	Frequency	Publication (see QRL Key)	Text reference and remarks
AIRPORTS (*contd.*)				
Transport to and from the airport (*contd.*)				
Survey of parked cars (*contd.*)				
Cars parked morning and afternoon on a peak weekday	By major airport, area. Heathrow	1967	[QRL 81]	2.2.1, 3.3
Cars parked at off airport parking area	Heathrow	1967	[QRL 81]	2.2.1, 3.3
Cars parked in central terminal area and available spaces	By location and time of day. Heathrow	1967	[QRL 81]	2.2.1, 3.3
Cars parked outside the terminal buildings	By time of day. Heathrow	1967	[QRL 81]	2.2.1, 3.3
Percentage of cars observed stopping for various periods outside the terminal buildings	Heathrow	1967	[QRL 81]	2.2.1, 3.3
Parking characteristics at staff multi-storey car park and at north side staff car park	Heathrow	1967	[QRL 81]	2.2.1, 3.3
Parking characteristics at north side of spectator car park	Heathrow	1967	[QRL 81]	2.2.1, 3.3
Survey of movements associated with air freight				
Trips to work	Freight employees by airport area. Heathrow	1967	[QRL 81]	2.2.1, 3.3
	Freight employees by last mode of transport. Heathrow	1967	[QRL 81]	2.2.1, 3.3
Inbound and outbound trips by vehicles collecting or delivering freight	By time of arrival and by mode. Heathrow	1967	[QRL 81]	2.2.1, 3.3
	By vehicle type and hour of day. Heathrow	1967	[QRL 81]	2.2.1, 3.3
Internal airport movements by vehicles collecting or delivering freight	By origin/destination major airport area. Heathrow	1967	[QRL 81]	2.2.1, 3.3
Inbound miscellaneous vehicle trips to the freight sheds	By hour of day. Heathrow	1967	[QRL 81]	2.2.1, 3.3
Numbers of collections and delivery calls made at cargo sheds	By vehicle type and hour of day. Heathrow	1967	[QRL 81]	2.2.1, 3.3

QUICK REFERENCE LIST

Numbers of collections or deliveries of air freight loads	By weight and carrying capacity of vehicle. Heathrow	1967	[QRL 81]	2.2.1, 3.3
Origins and destinations of inbound trips by vehicles collecting or delivering air freight	Heathrow	1967	[QRL 81]	2.2.1, 3.3
Origin and destination of vehicle trips to and from freight agents	Heathrow	1967	[QRL 81]	2.2.1, 3.3
Origins of import and export air freight loads collected from and delivered to freight sheds	By weight of load. Heathrow	1967	[QRL 81]	2.2.1, 3.3
Coach survey				
Air terminal coaches: between Central London and Heathrow airport	Coaches and passengers by hour. Heathrow	1967	[QRL 81]	2.2.1, 3.3
Air terminal coaches from Central London to airport	Coaches and passengers by in-town terminal. Heathrow	1967	[QRL 81]	2.2.1, 3.3
	Coach passengers and riders by in-town terminal. Heathrow	1967	[QRL 81]	2.2.1, 3.3
Charter coaches carrying air passengers	Number of coaches and passengers. Heathrow	1967	[QRL 81]	2.2.1, 3.3
Rail-link coach services	Number of coaches and passengers. Heathrow	1967	[QRL 81]	2.2.1, 3.3
Coaches bringing spectators to airport	Origin and number of passengers. Heathrow	1967	[QRL 81]	2.2.1, 3.3
Spectator car-park-shuttle coach service	Number of coaches and one-way passengers. Heathrow	1967	[QRL 81]	2.2.1, 3.3
	One-way passengers per average day, per month. Heathrow	1967	[QRL 81]	2.2.1, 3.3
Staff car-park-shuttle coach service	Number of coaches and passengers into central terminal area. Heathrow	1967	[QRL 81]	2.2.1, 3.3
Taxi survey				
Taxis entering the central terminal area	Full and empty taxis, by destination. Heathrow	1967	[QRL 81]	2.2.1, 3.3
	By origin area. Heathrow	1967	[QRL 81]	2.2.1, 3.3
	By number of passengers. Heathrow	1967	[QRL 81]	2.2.1, 3.3
(Taxi passengers)	By purpose. Heathrow	1967	[QRL 81]	2.2.1, 3.3
Miscellaneous				
Origin and destination of surface journeys to and from the airport made by air passengers	By flight type, flight purpose, area of origin, and destination, residency, weekday, Sunday. Heathrow	1971	[QRL 129]	2.2.1, 3.3

234 CIVIL AVIATION

Descriptive title	Breakdown	Frequency	Publication (see QRL Key)	Text reference and remarks
AIRPORTS (contd.)				
Transport to and from the airport (contd.)				
Miscellaneous (contd.)				
Probable use of the Piccadilly line	By UK and non-UK residents, trip purpose and household car ownership. Heathrow	1971	[QRL 129]	2.2.1, 3.3
Modal split of air-passenger journeys	By UK and non-UK residents, by district, weekday and Sunday. Gatwick	1971	[QRL 128]	2.2.1, 3.3
Passengers entering and leaving the airport by public transport over a 24-hour period	By bus stop, all buses, by rail, alighting, boarding, total weekday and Sunday. Gatwick	1971	[QRL 128]	2.2.1, 3.3
Hourly variation in number of public transport passengers entering and leaving the airport	Weekday, Sunday, by hour and type of passengers. Gatwick	1971	[QRL 128]	2.2.1, 3.3
Number of public transport passengers	By mode and purpose 1971, weekday and Sunday. Gatwick	1971	[QRL 128]	2.2.1, 3.3
Internal traffic	Matrix, 24-hour vehicular flow. Weekday and Sunday by airport areas. Gatwick	1971	[QRL 128]	2.2.1, 3.3
(Internal vehicles movement)	Between main airport areas 6 a.m.–10 p.m. Heathrow	1971	[QRL 129]	2.2.1, 3.3
Summary of 1971 car-parking statistics	By type of car park and trip purpose, and peak accumulation of parked cars. Gatwick	1971	[QRL 128]	2.2.1, 3.3
Peak-hour person movements	Inbound and outbound by journey purpose. Gatwick	1971	[QRL 128]	2.2.1, 3.3
	Inbound and outbound by journey purpose and mode of transport. Gatwick	1971	[QRL 128]	2.2.1, 3.3
Hourly variation in number of person trips into and out of the airport	By purpose August-Sundays. Gatwick	1971	[QRL 128]	2.2.1, 3.3
Peak-hour goods vehicle movements	By vehicle use. Gatwick	1971	[QRL 128]	2.2.1, 3.3
Traffic-flow figures				
Comparison of peak-hour, busy-day vehicle-flow figures	For main tunnel (inbound). Heathrow	Annual, compares given year and 3 years previously	[QRL 113]	2.2.1, 3.3

QUICK REFERENCE LIST

Total passenger throughput and total vehicles leaving the central terminal area	By year and percentage increase since 1971. Heathrow	Annual	[QRL 113]	2.2.1, 3.3
Diurnal traffic-flow patterns	Vehicles inbound via the main tunnel, by three categories of vehicle and time period	Annual	[QRL 113]	2.2.1, 3.3
Vehicles entering the central terminal area via the main tunnel	By category of vehicle. Heathrow	Annual	[QRL 113]	2.2.1, 3.3
Weekly totals of vehicular traffic, inbound via the main tunnel	Heathrow	Annual	[QRL 113]	2.2.1, 3.3
Peak-hour/busy-day traffic flow as a percentage and previous year's traffic flow	By road. Heathrow	Annual	[QRL 113]	2.2.1, 3.3
Traffic-flow diagrams	By area of airport, a.m. or p.m. Heathrow	Annual	[QRL 113]	2.2.1, 3.3
Traffic-flow data	By area of airport, type of vehicle and various dates and times of day	Annual	[QRL 113]	2.2.1, 3.3
Primary mode of transport: by airport	Scottish and Central English airports 1970 and 1975		[QRL 102]	2.2.1, 3.3
	Heathrow and Gatwick 1965 for passengers departing from and arriving by origin and destination in UK		[QRL 130]	2.2.1, 3.3
Primary mode of transport: by planning region of origin and destination	Percentage of passengers by various modes	1972	[QRL 103]	2.2.1, 3.3
	By region of origin and destination and airports			2.2.1, 3.3
Primary mode of transport: by secondary mode of transport	By airport. Scottish and Central England airports	1975	[QRL 102]	2.2.1, 3.3
Passengers using only one mode of transport	By airport and per cent of passengers	1975	[QRL 102]	2.2.1, 3.3
Passengers not being met/seen off	By primary mode of transport, by airport	1975	[QRL 102]	2.2.1, 3.3
Passengers travelling alone	By primary mode of transport, by airport	1972	[QRL 102]	2.2.1, 3.3
Type of passenger: by mode of transport	All terminating passengers London airports	1972	[QRL 101]	2.2.1, 3.3
	Foreign terminating passengers London airports (inwards and outwards)	1972	[QRL 101]	2.2.1, 3.3
	UK terminating passengers London airports (inwards and outwards)	1972		2.2.1, 3.3
	Origin and destination in South-east, London airports	1972		2.2.1, 3.3
Type of passenger: by mode of transport				
(Per cent)	Business and leisure total London airports	1972	[QRL 101]	2.2.1, 3.3
(Per cent)	Business and leisure. Gatwick and Heathrow	1972	[QRL 101]	2.2.1, 3.3

Descriptive title	Breakdown	Frequency	Publication (see QRL Key)	Text reference and remarks
AIRPORTS (*contd.*)				
Transport to and from the airport (*contd.*)				
Passengers: origin and destination (See also **Tourism**: Journey purpose by nationality) and **Miscellaneous total figures:** Percent of passengers UK or non-UK)				
(Per cent)	UK, non-UK, total by individual Scottish airports (BAA airports)	1968	[QRL 101]	2.2.1, 3.3
(Per cent)	UK, non-UK, total by individual South-east airports (BAA airports)	1968	[QRL 101]	2.2.1, 3.3
Time spent travelling to and from airport	Planning regions to three London airports	1968	[QRL 101]	2.2.1, 3.3
	Terminal passengers by airport, per cent up to and over 1½ hours (BAA London airports)	1968	[QRL 101]	2.2.1, 3.3
Mode of transport used between airport and railway station	Scottish and Central England airports. Per cent of total terminating passengers	1975	[QRL 102]	2.2.1, 3.3
NOISE				
General				
Annoyance due to aircraft noise	General and night-time—mean score	1967	[QRL 117]	2.1.10, 3.3.2
	By class	1967	[QRL 117]	2.1.10, 3.3.2
	By age group	1967	[QRL 117]	2.1.10, 3.3.2
	Compared with other noise in London	1968	[QRL 83]	2.1.10, 3.3.2
	Helicopter noise compared with other noise in Central London (large number of detailed tables)	1976	[QRL 6]	2.7, 3.3.2
Soundproofers	By social class	1967	[QRL 117]	2.1.10, 3.3.2
	Relationship of annoyance to soundproofing	1967	[QRL 117]	2.1.10, 3.3.2
	Fear of aircraft	1967	[QRL 117]	2.1.10, 3.3.2
Type of noises heard in the neighbourhood		1967	[QRL 117]	2.1.10, 3.3.2
Awareness of aircraft noise	By social class	1967	[QRL 117]	2.2.10, 3.3.2

QUICK REFERENCE LIST

Proportion of population in 10-mile radius exposed at each PNdB level		1967	[QRL 117]	2.1.10, 3.3.2
No. of aircraft heard per day in 10-mile radius		1967	[QRL 117]	2.1.10, 3.3.2
Intercorrelations between annoyance number and loudness of aircraft		1967	[QRL 117]	2.1.10, 3.3.2
Mean annoyance scores of those in different noise and no. strata (10-mile radius)		1967	[QRL 117]	2.1.10, 3.3.2
Self-assessment of acclimatization to aircraft noise		1967	[QRL 117]	2.1.10, 3.3.2
Self-rating on acclimatization to noise and mean annoyance scores		1967	[QRL 117]	2.1.10, 3.3.2
Relationship between noise annoyance and length of residence in area		1967	[QRL 117]	2.1.10, 3.3.2
Proportion experiencing each type of disturbance at various levels of annoyance		1967	[QRL 117]	2.1.10, 3.3.2
Wishes to move from area	By reason including aircraft noise	1967	[QRL 117]	2.1.10, 3.3.2
	By reason including aircraft noise	1961	[QRL 92]	2.1.10, 3.3.2
Noise level	By number of aircraft	1967	[QRL 117]	2.1.10, 3.3.2
Comparisons of results on questions common to two surveys of aircraft noise annoyance		1961 and 1967	[QRL 117, 92]	2.1.10, 3.3.2
Other tables involving manipulation of data		1967	[QRL 117]	2.1.10, 3.3.2
The number of informants	By noise level and number of aircraft per day	1961	[QRL 92]	2.1.10, 3.3.2
The number of people with various annoyance ratings	By noise level and number of aircraft per day	1961	[QRL 92]	2.1.10, 3.3.2
Relation between average annoyance and perceived noise levels		1961	[QRL 92]	2.1.10, 3.3.2
Relation between annoyance rating and noise and number index	Obtained from social survey and Farnborough experiments	1961	[QRL 92]	2.1.10, 3.3.2
Percentage of people disturbed	By various types of disturbance	1961	[QRL 92]	2.1.10, 3.3.2

238   CIVIL AVIATION

Descriptive title	Breakdown	Frequency	Publication (see QRL Key)	Text reference and remarks
NOISE (*contd.*)				
General (*contd.*)				
Number of times per 100 people questioned that aircraft noise and other things affecting local living conditions were disliked (Things disliked about the neighbourhood) (including aircraft noise)		1961	[QRL 92]	2.1.10, 3.3.2
		1967	[QRL 117]	2.1.10, 3.3.2
Percentage of people wishing to change their living conditions	By various reasons	1961	[QRL 92]	2.1.10, 3.3.2
Percentage of people rating their area as poor or very poor	By various reasons	1961	[QRL 92]	2.1.10, 3.3.2
Percentage of people liking their area less now than in the past		1961	[QRL 92]	2.1.10, 3.3.2
Data showing the distribution over noise levels of the total population and the seriously annoyed populations		1961	[QRL 92]	2.1.10, 3.3.2
Number of airport authorities which make specific arrangements for reducing aircraft noise	By nature of specific arrangements	1961	[QRL 92]	2.1.10, 3.3.2
Comparative judgement of different noise	By decibels, type of noise and judgement	1961	[QRL 92]	2.1.10, 3.3.2
Outdoor judgements	On the category scale of intrusiveness plotted against sound level and perceived noise level. For types of aircraft. For 2 days	1961	[QRL 92]	2.1.10, 3.3.2
	The category scale of noisiness plotted against a combined measure of sound level and duration. For types of aircraft	1961	[QRL 92]	2.1.10, 3.3.2
Indoor judgements	On the category scale of intrusiveness plotted against the difference between the level of aircraft noise and that of the prevailing film sound track by type of aircraft	1961	[QRL 92]	2.1.10, 3.3.2

QUICK REFERENCE LIST

Noise by aircraft type	Departure and arrival noise levels (PNdB) for temporary and fixed measuring sites. Concorde	1976	[QRL 91]	2.1.10, 3.3.2
	Departure and arrival durations, 10 dB down for temporary measuring sites. Concorde	1976	[QRL 91]	2.1.10, 3.3.2
	Departure and arrival durations, above 90 PNdB for temporary measuring sites. Concorde	1976	[QRL 91]	2.1.10, 3.3.2
	Incidence of high noise levels (greater than 110 PNdB) recorded at fixed noise monitoring sites. Concorde	1976	[QRL 91]	2.1.10, 3.3.2
	Helicopters by cruising altitude (two levels)—sound level	1961	[QRL 92]	2.1.10, 3.3.2
	By type of aircraft and (PNdB–dBA) for Farnborough and Fleming's data	1961	[QRL 92]	2.1.10, 3.3.2
	Contours of maximum sound level dBA for a Belvedere helicopter taking off and landing	1961	[QRL 92]	2.1.10, 3.3.2
	Various levels of aircraft sounds judged equally noisy	1972	[QRL 8]	2.7, 3.3.2
Noise by aircraft type	Standard deviations in dB, for levels used for noise ratings. For aircraft noises judged equally noisy	1972	[QRL 8]	2.7, 3.3.2
Noise map	London (Heathrow) airport and surrounding area	1961	[QRL 92]	2.1.10, 3.3.2
	By airport, aircraft type, and runway. Take-off and landing	1976	[QRL 90]	2.1.10, 3.3.2
	Effect of scheduled Concorde movements on noise exposure (NNI) around Heathrow	1976	[QRL 91]	2.1.10, 3.3.2
The noise effects of extending Luton airport	By year, configuration NNI strata, number of people in strata, number above 50 NNI, number of people affected in strata	1969	[QRL 9]	2.7, 3.3.2
Concorde departures	By date, runway, destination, weight tonnes, temporary sites (four noise levels PNdB), fixed sites (highest level and site), number of complaints	1976	[QRL 91]	2.1.10, 3.3.2
Concorde arrivals	By date, runway, origin, weight tonnes, mobile sites and (six noise levels PNdB), fixed sites highest level and site), number of complaints	1976	[QRL 91]	2.1.10, 3.3.2

Descriptive title	Breakdown	Frequency	Publication (see QRL Key)	Text reference and remarks
NOISE (*contd.*)				
Night operations				
Comparison of noise footprints	For night operations—take-off and landing. By aircraft type	Monthly	[QRL 90]	2.1.10, 3.3.2
Area within 95 and 105 PNdB	By aircraft type, departure, and landing	Monthly	[QRL 90]	2.1.10, 3.3.2
Population within 95 and 105 PNdB	By airport and aircraft type—departure and landing separately	Monthly	[QRL 90]	2.1.10, 3.3.2
Present hours of night restrictions	By airport	For two seasons Annual	[QRL 90]	2.1.10, 3.3.2
Summer night jet movements	By airport giving quota, arrivals and departures total and average number per night, and total movements	Annual	[QRL 90]	2.1.10, 3.3.2
Winter night jet movements	By airport by quota, arrivals and departures, actual movements	Annual	[QRL 90]	2.1.10, 3.3.2
Summer night non-jet movements	By airport. By arrivals and departures, total movements	Annual	[QRL 90]	2.1.10, 3.3.2
Winter night non-jet movements	By airport. By arrivals and departures, total movements	Annual	[QRL 90]	2.1.10, 3.3.2
Aircraft noise at night	By loudness and number of flights per day and per cent of population exposed at each level by night and day	1967	[QRL 117]	2.1.10, 3.3.2
	Relation between night annoyance and sleeping pattern	1967	[QRL 117]	2.1.10, 3.3.2
	Relation between night annoyance and exposure to aircraft	1967	[QRL 117]	2.1.10, 3.3.2
Complaints				
Complaints received	London airport by year	1961	[QRL 92]	2.1.10, 3.3.2
	By number of complainants and number of complaints	Oct. 1968–Mar. 1969	[QRL 3]	2.1.10, 3.3.2
	Distribution over successive months: by number of complainants and number of complaints	Oct. 1968–Mar. 1969	[QRL 3]	2.1.10, 3.3.2
	By area, number of complaints and number of complainants	Oct. 1968–Mar. 1969	[QRL 3]	2.1.10, 3.3.2
	By Concorde departure and arrival	Oct. 1968–Mar. 1969	[QRL 3]	2.1.10, 3.3.2

QUICK REFERENCE LIST

The distribution of complainants	Classified by noise level and number of aircraft per day	1961	[QRL 92]	2.1.10, 3.3.2
	By aircraft type and number and per cent complaints, and number and per cent of movements	Oct. 1968–Mar. 1969	[QRL 3]	2.1.10, 3.3.2
	By aircraft type, take-off and landing, night and day, number and per cent of complaints and number and per cent of movements	Oct. 1968–Mar. 1969	[QRL 3]	2.1.10, 3.3.2
	By landings and take-offs together by aircraft type	Oct. 1968–Mar. 1969	[QRL 3]	2.1.10, 3.3.2
	By aircraft type, take-off and landing, day and night	Oct. 1968–Mar. 1969	[QRL 3]	2.1.10, 3.3.2
The distribution of complaints over complainants	Number of complaints and number of complainants	Oct. 1968–Mar. 1969	[QRL 3]	2.1.0, 3.3.2
Analysis of Concorde complaints data		1976	[QRL 91]	2.1.10, 3.3.2
PERSONNEL				
Number				
Pilots and co-pilots	By airline and sex	Annual	[QRL 51]	1974 onwards, 2.1.3, 3.4
	By airline	Annual	[QRL 141]	2.3.4, 3.4
	By international scheduled airline—mid-year and end of year	Annual	[QRL 61]	2.3.1, 3.4
	By domestic scheduled airline—mid-year and end of year	Annual	[QRL 61]	2.3.1, 3.4
Other cockpit personnel	By airline and sex	Annual	[QRL 51]	1974 onwards, 2.1.3, 3.4
	By airline	Annual	[QRL 141]	2.3.4, 3.4
	By international scheduled airline—mid-year and end of year	Annual	[QRL 61]	2.3.1, 3.4
	By domestic scheduled airline—mid-year and end of year	Annual	[QRL 61]	2.3.1, 3.4
Cabin attendants	By airline and sex	Annual	[QRL 51]	1974 onwards, 2.1.3, 3.4
	By airline	Annual	[QRL 141]	2.3.4, 3.4
	By international scheduled airline—mid-year and end of year	Annual	[QRL 61]	2.3.1, 3.4
	By domestic scheduled airline—mid-year and end of year	Annual	[QRL 61]	2.3.1, 3.4
Maintenance and overhaul personnel	By airline and sex	Annual	[QRL 51]	1974 onwards, 2.1.3, 3.4

CIVIL AVIATION

Descriptive title	Breakdown	Frequency	Publication (see QRL Key)	Text reference and remarks
PERSONNEL (contd.) Number (contd.)				
	By airline	Annual	[QRL 141]	2.3.4, 3.4
	By international scheduled airline—mid-year and end of year	Annual	[QRL 61]	2.3.1, 3.4
	By domestic scheduled airline—mid-year and end of year	Annual	[QRL 61]	2.3.1, 3.4
Traffic and sales personnel	By airline and sex	Annual	[QRL 51]	1974 onwards, 2.1.3, 3.4
	By airline	Annual	[QRL 141]	2.3.4, 3.4
	By international scheduled airline—mid-year and end of year	Annual	[QRL 61]	2.3.1, 3.4
	By domestic scheduled airline—mid-year and end of year	Annual	[QRL 61]	2.3.1, 3.4
All other personnel	By airline and sex	Annual	[QRL 51]	1974 onwards, 2.1.3, 3.4
	By airline		[QRL 141]	2.3.4, 3.4
	By international scheduled airline—mid-year and end of year		[QRL 61]	2.3.1, 3.4
	By domestic scheduled airline—mid-year and end of year	Annual	[QRL 61]	2.3.1, 3.4
All personnel	By region, end of June and end of December. UK airline personnel	Annual	[QRL 51]	1974 onwards, 2.1.3, 3.4
All personnel	By airline. International scheduled airlines	Annual	[QRL 61]	2.3.1, 3.4
	By airline	Annual	[QRL 141]	2.3.4, 3.4
	By airline. Domestic scheduled airlines	Annual	[QRL 61]	2.3.1, 3.4
	By international scheduled airlines, mid-year and end of year	Annual	[QRL 61]	2.3.1, 3.4
	By domestic scheduled airline, mid-year and end of year	Annual	[QRL 61]	2.3.1, 3.4
Percentage change on last year	By airline	Annual	[QRL 141]	2.3.4, 3.4
Employment figures	Air transport	Annual	[QRL 137]	1.3.6, 3.4
	Air transport. By sex and full or part-time	Annual	[QRL 137]	1.3.6, 3.4
	Air transport. By region	Annual	[QRL 137]	1.3.6, 3.4
	Air transport for UK and Great Britain	Annual	[QRL 28]	1.3.6, 3.4
	Air transport, UK and Great Britain	Annual	[QRL 28]	1.3.6, 3.4
Unemployed	Air transport. UK and Great Britain by sex	1977	[QRL 54]	2.1.14, 3.4

QUICK REFERENCE LIST

Expenditure
Pilots and co-pilots

Average expenditure per head	By airline	Annual	[QRL 51]	1974 onwards, 2.1.3, 3.4
Average annual remuneration	By international and domestic scheduled airline separately. £ and US dollars	Annual	[QRL 61]	2.3.1, 3.4
Total expenditure in US dollars	By international and domestic scheduled airline separately	Annual	[QRL 61]	2.3.1, 3.4
Average expenditure per year percentage change over last year	By airline	Annual	[QRL 51]	1974 onwards, 2.1.3, 3.4

Other cockpit personnel

Average expenditure per year	By airline	Annual	[QRL 51]	1974 onwards, 2.1.3, 3.4
Average annual remuneration	By international and domestic scheduled airline separately. £ and US dollars	Annual	[QRL 61]	2.3.1, 3.4
Total expenditure in US dollars	By international and domestic scheduled airline separately	Annual	[QRL 61]	2.3.1, 3.4
Average expenditure per head percentage change over last year	By airline	Annual	[QRL 51]	1974 onwards, 2.1.3, 3.4

Cabin attendants

Average expenditure per head	By airline	Annual	[QRL 51]	1974 onwards, 2.1.3, 3.4
Average annual remuneration	By international and domestic scheduled airline separately. £ and US dollar	Annual	[QRL 61]	2.3.1, 3.4
Total expenditure in US dollars	By international and domestic scheduled airlines separately	Annual	[QRL 61]	2.3.1, 3.4
Average expenditure per head percentage change over last year	By airline	Annual	[QRL 51]	1974 onwards, 2.1.3, 3.4
Maintenance and overhaul personnel	Average expenditure per head. By airline and year	Annual	[QRL 51]	1974 onwards, 2.1.3, 3.4
	Average annual remuneration. By international and domestic scheduled airlines separately. £ and US dollars	Annual	[QRL 61]	2.3.1, 3.4
	Total expenditure in US dollars. By international and domestic scheduled airline separately	Annual	[QRL 61]	2.3.1, 3.4
	Average expenditure per head percentage change over last year. By airline and year	Annual	[QRL 51]	1974 onwards, 2.1.3, 3.4

244 CIVIL AVIATION

Descriptive title	Breakdown	Frequency	Publication (see QRL Key)	Text reference and remarks
PERSONNEL (contd.) **Expenditure** (contd.) *Cabin attendants* (contd.)				
Traffic and sales personnel	Average expenditure per head. By airline and year	Annual	[QRL 51]	1974 onwards, 2.1.3, 3.4
	Average annual remuneration. By international and domestic scheduled airline separately. £ and US dollars	Annual	[QRL 61]	2.3.1, 3.4
	Total expenditure in US dollars. By international and domestic scheduled airline separately	Annual	[QRL 61]	2.3.1, 3.4
	Average expenditure per head percentage change over last year. By airlines year	Annual	[QRL 51]	1974 onwards, 2.1.3, 3.4
All other personnel	Average expenditure per head. By airline and year	Annual	[QRL 51]	1974 onwards, 2.1.3, 3.4
	Average annual remuneration. By international and domestic scheduled airline separately. £ and US dollars	Annual	[QRL 61]	2.3.1, 3.4
	Total expenditure in US dollars. By international and domestic scheduled airline separately	Annual	[QRL 61]	2.3.1, 3.4
	Average expenditure per year percentage change over last year. By airline and year	Annual	[QRL 51]	Since 1974, 2.1.3, 3.4
All personnel	Total expenditure per head in US dollars. By international and domestic scheduled airline separately	Annual	[QRL 61]	2.3.1, 3.4
(Aircrew)	Total expenditure £s. By airline	Dec. 1974	[QRL 64]	2.6, 3.4
	Cost per ton/kilometre capacity. By airline	Dec. 1976	[QRL 64]	2.6, 3.4
Airport workers				
No. of workers at the airport	By occupation (six categories), sex and airport	(132 in 1975) (133 in 1976)	[QRL 132, 133]	2.2.1, 3.4
	By occupation (three categories) and employer	1969	[QRL 106]	2.7, 3.4
Proportion of workers present on a typical weekday	By occupation and airport	(132 in 1975) (133 in 1976)	[QRL 132, 133]	2.2.1, 3.4

QUICK REFERENCE LIST

Place of residence of workers	By airport, area and place	(132 in 1975) (133 in 1976)	[QRL 132, 133]	2.2.1, 3.4
Length of time lived at present address	By time period and airport	(132 in 1975) (133 in 1976)	[QRL 132, 133]	2.2.1, 3.4
Length of time worked at the airport	By time period and airport	(132 in 1975) (133 in 1976)	[QRL 132, 133]	2.2.1, 3.4
Modes of travel to the airport	By mode and airport	(132 in 1975) (133 in 1976)	[QRL 132, 133]	2.2.1, 3.4
Approximate number of workers who bring car to work (on a typical day)	By airport	1975	[QRL 132]	2.2.1, 3.4
Where car drivers enter the airport	By entry point, percentage, no. on typical weekday, and airport	1975	[QRL 133]	2.2.1, 3.4
	By entry point and percentage	1976	[QRL 132]	2.2.1, 3.4
Where drivers park	By parking place, percentage no. on typical weekday and a rport	1976	[QRL 133]	2.2.1, 3.4
	By parking place and percentage	1975	[QRL 132]	2.2.1, 3.4
Use of car at lunchtime	Percentage who use car by airport	1976	[QRL 133]	2.2.1, 3.4
Time of starting and finishing work	By time period and airport	(132 in 1975) (133 in 1976)	[QRL 132, 133]	2.2.1, 3.4
Age of workers	Percentage by age period and airport	(132 in 1975) (133 in 1976)	[QRL 132, 133]	2.2.1, 3.4
Household size	Percentage by no. of people and airport	(132 in 1975) (133 in 1976)	[QRL 132, 133]	2.2.1, 3.4
No. of children under 16 in household	Percentage by no. of children and airport	(132 in 1975) (133 in 1976)	[QRL 132, 133]	2.2.1, 3.4
Number of industrial employees	By airport	1969	[QRL 106]	2.7, 3.4
	By occupational group in detail on 1 April 1969. Four BAA London airports separately	1969	[QRL 106]	2.7, 3.4
	By occupational group in detail on 1 May 1969. Local authority airports separately	1969	[QRL 106]	2.7, 3.4
	By occupational group in detail on 1 May 1969. Local authority airports (Scotland) separately	1969	[QRL 106]	2.7, 3.4
	By occupational group in detail on 1 July 1969. Board of Trade airports	1969	[QRL 106]	2.7, 3.4
	By occupational group in detail on 1 July 1969. Board of Trade airports separately	1969	[QRL 106]	2.7, 3.4

CIVIL AVIATION

Descriptive title	Breakdown	Frequency	Publication (see QRL Key)	Text reference and remarks
PERSONNEL (*contd.*)				
Pay				
Basic pay for 40-hour week 14 May 1969	By occupational group and airport owner	1969	[QRL 106]	2.7, 3.4
Hourly and weekly earnings and hours worked for pay week including 14 May 1969	By occupational group and airport owner	1969	[QRL 106]	2.7, 3.4
Overtime as percentage of basic earnings April 1968–March 1969	By airport owner	1969	[QRL 106]	2.7, 3.4
Hourly and weekly earnings hours worked for pay week including 14 May 1969	By occupational group and airport owner	1969	[QRL 106]	2.7, 3.4
Hourly and weekly rostered earnings and hours worked for pay week including 14 May 1969	By occupational group and airport owner	1969	[QRL 106]	2.7, 3.4
Hourly and weekly unscheduled overtime earnings and hours worked for pay week including 14 May 1969	By occupational group and airport owner	1969	[QRL 106]	2.7, 3.4
Distribution of average weekly earnings of all employees for pay week including 14 May 1969	By earnings category and airport owner	1969	[QRL 106]	2.7, 3.4
Distribution of average weekly earnings of all operatives for pay week including 14 May 1969	By earnings category group and airport owner	1969	[QRL 106]	2.7, 3.4
Distribution of average weekly earnings of all firemen for pay week including 14 May 1969	By earnings category and airport group	1969	[QRL 106]	2.7, 3.4
Distribution of average weekly earnings of all craftsmen for pay week including 14 May 1969	By earnings category and airport group	1969	[QRL 106]	2.7, 3.4
Hourly and weekly earnings and hours worked of Ministry of Public Building and Works industrial employees working full time at Edinburgh and Aberdeen airports for pay week including 14 May 1969	By occupational group and type of hours worked	1969	[QRL 106]	2.7, 3.4

Miscellaneous

Airline staff productivity as a function of average passenger journey	By passenger per employee, average stage distance (km) and airline	Dec. 1976	[QRL 64]	2.6, 3.4

FINANCE

Profit and loss accounts (statement)	Total for UK airlines	Annual	[QRL 51]	1968 onwards, 2.1.12, 3.5
	By individual airline	Annual	[QRL 51]	1968 onwards, 2.1.12, 3.5
Profit and loss accounts (Statement)	By airline. US $ and £s	Annual	[QRL 60]	2.3.1, 3.5
	Total for UK airlines	1968–74 Annual	[QRL 66]	1974 onwards, 2.1.12, 3.5
	By airline	1972, 1973 Annual	[QRL 66]	1974 onwards, 2.1.12, 3.5
	Total for UK airlines: all airlines, public sector, private sector	Annual	[QRL 45]	2.1.12, 3.5
	By airline	Annual	[QRL 45]	2.1.12, 3.5
	By airline non-scheduled operators. US $	Annual	[QRL 122]	2.3.1, 3.5
	By airline, non-scheduled operators. US $ and £s	Annual	[QRL 122]	2.3.1, 3.5
Balance sheet	Total for UK airlines	Annual	[QRL 51]	1968 onwards, 2.1.12, 3.5
	By airline	Annual	[QRL 51]	1968 onwards, 2.1.12, 3.5
	By airline. US $ and £s	Annual	[QRL 60]	2.3.1, 3.5
	Total for UK airlines	1968–73 Annual	[QRL 66]	2.1.12, 3.5
	By airline	1972–73 Annual	[QRL 66]	2.1.12, 3.5
	Total for UK airlines: all airlines, public sector, private sector	Annual	[QRL 45]	2.1.12, 3.5
	By airline	Annual	[QRL 45]	2.1.12, 3.5
	By airline, non-scheduled operators. US $	Annual	[QRL 122]	2.3.1, 3.5
	By airline, non-scheduled operators. US $ and £s	Annual	[QRL 122]	2.3.1, 3.5
Appropriation account	Total for UK airlines	Annual	[QRL 51]	2.1.12, 3.5
	By airline	Annual	[QRL 51]	2.1.12, 3.5
	Total for UK airlines	1968–71 Annual	[QRL 66]	2.1.12, 3.5
	By airline	1972–7 Annual	[QRL 66]	2.1.12, 3.5

CIVIL AVIATION

Descriptive title	Breakdown	Frequency	Publication (see QRL Key)	Text reference and remarks
FINANCE (contd.)				
Financial resources	Total for UK airlines. By private and public sector, assets and liabilities	Annual	[QRL 51, 66]	2.1.12, 3.5
Revenue, expenses and profits	Total for UK airlines. By private and public sector and all airlines	Annual	[QRL 51, 66]	2.1.12, 3.5
Trends in operating costs and revenues	Total for UK airlines, by year 1968–75	Annual	[QRL 51, 66]	2.1.12, 3.5
Financial results	By airline giving operating revenue, operating expense, operating profit (or loss), and net profit (or loss). US $	Annual	[QRL 141]	2.3.4, 3.5
	By airline, giving assets, operating revenue and operating result, US $. Total operations of non-scheduled operators	Annual	[QRL 122]	2.3.1, 3.5
Assets	Detailed breakdown, by airline	Annual	[QRL 45]	2.3.1, 3.5
Liabilities	Detailed breakdown, by airline	Annual	[QRL 45]	2.3.1, 3.5
Operating revenues	By type of service. By no. and per cent by airline	Annual	[QRL 45]	2.3.1, 3.5
	By tonne km performed and tonne km available. By type of service. By airline	Annual	[QRL 45]	2.3.1, 3.5
Direct operating expenses	No. and per cent detailed breakdown by airline	Annual	[QRL 45]	2.3.1, 3.5
	Per tonne km performed and available. Detailed breakdown by airline	Annual	[QRL 45]	2.3.1, 3.5
Indirect and total operating expenses	No. and per cent detailed breakdown by airline	Annual	[QRL 45]	2.3.1, 3.5
	Per tonne km performed and available. Detailed breakdown by airline	Annual	[QRL 45]	2.3.1, 3.5
Operating result and non-operating items	Detailed breakdown by airline	Annual	[QRL 45]	2.3.1, 3.5
Net profit (or loss) and statement of retained earnings	Detailed breakdown by airline	Annual	[QRL 45]	2.3.1, 3.5
Invisible trade	Civil Aviation by UK and overseas airlines, credits and debits and net	Annual	[QRL 138]	2.1.13, 3.5
Consumers, expenditure at current prices	On air travel	Annual	[QRL 88]	2.1.13, 3.5

QUICK REFERENCE LIST

Treasury analysis of public expenditure	Nationalized industries—airways and airports	Annual	[QRL 88]	2.1.13, 3.5
Local authority: capital account expenditure	On harbours, docks and aerodromes (as one figure)	Annual	[QRL 88]	2.1.13, 3.5
Gross domestic fixed capital formation	At current and 1970 prices, by type of asset, private and public sector, vehicles, ships, and aircraft as one figure	Annual	[QRL 88]	2.1.13, 3.5
	At current prices by type of asset, aircraft	Annual	[QRL 88]	2.1.13, 3.5
	At 1970 prices by type of asset, railway, rolling stock, ship and aircraft as one figure	Annual	[QRL 88]	2.1.13, 3.5
Gross capital stock	By industry, air transport and type of asset	Annual	[QRL 88]	2.1.13, 3.5
	At 1970 replacement cost by industry (air transport)	Annual	[QRL 88]	2.1.13, 3.5
	At 1970 replacement cost by type of asset—railway stock, ships and aircraft as one figure	Annual	[QRL 88]	2.1.13, 3.5
Air fares	By European route, type of fare giving cost per mile	1976	[QRL 64]	2.6, 3.5

INDIVIDUAL STUDIES
Individual airports

Ballykelly	Domestic passengers through Belfast by route	1970	[QRL 32]	2.2.2, 3.2.1
	Holiday passengers by residence and destination. Northern Ireland	1970	[QRL 32]	2.2.2, 3.2.1
	Traffic forecasts by route and type of service	Up to 1975/6	[QRL 32]	2.2.2, 3.2.3
	Airfield details. Ballykelly	1970	[QRL 32]	2.2.2, 3.3
	Cost and revenue figures. Ballykelly	1970	[QRL 32]	2.2.2, 3.5
Biggin Hill	Revenue and cost summary (estimates)	1973, 78, 83	[QRL 58]	2.2.2, 3.5
	Expenditure estimates	1973, 78, 83	[QRL 58]	2.2.2, 3.5
	General aviation movements (includes estimates)	1965–91	[QRL 5]	2.2.2, 3.2.1
Birmingham	Passenger traffic by purpose, origin and income		[QRL 5]	2.2.2, 3.2.1
	Business passengers by type of industry		[QRL 5]	2.2.2, 3.2.1
	Passenger forecasts	Up to 1991	[QRL 5]	2.2.2, 3.2.1
	Time spent by passengers after check-in, before take-off	1975	[QRL 5]	2.2.2, 3.2.1
	Standard busy rate figures	1975	[QRL 5]	2.2.2, 3.2.3
	Freight forecasts	Up to 1991	[QRL 5]	2.2.2, 3.2.2
	Traffic movements to and from airport, and car-parking figures	1975	[QRL 5]	2.2.2, 3.3.1

250 CIVIL AVIATION

Descriptive title	Breakdown	Frequency	Publication (see QRL Key)	Text reference and remarks
INDIVIDUAL STUDIES (*contd.*)				
Individual airports (*contd.*)				
	Details about proposed terminal complex	1975	[QRL 5]	2.2.2, 3.3
	Construction cost estimates	1975	[QRL 5]	2.2.2, 3.5
	Passengers: detailed breakdown	1967	[QRL 4]	2.2.2, 3.2.1
	Business passengers: detailed breakdown	1967	[QRL 4]	2.2.2, 3.2.1
	Non-business passengers: detailed breakdown	1967	[QRL 4]	2.2.2, 3.2.1
	Interline passengers	1967	[QRL 4]	2.2.2, 3.2.1
	Reason for choosing air travel	1967	[QRL 4]	2.2.2, 3.2.1
Bournemouth–Hurn	NNI contours 1971, and forecast NNI contours for 1985, given two hypotheses	1971 & 1985	[QRL 33]	2.2.2, 3.3.2
	Actual or estimated net revenue counts for 1969/70 to 1972/3	1969/70–1972/3	[QRL 33]	2.2.2, 3.5
Bristol	Summary of expenditure and income forecasts		[QRL 33]	2.2.2, 3.5
	Private aircraft movements	1971	[QRL 34]	2.2.2, 3.1
	Business trip by origin and destination	1971	[QRL 34]	2.2.2, 3.2.1
	Freight movements and forecast of air cargo growth up to 1980	1971–80	[QRL 34]	2.2.2, 3.2.2
	Passenger and aircraft movements by type of service and destination and forecasts by type of service	1971 onwards	[QRL 34]	2.2.2, 3.2.1, 3.2.3
	NNI contours for Lulsgate and Filton + forecasts up to 1980	1971–80	[QRL 34]	2.2.1, 3.3.2
	Types of institution affected by aircraft noise	1971	[QRL 34]	2.2.2, 3.3.2
	Cost-benefit study of developing Lulsgate airport	1971	[QRL 34]	2.2.2, 3.5
	Development construction costs of Lulsgate airport	1971	[QRL 34]	2.2.2, 3.5
Gatwick	See also **Transport to and from the airport**			
	Diagrams on air transport movements forecasts, passenger forecasts, average number of seats per aircraft	1970–2000	[QRL 82]	2.2.2, 3.2.1, 3.2.2
	Diagrams on noise annoyance in the area	1970	[QRL 82]	2.2.2, 3.3.2
	General aviation by purpose, type of aircraft and origin	1972	[QRL 68]	2.2.2, 3.1
	Departures by airway and aircraft type	1972	[QRL 68]	2.2.2, 3.1.3

Goole–Thorne	Total movements by type of movement and destination	1972	[QRL 68]	2.2.2, 3.1.3
	Radar maps, map showing height of outbound flights	1972	[QRL 68]	2.2.2
	Noise reading by place. Noise maps	1972	[QRL 68]	2.2.2, 3.3.2
	Departing air passengers (detailed breakdown)	1966	[QRL 81]	2.2.2, 3.2.1
	Estimated passenger-traffic levels	1980–2000	[QRL 71]	2.2.2, 3.2.1
	Passenger and aircraft movements at Standard Busy Rate	1980–2000	[QRL 71]	
Heathrow	See also **Transport to and from airport**			
	Figures on distribution of vehicle journeys from Heathrow for passenger, staff and air freight, business trips and spectators	1975	[QRL 72]	2.2.1, 3.3.1
	Employment occupation categories	1975	[QRL 72]	2.2.1, 3.4
	No. of staff employed by location	1967–75	[QRL 72]	2.2.1, 3.4
	Cost-benefit summary of transport links to Heathrow airport	1971	[QRL 110]	2.7, 3.3.1
	Figures for Heathrow on passenger and air transport	1967 & 1972	[QRL 106]	2.2.2, 3.2.1, 3.2.3
	Detailed survey of local employers by type of firm and advantages and disadvantages of proximity to airport	1972	[QRL 106]	2.2.2, 3.3.3
	Local hotels proposed and existing	1973	[QRL 106]	2.2.2, 3.3.3
	Employment of local residents in area. Commuting distance	1951–66	[QRL106]	2.2.2, 3.3.3
	Employees at Heathrow	1969	[QRL 106]	2.2.2, 3.4
	Passenger reporting pattern by type of passenger	1975	[QRL 112]	2.6, 3.1
	Passenger queueing times	1975	[QRL 112]	2.6, 3.1
	No. of trolleys and porters used and available per passenger per coachload	1975	[QRL 112]	2.6, 3.1
	Complaints received by AUC	1975	[QRL 112]	2.6, 3.1
	Mode of travel to and between terminals	1975	[QRL 112]	2.6, 3.1
	Passenger time through the airport	1973	[QRL 73]	2.2.2, 3.1
	Arrival times at airport before flight and effect of 'Have a go' system, 'Gate check in' system on these	1973	[QRL 73]	2.2.2, 3.1
	Travel agents' latest reporting times for departing passengers	1973	[QRL 73]	2.2.2, 3.1
	Waiting time at check in	1973	[QRL 73]	2.2.2, 3.1
	Connection times for transfer passengers	1973	[QRL 73]	2.2.2, 3.3.4

252   CIVIL AVIATION

Descriptive title	Breakdown	Frequency	Publication (see QRL Key)	Text reference and remarks
INDIVIDUAL STUDIES (*contd.*)				
Individual airports (*contd.*)				
	Transfer time between terminals	1973	[QRL 73]	2.2.2, 3.3.4
	Time spent by passengers getting to baggage hall and waiting for baggage	1973	[QRL 73]	2.2.2, 3.1
	Passengers by type and terminal	1973	[QRL 73]	2.2.2, 3.1
	Queueing times by type of passenger	1973	[QRL 73]	2.2.2, 3.1
	Baggage time from aircraft to airport	1973	[QRL 73]	2.2.2, 3.1
	Car-park capacity, future requirements and time cars parked	1973	[QRL 73]	2.2.2, 3.3.1
	Cost-benefits of 'Have a go' system and 'Gate check in' system	1973	[QRL 73]	2.2.2, 3.1
	Cost-benefits of baggage handling	1973	[QRL 73]	2.2.2, 3.5
	Cost-benefit of increased manning	1973	[QRL 73]	2.2.2, 3.5
	Cost-benefit analysis of changing connecting time for transfer passengers	1973	[QRL 73]	2.2.2, 3.5
	Immigration staff costs	1973	[QRL 73]	2.2.2, 3.5
	Departing air passengers (detailed) breakdown	1966	[QRL 80]	
Lee-on-Solent	Estimation of cost and revenue for civil complex	1972–8	[QRL 78]	2.2.2, 3.5
Liverpool	Existing accommodation affected by aircraft noise and action necessary	1973	[QRL 56]	2.2.2, 3.3.2
	Assessment of number of dwellings affected by aircraft noise	1973	[QRL 56]	2.2.2, 3.3.2
	NNI contours for the region	1973	[QRL 56]	2.2.2, 3.3.2
	Manchester airport, present noise/traffic conditions	1973	[QRL 56]	2.2.2, 3.3.2
	Previous passenger forecasts	1966 & 1968	[QRL 79]	2.2.2, 3.2.1
	Estimates of growth and business and tourism by population	From 1971	[QRL 79]	2.2.2, 3.2.1
	Passengers: summary and estimates for Liverpool, neighbouring airports by origin and destination, business and tourism, scheduled and charter	1971	[QRL 79]	2.2.2, 3.2.1
	Air freight: scheduled and charter by destination and origin and cost. Liverpool and Manchester compared with London	1971	[QRL 79]	2.2.2, 3.2.2

Luton	Aircraft movements: busy period forecasts for Liverpool and Manchester	From 1971	[QRL 79]	2.2.2, 3.2.3
	Survey of firms' opinions about air transport	1969	[QRL 85]	2.2.2, 3.2.1
	Forecasts of aircraft passenger and freight movements	Up to 1980	[QRL 85]	2.2.2, 3.2.1, 3.2.2
	Daily traffic pattern for passenger and aircraft movements	1969	[QRL 85]	2.2.2, 3.2.1, 3.2.3
	Forecast for 1980 of airport users' ground transport movements	Up to 1980	[QRL 85]	2.2.2, 3.3.1
	Night movements and cost of restricting night flying	1969	[QRL 85]	2.2.2, 3.3.2
	Cost estimates of development	1969	[QRL 85]	2.2.2, 3.5
	Cost-benefit analysis	1969	[QRL 85]	2.2.2, 3.5
Newcastle	See also Northern region airport study			
	Figures and estimates for total passengers, passengers to aircraft ratio and aircraft movements	1980	[QRL 89]	2.2.2, 3.2.1
	Passenger and aircraft flows at typical busy hours	1972	[QRL 89]	2.2.2, 3.2.1, 3.2.3
	Simulation figures on passengers in terminal building	1972	[QRL 89]	2.2.2, 3.2.1
	Costs of extending terminal apron	1972	[QRL 89]	2.2.2, 3.5
	Time between arrival at airport and take-off—by type of traveller	1972	[QRL 89]	2.2.2, 3.2.1
	Ratio of friends and relative to air passengers	1972	[QRL 89]	2.2.2, 3.1
	Visitors to airport by arrival time	1972	[QRL 89]	2.2.2, 3.1
	Passengers' flow rate—terminal to aircraft	1972	[QRL 89]	2.2.2, 3.1
	Baggage flow rates from aircraft	1972	[QRL 89]	2.2.2, 3.1
	Travel to airport by mode and type of traveller	1972	[QRL 89]	2.2.2, 3.1
	Parking times at airport, by purpose of visit of car occupants	1972	[QRL 89]	2.2.2, 3.1
Norwich	Passenger and aircraft movements at Cambridge airport	1968–73	[QRL 57]	2.2.2, 3.2.1, 3.2.3
	Estimates of potential passenger movements and air traffic movements at Norwich airport by type of service	1973–4, 1985, 1990	[QRL 57]	2.2.2, 3.2.1, 3.2.3
	No. of dwellings and population within NNI contours	1974	[QRL 57]	2.2.2, 3.3.2
	Costs due to noise, land value and access for five villages around Norwich	1974	[QRL 57]	2.2.2, 3.2.1

Descriptive title	Breakdown	Frequency	Publication (see QRL Key)	Text reference and remarks
INDIVIDUAL STUDIES (*contd.*)				
Individual airports (*contd.*)				
Tees-side	Probable average passenger loading based on a daily schedule return service between Tees-side and other UK destinations, and Tees-side and the Netherlands	Estimate made 1972	[QRL 55]	2.2.2, 3.2.1
	Breakdown of air cargo from Tees-side	1971	[QRL 55]	2.2.2, 3.2.2
	Air transport movements Tees-side	1972	[QRL 55]	2.2.2, 3.2.3
	Estimates of inclusive tour flights by destination	Estimate made 1972	[QRL 55]	2.2.2, 3.2.3
	Use of air transport by firms in the area	1967	[QRL 23]	2.2.2, 3.2.1
	Probable air services	1967/8	[QRL 23]	2.2.2, 3.2.3
	Estimates of holiday travel	1972	[QRL 134]	2.2.2, 3.2.1
Airports by region				
Central England				
East Midlands, Manchester, Birmingham, Leeds/Bradford, Blackpool and four proposed new airports (North Cheshire, West Midlands, Notts./Yorks. and Finningley)	Estimated traffic at six airports by airport system	1990	[QRL 16]	2.2.2, 3.2.3
	Estimated population living within 35 NNI zone in 1990 by airport system	1990	[QRL 16]	2.2.2, 3.3.2
	Increase in NNI levels by airport and airport system	1975	[QRL 16]	2.2.2, 3.3.2
	Percentage cost of developing an airport, by item	1975	[QRL 16]	2.2.2, 3.5
	Costs and benefit of various projected airport systems	1975	[QRL 16]	2.2.2, 3.5
Birmingham, Blackpool, East Midlands, Leeds/Bradford, Liverpool and Manchester, (Coventry and Birmingham)	Passenger movements	1974	[QRL 49]	2.2.2, 3.2.1
	Freight	1974	[QRL 49]	2.2.2, 3.2.1
	Aircraft movements	1974	[QRL 49]	2.2.2, 3.2.3
	Figures on danger from airports	1974	[QRL 49]	2.2.2, 3.3
	Figures on 'trial sites' in Central England	1974	[QRL 49]	2.2.2, 3.3
	Figures on noise nuisance in airport areas	1974	[QRL 49]	2.2.2, 3.3.2
	Figures on employment in area	1974	[QRL 49]	2.2.2, 3.3.3
	Analysis of airline costs, revenues and profit	1974	[QRL 49]	2.2.2, 3.5
London airports	See also PASSENGERS: Origin and destination See also PERSONNEL			

	Quantitative report on survey on the role of London airports in meeting the business and social needs of the consumer	1973	[QRL 114]	2.7, 3.2.1
Heathrow, Gatwick, Stansted, Luton, Southend, Westland Heliport	Airport figures on aircraft movements, passengers, and freight	Annual since 1966	[QRL 27]	2.7, 3.2.1, 3.2.2, 3.2.3
Heathrow, Gatwick, Stansted, Luton	Passenger forecasts up to 1990	Estimated 1975–90	[QRL 21]	2.2.2, 3.2.1
	Passenger by type of service and airport	1974	[QRL 21]	2.2.2, 3.2.1
	Origin and destination of passengers	1972	[QRL 21]	2.2.2, 3.2.1
	Aircraft movements by airport	1974	[QRL 21]	2.2.2, 3.2.3
	Road and rail traffic by airport	1975–90 (Estimates)	[QRL 21]	2.2.2, 3.3.1
	NNI contours by airport, present and forecasts up to and population within contours	1975–90 (Estimates)	[QRL 21]	2.2.2, 3.3.2
	Employment by airport and employer	1975	[QRL 21]	2.2.2, 3.4
	Passenger forecasts by type of passenger	Estimates up to 1985	[QRL 110]	2.2.2, 3.2.1
Heathrow and Gatwick	Air transport movement forecasts by type of movement	Estimates up to 1985	[QRL 110]	2.2.2, 3.2.3
	Delays	Estimates up to 1974, 76, 78	[QRL 110]	2.2.2, 3.1
	Changes to operators' schedules	1965–8	[QRL 110]	2.2.2, 3.1
	Rescheduling forecasts	1974, 76, 78 (Estimates)	[QRL 110]	2.2.2, 3.1
	Gatwick, spare capacity	Estimate up to 1978	[QRL 110]	2.2.2, 3.1
	See also PASSENGERS: Origin and destination			
Midlands (West Midlands) Birmingham and East Midlands airports	General aviation forecasts	1973 onwards	[QRL 86]	2.2.2, 3.1
	General aviation movements	1973	[QRL 86]	2.2.2, 3.1
	Passengers by residence, type of passenger and type of service and by origin and destination, income and route	1973	[QRL 86]	2.2.2, 3.2.1
	Passenger and air cargo forecasts	1973	[QRL 86]	2.2.2, 3.2.2
	Air cargo by commodity group and destination	1973	[QRL 86]	2.2.2, 3.2.2
	Aircraft movements by type of service	1973	[QRL 86]	2.2.2, 3.2.3
	Pollution by aircraft type	1973	[QRL 86]	2.2.2, 3.3
	Surface transport by mode and flows and cost. Car parking	1973	[QRL 86]	2.2.2, 3.3.1

256   CIVIL AVIATION

Descriptive title	Breakdown	Frequency	Publication (see QRL Key)	Text reference and remarks
INDIVIDUAL STUDIES (*contd.*)				
Airports by region (*contd.*)				
Midlands (*contd.*)				
	NNI contours for Birmingham airport and East Midlands airport	1973	[QRL 86]	2.2.2, 3.3.2
	Employment forecasts by airport	1973	[QRL 86]	2.2.2, 3.4
	Cost-benefit analysis	1973	[QRL 86]	2.2.2, 3.5
Midlands				
Seighford, Manchester and Birmingham airports	Forecasts for passenger, cargo and aircraft movements—Seighford	1968–81	[QRL 18]	2.2.2, 3.2.1, 3.2.2, 3.2.3
	Firms using air transport. Seighford area	1968	[QRL 18]	2.2.2, 3.2.1
	Journey times including surface transport by route	1968	[QRL 18]	2.2.2, 3.3.1
	Noise levels by aircraft type	1968	[QRL 18]	2.2.2, 3.3.2
	Cost of the development of Seighford airport	1968	[QRL 18]	2.2.2, 3.5
North				
Carlisle, Newcastle, Tees-side	Forecasts of passenger movements by type of service and airport	1974–90	[QRL 96]	2.2.2, 3.2.1
	Survey of firms' views of their future use of air transport	1974	[QRL 96]	2.2.2, 3.2.1
	Passengers, freight and air transport movements, Newcastle and Tees-side airport combined	1974	[QRL 96]	2.2.2, 3.2.1, 3.2.2, 3.2.3
	Forecasts of air transport movements Newcastle and Tees-side	1974	[QRL 96]	2.2.2, 3.2.3
	Aircraft capacity and road factors, effects of closing various airports	1974	[QRL 96]	2.2.2, 3.3.1
	Map of time travel contours and time indifference lines	1974	[QRL 96]	2.2.2, 3.3.1
	NNI contours	Estimates 1980	[QRL 96]	2.2.2, 3.3.2
	Meteorological data	1974	[QRL 96]	2.2.2, 3.3
	Cost benefit analysis of closing various airports	1974	[QRL 96]	2.2.2, 3.5
North-east				
	See also PASSENGERS: **Origin and destination**			
	Air traffic movements Woolsington (Newcastle) airport	1958–62	[QRL 95]	2.2.2, 3.2.3

QUICK REFERENCE LIST

Region/Category	Description	Date	Source	Reference
Northern Ireland	See also PASSENGERS: Origin and destination			
North Lancashire Manchester, Liverpool and Blackpool	General aviation movements	1968	[QRL 15]	2.2.2, 3.1
	Passengers by type of service, Manchester, Blackpool and Liverpool	1968	[QRL 15]	2.2.2, 3.2.1
	Use of air transport by firms	1968	[QRL 15]	2.2.2, 3.2.1
	Forecasts of passenger and cargo movements, North Lancashire airport and Blackpool	1981	[QRL 15]	2.2.2, 3.2.1, 3.2.2
	Travel time contours for Lancashire	1968	[QRL 15]	2.2.2, 3.3.1
	Noise contour map. Blackpool airport	1968	[QRL 15]	2.2.2, 3.3.2
	Cost-benefit analysis of various proposals	1968	[QRL 15]	2.2.2, 3.5
North-west (Ireland)	Projection of visit or groups visiting Donegal by nationality (excluding visits from Northern Ireland or Eire)	1964 & estimates for 1970 & 1980	[QRL 97]	2.2.2, 3.2.1
Scotland	See also PASSENGERS: Origin and destination See also PERSONNEL			
Scottish Highland and Island airports	Passengers by airport and journey purpose, per cent	1962/3 & 1972/3	[QRL 24]	2.2.2, 3.2.1
	Traffic and operating statistics, detailed breakdown. By route	1968/9 & 1972/3	[QRL 24]	2.2.2, 3.2.3
	Aircraft movements by airport	1962/3 & 1973	[QRL 24]	2.2.2, 3.2.3
	Routes and services	1939, 50, 63, 73	[QRL 24]	2.2.2, 3.2.3
	Forecasts of traffic demand	1974–86	[QRL 24]	2.2.2, 3.2.3
	Aircraft punctuality	1972/3	[QRL 24]	2.2.2, 3.2.3
	Financial results by airport (detailed breakdown) sector for Loganair	1972/3	[QRL 24]	2.2.2, 3.5
	Operating costs by type of aircraft	1974	[QRL 24]	2.2.2, 3.5
Scotland and the North-west	See also PASSENGERS: Origin and destination			
South-east	See also PASSENGERS: Origin and destination			
Heathrow, Gatwick, Luton and Stansted	Annual passenger throughput and generated employment for South-east airways—estimates	Early 1980s	[QRL 118]	2.2.2, 3.2.1
	Population changes in relation to the South-east airports	1951–73	[QRL 118]	2.2.2, 3.3
South-east General Aviation	Aircraft movement projections	1974–85	[QRL 126]	2.1.11, 3.1
	Aircraft movements by type of movement	1960–73	[QRL 126]	2.1.11, 3.1

CIVIL AVIATION

Descriptive title	Breakdown	Frequency	Publication (see QRL Key)	Text reference and remarks
INDIVIDUAL STUDIES (contd.)				
Airports by region (contd.)				
South-east (contd.)				
	Aircraft utilization by UK registered light aircraft	1963–70	[QRL 126]	2.1.11, 3.1
	Pilots' licences current	1973	[QRL 126]	2.1.11, 3.1
	Gliding-club data	1959–73	[QRL 126]	2.1.11, 3.1
	Ownership of aircraft. Detailed breakdown by region, use of aircraft, etc.	1973	[QRL 126]	2.1.11, 3.1
	Members of flying clubs and groups. Detailed breakdown	1973	[QRL 126]	2.1.11, 3.1
South Wales and South-west England	Forecast of passengers by airport	1988	[QRL 67]	2.2.2, 3.2.1
Exeter, Bristol, Glamorgan, Southampton and Hurn	Passengers by type of service and airport	1973	[QRL 67]	2.2.2, 3.2.1
	Estimated effect on major cost items of increasing the number of airports in the area	1976	[QRL 67]	2.2.2, 3.5
	Estimated population within NNI contour. Five airports	1976	[QRL 67]	2.2.2, 3.3.2
	Effect of changing fares on airport revenue	1976	[QRL 67]	2.2.2, 3.5
	Passenger and aircraft movements	1973	[QRL 17]	2.2.2, 3.2.1, 3.2.3
	Forecasts of passenger traffic	1972–80, 1980–90 & 1988	[QRL 17]	2.2.2, 3.2.1
	Cost-benefit analysis by airport	1975	[QRL 17]	2.2.2, 3.5
	Noise costs by airport	1975	[QRL 17]	2.2.2, 3.3.2
	Forecasts of aircraft movements by airport	1988	[QRL 17]	2.2.2, 3.2.3
	Capital costs by airport	1975	[QRL 17]	2.2.2, 3.5
	NNI contours by airport	1973 (& 1988 Estimate)	[QRL 17]	2.2.2, 3.3.2
South-west England	Diagrams giving forecasts passenger movements and diagram of relation between peak hour and annual passengers: by type of passenger	1968–90	[QRL 121]	2.2.2, 3.2.1
Exeter airport and California Cross as a potential site				
South Hampshire	Recent movements at Eastleigh, Hurn, Portsmouth for terminal passengers and transport and aircraft	1963–9	[QRL 120]	2.2.2, 3.2.1, 3.2.3
Possible airport sites around Southampton particularly Eastleigh and Hurn	Estimate of population affected by noise	1980	[QRL 120]	2.2.2, 3.3.2

QUICK REFERENCE LIST

	Cash-flow analysis by capital and operating costs and revenue. Hurn and Eastleigh	Estimates 1972–82	[QRL 120]		2.2.2, 3.5
Wales	See PASSENGERS: **Origin and destination**				
Yorkshire (and Humberside) mainly Leeds/Bradford and Hull	Passenger forecasts Yeadon and Brough	1970, 1975 & 1980	[QRL 20]		2.2.2, 3.2.1
	Use of air transport by firms in the area	1967	[QRL 20]		2.2.2, 3.2.1
	Cargo forecasts Yeadon and Brough	1967–80	[QRL 20]		2.2.2, 3.2.2
	Passengers and aircraft movements, by airport	1967	[QRL 20]		2.2.2, 3.2.1, 3.2.3
	Journey time including surface transport. By route	1967	[QRL 20]		2.2.2, 3.3.1
	Travel time forecast map costs of various developments	1980	[QRL 20]		2.2.2, 3.3.1
	General aviation movements and forecasts. Leeds/Bradford	1980 & 1990	[QRL 19]		2.2.2, 3.1
	Passenger forecasts by type of traffic and destination and Ainsley, Yorkshire	1970, 1980 & 1990	[QRL 19]		2.2.2, 3.2.1
	Passenger time and cost savings Yeaden 1970	1970 (& Balne Moor estimate 1990)	[QRL 19]		2.2.2, 3.2.1
Five possible sites for Yorkshire airport: Balne Moor, Church Fenton, Elvington, Wintersett, Leeds/Bradford	No. of people and buildings affected by each NNI band, five possible sites for a Yorkshire airport	Estimates 1980 & 1990	[QRL 19]		2.2.2, 3.3.2
	Employment generated by an airport	1972	[QRL 19]		2.2.2, 3.3.3
	Trading profits of selected UK airports	1972	[QRL 19]		2.2.2, 3.5
	Cost effects of a Yorkshire airport	1972	[QRL 19]		2.2.2, 3.5
	Cost of noise for each site	Estimates 1980 & 1990	[QRL 19]		2.2.2, 3.5
	Environmental costs of an airport at five sites	1972	[QRL 19]		2.2.2, 3.5
	Cost-benefit analysis of five possible sites	1972	[QRL 19]		2.2.2, 3.5
Yorkshire and the North-east	Origin and destination of passengers	1964	[QRL 109]		2.2.2, 3.2.1
	Passengers—Yeadon and Woolsington. 1962 by month	1962 by month	[QRL 109]		2.2.2, 3.2.1
	Air freight movements 1962. Yeadon and Woolsington by month	1962 by month	[QRL 109]		2.2.2, 3.2.2
	Operations from NE airports Aug./Sept. 1963. Leeds/Bradford and Woolsington	1963 Aug.–Sept.	[QRL 109]		2.2.2, 3.2.3
	Estimate of average yearly cost of operating Middleton-St-George airport	1964	[QRL 109]		2.2.2, 3.5

CIVIL AVIATION

Descriptive title	Breakdown	Frequency	Publication (see QRL Key)	Text reference and remarks
INDIVIDUAL STUDIES (*contd.*)				
Airports by region (*contd.*)				
British airports: authority airports				
Heathrow, Gatwick, Stansted, Glasgow, Edinburgh, Prestwick, and Aberdeen (1977) (fewer airports earlier: see Appendix 1 on coverage)	Passengers: by airport, type of service, terminal and transit	Annual & Monthly	[QRL 35]	2.2.1, 3.2.1
	Passengers: aircraft movements and cargo, origin and destination	Annual	[QRL 35]	2.2.1, 3.2.1, 3.2.2, 3.2.3
	Average passenger per aircraft, by airport and type of service		[QRL 35]	2.2.1, 3.2.1
	Cargo and mail by airport, type of service year and month		[QRL 35]	2.2.1, 3.2.2
	Aircraft movements by type, airport, year and month		[QRL 35]	2.2.1, 3.2.3
	Air transport movements by airport and type of plane		[QRL 35]	2.2.1, 3.2.3
	Personnel—by airport, type of employee and year		[QRL 35]	2.2.1, 3.4
	Visible trade through UK airports—by airport		[QRL 35]	2.2.1, 3.5
	Financial data—detailed breakdown total for BAA and by individual airport		[QRL 35]	2.2.1, 3.5
Regional airports	Passengers by type and by airport	1973–4 (Estimate 1990)	[QRL 21]	2.2.2, 3.2.1
	Regional propensity to fly	1973	[QRL 21]	2.2.2, 3.2.1
	Origin and destination by passenger type	1972 & 1973	[QRL 21]	2.2.2, 3.2.1
	Freight by airport and type of service	1974	[QRL 21]	2.2.2, 3.2.2
	Air transport movements by Scottish airport and type of service	1973, 1974, 1975 and estimate for 1980	[QRL 21]	2.2.2, 3.2.3
	Possible airport capacities. By airport	1990	[QRL 21]	2.2.2, 3.3
	NNI contours by airport and population within those contours	1973 or 1974, estimate 1990	[QRL 21]	2.2.2, 3.3.2
	Financial data by airport	1972-3–1974-5	[QRL 21]	2.2.2, 3.5
Airlines				
British European Airlines (BEA passengers)	Proportion of business travel by region	1966/7	[QRL 26]	2.2.2, 3.2.1
	Passengers and passenger miles by type of passenger, main markets and type of traffic	1966/7	[QRL 26]	2.2.2, 3.2.1
British United Airlines (BUA passengers)	Origin and destination for passenger journeys at Gatwick, Glasgow, Edinburgh and Belfast	1968	[QRL 75]	2.2.2, 3.2.1

QUICK REFERENCE LIST

British Airways	Analysis of sale of tickets and convenience of flights by frequency of travel length of flight	1968	[QRL 75]	2.2.2, 3.2.1
	Operating and traffic statistics—detailed breakdown	Annual	[QRL 37]	2.4, 3.2.1, 3.2.2, 3.2.3
	Aircraft fleet	Annual	[QRL 37]	2.4, 3.2.3
	Route details	Annual	[QRL 37]	2.4, 3.2.3
	Manpower by division	Annual	[QRL 37]	2.4, 3.4
	Financial data. Detailed breakdown	Annual	[QRL 37]	2.4, 3.5
Miscellaneous				
North Atlantic traffic forecasts: ICAO	Passenger, cargo and mail by type of flight	1965	[QRL 94]	2.3.1, 3.2.1, 3.2.2
	Seasonal variation—passenger and factors on the route	1965	[QRL 94]	2.3.1, 3.2.1
North Atlantic air traffic forecasts: NATS	Passenger forecasts	Annual	[QRL 93]	2.1.8, 3.2.1
	Freight forecasts	Annual	[QRL 93]	2.1.8, 3.2.2
	Flights by type of equipment	Annual	[QRL 93]	2.1.8, 3.2.3
	Number of busy day flights on each axis by the hour	Annual	[QRL 93]	2.1.8, 3.2.3
Inter-city modal split in Great Britain, Air versus Rail Routes: London–Glasgow London–Manchester London–Liverpool London–Birmingham Glasgow–Manchester	Journey time and purpose by route	1971	[QRL 74]	2.2.2, 3.2.1
	Passengers: detailed breakdown	1971	[QRL 74]	2.2.2, 3.2.1
	Travellers having car available	1971	[QRL 74]	2.2.2, 3.2.1
	Passengers on work and non-work journeys—detailed breakdown	1971	[QRL 74]	2.2.2, 3.2.1
	Alternative mode of transport considered	1971	[QRL 74]	2.2.2, 3.2.1
	Household income by route and type of passenger	1971	[QRL 74]	2.2.2, 3.2.1
	Surface transport to and from terminal. Travel distances to terminal. Waiting times at origin terminals	1971	[QRL 74]	2.2.2, 3.3.1
	Probability curves based on the discriminant function, total cost, travel time saved. By route	1971	[QRL 74]	2.2.2, 3.5
British air transport in the seventies (Edwards Report)	Passengers detailed breakdown and forecasts	1958–68	[QRL 36]	1.3.1, 2.7, 3.2.1
	Freight detailed breakdown and forecasts	1958–68	[QRL 36]	1.3.1, 2.7, 3.2.2
	Aircraft detailed breakdown and forecasts and comparison with other world	1958–68	[QRL 36]	1.3.1, 2.7, 3.2.3
	Minister's refusal of licences	1960–8	[QRL 36]	1.3.1, 2.7, 3.2.3
	Accidents by airlines	1963–7	[QRL 36]	1.3.1, 2.7, 3.2.4
	Manpower productivity 1967 and data by airlines	1959–68	[QRL 36]	1.3.1, 2.7, 3.4
	Financial data by airline (detailed breakdown)	1958–67	[QRL 36]	1.3.1, 2.7, 3.5

CIVIL AVIATION

Descriptive title	Breakdown	Frequency	Publication (see QRL Key)	Text reference and remarks
INDIVIDUAL STUDIES (*contd.*)				
Miscellaneous (*contd.*)				
	Contribution of civil aviation to balance of payments	1968	[QRL 36]	1.3.1, 2.7, 3.5
	Aviation infrastructure. Financial results	1968	[QRL 36]	1.3.1, 2.7, 3.5
The Commission on the Third London Airport (Roskill Commission)	Individual studies on:			
	Effects on Coventry Gliding Club	1971	[QRL 53]	2.1.4, 2.7, 3.1
	Passenger estimates	1971	[QRL 53]	2.1.4, 2.7, 3.1
Four possible airport sites: Foulness, Nuthampstead, Cutlington and Thurleigh	General cargo	1971	[QRL 53]	2.1.4, 2.7, 3.2.2
	Aircraft movement estimates	1971	[QRL 53]	2.1.4, 2.7, 3.2.3
	Proximity of aircraft	1971	[QRL 53]	2.1.4, 2.7, 3.2.3
	Airport performance	1971	[QRL 53]	2.1.4, 2.7, 3.3
	Road traffic to London	1971	[QRL 53]	2.1.4, 2.7, 3.3.1
	Revenue	1971	[QRL 53]	2.1.4, 2.7, 3.5
	Birds	1971	[QRL 53]	2.1.4, 2.7, 3.5
	Cost and benefits associated with each of four possible airport sites in terms of:			
	Surface transport	1971	[QRL 53]	2.1.4, 2.7, 3.5
	Noise contours	1971	[QRL 53]	2.1.4, 2.7, 3.5
	Population, housing and employment in the area, and value of agricultural land	1971	[QRL 53]	2.1.4, 2.7, 3.5
Statistical appraisal of non-scheduled commercial operations with large aircraft 1968. ICAO	Comparison of scheduled and non-scheduled traffic	1968	[QRL 123]	2.3.1, 3.2.1
	Comparison of passengers by country	1968	[QRL 123]	2.3.1, 3.2.1
	Comparison of tonne-km by country	1968	[QRL 123]	2.3.1, 3.2.3

Quick Reference List Key to Publications

Reference number	Author or organization responsible	Title	Publisher	Frequency or date of publication	Remarks
[QRL 1]	Barker, C. B. and Morgan, S. L.	An Analysis of the Civil Airmiss Situation in the U.K. and its Relation to Collision Risk (Paper 75001)	CAA, London	1975	
[QRL 2]	Belcher, B. A. and Penna, B. D. M.	A Statistical Study of Mid-air Collisions Involving Public Transport and Executive Jet 1926–1975 Worldwide	CAA, London	1976	
[QRL 3]	Culver, H. A.	Analysis of Aircraft Noise Complaints, October 1968–March 1969	Board of Trade, London	1969	CAA library
[QRL 4]	Doganis, Rigas S.	Who travels by air: A survey of air passengers at Birmingham airport	Unpublished (Department of Transportation & Environmental Planning, University of Birmingham)	1967	CAA library
[QRL 5]	Maudsley, J. A. & Gordon, J. A.	Birmingham Airport 1971–91	Unpublished	1975	CAA library
[QRL 6]	Morton-William, J. and Berthoud, R.	Helicopter noise in Central London	Unpublished	1970	CAA library
[QRL 7]	Pooley, Robert	United Kingdom and Ireland Air Touring Flight Guide	Airtour Associates International Ltd.	Annual 1964 onwards	
[QRL 8]	Schultz, T. J.	Community Noise Ratings	Applied Science Publishers Ltd., London	1972	
[QRL 9]	Waters, C. S.	The noise effects of extending Luton Airport	Unpublished	1969	CAA library
[QRL 10]	Civil Aviation Authority (and predecessors, see text)	Accidents to Aircraft on the British Register	CAA, London, 1971 onwards HMSO, 1949–70	Annual 1949 onwards	

CIVIL AVIATION

Reference number	Author or organization responsible	Title	Publisher	Frequency or date of publication	Remarks
[QRL 11]	International Civil Aviation Organization	*Aircraft Accident Digest*	ICAO, Montreal	Annual 1951 onwards	Available from CAA library–British distributing agent
[QRL 12]	Civil Aviation Authority	*Air Freight Demand: a Survey of UK Shippers* (CAP 401)	CAA, London	1977	
[QRL 13]	International Civil Aviation Organization	*Airline Traffic* (earlier *Digest of Statistics on Traffic*)	ICAO, Montreal	1947 onwards	
[QRL 14]	Civil Aviation Authority	*Air Pilot* (CAP 32, 3 volumes)	CAA, London	Annual 1948 onwards	
[QRL 15]	Alan Stratford and associates	Airport and air service development in N. Lancashire	Unpublished	1968	CAA library
[QRL 16]	Civil Aviation Authority	*Airport Development in the Central England Area* (CAP 373)	CAA, London	1975	
[QRL 17]	Civil Aviation Authority, Economics & Statistics Division	*Airport Development in South Wales and the South West Region of England* (CAP 377)	CAA, London	1975	
[QRL 18]	Alan Stratford and associates	Airport facilities in the North of the West Midlands region	Unpublished	1968	CAA library
[QRL 19]	Metra Consulting Group	An airport for Yorkshire. The future of air transport facilities in Yorkshire	Unpublished	1972	CAA library
[QRL 20]	Alan Stratford and associates	An airport programme for Yorkshire and Humberside 1970–85	Unpublished	1967	CAA library
[QRL 21]	Department of Trade	*Airport Strategy for Great Britain* (in 2 parts)	HMSO, London	1975 and 1976	
[QRL 22]	National Air Traffic Services (pre-1969 National Air Traffic Control Services)	*Air Traffic Controlled by the UK Air Traffic Control Centres*	CAA 1971 onwards, pre-1970 unpublished	Annual 1966 onwards until 1974 Biennial 1974 onwards	Responsible authorities 1966–9 Board of Trade 1970 DTI Available. from CAA library. 1976 onwards—contact CG2 of CAA (see 'Useful Libraries and Bodies').

QUICK REFERENCE LIST

[QRL 23]	Alan Stratford and associates	Air traffic development at Tees-side Airport	Unpublished	1967	CAA library
[QRL 24]	Civil Aviation Authority	*Air Transport in the Scottish Highlands and Islands*	CAA, London	1974	
[QRL 25]	Air Transport Licensing Board	*Air Transport Licensing Board Annual Report*	Air Transport Licensing Board	Annual 1960/1–1971/2	
[QRL 26]	British European Airways	Analysis of BEA international and domestic traffic by main areas of sale and reasons for travel 1966/7	Unpublished	1967	CAA library
[QRL 27]	Director of Research and Intelligence, Greater London Council	*Annual Abstract of Greater London Statistics*	Greater London Council	Annual 1966 onwards	
[QRL 28]	Central Statistical Office	*Annual Abstract of Statistics*	HMSO, London	Annual 1956 onwards	
[QRL 29]	United Nations	*Annual Bulletin of Transport Statistics for Europe*	United Nations, New York	Annual 1952 onwards	
[QRL 30]	Airline Users Committee	*Annual Report*	CAA, London	1973/4 onwards	
[QRL 31]	HM Customs and Excise Commissioners	*Annual Statement of the Overseas Trade of the UK, Vol. V: Trade at Ports*	HMSO, London	Annual	Publication ceased at beginning of 1978. See companion review
[QRL 32]	Alan Stratford and associates	Ballykelly Development: a civil airport and industrial estate	Unpublished	1970	CAA library
[QRL 33]	Bournemouth County Borough Council, Dorset County Council	Bournemouth—Hurn Airport—report on airport development	Unpublished	1972	CAA library
[QRL 34]	Alan Stratford and associates	Bristol airport study	Unpublished	1971	CAA library
[QRL 35]	British Airports Authority	*British Airports Authority Annual Report and Accounts*	British Airports Authority, London	Annual 1965 onwards	HMSO until 1970–1
[QRL 36]	Edwards Committee	*British Air Transport in the Seventies* (Report of the Committee of Inquiry into Civil Air Transport)	HMSO, London	1969	BAA library

Reference number	Author or organization responsible	Title	Publisher	Frequency or date of publication	Remarks
[QRL 37]	British Airways	*British Airways Annual Report and Accounts*	British Airways, London	1972–3 onwards	BEA and BOAC Reports 1946–74, 1940–74
[QRL 38]	Department of Trade and Industry	*Business Monitor: C.A.1, Airport Activity*	HMSO, London	Monthly 1968–72	CAA library
[QRL 39]	Department of Trade and Industry	*Business Monitor: C.A.2, Air Passengers*	HMSO, London	Monthly 1968–72	CAA library
[QRL 40]	Department of Trade and Industry	*Business Monitor: C.A.3, Air Freight and Mail*	HMSO, London	Monthly 1968–72	CAA library
[QRL 41]	Department of Trade and Industry	*Business Monitor: C.A.4, Airline Operations*	HMSO, London	Monthly 1968–72	CAA library
[QRL 42]	Department of Trade and Industry	*Business Monitor: C.A.5, Airline Operations*	HMSO, London	Quarterly 1968–72	CAA library
[QRL 43]	Department of Trade and Industry	*Business Monitor: C.A.6, Domestic Passenger Traffic*	HMSO, London	Annual 1968 Quarterly 1969–72	CAA library
[QRL 44]	Department of Trade and Industry	*Business Monitor: C.A.7, Air Passengers—International and Cabotage*	HMSO, London	Annual 1968 Quarterly 1969–72	CAA library
[QRL 45]	Department of Trade and Industry	*Business Monitor: C.A.8, Airline Financial Statistics*	HMSO, London	Annual 1968–71	CAA library
[QRL 46]	Department of Trade and Industry	*Business Monitor: M.6, Overseas Travel and Tourism*	HMSO, London	Quarterly 1963 onwards	CAA library
[QRL 47]	Ministry of Aviation	Census of Civil Air Traffic 1961–64	Unpublished	Dec. 1961, July 1962 and Feb. and July 1963	CAA library
[QRL 48]	Board of Trade, Ministry of Defence, National Air Traffic Services	*Census of Civil Air Traffic, 19–25/7/1967*	Board of Trade, London	1968	CAA library
[QRL 49]	Metra Consulting Group	Central England Airport study	Unpublished	1974	CAA library
[QRL 50]	International Civil Aviation Organization	*Civil Aircraft on Register*	ICAO, Montreal	Annual 1961 onwards	

[QRL 51]	Civil Aviation Authority	*Civil Aviation Authority: Annual Statistics*	CAA, London	Annual 1973 onwards	
[QRL 52]	Civil Aviation Authority	*Civil Aviation Authority Monthly Statistics*	CAA, London	Monthly April 1973 onwards	
[QRL 53]	Roskill Commission	*The Commission on the Third London Airport* Vol. VIII and Vol. IX	HMSO, London	1971	
[QRL 54]	Department of Employment	*Department of Employment Gazette* (formerly Ministry of Labour Gazette 1924-68, Employment and Productivity Gazette 1968-70)	HMSO, London	Monthly 1924 onwards	
[QRL 55]	Tees-side Airport Joint Committee	The development of air services at Tees-side Airport	Unpublished	1972	CAA library
[QRL 56]	Director of Transportation and Basic Services Liverpool Corporation	The development of Liverpool Airport	Unpublished	1973	CAA library
[QRL 57]	Civil Aviation Authority	The development of Norwich Airport	Unpublished	1975	CAA library
[QRL 58]	Alan Stratford and associates	Development plan for Biggin Hill Airfield	Unpublished	1972	CAA library
[QRL 59]	International Civil Aviation Organization	*Digest of Statistics on Airport Traffic*	ICAO, Montreal	Annual 1960 onwards	
[QRL 60]	International Civil Aviation Organization	*Digest of Statistics on Financial Data*	ICAO, Montreal	Annual 1947 onwards	
[QRL 61]	International Civil Aviation Organization	*Digest of Statistics on Fleet—Personnel*	ICAO, Montreal	Annual 1947 onwards	
[QRL 62]	International Civil Aviation Organization	*Digest of Statistics on Traffic Flow*	ICAO, Montreal	1947 onwards	
[QRL 63]	British Tourist Authority	*Digest of Tourist Statistics*	British Tourist Authority, London	Irregular 1969 onwards	
[QRL 64]	Airline Users Committee	*European Air Fares*	CAA, London	1976	
[QRL 65]	Statistical Office of the European Communities	*European Economic Community Basic Statistics of the Community*	Statistical Office of the European Communities	Annual 1959 onwards	

Reference number	Author or organization responsible	Title	Publisher	Frequency or date of publication	Remarks
[QRL 66]	Civil Aviation Authority	*Financial Results—UK Airlines 1968–74 (CAP 376)*	CAA, London	1975	
[QRL 67]	Civil Aviation Authority	*Future Airport Development in S. Wales and the SW of England (CAP380)*	CAA, London	1976	
[QRL 68]	Alan Stratford and associates	Gatwick air traffic and the environment	Unpublished	1972	CAA library
[QRL 69]	Civil Aviation Authority	*General Aviation Flight Guide*	CAA, London	1971	
[QRL 70]	Association of European Airlines	General development of air transport in Europe 1968–72	Unpublished (issued by Association of European Airlines Brussels)	1974	CAA library
[QRL 71]	West Riding Town and County Planning Committee	Goole–Thorne regional airport	Unpublished	1968	CAA library
[QRL 72]	British Airports Authority	*Heathrow Airport London Master Development Plan Report*	British Airports Authority	1976	CAA library
[QRL 73]	Metra Consulting Group	*Heathrow Passenger and Baggage Survey*	Department of Trade and Industry	1973	
[QRL 74]	University of Leeds	Intercity modal split in Great Britain: Air v. Rail	Unpublished	1971	CAA library
[QRL 75]	British United Airways	Interjet passenger survey	Unpublished	1968	CAA library
[QRL 76]	Civil Aviation Authority	*International Register of Civil Aviation*	CAA, London	Annual	
[QRL 77]	Macdonald and Jane's Publishers Ltd.	*Jane's All the World's Aircraft*	Macdonald and Jane's Publishers Ltd.	Annual 1909 onwards	
[QRL 78]	Frederick Snow and Partners, and Alan Stratford Associates	Lee-on-Solent: A joint airport for civil and naval use	Unpublished	1971	CAA library

[QRL 79]	Scott Wilson Kirkpatrick and partners	Liverpool Airport—market research	Unpublished	1971	CAA library
[QRL 80]	Freeman, Fox and associates	London Airport's traffic study: Gatwick Airport	Unpublished	1967	CAA library
[QRL 81]	Freeman, Fox and associates	London Airport's traffic study: Heathrow Airport	Unpublished	1967	CAA library
[QRL 82]	Surrey County Council	*London Gatwick Airport: An Environmental Study*	Surrey County Council	1970	CAA library
[QRL 83]	Ministry of Public Building and Works	*London Noise Survey*	HMSO, London	1968	CAA library
[QRL 84]	Department of Trade and Industry	*London Origin and Destination Survey, 1/8–4/12/72*	HMSO, London	1973	CAA library
[QRL 85]	Snow, Frederick and partners	Luton Airport development	Unpublished	1969	CAA library
[QRL 86]	Atkins Planning (in association with Atkins research and development and Alan Stratford and associates)	Midlands Airport study	Unpublished	Summary and Report 1973	CAA library
[QRL 87]	Softward Sciences Ltd. (for National Air Traffic Services, Civil Aviation Authority and Ministry of Defence)	National census of UK air traffic	Unpublished	1974	CAA library
[QRL 88]	Central Statistical Office	*National Income and Expenditure (Blue Book)*	HMSO, London	Annual 10-year periods 1946/51 onwards	
[QRL 89]	Frederick Snow and partners	*Newcastle Airport: Terminal User Survey and Study for Future Expansion*		1971 and 1972	CAA library
[QRL 90]	Department of Trade	*Night Disturbance from Aircraft Noise at Heathrow and Gatwick*	Department of Trade, London	1977	
[QRL 91]	Civil Aviation Authority	*Noise Data from the First Year of Scheduled Concorde Operations at Heathrow Airport, London (Paper 7707)*	CAA, London	1977	
[QRL 92]	Wilson Committee	*Noise: Final Report*	HMSO, London	1963	

Reference number	Author or organization responsible	Title	Publisher	Frequency or date of publication	Remarks
QRL 93]	National Air Traffic Services (formerly National Air Traffic Control Services)	*North Atlantic Traffic: Air traffic forecasts* (prepared jointly for the North Atlantic Systems Planning Group by Canada, the United States and the United Kingdom)	CAA	Annual 1965–75	
[QRL 94]	International Civil Aviation Organization	*North Atlantic Traffic Forecasts*	ICAO, Montreal	1966	
[QRL 95]	Frederick Snow and partners	North-east Regional airport: report on future developments	Unpublished	1963	CAA library
[QRL 96]	Alan Stratford and associates	Northern Region airport study	Unpublished	1974	CAA library
[QRL 97]	James Munce Partnership	North-west airport feasibility study	Unpublished	1969	CAA library
[QRL 98]	Aviation, Economics and Aircraft Branch (Civil Aviation Department, pre-1963)	Operating and traffic statistics of UK airlines	Mimeographed	Annual post-war–1967	CAA library (pre-1965 figures Ministry of Aviation, post-1965 Board of Trade)
[QRL 99]	Civil Aviation Authority	*Origins and Destinations of Passengers at UK Airports* (CAP 363)	CAA, London	1975	
[QRL 100]	Department of Trade and Industry	*Passengers at Airports in Scotland and the North-west* (origins and destinations survey 8/6–4/10/1970)	HMSO, London	1972	
[QRL 101]	Board of Trade	*Passengers at London's Airports* (origins and destinations survey 15/8–14/11/1968)	HMSO, London	1970	
[QRL 102]	Civil Aviation Authority	*Passengers at Major Airports in Scotland and Central England*, CAP 394 (Origins and Destinations Survey, July–November 1975)	CAA, London	1976	

[QRL 103]	Department of Trade and Industry	*Passengers in Wales, West Midlands, North-east and Northern Ireland* (Origins and Destinations Survey, 7/6–4/10/71)	HMSO, London	1972	
[QRL 104]	Department of the Environment (1971–3) (Ministry of Transport, 1968)	*Passenger Transport in Great Britain* (PTGB)	HMSO, London	Annual 1949–73	Information now appears in *Transport Statistics Great Britain* [QRL 137]
[QRL 105]	British Airports Authority	Patterns of Traffic at the British Airports Authorities Airports	Unpublished	Annual 1969 onwards	Aviation Statistical Service Room J.1
[QRL 106]	National Board for Prices Incomes	*Pay of Ground Staff at Aerodromes* (Parliamentary paper Cmnd.4182)	HMSO, London	1969	
[QRL 107]	Heathrow Area Working Party	Planning implications of airport generated uses	Unpublished	1973	CAA library
[QRL 108]	British Airports Authority	Quarterly analysis	Unpublished	1967/68 onwards	Aviation Statistical Service Room J.1
[QRL 109]	Alan Stratford and associates	A regional airport for Yorkshire and the North-east	Unpublished	1964	CAA library
[QRL 110]	Department of Trade and Industry	*Report of the Working Party on Traffic and Capacity at Heathrow* (CAP 349)	HMSO, London	1971	
[QRL 111]	Transport Co-ordinating Council for London—Interchanges	Report on links for Heathrow Airport	Unpublished	July 1967	CAA library
[QRL 112]	Airline Users Committee	*Report on the Monitoring of Arrangements at West London Terminal and Terminal 1 at Heathrow*	CAA, London	1975	
[QRL 113]	British Airports Authority	Road traffic survey : Heathrow	Unpublished	Annual 1972 onwards	BAA library and Road Administrator Heathrow Airport
[QRL 114]	London Chamber of Commerce and Industry	The role of the London airports in meeting the business and social needs of the consumer	Unpublished	July 1973	CAA library
[QRL 115]	Association of European Airlines (formerly European Airlines Research Bureau)	*Scheduled Intra-European Passenger and Cargo Traffic of AEA Member Airlines*	Association of European Airlines Paris (and Airlines Research Bureau)	Monthly EARB until 3/1973, AEA 4/1973 onwards	CAA library

Reference number	Author or organization responsible	Title	Publisher	Frequency or date of publication	Remarks
[QRL 116]	British Airports Authority	*Scottish Airports*, Origin and Destination Survey	British Airports Authority, London	1975	
[QRL 117]	Office of Population Censuses and Surveys	*Second Survey of Aircraft Noise Annoyance round London (Heathrow) Airport*	HMSO, London	1971	
[QRL 118]	Standing Conference on London and South East Regional Planning	South-east airports	Unpublished	1976	CAA library
[QRL 119]	British Airports Authority	*South-east Airports*, Origin and Destination Survey	British Airports Authority, London	1975	
[QRL 120]	Frederick Snow and Alan Stratford	South Hampshire airport study	Unpublished	1969–70	CAA library
[QRL 121]	Frederick Snow and partners	South-west Regional airport survey	Unpublished	1968	CAA library
[QRL 122]	International Civil Aviation Organization	*Special Digest of Statistics on Non-scheduled Air Transport*	International Civil Aviation Organization, Montreal	Annual 1971	
[QRL 123]	International Civil Aviation Organization	*Statistical Appraisal of Non-scheduled Commercial Operations with Large Aircraft 1968*	International Civil Aviation Organization	1971	
[QRL 124]	European Civil Aviation Conference	*Statistics of Non-scheduled Traffic Reported in ECAC States*	European Civil Aviation Conference		
[QRL 125]	Western European Airports Association and International Civil Airports Association	Statistiques de trafic	Unpublished	Monthly	CAA library
[QRL 126]	Civil Aviation Authority	*A Study of General Aviation in the South-east of England*	CAA, London	1974	

QUICK REFERENCE LIST

[QRL 127]	Civil Aviation Economics and Statistics Branch, Board of Trade (formerly Civil Aviation Dept.)	Summary of activity at aerodromes in the UK and Channel Islands	Mimeographed	Monthly with Annual summary post-war up to 1967	CAA library (Ministry of Aviation pre-1965 and Board of Trade post-1965)
[QRL 128]	Freeman, Fox and associates	Surface transport study at Gatwick	Unpublished	1971	BAA library
[QRL 129]	Jamieson and Mackay	Surface transport study at Heathrow	Unpublished	1971	BAA library
[QRL 130]	Aviation Economics and Aircraft Branch, Ministry of Aviation	A survey of passenger transport at London's airports, summer 1965	Unpublished	1966	CAA library
[QRL 131]	British Airports Authority	*Survey of Transfer Passengers—Heathrow Summary of Results*	British Airports Authority, London	1976	
[QRL 132]	Operational Research Department, British Airports Authority	Survey on airport workers—Heathrow, Gatwick, and Stansted	Unpublished	1975	Available from BAA and CAA library
[QRL 133]	Operational Research Department, British Airports Authority	Survey on airport workers—Aberdeen, Edinburgh, Glasgow and Prestwick	Unpublished	1975	Available from BAA and CAA library
[QRL 134]	Firma International Advertising Agency	Tees-side airport holiday survey	Unpublished	1972	CAA library
[QRL 135]	Organization for European Cooperation and Development	*Tourism Policy and International Tourism in OECD Member Countries*	OECD	Annual	
[QRL 136]	Association of European Airlines (formerly EARB)	*Traffic and Operating Data of AEA Airlines*	AEA	Annually for 4 years 1973–7	
[QRL 137]	Department of Transport	*Transport Statistics Great Britain* (replaces *Highway Statistics* and *Passenger Transport Great Britain*)	HMSO, London	Annual	CAA library
[QRL 138]	Central Statistical Office	UK Balance of Payments (Pink Book)	HMSO, London	Annual 10-year periods 1946 onwards	
[QRL 139]	Department of Transportation, Federal Aviation Authority	*US Civil Aircraft Register*	Federal Aviation Authority	Half-yearly post-war	
[QRL 140]	Civil Aviation Authority	*World Airline Accident: Summary*	CAA, London	1946 onwards	
[QRL 141]	International Air Transport Association	*World Air Transport Statistics*	International Air Transport Association	Annual 1957 onwards	

SELECT BIBLIOGRAPHY

[B 1] Brearley, R. E. G. *Wind Shear: A Select Bibliography*, Civil Aviation Authority, London, Jan. 1976.
[B 2] Brooker, P. and Ingram, T. *Collision Risk in the Air Traffic Systems: The Derivation of the Longitudinal/Vertical Overlap Factor P_{xz} for Parallel Tracks*, Paper 77004, Civil Aviation Authority, London, 1977.
[B 3] Brooker, P. and Ingram, T. *Target Levels of Safety for Controlled Airspace*, Paper 77002, Civil Aviation Authority, London, 1977.
[B 4] Coe, G. J. and Goldstein, M. G. *A Study of Traffic Subject to Flow Regulations at 'Victor Romeo' on Airway Amber 1—Summer 1975*, Paper 76018, Civil Aviation Authority, London, 1976.
[B 5] Deakin and Seward. *Productivity in Transport*, University of Cambridge, Department of Applied Economics, Paper 17, Cambridge University Press, 1969.
[B 6] Douganis and Thompson. *The Economics of British Airports*, May 1973 (CAA Library).
[B 7] Foulkes, Nigel. *Quiet Aircraft Symposium—Some Social Aspects of Major Airports*, Local Authorities Aircraft Noise Council and UK Federation Against Aircraft Nuisance, 1972.
[B 8] Hart, P. E. *Population Densities and Optimal Aircraft Flight Paths*, University of Reading Discussion papers in Economics No. 37, Oct. 1972 (CAA Library).
[B 9] Hedges, M. J. *An Investigation into Poor Braking Action because of Extensive Pounding on the Runway at an International Airport*, Paper No. 75036, Civil Aviation Authority, London, September 1975.
[B 10] McKennell, A. C. *Aircraft Annoyance round London (Heathrow) Airport*, COI, London, 1963.
[B 11] McKennell, A. C. 'Methodological problems in a survey of aircraft noise annoyance', *The Statistician*, Part I, pp. 1–33, 1970.
[B 12] Middleton, V. T. C. 'Tourism policy in Britain', Special Report No. 1 in *International Tourism Quarterly*, Economics Intelligence Unit, 1974.
[B 13] Yacoumis, J. 'Air inclusive tour marketing', Special Report No. 2 in *International Tourism Quarterly*, Economics Intelligence Unit, 1975.
[B 14] Yeowart, N. S., 'An acceptable exposure level for aircraft noise in residential communities', *Journal of Sound and Vibration*, **25**, Part II, pp. 243–354, 1972.
[B 15] *ABC Cargo Guide*, ABC Travel Guides Ltd., Monthly, Jan. 1958 onwards.
[B 16] *ABC World Airways Guide*, ABC Travel Guides Ltd., Monthly 1934 onwards.
[B 17] *Action against Aircraft Noise: Progress Report*, Department of Trade and Industry, HMSO, London, 1973.
[B 18] *Aerodrome Fire and Rescue Services: Report on the Regulations for Aerodrome Fire and Rescue Services*, Civil Aviation Authority, London, May 1972.
[B 19] *Aircraft Engine Noise Research*, Noise Advisory Council, HMSO, London, 1974.
[B 20] *Aircraft Noise: Flight Routing near Airports*, Noise Advisory Council, HMSO, London, 1971.
[B 21] *Aircraft Noise in the Neighbourhood of London, Heathrow Airport, 1967*, Department of Trade and Industry, 1971.
[B 22] *Aircraft Noise: Review of Aircraft Departure Routing Policy*, Noise Advisory Council, HMSO, 1974.
[B 23] *Aircraft Noise: Selection of Runway Sites for Mapline Airport*, Noise Advisory Council, HMSO, London, 1972.
[B 24] *Aircraft Noise: Should the Noise and Number Index be Revised?*, Noise Advisory Council, HMSO, London, 1972.
[B 25] *Airport Planning: An Approach on a National Basis*, Civil Aviation Authority, London, 1972.
[B 26] *Airports: The Challenging Future*, Proceedings of the 5th World Conference on Technological and Economic Change, Institute of Civil Engineers, London, Mar. 1976.
[B 27] 'Air transport', *Economic Trends*, Aug. 1969.
[B 28] *Air Transport World*, Penton/IPC Reinhold, Reinhold Publishing Co. Inc., monthly.

SELECT BIBLIOGRAPHY

[B 29] *Civil Aviation Authority: Annual Report and Accounts*, Civil Aviation Authority, London, 1972/3.
[B 30] *Civil Aviation Authority—its Work and Finances*, Civil Aviation Authority, London, April 1976 (free on request from CAA library).
[B 31] *Civil Aviation Statistics Bibliography*, Department of Trade and Industry, 1972 (CAA library).
[B 32] 'Commercial aircraft survey' in *Flight International*, occasional.
[B 33] *The Commission on the Third London Airport*, Roskill Commission, HMSO, London, 1971.
[B 34] *Comparative Examination of EARB and US Airlines*, European Airlines Research Bureau, Paris, 1970.
[B 35] *Digest of Statistics, Northern Ireland*, Statistics and Economics Unit, Department of Finance, Stormont, HMSO, Belfast, twice annually 1954 onwatds.
[B 36] *Digest of Welsh Statistics*, Welsh Office, HMSO, Cardiff, annual 1954 onwards.
[B 37] *Domestic Air Services Survey*, British Junior Chambers of Commerce, 1965 (CAA library).
[B 38] *Flight International*, I.P.C. Transport Press Ltd., weekly 1909 onwards.
[B 39] *Forecasts of Air Traffic and Capacity at Airports in the London Area*, Civil Aviation Authority, London, May 1973.
[B 40] *The Future Role of Regional Airports*, Airports International, Nov. 1974 (CAA library).
[B 41] *Gatwick Airport*, Ministry of Transport and Civil Aviation, June 1958 (CAA library).
[B 42] *Gatwick Airport London Master Plan Report*, British Airports Authority, London, July 1974 (CAA library).
[B 43] *General Aviation and Fairoaks Airfield*, Alan Stratford and Associates, Sept. 1970 (CAA library).
[B 44] 'Heathrow Airport: keeping traffic moving: a second consultative paper', British Airports Authority, 1976 (free on request BAA).
[B 45] *Heathrow Routings over Surrey*, Stratford, Alan and Associates, 1970 (CAA library).
[B 46] *ICAO Bulletin*, International Civil Aviation Organization, Montreal, monthly 1947 onwards.
[B 47] *Importance of Civil Air Transport to the UK Economy*, International Air Transport Association, Montreal, 1970.
[B 48] *International Air Freight Services: A Consultative Document*, CAP 379, Civil Aviation Authority, London, Sept. 1975.
[B 49] 'The International Passenger Survey', *Board of Trade Journal*, Aug. 1962.
[B 50] *Manual on the ICAO Statistical Programme—A Guide for Reporting and Using ICAO Civil Aviation Statistics*, International Civil Aviation Organization, Montreal, 1973.
[B 51] *Monthly Digest of Statistics*, Central Statistical Office, HMSO, London, 1946 onwards.
[B 52] *Newcastle Airport*, North East Regional Airport Committee, 1967 (CAA library).
[B 53] *Newcastle Airport: Report on Future Development*, Frederick Snow and Partners, 1974 (CAA library).
[B 54] *Noise Alleviation of Large Subsonic Jet Aircraft*, National Aeronautic Space Agency, Washington, Oct. 1968.
[B 55] 'Overseas travel and tourism 1974–75', *Trade and Industry*, 2 Jan. 1976.
[B 56] *Preliminary Data for Forecasting Aircraft Noise in Selecting Foulness Airport Site*, Department of Trade and Industry, London, 1971 (DTI library).
[B 57] *Report into an Inquiry into the Proposed Development of Gatwick Airport*, Parliamentary paper, Cmnd. 9215, HMSO, London, July 1954 (CAA library).
[B 58] *Report of the Noise Abatement Committee*, Ministry of Civil Aviation, 1953 (CAA library).
[B 59] *Review of the Economic Development of the Airlines of ECAC Member States*, European Civil Aviation Conference, Paris, 1968.
[B 60] *Scottish Abstract of Statistics*, The Scottish Office, HMSO, annual 1971 onwards.
[B 61] *Some Notes on the Origin and Destination Surveys of Air Passengers*, Department of Trade and Industry, 1973 (CAA library).
[B 62] *Standard Method for the Estimation of Direct Operating Costs of Aircraft*, Report No. 3, Society of Aircraft Constructors, 1959 (CAA library).
[B 63] *A Study of the Effects of Aircraft Noise upon the Royal Borough of Kensington and Chelsea*, Chelsea and Kensington Action Committee on Aircraft Noise, 1963 (CAA library).
[B 64] *Symposium on Noise in Transportation*, Noise Advisory Council, 1974 (CAA library).
[B 65] *Ulster Year Book*, Northern Ireland Information Service, HMSO, Belfast, 1926 onwards.
[B 66] *World Survey of Aviation*, Aviation Studies Atlantic, Report Supplement No. 182, Feb. 1970 (CAA library).

COVERAGE OF PUBLICATIONS

[QRL 7] Robert Pooley: *Air Touring Flight Guide*. Annual
Civil airports: UK, Isles of Barra, Wight, Benbecula, Mull, Man, Skye, Scilly Isles, Jersey, Guernsey, North Ronaldsay.
Private airports: UK, Shetland Isles.
Heliports: UK, Hayling Island.

[QRL 13] *Airline Traffic ICAO*. Annual and monthly figures
Covers airlines: Air Bridge carriers, Air Freight, Alidair.
British Airways: (Helicopters, Cambrian, Channel Islands, European, North East, Overseas), British Caledonian, Brymon, Cathay, Pacific, Intra Airways, JF Airlines, Scottish Airways, Air Anglia, Aurigny, BIA, British Airferries, British Midland, Channel Airways, Dan Air, Loganair, Saggitair, Skyways International, Domestic Airlines.

[QRL 14] *Air Pilot* (see [QRL 69]).
Airports.

[QRL 21] *Airport Strategy for Great Britain*
Airports.
Part 1: London Heathrow, Gatwick, Stansted, Luton.
Part 2: Regional airports: England: Birmingham, Blackpool, Bournemouth, Bristol, Carlisle, Coventry, East Midlands, Exeter, Humberside, Leeds/Bradford, Liverpool, Manchester, Newcastle, Norwich, Southampton, Tees-side. Wales: Glamorgan. Scotland: Aberdeen, Edinburgh, Glasgow, Prestwick.

[QRL 24] *Air Transport at the Scottish Highlands and Islands*, CAA
Covers airports: Aberdeen, Benbecula, Inverness, Islay, Kirkwell, Stornoway, Sumburgh, Tiree and Wick, and additional places in Scotland when details of routes given.

[QRL 31] *Annual Statement of the Overseas Trade of the UK*
Covers airports: Belfast, Gatwick, Glasgow, London (incl. Northolt), Manchester, Prestwick, Southend, all other airports.

[QRL 35] *British Airports Authority Annual Report*
1977. Heathrow, Gatwick, Stanstead, Glasgow, Edinburgh, Prestwick, Aberdeen.

[QRL 38] *C.A. 1*. Monthly. (January 1972)
Covers airports: Heathrow, Gatwick, Stansted, Westland Heliport, Aberdeen, Ashford, Belfast, Benbecula, Birmingham, Blackpool, Bournemouth, Bristol, Cambridge, Coventry, East Midlands, Edinburgh, Glamorgan, Glasgow, Gloucester, Hawarden, Inverness, Islay, Isle of Man, Kirkwall, Leeds/Bradford, Liverpool, Luton, Lydd, Manchester, Newcastle, Penzance Heliport, Portsmouth, Prestwick, Scilly Isles, Southampton, Southend, Stornoway, Sumburgh, Swansea, Tees-side, Tiree, Wick, Alderney, Jersey, Guernsey.

[QRL 39] *C.A.2.* Monthly
Covers airports: As C.A.1.

[QRL 40] *C.A.3.* Monthly
Covers airports: As C.A.1.

[QRL 41] *C.A.4.* Monthly
Covers airlines: BOAC, BEA, Independent airlines (as one figure).

[QRL 42] *C.A.5.* Quarterly
Covers airlines: BOAC, BEA, BEA Helicopters, Air Anglia, Aurigny Air Services, British Air Ferries, British Caledonian Airways, BIA, British Midland Airways, Cambrian Airways, Dan Air Services, Intra Airways, JF Airlines, Loganair, North East Airlines, Skyways International, Air Freight, Saggitair, BEA airtours, Air London, Britannia Airways, Brymon Aviation, Channel Airways, Court Line Aviation, Donaldson International Airways, Eagle Flying Service, Fairflight Charter, Haywards Aviation, Humber Airways, Invicta Airlines, Island Air Charter, Kestrel Aviation, Laker Airways, Lloyd International Airways, Lowland

COVERAGE OF PUBLICATIONS

Air Services, McAlpine Aviation, Midland Air Cargo, Monarch Airlines, Northair Airlines, Northeast Airlines, Northern Executive Aviation, Shoreham Aviation, Thurston Aviation, Tradewinds Airways, Trans Meridian Air Cargo, Vernair Transport (1st quarter 1972).

[QRL 43] *C.A.6.* Quarterly
Covers airports: As C.A. 1 (Channel Islands not covered separately).

[QRL 44] *C.A.7.* Quarterly
As C.A.1. Channel Islands not covered separately.

[QRL 45] *C.A.8.* Annual (January 1972)
Covers airlines: Aurigny Air Services, Britannia Airways, British Air Services, BEA, BEA Airtours, British Island Airways, BOAC, British Caledonian Airways, Laker Airways, Monarch Airlines (1971).

[QRL 51] *CAA Annual Statistics*
Airlines: British Airways (Overseas, European, Helicopters, Channel Islands, Scottish, Cambrian, Northeast), British Caledonian, Air Anglia, Air Bridge Carriers, Aurigny Air Services, British Air Ferries, British Island Airways, British Midland Airways, Brymon Airways, Dan Air Services, Intra Airways, Loganair, Air Freight, Alidair, Beecham Imperial, Bristow Helicopters, Britannia Airways, British Executive Air Services, Eagle Flying Services, Fairflight Charters, Green Shield Stamp, Haywards Aviation, IOS Aircraft, International Aviation Service, Invicta International Airlines, Laker Airways, MAM Aviation, Management Aviation, McAlpine Aviation, McDonald Aviation, Merlot Aviation, Monarch Airlines, Moseley Aviation, Northern Air Taxis, Northern Executive Aviation, Peters Aviation, Ryburn Aviation, Thurston Aviation, Tradewinds Airways, Trans Meridian Air Cargo, Vernair Transport.
Airports: Gatwick, Heathrow, Luton, Southend, Stansted, Westland Heliport, Leeds/Bradford, Liverpool, Manchester, Birmingham, Coventry, East Midlands, Newcastle, Tees-side, Bristol, Glamorgan, Swansea, Blackpool, Bournemouth, Cambridge, Exeter, Gloucester/Cheltenham, Hawarden, Isles of Scilly, Lydd, Manston, Norwich, Penzance Heliport, Southampton, Edinburgh, Glasgow, Prestwick, Aberdeen, Benbecula, Inverness, Islay, Kirkwall, Stornoway, Sumburgh, Tiree, Wick, Belfast, Isle of Man, Alderney, Jersey, Guernsey.

[QRL 59] *Digest of Statistics on Airport Traffic ICAO.* Annual (and monthly)
Covers airports: London, Gatwick, Heathrow, Luton, Manchester.

[QRL 60] *Digest of Statistics on Financial Data ICAO.* Annual
Covers airlines: Air Anglia, Air Bridge Carriers (domestic), Aurigny, British Airways (as one figure), British Air Ferries, British Caledonian, British Midland, Brymon Airways, Intra Airways.

[QRL 61] *Digest of Statistics on Fleet-Personnel ICAO.* Annual
Covers airlines: Air Anglia, Air Freight, Aurigny, British Air Ferries, British Airways (Cambrian, Channel Islands, European, Northeast, Overseas), British Caledonian, BIA, British Airways (Helicopters, Scottish), Loganair.

[QRL 62] *Digest of Statistics on Traffic Flow ICAO.* Monthly for certain months
Covers airlines: Air Anglia, Air Freight, Aurigny, BIA, British Airways (Cambrian, Channel Islands, European, North East, Overseas), British Air Ferries, British Caledonian, British Midland, Brymon Airways, Cathay Pacific, Dan Air Services, Intra Airways.

[QRL 66] *Financial Results—UK Airlines 1968–74.* CAA
Covers airlines: Air Anglia, Air Freight, Aurigny Air Services, Britannia Airways, British Caledonian, British Island Airways, British Midland, Brymon Aviation, Dan Air Services, International Aviation Services, Intra Airways, Laker Airways, Loganair, Monarch Airlines, Tradewinds, Invicta International.
British Airways (Overseas, European, Helicopters, British Airtours, Cambrian, Channel Islands, North East, Scottish). Trans Meridian Air Cargo. Air Bridge.

[QRL 69] *General Aviation Flight Guide*
Covers airports: UK, Isle of Man, Walney, Benbecula, Eday, Fair Isle, Hull, Shetland Isles, Orkney Isles, Skye, Guernsey, Jersey.

[QRL 99] *Origins and Destinations of Passengers at UK Airports*
Heathrow, Gatwick, Luton, Manston and Southampton 1968.
Cardiff, Birmingham, East Midlands, Newcastle, Belfast and Bristol 1971.
Heathrow, Gatwick, Luton, Southend and Stansted 1972.
Glasgow, Edinburgh, Prestwick, Blackpool, Liverpool, Manchester, Leeds/Bradford 1970.

[QRL 100] *Passengers at Airports in Scotland and the North West*
Covers airports: Leeds, Bradford, Blackpool, Liverpool, Manchester, Edinburgh, Glasgow, Prestwick.

[QRL 102] *Passengers at Airports in Scotland and Central England*
Aberdeen, Edinburgh, Glasgow, Prestwick, Manchester, Birmingham and East Midlands.

[QRL 103] *Passengers in Wales, West Midlands, North East and Northern Ireland*
Covers airports: Belfast, Birmingham, Bristol, Cardiff, East Midlands, Newcastle.

[QRL 104] *Passenger Transport in Great Britain*
Domestic Scheduled Air Services within and between the UK, Channel Isles and Isle of Man (as one figure—source CAA).

[QRL 105] *Patterns of Traffic at BAA Airports*
Covers airports: Heathrow, Gatwick, Stansted, Prestwick, Edinburgh.

[QRL 106] *Pay of Ground Staff at Aerodromes.* Cmnd. 4182, 1969
Coverage: Airports.
British Airports Authority airports: London (Heathrow), London (Gatwick), Stansted, Prestwick.
Local Authority airports: Glasgow, Manchester, Birmingham, Liverpool, Southend, Bournemouth, Bristol, Glamorgan, Leeds/Bradford, Luton, East Midlands, Newcastle, Blackpool, Coventry, Gloucester/Cheltenham, Norwich, Portsmouth, Swansea, Tees-side, Sunderland.
Board of Trade airports: Belfast, Edinburgh, Aberdeen, Benbecula, Inverness, Islay, Kirkwall, Stornoway, Sumburgh, Tiree, Wick.

[QRL 108] *BAA Quarterly Analysis*
Covers airports: Heathrow, Gatwick, Stansted, Prestwick, Edinburgh, Aberdeen and Glasgow.

[QRL 115] *Scheduled Intra European Passenger and Cargo Traffic of AEA Member Airline.* Monthly
By country.

[QRL 116] *Scottish Airports: O & D*
Covers airports: Glasgow, Edinburgh, Prestwick, Aberdeen.

[QRL 119] *South East Airports: O & D*
Covers airports: Gatwick, Luton and Heathrow (by terminals).

[QRL 122] *Special Digest of Statistics on Non-scheduled Air Transport.* Annual (and monthly)
Covers airlines: Alidair, British Airtours, Britannia, IAS Cargo, Invicta International, Laker, Monarch, Tradewinds, Trans Meridian.

[QRL 124] *Statistics of Non-scheduled Traffic Reported in ECAC States*
By country.

[QRL 125] *Statistiques de Trafic.* Monthly with annual summary
Covers airports: London: Heathrow, Gatwick, Stansted, Glasgow–Prestwick, Edinburgh.

[QRL 130] *A Survey of Passenger Transport at London's Airports*
Heathrow and Gatwick.

[QRL 132] *Survey of Airport Workers*
Covers airports: Heathrow, Gatwick and Stansted.

[QRL 133] *Survey of Airport Workers*
Covers airports: Aberdeen, Edinburgh, Glasgow, Prestwick.

[QRL 136] *Traffic and Operating Data of AEA Airlines.* Annual
Covers airlines: British Airways (European, Overseas), British Caledonian.

[QRL 137] *Transport Statistics Great Britain*
UK airways as one figure.
Airports as [QRL 50] plus Ashford. Channel Islands airports not covered separately. A figure called 'All other airports' presumably includes or consists solely of them as one figure.

[QRL 141] *World Air Transport Statistics IATA.* Annual
Covers airlines: British Airways, British Caledonian.

USEFUL LIBRARIES AND BODIES

For the main unpublished materials referred to in this review as well as published material by the CAA and international agencies the best library to visit is the CAA's

>Aviation House,
>129 Kingsway,
>London W.C.2.

The library is open to the public by request and staff are very helpful with enquiries. Free publications by the CAA and AUC are available and orders can be placed for ICAO publications. For 1976 and subsequent analyses of [QRL 22] Air Traffic Control data, contact

>C.G.2 (Stats) T1114,
>Space House,
>43–59 Kingsway,
>London W.C.2

because of the detailed and specialized nature of the material.

For detailed work on the BAA, it is best to visit its library at

>2 Buckingham Gate,
>London S.W.1.

The unpublished material mentioned in the review may be obtained at the same address from the Statistical Service, Room J.1.

LIST OF APPENDICES

1. (a) Monthly airline return of air traffic by sector
   (b) Monthly airline return of air traffic
   (c) Monthly airline return of scheduled air traffic—point to point
   (d) Monthly airline return of non-scheduled air traffic—point to point
   (e) Class 5 licences—monthly airline return of air traffic
   (f) Quarterly airline fleet return
   (g) Quarterly airline return of personnel

2. Flight Information Strip
   (a) Examples of 'filled-in' flight strips
   (b) Note on monthly movements for December 1977 showing the way data are collected

3. (a) Quarterly/Annual airline profit and loss statement
   (b) Annual airline appropriation account
   (c) Airline balance sheet
   (d) Quarterly airline balance of payments return—overseas sterling area
   (e) Quarterly airline balance of payments return—EEC and non-sterling area

Appendix 1

(a)
Civil Aviation Authority
MONTHLY AIRLINE RETURN OF AIR TRAFFIC BY SECTOR

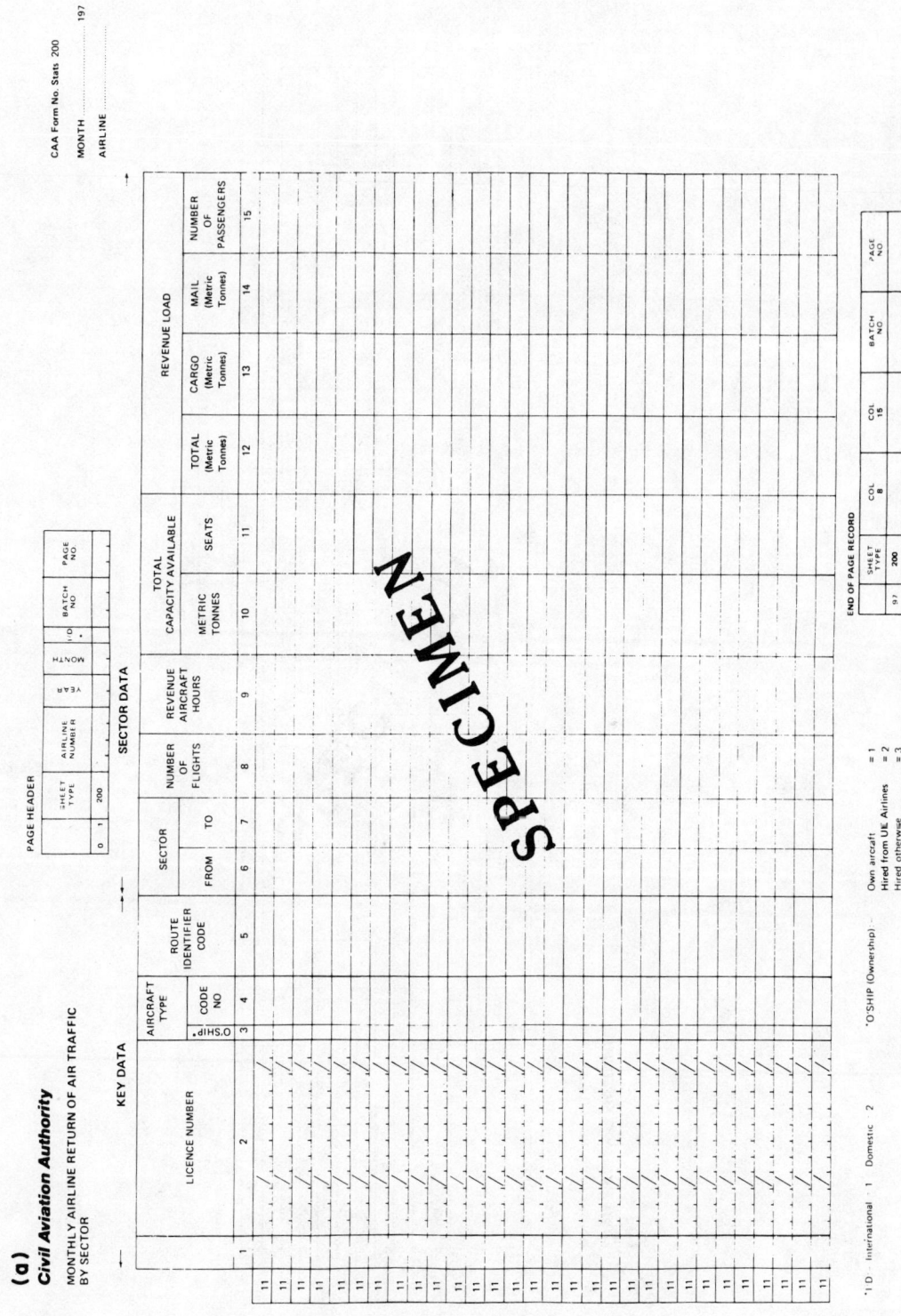

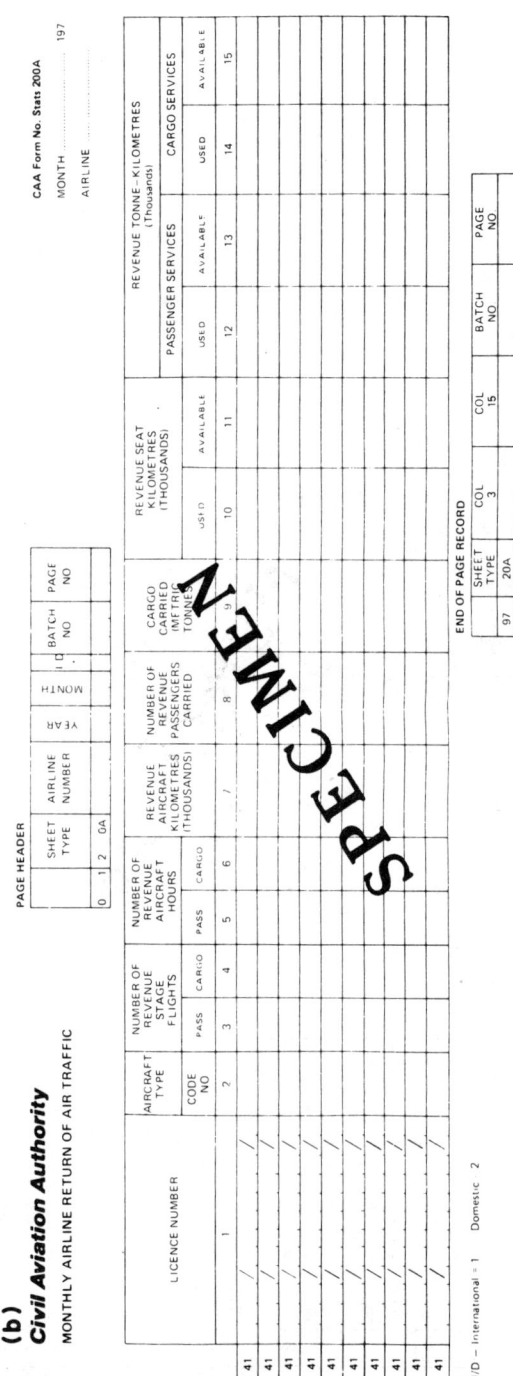

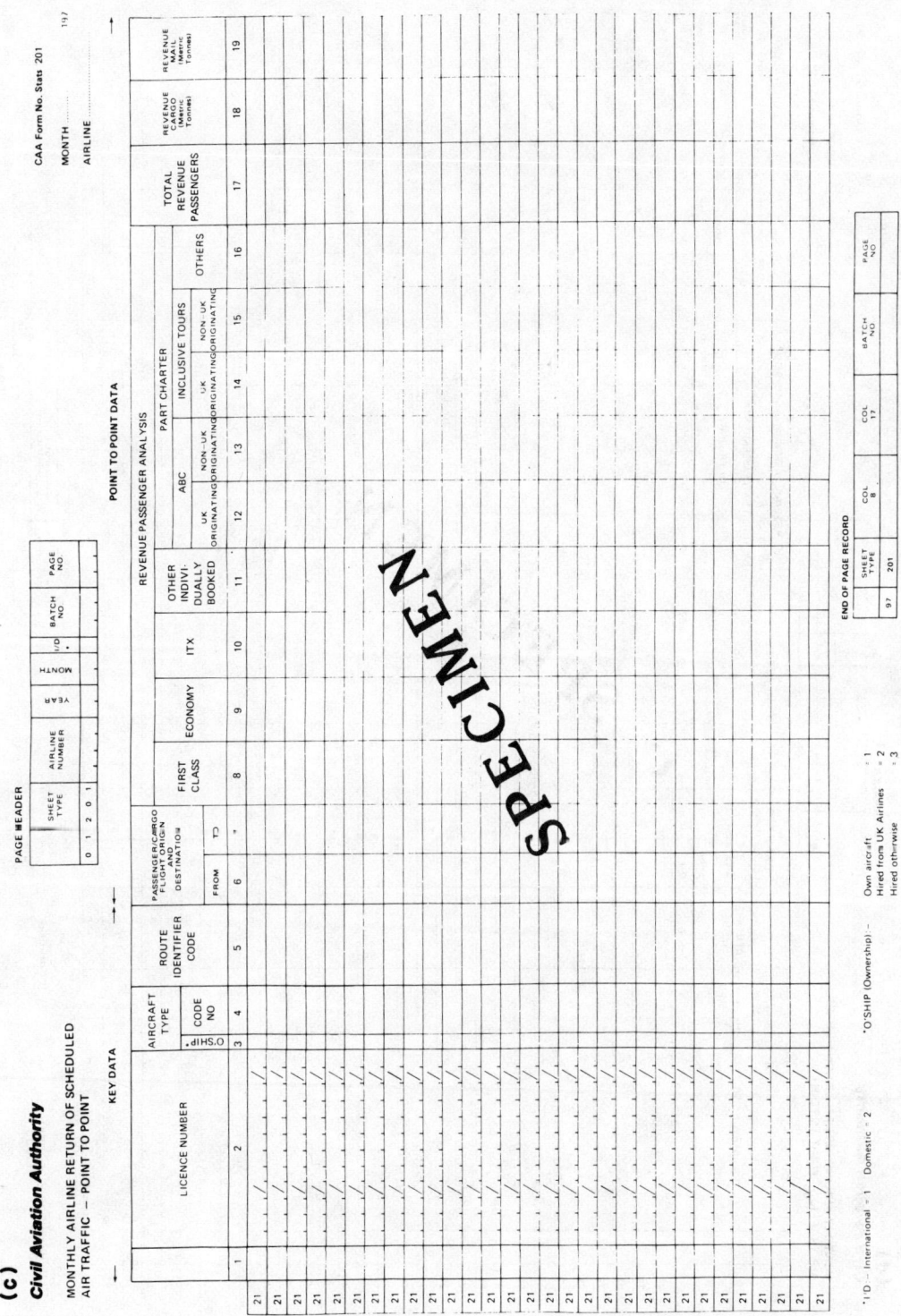

(d)
Civil Aviation Authority

MONTHLY AIRLINE RETURN OF NON-SCHEDULED
AIR TRAFFIC — POINT TO POINT

SPECIMEN

CAA Form No. Stats 202

MONTH .... 197...
AIRLINE ....

*I/D — International = 1   Domestic = 2   *O'SHIP (Ownership) —   Own aircraft = 1
                                                                      Hired from UK Airlines = 2
                                                                      Hired otherwise = 3

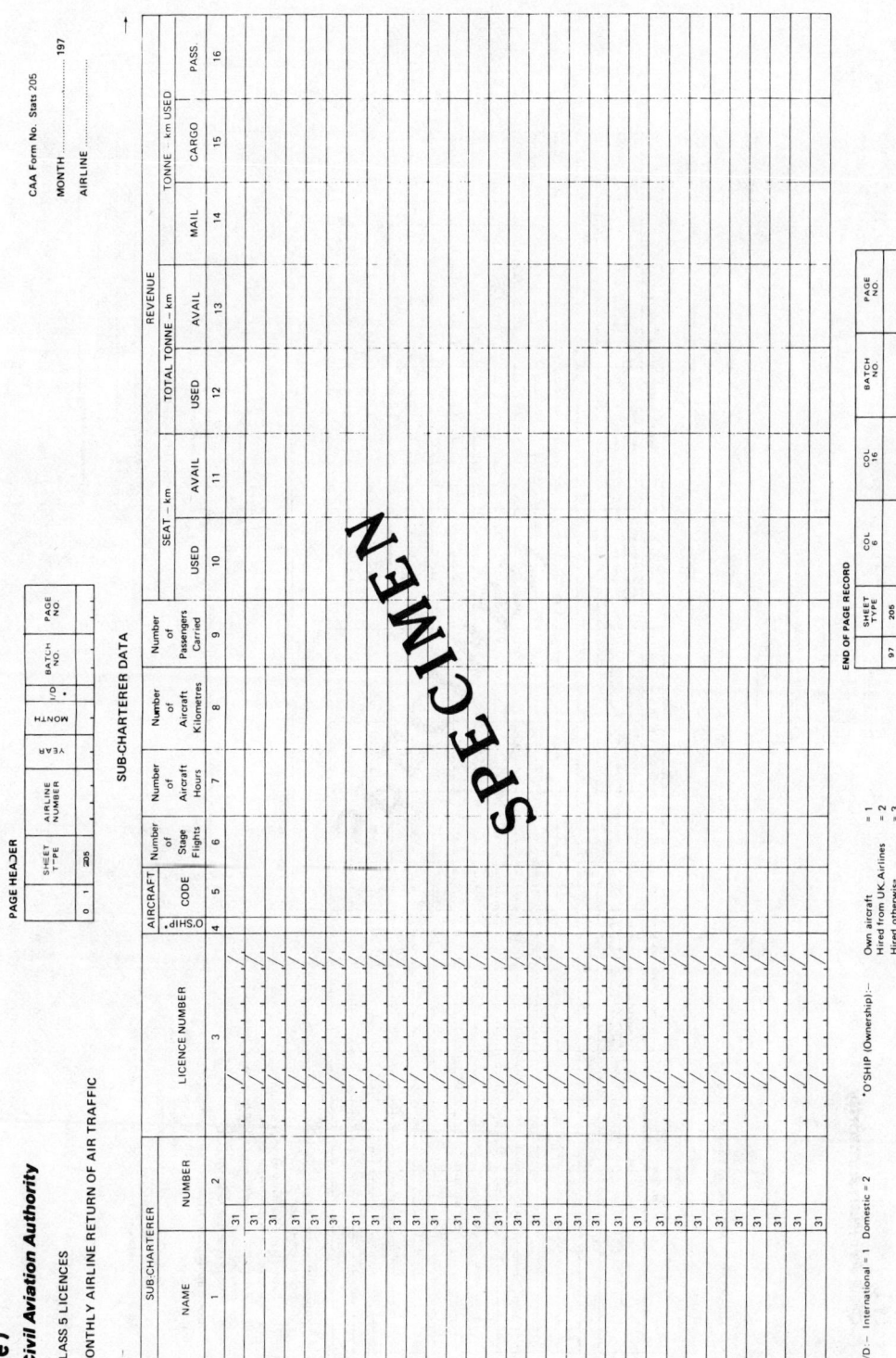

(f) Civil Aviation Authority

CAA Form No. Stats 25.3

QUARTERLY AIRLINE FLEET RETURN

Airline _____

PAGE HEADER

AIRLINE	YY	Q
F	0	

COLS 1-6 OF ALL CARDS

AIRLINE	
F	1

Quarter ended _____ 197___

Aircraft type			Number of Aircraft of each type				Size of Aircraft			Utilization of Aircraft flown during each type			
Manufacturer and model	C.A.A. Code No.	Category of Use*	In fleet at beginning of quarter	Acquired during quarter	Disposed of during quarter	In fleet at end of quarter	Number of installed passenger seats minimum	Number of installed passenger seats maximum	Average of maximum take-off weights (tonnes)	Number of aircraft departures during quarter (Revenue and Non-revenue)	Aircraft hours flown during quarter (Revenue and Non-revenue)	Weight of fuel consumed (tonnes)	Aircraft days available
a	b	c*	d	e	f	g	h	i	k	l	m	n	o
7	9	10	11 12	13 14	15 16	17 18	19 21	22 24	25 V 28	29 33	34 39	40 45	46 49

REMARKS

*Category of use refers to the air transport uses for which each aircraft is built. Report one of these codes:
1. Aircraft built primarily for passenger transport
2. Aircraft built to carry freight loads only
3. Aircraft readily convertable to carry all freight loads — or regular passenger loads
4. Aircraft other than for air transport

Address the completed return to: Civil Aviation Authority
Ec/S Division, Room T409
Space House, 43/59 Kingsway
London WC2B 6TE

For enquiries telephone: 01-379 7311 exts 2223, 2474

SEE BOOKLET FOR GUIDANCE ON COMPILATION

Signature of compiler _____

Compiler's name (CAPS) _____

Full address _____

Telephone Number _____ Ext _____

070476

SPECIMEN

(g)
Civil Aviation Authority

PAGE HEADER

AIRLINE		YY	Q
F		O	

CAA Form No. Stats 254

COLS 1–5 ALL CARDS

	AIRLINE
F	

QUARTERLY AIRLINE RETURN OF PERSONNEL

Airline _____   Quarter ended _____ 197___

PART I – EMPLOYED IN THE UNITED KINGDOM AND OVERSEAS

Category of Personnel	Number of personnel at end of quarter		Total expenditure in quarter for each category
	Male	Female	
a	b	c	d
1 Pilots and Co-pilots	1	2	3
2 Other cockpit personnel			
3 Cabin attendants			
4 Maintenance and overhaul personnel			
5 Traffic and sales personnel			
6 All other personnel			
7 Total personnel (Home and abroad)			
8 Employer superannuation contribution			

PART II – EMPLOYED IN GREAT BRITAIN ONLY

	Number of personnel at end of quarter		Number of females employed part-time * (also included under c)
	Male	Female	
a	b	c	d
1 North	4	5	6
2 Yorkshire and Humberside			
3 East Midlands			
4 East Anglia			
5 South East			
6 South West			
7 West Midlands			
8 North West			
9 Wales			
10 Scotland			
11 Total personnel (Great Britain only)			

*Part-time employment is defined as being not more than 30 hours a week

Turnover of Personnel (Great Britain only)	
a	b
12 Number engaged during quarter (male)	7
13 Number leaving during quarter (male)	
14 Number engaged during quarter (female)	
15 Number leaving during quarter (female)	

REMARKS

SPECIMEN

Address the completed return to :   Civil Aviation Authority
Ec/S Division, Room 622
Aviation House, 129 Kingsway
London WC2B 6NN

For enquiries telephone: 01-405 6922 ext.244

Signature of compiler _____

Compiler's name (CAPS) _____

Full address _____

Telephone Number _____ Ext _____

SEE BOOKLET FOR GUIDANCE ON COMPILATION

APPENDIX 2

FLIGHT INFORMATION STRIPS

(a) Examples of "filled-in" flight strips

WARNING STRIP FORMATS

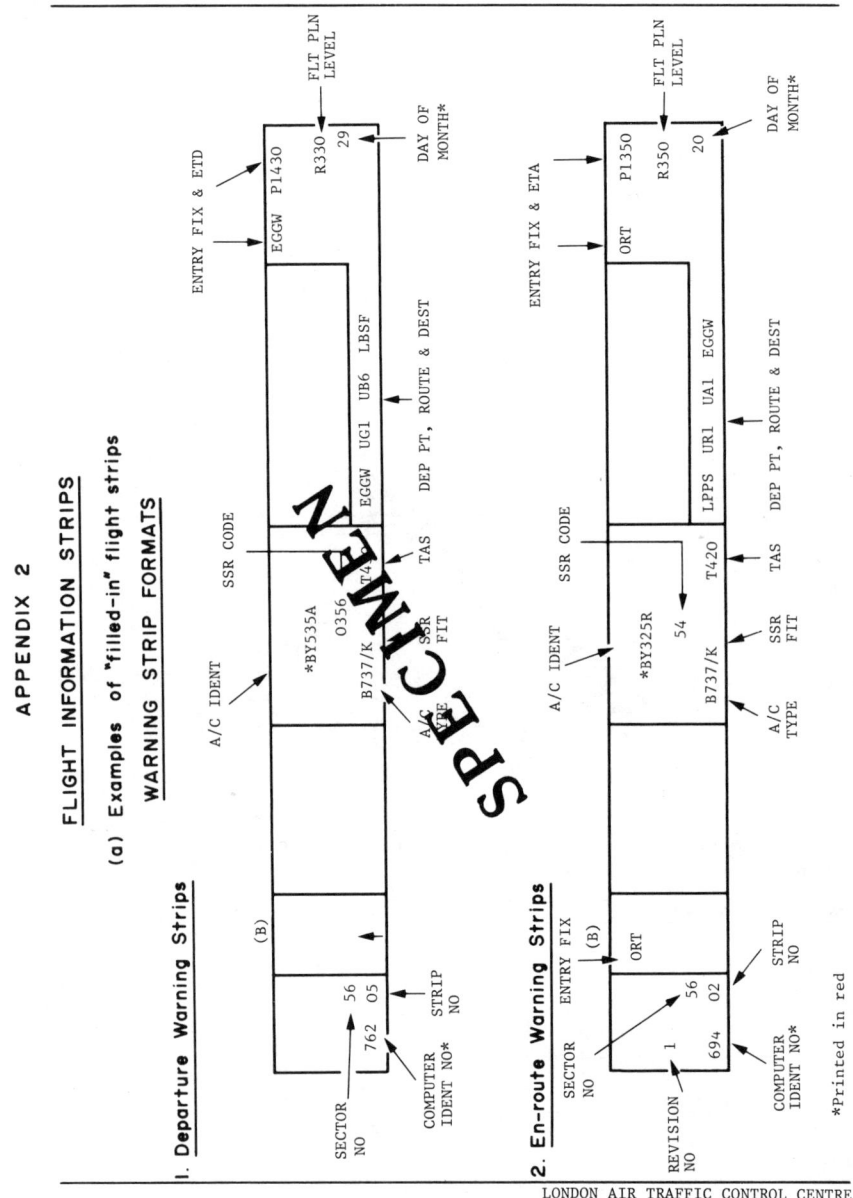

LONDON AIR TRAFFIC CONTROL CENTRE

APPENDICES

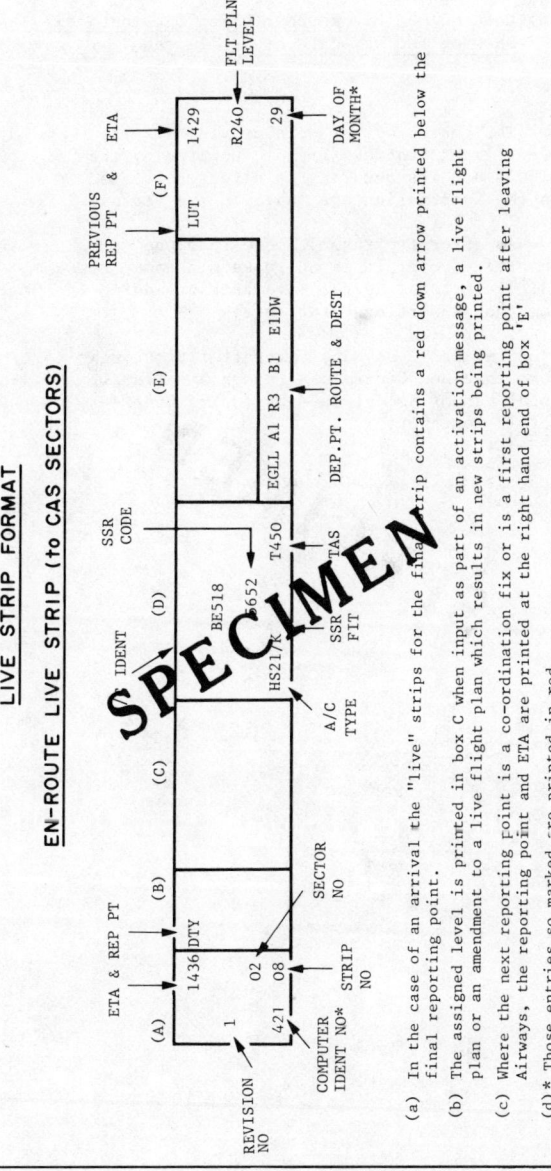

LONDON AIR TRAFFIC CONTROL CENTRE

B.1

(b) <u>Note on monthly movements for December 1977 showing the way data are collected</u>

1. The source of the data provided is the used Flight Progress Strips supplied by the ATCC's and its accuracy is directly related to the information available on the Strips.

2. As aircraft traverse more than one Reporting Point it is not possible to calculate total Sector movements by adding together Reporting Point totals.

3. Similarly, as many aircraft fly through more than one Centre's airspace a national total cannot be obtained by adding Centre totals together.

APPENDICES

B.2 NATIONAL AIR TRAFFIC SERVICES

Controlled Movements at selected Reporting Points (estimates based on a seven day count) by L.A.T.C.C. for DECEMBER 1977

BRISTOL STRUMBLE SECTOR 20		KNI	STU	LA/COM			
FL 250+	C	753	1931	2121			
	M	13	128	190			
FL 245−	C	469	328	757			
	M	62	22	230			
TOTAL		1297	2409	3298			

CLACTON		CIN/BRA	LSD	GAB			
FL 250+	C	1563	3056	1382			
	M	230	40	−			
FL 245−	C	1120	2414	−			
	M	248	−92	−			
TOTAL		3161	5302	1382			

NORTH SEA		BLU	NEW				
FL 250+	C	3175	656				
	M	283	84				
FL 245−	C	616	−				
	M	89	−				
TOTAL		4163	740				

POLE HILL IRISH SEA		WAL	LFY	BEL			
FL 250+	C	4406	2037	664	593		
	M	292	93	58	195		
FL 245−	C	1807	979	722	660		
	M	226	155	−	102		
TOTAL		6731	3264	1444	1550		

(POL/OLD column: 4406, 292, 1807, 226, 6731)

SECTOR 23 CARDIFF		MER	BHD	LND	LIZ
FL 250+	C	700	722	1364	673
	M	204	18	120	31
FL 245−	C	−	173	31	31
	M	−	35	22	13
TOTAL		904	948	1537	748

DCVER		DVR			
FL 250+	C	2994			
	M	323			
FL 245−	C	2174			
	M	257			
TOTAL		5748			

LYDD		SGT	CLF		
FL 250+	C	1851	2440		
	M	283	9		
FL 245−	C	788	1258		
	M	93	4		
TOTAL		3015	3711		

DAVENTRY		HON	DTY	HUC	
FL 250+	C	2405	3096	407	
	M	40	62	18	
FL 245−	C	1926	2170	−	
	M	75	173	−	
TOTAL		4446	5501	425	

SEAFORD WORTHING		DPE	VR	ETT	NEV
FL 250+	C	403	2245	828	−
	M	−	84	18	−
FL 245−	C	961	120	102	93
	M	13	44	31	−
TOTAL		1377	2493	979	93

HURN		IBY/FAW	ORT*		
FL 250+	C	3534	−		
	M	332	−		
FL 245−	C	1594	899		
	M	128	22		
TOTAL		5588	921		

TMA (NORTH) Inbounds only			
BNN	LAM	BKY	
2303	4216	1337	

TMA (SOUTH) Inbounds only			
OCK	BIG	MAY	
2285	2569	3817	

F.I.R.		
CIVIL	MILITARY	TOTAL
4863	208	5071

NOTE: DCS is counted by ScATCC.
* Bournemouth Zone Traffic only
C = Civil. M = Military.

(TOTALS OVERLEAF)

ATCEU Statistics
Issued by C(G)2.

SPECIMEN

ESTIMATED TOTAL MOVEMENTS FOR AWYS/ADRS/UIRS

CIVIL	MILITARY	TOTAL
49,847	3,983	53,830

Appendix 3

(a) Civil Aviation Authority

COMMERCIAL IN CONFIDENCE
(when wholly or partly completed)

QUARTERLY/ANNUAL AIRLINE
PROFIT AND LOSS STATEMENT

PAGE HEADER

AIRLINE		YY	Q
S		O	

COLS 1–5 ALL CARDS

AIRLINE	
S	

CAA Form No. Stats 250

Airline _____   Quarter/Year ended _____ 197___

Description		Amount (£000)
REVENUES		
1 Scheduled Passenger (individually booked seats direct to passenger)	1	
2 Scheduled Passenger (all block-booked seats, including part-charter)		
3 Scheduled Excess baggage		
4 Scheduled Freight and diplomatic bags		
5 Scheduled Mail		
6 Non-scheduled flights (a) Inclusive tours		
(b) ABC other than part-charter		
(c) Affinity groups		
(d) Cargo		
(e) Other		
7 Incidental revenue		
8 TOTAL OPERATING REVENUES		
EXPENSES		
9 Flight crew salaries and expenses	2	
10 Aircraft fuel and oil		
11 Flight equipment insurance		
12 Uninsured losses		
13 Rental of flight equipment		
14 Flight crew training (when not amortised)		
15 Flight expenses other than Items 9 to 14		
16 Maintenance and overhaul		
17 Depreciation of aircraft fleet (including spares)		
18 Depreciation of ground property and equipment		
19 Amortisation of development and pre-operating costs		
20 Flight crew training (when amortised)	3	
21a Landing and departure fees		
21b Aerodrome, En route, and other Navigation service charges		
22 Station and ground expenses other than 21		
23a Passenger services — cabin staff and other flight expenses		
23b Passenger services — other passenger service costs		
24 Ticketing, sales and promotion		
25 General and administrative		
26 Other operating expenses		
27 TOTAL OPERATING EXPENSES		
27a (of which services bought in under 16, 24 and 25 above)		
28 OPERATING PROFIT (OR LOSS)		
29 Profit or loss on disposal of fixed assets	4	
30 Interest payable less receivable (Net)		
31 Direct subsidies from public funds		
32 Other payments from public funds		
33 Dividends receivable		
34 Other non-operating items		
35 NON-OPERATING ITEMS (balance)		
36 PROFIT OR LOSS (−) BEFORE TAXATION		

SPECIMEN

REMARKS

Address the completed return to: Civil Aviation Authority
Ec/S Division, Room 611
Aviation House, 129 Kingsway
London WC2B 6NN
for enquiries telephone: 01-405 6922 ext 411

Signature of compiler _____

Compiler's name (CAPS) _____

Full address _____
_____
_____

Telephone Number _____ Ext _____

SEE BOOKLET FOR GUIDANCE ON COMPILATION

(b)
Civil Aviation Authority

COMMERCIAL IN CONFIDENCE
ANNUAL AIRLINE APPROPRIATION ACCOUNT

Airline _____

PAGE HEADER

AIRLINE NO	YY
A	

COLS 1-5 ALL CARDS

AIRLINE NO
A

CAA Form No. Stats 251

Year ended _____ 197____

	DESCRIPTION	AMOUNT (£000)		AMOUNT (£000)
1	Profit (or Loss) before Taxation		1	
2	Taxation			
3	Profit (or Loss) after Taxation			
4	Exceptional items and prior year adjustments (SPECIFY) _____			
5	Transfers from reserves (SPECIFY) _____			
6	Available for appropriation			
7	Dividends			
8	Transfers to reserves (SPECIFY) _____			

SPECIMEN

REMARKS

Address the completed return to: Civil Aviation Authority
Ec/S Division, Room 611
Aviation House, 129 Kingsway
London WC2B 6NN

For enquiries telephone: 01-405 6922 Ext 411

Signature of compiler _____

Compiler's name (CAPS) _____

Full address _____

Telephone Number _____ Ext _____

SEE BOOKLET FOR GUIDANCE ON COMPILATION

APPENDICES

(c)
Civil Aviation Authority

COMMERCIAL IN CONFIDENCE
(when wholly or partly completed)

PAGE HEADER

	AIRLINE		Y Y
B		0	

CAA Form No. Stats 252

COLS 1 5 ALL CARDS

	AIRLINE
B	

AIRLINE BALANCE SHEET

AIRLINE _____

Parent Company _____

Ultimate holding company (where applicable) _____

As at _____ 197 _____

Based on Audited/Draft Accounts (delete as appropriate)

SPECIMEN

ASSETS EMPLOYED

1 **OPERATING EQUIPMENT AND PROPERTY**
  Aircraft fleet (including spares)
  Less: provision for amortisation and depreciation
  Aircraft fleet after depreciation
  Property and other equipment
  Less: provisions for amortisation and depreciation
  Property and other equipment after depreciation
  Payments on account of aircraft under construction

2 **INTERESTS IN GROUP COMPANIES**
  Shares
  Advances and debts not currently receivable

3 **TRADE INVESTMENTS**
  Shares
  Advances and debts not currently receivable

4 **CURRENT ASSETS**
  Stores and work in progress
  Debtors and prepayments
  Short term loans and deposits
  Bank balance and cash
  Group companies' advances and
   debts currently receivable
  Other items (specify)   (£000)
  TOTAL CURRENT ASSETS

5 **LESS: CURRENT LIABILITIES**
  Creditors and accruals
  Traffic revenue received in advance
  Taxation
  Dividends
  Bank overdrafts
  Instalments of borrowings and hire purchase liabilities
   repayable within one year
  Group companies advances and debts currently payable
  Other items (specify)   (£000)

  TOTAL CURRENT LIABILITIES
  TOTAL NET CURRENT ASSETS

6 **UNAMORTISED COSTS**
  Pre-operational training and development
  Other items (specify)   (£000)

7 **OTHER ASSETS** (specify)   (£000)

TOTAL ASSETS
FINANCED BY:—

8 **SHAREHOLDERS FUND**
  Share capital
  Share premium account
  Reserves: Capital
   Self-insurance
   Revenue
   Other

9 **BORROWINGS ETC.** (repayable more than
  one year ahead)
  Advances from other Group companies
  Bank loans
  Other loans
  Hire purchase liabilities

10 **DEFERRED LIABILITIES**   (£000)
  Taxation
  Other (specify) _____

TOTAL LIABILITIES

REMARKS

Address the completed return to: Civil Aviation Authority
Ec/S Division, Room 611
Aviation House, 129 Kingsway
London WC2B 6NN

For enquiries telephone: 01 405 6922   Ext 411

Signature of compiler _____
Compiler's name (CAPS) _____
Full address _____
Telephone Number _____ Ext _____

295

(d)

Civil Aviation Authority

COMMERCIAL IN CONFIDENCE
(when wholly or partly completed)

QUARTERLY AIRLINE BALANCE OF PAYMENTS RETURN

Airline _____

PAGE HEADER

AIRLINE	YY	Q
M	O	

CAA Form No. Stats 255A

COLS 1-6 ALL CARDS

AIRLINE	
M	1

Quarter ended _____ 197____

OVERSEAS STERLING AREA

Geographical Area		REVENUE (£000)						EXPENDITURE (£000)			
		Passenger and excess baggage		Mail	Freight	Pool Receipts	Other	Total	(1) Fuel and Oil	Pool Payments	Other	Total
		Scheduled	Non-scheduled									
(a)	7 9	10 (b) 15	16 (c) 21	22 (d) 27	28 (e) 33	34 (f) 39	40 (g) 45	46 (h) 51	52 (j) 57	58 (k) 63	64 (l) 69	70 (m) 76
Australia	010											
Bahamas	020											
Bangladesh	030											
Bermuda	040											
Sri Lanka	050											
Cyprus	060											
East Africa (2)	070											
East Caribbean (3)	080											
Fiji	090											
Ghana	100											
Gulf (4)	110											
Hong Kong	120											
Iceland	130											
India	140											
Jamaica	150											
Jordan	160											
Malawi	170											
Malta	180											
New Zealand	190											
Nigeria	200											
Pakistan	210											
South Africa	220											
South East Asia (5)	230											
Others	490											
TOTAL	499											

SPECIMEN

NOTES:
(1) Value of fuel and oil uplifted abroad but paid for in the UK. Any expenditure abroad on fuel and oil should be included in 'Other'.

(2) Kenya, Uganda, Tanzania, Mauritius, Seychelles and Zambia.

(3) Trinidad and Tobago, Barbados, Guyana, Leeward Islands and Windward Islands.

(4) Kuwait, United Arab Emirates, Bahrain, Oman, Qatar

(5) Malaysia, Singapore and Brunei.

Address the completed return to: Civil Aviation Authority
Ec/S Division, Room 611
Aviation House, 129 Kingsway
London WC2B 6NN

For enquiries telephone: 01-405 6922 ext. 257

Signature of compiler _____

Compiler's name (CAPS) _____

Full address _____

Telephone Number _____ Ext _____

APPENDICES

(e) Civil Aviation Authority

COMMERCIAL IN CONFIDENCE
(when wholly or partly completed)

QUARTERLY AIRLINE BALANCE OF PAYMENTS RETURN

CAA Form No. Stats 255B

PAGE HEADER: AIRLINE N / O / YY / Q

COLS 1 6 ALL CARDS: AIRLINE N / 1

Airline _____ Quarter ended _____ 197___

EEC AND NON STERLING AREA

Geographical Area		REVENUE (£000)							EXPENDITURE (£000)			
		Passenger and excess baggage		Mail	Freight	Pool Receipts	Other	Total	(1) Fuel and Oil	Pool Payments	Other	Total
		Scheduled	Non-scheduled									
(a)	79	10 (b) 15	16 (c) 21	22 (d) 27	28 (e) 33	34 (f) 39	40 (g) 45	46 (h) 51	52 (j) 57	58 (k) 63	64 (l) 69	70 (m) 76
Belgium	510											
Denmark	520											
France	530											
Gibraltar	540											
Irish Republic	550											
Italy	560											
Luxembourg	570											
Netherlands	580											
West Germany	590											
EEC TOTAL	600											
Austria	610											
Burma	620											
Canada	630											
Central America (2)	640											
Czechoslovakia	650											
Finland	660											
Greece	670											
Iran	680											
Iraq	690											
Israel	700											
Japan	710											
Lebanon	720											
Mexico	730											
North Africa (3)	740											
Norway	750											
Poland	760											
Portugal	770											
Saudi Arabia	780											
South America (4)	790											
South East Asia (5)	800											
Spain	810											
Sweden	820											
Switzerland	830											
Syria	840											
Turkey	850											
USA	860											
USSR	870											
Yugoslavia	880											
Others	998											
NON EEC TOTAL	999											

SPECIMEN

NOTES:

(1) Value of fuel and oil uplifted abroad but paid for in the UK. Any expenditure abroad on fuel and oil should be included in 'Other'.

(2) Honduras, Nicaragua, El Salvador, Panama, Costa Rica and Guatemala.

(3) Morocco, Algeria, Tunisia, Libya, Egypt, Sudan, Ethiopia and Somalia.

(4) Ecuador, Peru, Bolivia, Chile, Colombia, Venezuela, Brazil, Argentina, Paraguay and Uruguay.

(5) Cambodia, Laos, Thailand and Vietnam.

Address the completed return to: Civil Aviation Authority
Ec/S Division, Room 611
Aviation House, 129 Kingsway
London WC2B 6NN

For enquiries telephone: 01-405 6922 ext. 257

Signature of Compiler _____
Compiler's name (CAPS) _____
Full address _____
_____
Telephone Number _____ Ext _____

SUBJECT INDEX

Aberdeen airport, 1.3.2; 2.2.1
Accident avoidance, 2.1.8
Accidents, 1.3.1; 2.1.1; 2.1.9; 2.3.1; 3.2.4
Accidents, cause of, 2.1.9; 3.2.4
Accidents to private aircraft, 4.2.2
Air Anglia, 2.2.2
Air clubs, 1.3.3; 1.3.4; 1.3.6; 2.1.8; 2.1.11; 3.1; 4.2.2
Air congestion, 2.1.8
Air freight demand, 2.1.5; 3.2.2; 4.1
Air traffic control, 1.3.4; 2.1.8; 3.2.3; 4.1
Air traffic control data publication, 2.1.1; 2.1.8
Air traffic control sectors, 2.1.8
Air transport employees, 2.1.14; 3.3.3; 3.4
Air Transport Licensing Board, 1.3.1; 1.3.3
Air travel, expenditure on, 2.1.13
Air travel in national income, 2.1.13
Aircraft, licensing of, 1.3.1; 1.3.3; 3.2.3
Aircraft manufacturing, 1.2
Aircraft movements, 2.1.2; 3.2.3
Aircraft, ownership of, 1.3.3; 2.1.3; 2.4; 3.1; 3.2.3
Aircraft, registration of, 1.3.3; 2.3.1; 3.2.3
Aircraft, stock of, 2.1.3; 2.4; 3.2.3
Aircraft, weight of, 1.3.3
Airline balance sheets, 2.1.12; 2.4
Airline employees, 1.3.6; 2.3.1; 2.4; 3.4
Airline profit and loss statements, 2.1.12
Airline Users Committee, 2.6
Airlines annual reports, 2.4; 3.4
Airlines, financial data from, 2.1.12; 2.3.1; 3.5
Air-miss working groups, 2.1.9
Airport employees, 1.3.6; 2.2.1; 3.3.3
Airports, British Airports Authority owned, 1.3.2; 2.2.1
Airports, Civil Aviation Authority run, 1.3.2
Airports, licensing of, 1.3.1; 1.3.2
Airports, lists of, 1.3.2
Airports, ownership of, 1.3.2
Alan Stratford and Associates, 2.2.2
Association of European Airlines, 2.3.2
Atkins Planning, 2.2.2

Baggage at Heathrow, passengers', 2.2.2; 2.6
Baggage, excess, 3.2.2
Baggage, passengers', 2.2.1; 3.2.1
Balance of payments, travel in the, 1.3.1; 2.1.5; 2.1.13; 4.1
Balance, rail–air travel, 2.2.2
Balance, sea–air travel, 2.1.5

Balance sheets, airline, 2.1.12; 2.4
Ballykelly, 2.2.2
Belfast airport, 2.1.4
Biggin Hill, 2.2.2
Birmingham airport, 1.3.2; 2.1.4; 2.2.2
Board of Trade, 1.3.1; 2.1.1; 2.1.3; 2.1.8; 2.1.9; 2.1.10; 4.1
Bonded warehouses, cargo in, 2.1.7
Bournemouth airport, 2.2.2
Bristol airport, 2.1.4; 2.2.2
British Airline Pilots Association, 3.3.2
British Airports Authority creation, 1.3.1; 2.2.1
British Airports Authority employees, 1.3.6; 2.2.1; 3.3.1; 3.3.3
British Airports Authority owned airports, 1.3.2; 2.2.1
British Airways, 2.3.2; 2.3.4; 2.3.5; 2.4
British Caledonian, 2.2.3; 2.3.4; 2.3.5
British European Airways, 2.2.2
British Home Tourism Survey, 2.5
British National Travel Survey, 2.5
British Overseas Airways Corporation, 2.3.2; 2.4
British residents, journeys of, 2.1.5
British Tourist Authority, 2.5; 3.2.1
British United Airways, 2.4
Building, cost of, 2.2.2; 3.5
Building research station, 3.3.2
Business monitors, 2.1.1, 2.1.2; 2.1.5
Business passengers, 2.2.1; 2.2.2; 3.2.1

Canada, 2.3.5
Cardiff airport, 2.1.4
Cargo in bonded warehouses, 2.1.7
Cargo in transit, 2.1.7; 3.2.2
Cargo, weight of, 2.1.2; 2.1.6; 3.2.2
Carlisle airport, 2.2.2
Catering at airports, 1.3.6
Cause of accidents, 2.1.9; 3.2.4
Census of all traffic, 1.3.4; 2.1.8; 2.1.11; 3.1; 3.2.2
Centre for Transport Studies—University of Leeds, 2.2.2
Changes in publication over time, 2.1.1
Channel Islands, 2.1.2; 3.1
Charter flights, 2.1.2; 2.1.3; 4.1
Civil Aviation Authority creation, 1.3.1; 4.1
Civil Aviation Authority publications, 2.1.1; 2.1.2; 2.1.3
Civil Aviation Authority run airports, 1.3.2
Class 5 licences, 2.1.3

Cleaners at airports, 1.3.6
Collision risk, 2.1.9; 3.2.4
Commercial movements, 2.1.2; 2.3.3; 3.2.3
Commodity data, 2.1.6; 2.1.7; 3.2.2
Company stores, 3.2.2
Complaints about air transport, 2.6; 2.7
Complaints, noise, 2.1.10
Complimentary passengers, 2.1.3
Concorde noise, 2.7
Congestion, air, 2.1.8
Controlled aircraft, surveys of, 1.3.4; 2.1.8
Corporation flights, 2.1.2
Cost of buildings, 2.2.2; 3.5
Cost-benefit studies, 2.2.2; 3.3; 3.5
Crew, 2.1.2; 2.1.3; 3.2.1
Customs and Excise, HM, 2.1.7; 3.2.2

Definition of Civil Aviation, 1.2
Definition of passenger in airline data, 2.1.3; 3.2.1
Definition of passenger in airport data, 2.12.; 3.2.1
Definition of passenger in origin and destination surveys, 2.1.4; 3.2.1
Density, traffic, 2.1.8; 3.2.3
Department of Trade and Industry, 1.3.1; 2.1.1; 2.1.2; 2.1.4; 2.1.5; 2.1.8; 2.1.9; 2.1.10; 2.1.12; 2.2.2; 3.2.1; 3.3.1; 3.3.2; 4.1
Destination surveys, origin and, 2.1.1; 2.1.4; 2.1.5; 2.2.1; 2.2.2; 3.2.1; 3.3.1; 4.1; 4.2.1
Diplomatic bags, 3.2.2

East Midlands airport, 2.1.4
Edinburgh airport, 2.2.1; 2.3.3
Edwards Report, 1.3.1; 2.1.1; 2.7
Employees, air transport, 2.1.14; 3.3.3; 3.4
Employees, airline, 1.3.6; 2.3.1; 2.4; 3.4
Employees, airport, 1.3.6; 2.2.1; 3.3.3
Employees, British Airports Authority, 1.3.6; 2.2.1; 3.3.1; 3.3.3
Employees, hours worked by BAA, 2.2.1
Employees, pay of airport, 2.7
Employees, travel-to-work habits, 2.2.1; 3.3.1
Environmental effect of airports, 3.3; 4.2.2
Eurocontrol, 2.3.5
European Airlines Research Bureau, 2.3.2
European Civil Aviation Conference, 2.3.2
European Economic Community, 2.3.5
Excess baggage, 3.2.2
Expenditure on air travel, 2.1.13
Exports and imports, 2.1.7

Facilities, 4.2.2
Facilities around airport, transport, 2.1.4; 2.2.1; 2.7; 3.3.1; 4.2.2
Fare-paying passengers, 2.1.2; 2.1.3; 2.1.4; 3.2.1
Fares, 2.6
Financial data from airlines, 2.1.12; 2.3.1; 3.5
Flight, length of, 2.3.2
Flight level, 2.1.8
Flight strips, 1.3.4; 2.1.8
Flying Schools, 2.1.8; 2.1.11
Foreigners visiting UK, 2.1.5; 2.3.5
Freight assignments, urgency of, 2.1.6

Freight carried, 2.1.3; 2.1.6; 2.3.3; 3.2.2
Freight demand, air, 2.1.5; 3.2.2; 4.1
Freight load, size of, 2.1.6
Freight services, licensing of air, 2.1.6
Freight traffic, 2.1.2; 2.1.6; 2.3.2; 2.3.3; 3.2.2
Freight users, 2.1.6; 4.1
Freight, value of, 2.1.7; 3.2.2

Gatwick airport, 2.1.4; 2.2.1; 2.2.2; 2.3.1; 2.3.3; 2.7; 3.3.1
Gatwick airport, noise at, 2.2.2
General aviation, 1.3.3; 1.3.5; 2.1.8; 2.1.11; 3.1; 4.2.2
Glasgow airport, 2.2.1; 2.3.3
Gliding clubs, 1.3.4; 1.3.6; 2.1.8; 2.1.11; 4.2.2
Greater London Council, 2.2.1
Gross domestic fixed capital formation, 2.1.13

Handicapped, 2.6
Heathrow airport, 2.1.4; 2.1.10; 2.2.1; 2.3.1; 2.3.3; 2.7; 3.3.1
Heathrow, noise at, 3.3.2
Heathrow, passengers' baggage at, 2.2.2; 2.6
Helicopter noise, 2.7
Heliport, Westland, 2.7
Hiring private aircraft, 1.3.2
Historic series, 2.3.1
HM Customs and Excise, 2.1.7; 3.2.2
Home Office, 1.3.1; 2.1.5
Hours worked by BAA employees, 2.2.1
Humberside, Yorkshire and, 2.2.2

Immigration, 1.3.1; 2.1.5
Imports, exports and, 2.1.7
In-flight surveys, 2.2.2; 2.4
Inclusive tours, 2.1.2
Income, air travel in national, 2.1.13
Incomes, National Board for Prices and, 2.7
Indulgence flights, 1.3.5
Inter-city routes, 2.2.2
Interline passengers, 2.1.4
International Air Transport Association, 2.3.4; 2.3.5
International airlines data, 2.3.1
International Civil Aviation Organization, 2.1.12; 2.3.1; 2.3.5; 3.2.1; 3.2.4; 3.4; 3.5
International passenger survey, 2.1.4; 2.1.5; 2.5; 3.2.1; 3.3.1

Japan, 2.3.5
Journeys of British residents, 2.1.5

Landings, 2.1.2; 2.1.8; 2.3.2
Lee-on-Solent, 2.2.2
Leeds/Bradford airport, 2.1.4
Length of flight, 2.3.2
Licences, Class 5, 2.1.3
Licensed pilots, list of, 3.4
Licensing Board, Air Transport, 1.3.1; 1.3.3
Licensing of air freight services, 2.1.6
Licensing of aircraft, 1.3.1; 1.3.3; 3.2.3

SUBJECT INDEX

Licensing of airports, 1.3.1; 1.3.2
List of licensed pilots, 3.4
Lists of airports, 1.3.2
Liverpool airport, noise at, 2.2.2
Local authority airports, 1.3.2
Loganair, 2.2.2
London Air Traffic Control area, 1.3.4; 2.1.8
London airport, third, 2.1.1; 3.3
London Chamber of Commerce and Industry, 2.7
London Interchanges, Transport Co-ordinating Council for, 2.7
Luton airport, 1.3.2; 2.1.4; 2.2.1; 2.2.2; 2.3.1; 2.7

Mail, 2.1.2; 2.3.2; 3.2.2
Mail, troops', 3.2.2
Manchester airport, 2.3.1
Manston airport, 2.1.4
Manufacturing, aircraft, 1.2
Methodology, 4.1
Metra, 2.2.2
Metric tons, 2.1.2; 3.2.2
Military aircraft, 1.3.4; 2.1.8
Ministry of Aviation, 1.3.1; 2.1.1; 2.1.4; 2.1.8; 2.1.9; 4.1
Ministry of Defence, 1.3.1
Ministry of Transport, 2.2.1

National Air Traffic services, 1.3.4; 2.1.1; 2.1.8; 2.1.9; 2.3.1; 3.2.3; 3.2.4; 4.1; 4.2.1
National Board for Prices and Incomes, 2.7
National income, air travel in, 2.1.13
National Physical Laboratory, 3.3.2
Navigators, 3.4
Near misses, 2.1.9; 3.2.4
Newcastle airport, 2.1.4; 2.2.2
Night, noise at, 2.1.10; 3.3.2
Noise, 2.1.10; 2.7; 3.3.2; 4.2.2
Noise Abatement Council, 3.3.2
Noise Advisory Council, 3.3.2
Noise at Gatwick airport, 2.2.2
Noise at Heathrow, 3.3.2
Noise at Liverpool airport, 2.2.2
Noise at night, 2.1.10; 3.3.2
Noise complaints, 2.1.10
Noise, Concorde, 2.7
Noise, helicopter, 2.7
Noise measurement responsibility, 2.1.1
Noise number index, 2.1.10; 3.3.2
Non-commercial movements, 2.1.2; 2.3.3; 3.1; 3.2.3
Non-fare-paying passengers, 2.1.2; 2.1.4; 3.2.1
Non-scheduled flights, 2.1.3; 2.3.1; 2.3.2
North Atlantic traffic, 1.3.4; 2.1.8; 2.3.1
North West Scottish airports, 2.1.4
Norwich airport, 2.2.2

Office of Population Censuses and Surveys, 2.1.5
Oil-industry passengers, 2.2.1, 2.2.2
Organization for Economic Co-operation and Development, 2.3.5

Origin and destination surveys, 2.1.1; 2.1.4; 2.1.5; 2.2.1; 2.2.2; 3.2.1; 3.3.1; 4.1; 4.2.1
Owned, type of aircraft, 2.1.3; 3.2.3
Ownership of aircraft, 1.3.3; 2.1.3; 2.4; 3.1; 3.2.3
Ownership of airports, 1.3.2

Passenger in airline data, definition of, 2.1.3; 3.2.1
Passenger in airport data, definition of, 2.1.2; 3.2.1
Passenger in origin and destination surveys, definition of, 2.1.4; 3.2.1
Passenger loadings, 2.1.3
Passenger survey, international, 2.1.4; 2.1.5; 2.5; 3.2.1; 3.3.1
Passengers at BAA airports, 2.2.1
Passengers' baggage, 2.2.1; 3.2.1
Passengers' baggage at Heathrow, 2.2.2; 2.6
Passengers, business, 2.2.1; 2.2.2; 3.2.1
Passengers, complimentary, 2.1.3
Passengers, fare-paying, 2.1.2; 2.1.3; 2.1.4; 3.2.1
Passengers, interline, 2.1.4
Passengers, non-fare-paying, 2.1.2; 2.1.4; 3.2.1
Passengers, oil industry, 2.2.1; 2.2.2
Passengers, terminal, 2.1.2; 2.1.4; 2.2.1; 2.3.3; 3.2.1
Passengers, transferring, 2.1.4; 2.2.1; 3.2.1
Passengers, transit, 2.1.2; 2.1.3; 2.1.4; 2.3.3; 3.2.1
Pay of airport employees, 2.7
Peak periods, 2.2.1
Pilots, list of licensed, 3.4
Preston air traffic control area, 2.1.8
Prestwick airport, 1.3.2; 2.2.1; 2.3.3
Private aircraft, 1.3.3; 2.1.11; 3.1; 4.2.2
Private aircraft, accidents to, 4.2.2
Private aircraft, hiring, 1.3.2
Productivity, staff, 2.6
Profit and loss statements, airline, 2.1.12
Publication, air traffic control data, 2.1.1; 2.1.8
Publication over time, changes in, 2.1.1
Publications, Civil Aviation Authority, 2.1.1; 2.1.2; 2.1.3

Quiet aircraft symposium, 4.2.2

Rail–air travel balance, 2.2.2
Regional demand, 2.2.2
Registration of aircraft, 1.3.3; 2.3.1; 3.2.3
Roskill Commission, 2.1.4; 2.7
Routes, inter-city, 2.2.2
Routes, traffic-controlled, 1.3.4; 2.1.8; 3.1
Runways, strength of, 2.2.2

Scheduled flights, 2.1.2; 2.1.3; 2.3.1
Schools, flying, 2.1.8; 2.1.11
Scotland air traffic control area, 1.3.4; 2.1.8
Scottish air, 2.2.2
Scottish airports, North-west, 2.1.4
Sea–air travel balance, 2.1.5
Sectors, air traffic control, 2.1.8
Shanwick air traffic control area, 1.3.4; 2.1.8
Short tons, 2.1.2; 3.2.2
Sir Frederick Snow and Partners, 2.2.2
Size of freight load, 2.1.6
Software Sciences, 2.1.8; 2.2.2

Sound contours, 2.1.10; 3.3.2
Southampton airport, 2.1.4
Southend airport, 2.1.4; 2.7
Staff productivity, 2.6
Stage flights, 2.1.3
Stansted airport, 2.1.4; 2.2.1; 2.3.3; 2.7; 3.3.1
Stock of aircraft, 2.1.3; 2.4; 3.2.3
Strength of runways, 2.2.2
Surface travel, 2.2.1
Surveys of controlled aircraft, 1.3.4; 2.1.8

Take-offs, 2.1.2; 2.1.8; 2.3.2
Terminal passengers, 2.1.2; 2.1.4; 2.2.1; 2.3.3; 3.2.1
Third London airport, 2.1.1; 3.3
Ticket bookers at airports, 1.3.6
Tonne-kilometre, 3.2.2
Tons, metric, 2.1.2; 3.2.2
Tons, short, 2.1.2; 3.2.2
Tourism, 2.1.5; 2.3.5; 3.2.1
Tours, inclusive, 2.1.2
Traffic-controlled routes, 1.3.4; 2.1.8; 3.1
Traffic density, 2.1.8; 3.2.3
Traffic patterns at BAA airports, 2.2.1
Transferring passengers, 2.1.4; 2.2.1; 3.2.1
Transit, cargo in, 2.1.7; 3.2.2
Transit passengers, 2.1.2; 2.1.3; 2.1.4; 2.3.3; 3.2.1

Transport Co-ordinating Council for London Interchanges, 2.7
Transport facilities around airport, 2.1.4; 2.2.1; 2.7; 3.3.1; 4.2.2
Travel in the balance of payments, 1.3.1; 2.1.5; 2.1.13; 4.1
Troops' mail, 3.2.2
Type of aircraft on routes, 2.1.8; 3.2.3
Type of aircraft owned, 2.1.3; 3.2.3

Uncontrolled traffic, 1.3.6; 2.1.8; 2.1.11; 3.1; 4.2.2
Unemployment, 2.1.14
United Nations, 2.3.5
Urgency of freight assignments, 2.1.6
USA, 2.3.5
USSR, 2.3.5

Value of freight, 2.1.7; 3.2.2
Vehicles carried, 3.2.2

Weight of aircraft, 1.3.3
Weight of cargo, 2.1.2; 2.1.6; 3.2.2
Western European Airports Association, 2.3.3
Westland heliport, 2.7
Wilson Committee, 2.1.10; 3.3.2

Yorkshire and Humberside, 2.2.2